W9-BVU-470

Empires, Nations, and Natives

Benoît de L'Estoile, Federico Neiburg,
and Lygia Sigaud, editors

EMPIRES, NATIONS, AND NATIVES

Anthropology and State-Making

Duke University Press   Durham & London

2005

TRENT UNIVERSITY LIBRARY
PETERBOROUGH, ONTARIO

© 2005 Duke University Press

All rights reserved

Printed in the United States of America

on acid-free paper ∞

Designed by C. H. Westmoreland

Typeset in Minion by Keystone

Typesetting, Inc.

Library of Congress Cataloging-in-

Publication Data appear on the last

printed page of this book.

CONTENTS

ACKNOWLEDGMENTS

This volume is the outcome of an intense process of international cooperation. In September 1997, the Museu Nacional (Federal University of Rio de Janeiro) hosted the French-Brazilian workshop Social Sciences, State and Society, organized by the institution's Postgraduate Program in Social Anthropology and by the Department of Social Sciences of the École Normale Supérieure (Paris). Also participating in the event were researchers from the Centre for the Sociology of Education and Culture and the Contemporary Brazil Studies Centre, both at the École des Hautes Études en Sciences Sociales (Paris). In observing a convergence of perspectives in our analyses of the complex links between the practices of social scientists and other social practices, we were stimulated to pursue a systematic analysis on the relations between the construction of anthropological knowledges and the building of states.

The starting point for this analysis was the application of the same set of questions to a universe of diverse situations and processes, distributed in time and space. After the Rio de Janeiro workshop we invited other colleges to take part in the project so as to widen the scope of the comparison. The result was the publication of a special issue of the *Revue de Synthèse* in 2000, which was titled "Anthropologies, États et populations." This issue contained six new articles, three essays, and an introduction in which for the first time we formulated the implications of the systematic comparison between the analyzed cases.

The present publication is based on this issue of the *Revue de Synthèse* and the volume *Antropologia, impérios e Estados nacionais,* published in Brazil in 2002. Nearly all of the chapters, including the introductory one, have been revised, with some considerably reworked for this edition, and three new chapters have been included (on North American anthropology, on Portuguese anthropology, and on British anthropology). An earlier version of the chapter by Federico Neiburg and Marcio Goldman was published in *Cultural Anthropology* 13:1 (1998) and in *Anuário Antropológico 97* (1998). An earlier version of the chapter by Omar Ribeiro Thomaz was published in *Mana: Estudos en Antropologia Social* 7:1 (2000).

We have benefited from the support of various institutions throughout the period of creating this volume: the Conselho Nacional de Desenvolvimento Científico e Tecnológico, the Fundação Universitária José Bonifácio, the Fundação de Amparo a Pesquisa do Estado do Rio de Janeiro, the Federal University of Rio de Janeiro, the Graduate Program in Social Anthropology (Museu Nacional), the École Normale Supèrieure, the École des Hautes Études em Sciences Sociales, the Maison des Sciences de l'Homme, and the Ministère des Affaires Étrangères. The work was also made possible thanks to the project "Internationalization and Transformation of National States (Economy, Society, Culture)," developed as part of a CAPES-COFECUB international cooperation agreement.

Among the many colleagues we wish to thank, we choose here for special mention those with whom we were able to discuss not only some of the essays included in the volume but also the general structure of the project: Eric Brian, Adam Kuper, Gerard Lenclud, and Sergio Miceli.

Marcela Coelho de Souza helped us by coordinating the work of translation and assuming the overall revision of the book. Translation of the chapters was undertaken by David Rodgers (the introduction and the essays by Thomaz, Souza Lima, Oliveira, and Pantaleón), Noal Mellott (the essay by L'Estoile; revised by David Rodgers), Kimberly Arkin (the essay by Weber), Janet Paweko and Leah Sophie Horowitz (the essay by Bensa; revised by David Rodgers), and Peter Gow (the essay by Neiburg and Goldman). We thank Judith Bovensiepen, Jack Murphy, Sarah Froning Deleporte, Alison Murray Levine, and John Tresch for their help in revising some of the chapters. We also thank Duke University Press's anonymous reviewers for their very helpful editorial comments.

Benoît de L'Estoile, Federico Neiburg,

and Lygia Sigaud

INTRODUCTION

Anthropology and the Government

of "Natives," a Comparative Approach

Two recent events help to illustrate some of the contrasting aspects of anthropology's present predicaments, including the way these predicaments are embedded in complex power relationships. At the meeting of the American Anthropological Association in San Francisco in November 2000, a large crowd of anthropologists packed into a conference room for a special session titled "Ethical Issues in Field Research among the Yanomami." The session had been convened by the association's ethics committee in the wake of the uneasiness stirred up by the publication of Patrick Tierney's controversial book, *Darkness in El Dorado*, which denounced the alleged misconduct by anthropologists among the indigenous Yanomami populations living on the borders of Brazil and Venezuela. The atmosphere in the conference room was dramatic. Beyond the troubling accusation of a grave breach of professional ethics lurked the potential damage to anthropology's public image, perhaps putting at risk the discipline's funding and even its access to the field: during the session, an anthropologist speaking on behalf of the Dirección de Assuntos Indigenas, the Venezuelan state agency in charge of indigenous populations, announced the agency's decision to place a moratorium on all research in indigenous areas by local and foreign researchers.

Less than three years later, during summer 2003, the prestigious Cartier Foundation for Contemporary Art hosted an exhibition in Paris titled "Yanomami, the Spirit of the Forest." The show displayed various works by contemporary artists invited to visit the Yanomami village of Watokiri in Brazil, through the mediation of French anthropologist Bruce Albert, along with the help of two nongovernmental organizations (NGOS): Survival International and the (Brazilian) Pro-Yanomami Commission. The exhibition was presented by Davi Kopenawa, a Yanomami shaman and leader, as a way of "making our voices heard" and thus gaining the support of powerful allies: "Only the people from afar want to know us and defend us. Their words are strong and they come to our aid. Thanks to them, people living nearby, who speak against us incessantly, will cease invading the forest" (Albert and Kopenawa 2003).

These two scenes highlight crucial aspects of anthropology's presence in the contemporary world. Challenged by intense criticism from within and from without and torn by ethical and political quandaries, anthropologists find themselves mediating between local groups and global audiences, while negotiating their relationships with state administrations, transnational agencies, and NGOs in the context of shifting regional politics and international power relationships that involve alliance building and boundary definition with patrons, journalists, artists, and the public.

While the scenes described above were especially dramatic, they echo similar situations in many other settings. The essays collected in this volume aim to shed light on the kinds of dilemmas currently faced by anthropologists by placing the issues in a larger framework through a historical and comparative approach. As part of the division of labor among the social sciences, anthropology historically specialized in the description and classification of human groups that frequently were viewed as primitive, backward, marginal, tribal, underdeveloped, or premodern (Wallerstein 1996). These peoples were identified by their exteriority and alterity vis-à-vis the world of civilization, science, and technology to which anthropologists supposedly belonged. Yet the work of anthropologists was only possible because such groups were already being absorbed into larger polities and subordinated—or in the process of subordination—by modern nation-states or empires, and consequently subjected to a range of policies spanning from preservation and protection to programs for planned social transformation and even domestication. The involvement of anthropologists in conceiving and implementing such policies has been a well-worn topic in terms of ethical and political debate, yet it has only rarely been taken up as an object of sociological analysis.

The essays in this book explore social situations located in a wide variety of settings: the production of difference and identity in South Africa; the place of anthropology in the construction of Mexican and Portuguese nationalism; the international migration of state policies relating to Amerindian peoples; the modernization projects undertaken by French colonial administration; the planning of British colonial development and of projects for eradicating poverty in Latin America; the repercussions of World War II on American anthropology and French folklore; the confrontation between contemporary architecture and indigenous cultural revival in the Pacific; and the entanglement of cultural identity, ethnic emergence, and access to land in contemporary Brazil. In all of these contexts, anthropologists have established relationships with the agents responsible for implementing policies and the groups these policies directly affect. Social groups and categories such as Amerindians, Kanak, Tikuna, Bushmen, Mexicans, Japanese, French, the poor, or the natives, as well as entities such as the state, the empire, the nation, and science, are all defined within these situations.

In this introductory essay, we examine this set of cases from a historical and comparative perspective, inspired by social studies of science and the historical ethnography of the state. Our aim is to provide a comprehensive overview of the relationships between the production of anthropological knowledge, the government of populations, and the building of empires and nation-states, moving beyond the typical and limited responses to these topics as either denunciation or engagement.

Critique, Commitment, and Expertise

Critique and commitment have been central issues in the history of anthropology. From the 1950s onward it became increasingly commonplace to accuse the discipline of working in the service of colonialism and the expansion of capitalism. In the aftermath of decolonization sharp critiques cropped up concerning the role of British anthropologists in the policy of indirect rule in Africa, the participation of French anthropologists in the administration of colonized populations (especially in Algeria), and the role of North American anthropologists in the overall policy of control and domination in Southeast Asia and Latin America.[1] In reply, arguments were made advocating the innocence of those accused and stressing the colonial administrations' absence of interest in and even open hostility toward anthropologists (Goody 1995; Loizos 1977). More recently, there has been an outburst of proposals to remodel anthropology as a tool for another kind of politics, one that propounds an "ethical" or "militant" anthropology. An example of this approach can be seen in the work of Nancy Scheper-Hughes (1995: 410), where she describes her "transformation from 'objective' anthropologist to politically and morally engaged *companheira.*"

While these debates are certainly crucial for us as practicing members of the discipline, it is not our aim here to try to define a moral stance or to elaborate principles for action. Instead, our aim is to help clarify the issues involved in the relations between anthropologists and colonial or postcolonial governments through a comparative and sociologically informed approach.

Abrupt reversals in political contexts often provide favorable conditions for denunciations. The end of the German occupation of France in 1944 and the subsequent fall of the authoritarian Vichy regime was just such a moment. As Florence Weber shows in her essay in this volume, prominent figures were denounced as traitors, and "folklore" quickly lost its credibility as a scientific discipline in the wake of its close association with the Vichy government's political program. Its heirs had to redefine their field of studies as the "ethnology of France." At the same time, the active participation of a handful of ethnologists in the so-called Musée de l'Homme network (one of the first resistance movements against German occupation) helped valorize a form of engagement that would later reach its most intense expression during the Algerian war of independence (1954–1962).

Denunciation may also be used as a weapon in the struggle between theoretical and political factions—a fact made apparent in Claudio Lomnitz's study of Mexican anthropology. Soon after the student uprisings of 1968, a group of young anthropologists published a book setting out new foundations for the discipline, while simultaneously exposing the complicity of anthropologists in supporting *indigenismo*, a set of policies ostensibly designed to integrate indigenous groups into Mexican society (Warman et al. 1970). In their view, the ideal of a "revolutionary anthropology" modeled after the 1910 revolution—a project focused on helping to build a *mestizo* Mexico, an Indianized nation—had been corrupted. Anthropology had turned into an instrument of domination, serving the reproduction of a capitalist system itself dependent on an authoritarian state. Twenty years later, several of these rebels had become recognized anthropologists occupying key positions both in academic institutions and in the state bodies responsible for the administration of indigenous populations. The careers of those in the 1968 generation—from denouncing the state to being co-opted by the state—bring to light a salient feature of Mexican anthropology's history. As Lomnitz demonstrates, the recruitment of anthropologists by state institutions in order to develop, direct, and scientifically legitimize government policies recurs frequently throughout the formation of Mexico as a nation-state. The state used the knowledge of society produced by anthropology to support its policies.

In the South African case, Adam Kuper's essay contrasts two trends of anthropology during the apartheid period. Afrikaans-speaking anthropologists identified and classified populations according to racial and cultural criteria, with the eventual aim of regulating the relations between the social groups that were classified and organized by means of their separation. Kuper reveals the intimate relationship between a classificatory science emphasizing the differences between groups and segregation as state policy. This relationship was reinforced by the social proximity between anthropologists of Afrikaner origin educated in Afrikaans-language universities, and the nationalists who conceived and implemented apartheid. At the opposite pole were the anthropologists working in English-speaking universities: these researchers tended to stress the unity of South African society, accusing their Afrikaner rivals of complicity with the system of apartheid. In the wake of the political changes of the 1990s, the heirs of this critical anthropology were invited to take part in developing and implementing policies for unifying and rebuilding the new South Africa, granting a new legitimacy to the use of anthropology in the service of the state.

The incorporation of researchers into state bureaucracy is but one aspect of the relationship between the production of knowledge and the development and implementation of policies. Other essays in this book explore various forms this relationship may take today, among them the figure of the expert. João Pacheco de Oliveira examines the role anthropologists began to perform as experts employed by the Brazilian state in the process of demarcating indigenous lands in the wake of the new democratic 1988 constitution. In this instance, the anthropologist acts on behalf of both the state and the indigenous groups who require his or her specialized knowledge in order to be legally recognized by the state (whose own recognition by the state derives from the juridical validity attributed to their official reports). Anthropologists also play a central role as mediators in the process of identifying and territorializing "ethnic groups," both working and competing with indigenous leaders, lawyers, and militants from nongovernmental organizations. Pacheco himself suggests a parallel with the role that some North American anthropologists came to play in defining "Indianness," such as in the famous Mashpee case (Clifford 1988).

The figure of the expert also appears in the involvement of anthropologists in large state-sponsored cultural projects. Alban Bensa, in his essay, reflects on his own participation in a joint project involving the French state and the Kanak nationalist movement in New Caledonia. In 1989, after a series of violent episodes, the French government and the Kanak leaders signed an agreement that included the creation of the Agency for Kanak Cultural Development and the construction of a Kanak cultural center. Renzo Piano, the world-renowned architect chosen to build the center, called on an anthropologist's services to meet what he perceived to be the project's most difficult challenge: to embody the Kanak past (the relations of the Kanak with their memory and their own way of representing their tradition) and to project Kanak culture into the future, in parallel with the nationalist movement's aspirations toward self-determination.

A comparison of these cases shows that anthropologists have frequently participated in the idealization and implementation of state policies. It is also clear that critical evaluations of this role historically have depended both on external political settings and on the discipline's own internal conflicts.[2] Pairs of terms such as innocence/complicity and resistance/collaboration—frequently invoked in the impassioned analyses of the social responsibility of anthropologists—must indeed be seen as categories of praise and accusation used by individuals and groups to legitimize their own positions. These must be regarded, therefore, not as analytical categories but as native ones. Sociological comprehension of the relational dynamic between anthropologists and states is only possible if we consider the structural (and structuring) nature of this relationship, instead of condemning it as pathological or deviant or praising it as heroic political activism.[3]

"Scientific" and "Political":
Practical Evaluations and Categories of Analysis

Denunciations of the political complicity of social scientists are frequently based on the supposed pollution of science by politics. Academics reflecting on the relationships between the production of scientific knowledge and political activities likewise commonly fall back on the opposition between science and politics. This recourse allows the behavior of individuals acting as scholars to be contrasted with their actions as citizens, which in turn fosters endless reflections on the difficulties met in reconciling the demands (experienced as potentially conflicting) of belonging to the scientific community and taking an active part in policy debates and conflicts.

This approach—exemplified by Raymond Aron's reading of Max Weber's lectures *Politik als Beruf* and *Wissenschaft als Beruf* (Aron 1959;[4] Weber 1958a and 1958b)—effectively amounts to a kind of commonsense understanding within the academic world. Yet it empties the relationship between science and politics of their historicity, treating them as a-temporal ethical problems to be resolved at a personal level. The figures of the scientist and the politician, far from being used in Weber's sense in an ideal-typical manner (as analytic tools), function as archetypes within a normative approach. The ritualistic citing of the founding father covers the issue with a sociological gloss when its apprehension is really based on moral considerations, self-justifications, and prescriptions.

Debates on the means and ends of the social sciences, as well as the attitudes to be adopted in response to demands from both public administrations and social movements, raise questions with which all scholars may legitimately be concerned. Max Weber himself adopted a normative posture in his epistemological writings, urging the researcher to distinguish sharply between the sphere of practical evaluations and the sphere of scientific analyses. Nonetheless, he made it abundantly clear that this separation represents an ideal norm and not an actual description of the world of science. Whenever a norm we consider true or valid (such as a mathematical or logical rule) is taken as an object of analysis, it must be treated following the same principles that guide the study of other values we ourselves may take to be false or mistaken (Weber 1949). This approach therefore entails analyzing values (including, obviously, the values of science) as practical judgments— as native categories or abstractions produced and used by researchers in their efforts to make sense of the world they inhabit.

Florence Weber's text provides us with an excellent example of the possibilities opened up by a critical approach to the academic commonsense opposition between science and politics. She asks how we can explain the simultaneous disappearance of both scientific folklore and militant regionalism in France after 1945. Her analysis boils down to three elements. First, neither folklore nor regionalism was invented by the Vichy regime allied with Nazi Germany: both of them existed beforehand, without any necessary coincidence between scientific activity and commitment to a political program. Second, just before the war, folklore was on the verge of acquiring institutional status as a scientific discipline. Third, the Vichy period paradoxically encouraged the dissociation between scientific and political activities. By distancing herself radically from narratives that identify heroes and traitors, *collaborateurs* and *résistants*, Weber describes how the passion for science lent meaning to the actions of individuals interested in studying folklore between 1930 and 1945, and she explains why they continued to adhere to a definition of science as a domain separate from politics.

This historical analysis stimulates us to reflect on the ways in which relationships between the political and scientific worlds are generally described (and prescribed) today. Two contrasting positions can be identified. At one pole are formulations that take policy-oriented research to be only a means for (real) science: academics are expected to clearly separate the activities they undertake as scientists (located in universities and research centers) from those they pursue as citizens or experts (taking part in the implementation of state policies) and to strategically use the latter to support their scientific activity. From this viewpoint, the development of a research project funded by a state agency, an NGO, or a foundation is but one way of providing the material conditions for advancing scientific knowledge.[5] The double output of research activity—the reports sent to funding agencies and the articles published in scientific journals—amounts to the materialization of this separation between the scientific and political worlds. At the opposite pole are those who stress the value of science in the service of policy, the need to rationalize the solution of social problems through the use of scientific knowledge, or in a more radical mood, the advocacy of politically committed research ("in the service of . . ."). In the first case, the target audience is made up of academics, and pure research is much more highly valued than applied research. In the second case, the hierarchy is inverted: the main audience includes statesmen, administrators, militants, or social movements, although the final product of the research may still be read by researchers in academic settings.[6]

These two ways of conceptualizing the relations between science and politics obviously refer to ideal types. They are based on notions of pure science and applied science that vary historically. Indeed, in real-world situations the same individual or group may strategically use one or the other argument in response to the given context, or adopt an intermediary position claiming the right to study practical problems as scientists—as Bronislaw Malinowski said in a seminar: "Practical problems are brought before us [by the colonial administrators], and we have to show how far they can be studied from a scientific point of view."[7] The autonomy of science in relation to politics therefore appears not as an absolute notion, one that could serve as a transhistorical criterion for classifying different scientific spaces or various individuals located within such spaces, but rather as a claim produced in particular historical conditions by specific social agents or groups. Jorge Pantaleón amply demonstrates the ambiguity of autonomy as an analytical category in his examination in this volume of the involvement of anthropologists in setting up and implementing NGO-sponsored social development policies in Latin America. Pantaleón points out the twofold use of the notion of autonomization by those anthropologists who study the world of NGOs in which they often themselves play an active role: the term is employed both as an analytical tool for understanding current developments in this field and as a goal for themselves as practitioners.

Comparative analysis thus shows that autonomy must be treated as a native category and never as an analytical one; for example, as one purporting to measure lesser or greater degrees of autonomy. Its meaning is situational, referring to the body in relation to which autonomy is claimed: the church, the university system, public administration, corporations, and the like. The definition of what constitutes science and what lies outside it (politics, for example) cannot be taken as a given: rather, it is a construction constantly being redefined and renegotiated over time (Shapin 1992). Thus an academic discipline may win its autonomy from other bodies of knowledge by allying itself with particular sectors of public administration; scientists may look beyond the national academic space in pursuit of greater autonomy vis-à-vis the local political context, developing what may appear, at least in the eyes of their adversaries, as a form of dependency on foreign science.

Here the sociology of religious specialists may be useful to help us create some distance from the preconceptions we share as members of an academic world. The comparison between intellectuals and the clergy is extremely pertinent: the cleric in fact comprises an ideal type of a specific relationship between a bureaucratic organization and forms of intellectual production. Weber's studies of the relationship between clerical and secular power thus help illuminate the debate over the uses of "pure science" as a value (see Weber 1968 [1922]: 1158–211). Inside religious space, the denunciation of involvement with the corrupting outer world of power and wealth is often made by appealing to an ideal of religious purity. Weber demonstrates this claim in his analysis of the denunciations made by various reformers contesting the establishment (for example, those urging monastic reforms in the name of a return to an original purity lost through overinvolvement with the secular world), as well as the denunciations made by the central hierocratic power (the pope) seeking to establish, in detriment to the secular lords, its control over the distribution of ecclesiastical positions. Perceived in this light, a number of values salient in the academic ethos appear structurally analogous to values in the clerical ethos.

Similarly, the clergy regularly turned to support from the secular power in order to defend their religious monopoly against various kinds of challenges (such as religious heresies). However, to ensure their autonomy in both material and intellectual terms, they made strenuous efforts to maintain their control over the access to clerical positions and the definition of ortho- doxy. Yet this does not mean that the church apparatus (in Weber's terms, the hierocracy) was necessarily exterior to the state.[8] In fact the crucial services it provided to the state, assuring both the legitimacy of its power and a supply of literate specialists to run the kingdom and educate the elites, boosted the hierocracy's ability to claim its autonomy from the secular power (Weber 1968 [1922]: 1173–176). Weber's analysis of the complex links between hierocracy and the secular state allows us, by analogy, to see that there is no necessary contradiction between demands for autonomy on one hand and persistent border conflicts on the other. Rather than trying to ascertain the various degrees of autonomy found in academic production (in our case, that of anthropologists), we draw on that analogy: first, to identify structural relations of solidarity and conflict between the worlds of science and policy; and, second, to understand these relations in terms of transformations in social configurations, as well as changes in modalities of interdependence, in the sense later developed by Norbert Elias (1989 [1968]).

The stereotyped opposition of scientific versus political thus conceals the existence of a series of constitutive relations between scientific practice and the state. By focusing on the moral dilemmas involved in the interplay between the activity of an individual as a researcher and his or her political engagement, it distracts attention from the central issue: namely, the very conditions of possibility of scientific practice, beginning with the key role of states in setting up and maintaining the institutions in which knowledge is produced. While academic common sense often laments the polluting ef- fects that the political world has on science, a comparative historical analysis reveals the mutual interdependence between the development and imple- mentation of state policies by administrative agents, and the knowledge about the populations they govern.

Anthropology: A Form of State Knowledge?

At this point, however, the overused concept of the state demands a closer examination. The term state in fact encompasses two dimensions of social reality. On one hand, the state can be seen as an entity that acts in the world, defining boundaries, identifying groups, legitimizing rights, and establishing relationships and hierarchies (for example, among the groups studied by the anthropologist), as well as recognizing forms of collective representation as authentic (such as the cultures of these populations). To this Durkheimian dimension of the analysis of the state (Durkheim 1975), we can add a further dimension—one we might call Weberian. In this case, the term state refers not to an agent but to a social field inhabited by individuals who, enmeshed in competitive and interdependent relationships, devise and implement policies intended to govern populations or resolve social problems (e.g., Weber 1968 [1922]: 1047–117).[9]

By taking these meanings and practices as objects of analysis throughout this book, we question the paradigmatic opposition of science and state as clearly distinct universes. Analyzing the actual relations between these worlds shows that their postulated separateness, though a widely held belief, fails to account for the diversity of observed empirical situations or for the social conditions that enable their particular configurations. Rather than assuming that knowledge producers are located a priori outside the state—thereby confronting the state as an Other—it is historically more appropriate and analytically more productive to take them as interested parties in the disputes surrounding the definition of the state and its role and the policies that it should carry out. In this light, the conflict between anthropologists and colonial civil servants, rather than expressing an antagonism between "men of knowledge" and "men of power," should be analyzed as one variant of the numerous contests existing within the space of the state: a conflict between state agents belonging to different sectors of the administrative machinery.[10]

In his essay in this volume Benoît de L'Estoile offers an ideal-typical distinction between two dimensions of science's involvement in the field of state action: instrumentalizing and legitimizing. In the first instance, academic discourses provide tools for "ordering" the natural and social worlds: they provide the "means of orientation" (Elias 1982) that enable the identification of populations and make sense of the endless flux of experience, thus informing the construction of the problems to which public policies endeavor to respond. In the second instance, science supplies a set of arguments capable of legitimizing the aims and means of such policies and those who implement them. Modern state support of academic institutions allows the state to claim a rational and objective dimension, evidenced by its strong connections with science.

Certainly this twofold dimension of instrumentalization and legitimization is not unique to anthropology. Indeed, it is even more apparent in the case of a discipline such as economics, whose specialists base their professional identity on combining theoretical sophistication with accurate forecasting.[11] By contrast, the professional identity prevalent among most anthropologists, at least today, tends to uphold the ideal of autonomy from the state, minimizing the existence of relations with the official world, or treating these simply as circumstantial interference to be eventually eliminated from the knowledge-producing process.

In his analysis of governmentality, Michel Foucault (1979) points out that the development of a "science of populations" comprises one of the main elements in the constitution of modern forms of government. Foucault is writing about political economy, but his expression science of populations applies equally well to anthropological knowledge. It must be pointed out, nonetheless, that the production of knowledge about subaltern populations has never been the monopoly of anthropologists.[12] Indeed, they are rarely the first to write about the peoples they study. Explorations, military campaign and travel narratives, missionary writings, administrative and medical reports, commissions of inquiry, military instruction manuals, and official statistics comprise a terrain of knowledge, discourses, and practices from which (and often against which) anthropology emerges.

The research undertaken on Afro-Brazilian populations during the interwar period is a prime example. Rooted in the debate on the "black issue" and orientated toward policy formulation, especially in the area of education and psychotherapy, these studies made distinctive use of scientific arguments. A figure such as Arthur Ramos—who was a medical doctor, psychiatrist, criminologist, and anthropologist instrumental in promoting the notion of Afro-Brazilian culture both as a field of academic study and as a national symbol—is typical of a professional space with blurred boundaries, capable of allowing the same person to be recognized as a specialist in areas that later became independent, and at the same time enabling him to occupy a series of positions in psychiatric and educational institutions, first in provincial Salvador da Bahia and later at the center of the federal state apparatus in Rio de Janeiro.[13] As the development of universities from the 1930s onward generated the conditions for the emergence of a new body of specialists, Ramos withdrew from administration (though he was to play a role in cultural diplomacy after the war at the Division for Social Sciences at UNESCO) in order to take up the country's first chair in physical and cultural anthropology. Thus, in different settings that he himself helped to transform, Ramos successively embodied the figures of state scientist and autonomous university academic.[14]

Far from simply being an archaic feature of the discipline's preinstitutional phase, Ramos's career may be taken as a key to analyzing other configurations where similar processes of disciplinary differentiation have unfolded. The hypothesis that academic discourses and debates on state policies develop, at least in part, within the same social space prevents us from taking as a given fact the distinction between these universes. The actual process involved in differentiating social roles can only be understood, therefore, by taking into account the division of labor between the various disciplines responsible for producing knowledge about the social world, as well as the conflicts over the monopoly for formulating and applying policies based on such knowledge.

In France during the interwar period, competition with other imperial powers and the challenge of the burgeoning of nationalist movements prompted the need to establish fresh grounds for legitimizing colonial domination. In line with these pressures, a new governmentality over the populations in overseas territories developed in which the sciences—in particular anthropology, the new "science of man"—played a key role. Based on a discussion of the Weberian notion of "rationalizing domination," Benoît de L'Estoile's essay describes various aspects of a convergence between scientific and bureaucratic-administrative forms of rationality. The colonial administration's attempts to devise techniques for identifying and describing populations spurred the growth of a body of ethnological knowledge that contributed to the development of an "ethnic" framework for reading the indigenous social world. In the metropole itself, arguments supporting "colonial action founded on reason" were developed in the context of an emerging alliance between individuals who, especially in the Colonial School that was training the colonial administrators, tried to establish themselves as professionals specializing in the administration of natives, and other individuals who sought recognition as specialists in the science of natives (in the Institute of Ethnology and the Museum of Man). In this case, the process of rationalizing domination resulted in creating both specialized fields and specialists who defined their distinctive identity in relations of dependency and competition.

Such a process was by no means limited to imperial situations. Antonio Carlos de Souza Lima's careful reconstruction in his essay suggests that the consolidation of anthropology as an academic and university discipline in

Brazil, especially from the 1960s onward, can only be comprehended by taking into account the participation of anthropologists in the formulation of state policies. Souza Lima shows how the importation of the Mexican model of indigenism, involving the active participation of anthropologists, contributed to the restructuring of state organizations in charge of governing Brazil's indigenous populations. The founding in the 1950s of a "studies section" within the Indian Protection Service (Serviço de Proteção ao Índio, or SPI), and later the creation of the Museum of the Indian, is a paradigmatic example of the creation within the state's administrative machinery of a specific body charged with producing and disseminating knowledge about indigenous populations.

In fact, the development of research organizations within indigenist agencies—whether in the Mexican or Brazilian version—is strikingly similar to the establishment of temporary or permanent schemes for ethnographic research by colonial governments, as in the creation of the Office for Colonial Scientific Research in France or, in 1925, of the ethnological section of the Department of Native Affairs in South Africa. These are examples of a process of specialization based on the division of labor between specialists of knowledge and administrative staff.[15] They shed light on other configurations in which the state administration (or parts of it) supports the development of autonomous academic institutions specializing in the production of knowledge about indigenous populations: ethnographic museums and expeditions, university departments, research institutes, academic societies, and the like.

In the United Kingdom, a case in point was the creation of the Colonial Social Science Research Council, an autonomous body responsible for allocating the large funds set up for social science research as part of the Colonial Development and Welfare Act of 1940, which envisaged such research as a necessary preliminary step to any social planning. David Mills, in his essay in this volume, shows how this considerable influx of money played a vital role in funding the academic success of British anthropology after World War II.

The very existence of a discipline dedicated to exploring the differences between human groups furnishes scientific confirmation of the need to design policies premised on such differences. Conversely, the need to develop specific policies in response to a population's distinctive traits comprises a strong argument for developing scientific knowledge about this population. There is thus a process of positive feedback between the establishment of groups that construct their professional identity as specialists in the administration of specific population groups (indigenists, colonial administrators, native affairs departments, minority-group managers, etc.) and the growth of a scholarly discourse taking these groups as objects. In other words, the existence of a scholarly undertaking such as a science of native peoples confers validity to the project of elaborating native policies that justify the existence of specialized agents and in turn contribute to singularizing those groups submitted to such policies. This in turn reinforces their status as a special object for anthropological studies. As a result, this circular process may culminate in the intensification of difference among the social groups under study.[16] The shared interest of these two types of specialists in indigenous peoples—those governing them and those studying them—creates the basis for an alliance, albeit one still troubled by border conflicts. This alliance underpins the support granted by certain sectors of the state to anthropologists' attempts to preserve a monopoly of knowledge regarding indigenous populations.

There is thus a vast array of positions corresponding to various configurations of interdependence that cannot be reduced to a single pattern of autonomy or dependence. These positions range from civil servants writing ethnographic studies of the populations they administrate, to academics conducting policy-oriented research funded by health programs or NGOs or training officials in charge of subaltern groups, to researchers working within public administrations. These diverse configurations produce different forms of circulation between administrative and anthropological knowledge, each of which contributes to distinct forms of objectifying the social world.

In a number of cases anthropology has therefore been a key agent in the construction and stabilization of grids capable of providing some order to the puzzling complexity of the social world. Kuper and Lomnitz reveal, for example, how in southern Africa and in Mexico the categories used to designate groups originally varied in response to local contexts. However, the combined demands for unifying official categories and statistics as well as standardizing scientific classifications (at a time when anthropology was thought of as the "natural science of societies") worked to stabilize the identities of the subaltern groups. Kuper highlights the complex development of population categories in South Africa and Botswana and examines some of their transformations: the interplay of terms of self-identification (autonyms) with names given by neighboring groups, sometimes taken up as administrative or academic denominations; the shift from categories based on status to those based on race; the oscillation between a biological or linguistic basis for determining the limits of such groups; the interaction between legal categories and statistical classifications; and the recent abandoning of ethnonyms held to be deprecatory. Such phenomena are part of a more general process. Beyond this particular case, census counts, ethnographic maps, ethnic and area files, ethnographic museums and films, tribal encyclopedias, and so forth all make up part of this process of transformation and crystallization, insofar as they contribute (or not) to providing scientific and legal backing to the existence of certain groups, which then may give rise to new collective identities while potentially denying such legitimacy to other groups.[17] In their essays, Pacheco, Bensa, and Pantaleón invite us to reflect on the role that anthropologists still play today in the crystallization and officialization of ethnic, sociopolitical, or cultural identities.

However, this division of labor between the production of scientific knowledge and the administration of subaltern groups is further complicated by the fact that anthropologists claim the role of spokespersons for those they study. As an early example, Bronislaw Malinowski (1937: viii) defended the idea that the anthropologist should become "not only the interpreter of the native, but also his champion." Such a claim made sense in a context where the subaltern groups were often without a voice and where in the field the anthropologist was often (and still is) seen as a mediator by those among whom he or she conducts research; that is, as someone who will be capable of transmitting a group's demands to authorities or facilitating the group's access to particular resources (money, goods, medical supplies, protection, etc.) and the attainment of prestige.

More recently, however, social transformations—not least the increasing literacy of the groups under study[18]—have produced profound changes in the interactions between researchers and those among whom they study, leading to a redefinition of the role of mediator. Ever more frequently, the anthropologist must negotiate his or her presence in the field and face probing questions about the benefits the people themselves will be able to gain from the research.[19] This change in the power relationships is certainly a key factor in understanding the growing pleas for advocacy within anthropology.

The mission of defending disempowered minorities fulfils an important role in the construction of anthropologists as a professional group. Thus, professional organizations such as the American Anthropological Association (AAA) or the Associação Brasileira de Antropologia (ABA) assume the function of promoting the discipline vis-à-vis public institutions,[20] acting as pressure groups looking to intervene in the definition of state policies so as to protect the rights of the subaltern populations studied by their affiliated members.[21] In the Brazilian case, especially at the end of the 1980s, anthropologists played a key role in the intense struggle to recognize the rights of indigenous populations in the new national constitution.[22]

Anthropologists are not, however, the only potential mediators between local populations and state administrations, international agencies, and nongovernmental organizations. In fact, they compete with members of other academic disciplines (sociologists, psychologists, economists, political scientists, jurists), other professional groups (physicians, lawyers, journalists, writers, artists, museum curators), political or union activists, indigenous organizations, and so on. At stake in such competition is not just the monopoly over the right to "tell the true story" but also the very definition of the problems requiring action from the state.[23]

Conceptualizing one's relationship with the state often assumes a central role in the self-definition of knowledge producers. Thus there are social scientists who work in the service of the state, others who conceive themselves to be acting in the service of populations and social groups whose definition depends on juridical recognition by the state, and others still who identify themselves as autonomous because they believe their relationship to the power of the state to be oppositional, although they may well be on the public payroll—or in Max Weber's apt expression, live "off the back of the state."[24]

The International Space of National Anthropologies

A major focus of this book is the emergence and specialization of distinct national traditions in anthropology. The case studies collected here, drawn from a range of sites within and beyond metropoles, suggest that the relations between the production of anthropological knowledge and the process of state building should be considered from at least three different vantage points: (1) the nature of the political units (nation-state, imperial state) within which a national anthropological tradition develops and toward whose construction it contributes; (2) the position occupied by each political unit within the international space and the transformations over time in the system of interdependence between states; and (3) the interplay between the emergence, maintenance, and transformation of specific national anthropological traditions and the international circulation of scientific theories and models for governing populations.

The notion of national anthropologies, as used for instance by Tomas Gerholm and Ulf Hannerz (1983), can carry two distinct meanings: the adjective "national" may refer to the distinction between nation-state and empire or to the opposition between the national sphere and international space. George W. Stocking gave substance to the first meaning by contrasting nation-building anthropologies with empire-building anthropologies. For example, the determinant factor in British anthropology—the paradigm of an empire-building anthropology—was "experience with dark-skinned 'others' in the overseas Empire" while the dominant feature in the anthropology produced in continental European countries was, by contrast, "the relation between national identity and internal 'otherness'" (1983: 172). National anthropologies were confined to the study of groups living within the national territory, while metropolitan anthropologies embraced a far wider area.

Taken in its second sense, the term national anthropology designates a discipline defined by its local character in contrast to an international anthropology, cosmopolitan in nature and practiced by researchers from diverse backgrounds, whose center is Anglo-American—and to a lesser degree French—anthropology. Seen from the viewpoint of this center, national anthropologies frequently add up to little more than residual forms destined to dissolve into international anthropology.

The analyses contained in this book point out that the alluring formula "science recognizes no boundaries" in fact conceals deep inequalities— beginning with inequalities among languages that virtually wipe off the map large portions of the world's anthropological literature. They also suggest that the circulation of ideas does not suppress power relations but may itself have the effect of constructing and reinforcing hierarchies. At the same time, the constant and frequently implicit slippage between the first and second sense in the volume edited by Gerholm and Hannerz has the side effect of reinforcing a dichotomy that equates one pair of terms, national and international, with another pair, peripheral and central. There is also an implicit hierarchy here (one constructed from the dominant position of the center, apparent in both Stocking 1983 and Gerholm and Hannerz 1983) that associates the scaling of the opposed terms with the supposed theoretical sophistication or naïveté of the anthropological traditions in question. Thus national anthropologies are held to be more modest in scale and content than metropolitan ones, while the latter are in turn assumed to provide the largest contribution to so-called international anthropology.[25] This schema underlies most histories of anthropology. One way to subvert this assumption would be to study the social conditions that generated these dichotomies, including the contributions of anthropologists themselves.

At another level, the distinction between national and imperial anthropologies also calls attention to varying degrees of centrality, within political communities, of the subaltern populations that have been the predominant object of anthropological knowledge. The "native problem" did not carry the same urgency when it related to populations in distant overseas territories as when these populations occupied a strategic place in the national space, albeit in a subaltern position, such as in Mexico, Brazil, or South Africa (see, e.g., Schapera 1939).

Mexican anthropology, for instance, can be described as a national or nation-centered anthropology (Elias 1989 [1968])[26] insofar as it has played a crucial role in the building of a nation-state by developing the ideological base of Mexican nationalism, the implementation of state policies premised on this ideology, and the creation of governmental institutions after the 1930s.[27] The Escuela Nacional de Antropología e Historia (ENAH) for a long time kept its monopoly over the training of anthropologists, thereby supplying the bulk of the Mexican anthropological establishment; the Instituto Nacional de Antropología e Historia (INAH) is at once one of the country's foremost research institutions and one of the most important sites for cultivating images of the nation that, highly valued by Mexican nationalism (the unique synthesis of ethnic mixing and modernity analyzed by Lomnitz), are disseminated throughout Mexico by anthropological and historical museums, headed by the National Museum of Anthropology.[28] Finally, the Instituto Nacional Indigenista (INI) is the most important state body dedicated to the creation and implementation of policies for governing indigenous populations. In fact, it supplies anthropologists with one of their main job opportunities. This case and others presented in this book demonstrate the centrality of the intellectuals' own contribution to the production of national feelings and national consciousness, as Max Weber proposed (1968 [1922]:925–26), and thus to the construction of those political entities we call nations.

Yet national feeling may sometimes be intimately associated with imperial feeling. As Omar Ribeiro Thomaz amply shows in his essay, Portugal provides a striking example of an anthropological tradition that is at once imperial, national, and peripheral. Modern Portuguese nationalism developed around the idea that the greatness of the nation resides in its identity as a people of navigators and empire builders. Its particular drama was its having been the first European country to build up an overseas empire and yet end up occupying only a marginal position among the European powers. As a result, twentieth-century Portuguese anthropology has been distinguished by a concern to celebrate the diversity and unity of this nation-empire and, simultaneously, by a desire to secure the recognition that Portugal was scientifically competitive at an international level (see also Thomaz 2002). The Portuguese experience may be contrasted with that of South Africa: while in Portugal nation-building was achieved by conceiving the empire as a union of disparate peoples, South Africa, at the edge of the British colonial empire, insisted on building a national state founded on the preservation of internal difference.

Nation building and empire building appear, then, not as two exclusive categories but rather as two poles in relation to which social configurations specifically located in time and geography move closer or further away. This idea allows us to avoid the pitfalls of essentializing the notions of center and periphery by linking the transformations occurring within particular anthropological traditions with the history of interdependence between states. Such a perspective suggests a perhaps predictable but nevertheless crucial pattern: the more a state has the capacity to project itself abroad (in colonial or hegemonic form), the more its anthropologists will tend to undertake fieldwork beyond national borders.

The case of U.S. anthropology studied in this volume by Federico Neiburg and Marcio Goldman thus offers a rare case of a shift from a nation-centered anthropology, focused essentially (like Mexican or Brazilian anthropologies) on nation building, to an imperial or metropolitan anthropology. From the middle of the nineteenth century, anthropologists in the United States had focused on the study of groups subjected to a process of subordination within the national territory. Anthropology essentially dealt with issues of internal politics. Until the 1930s, American anthropologists stressed the discipline's capacity to resolve what were viewed as practical problems, focusing its attention on the country's social and cultural diversity: "Indians," "Blacks," and "immigrants" from a variety of origins including small rural communities and large urban cities—as a whole making up an extremely diverse population.

The first projection of this national anthropology beyond its own borders took place during the interwar years in regions under U.S. influence such as Central America, the Caribbean, and the Pacific Islands. Robert Redfield's career may well serve to illustrate this process. His first research project was undertaken in the Department of Anthropology and Sociology at the University of Chicago and focused on Mexican immigrants. This project was developed under the auspices of the Local Community Research Committee, funded by the Rockefeller Foundation and set up by the sociologists Robert Park (Redfield's father-in-law) and Ernest Burgess to analyze the social problems of Chicago's highly diverse population. In the mid-1920s, Redfield abandoned this project and headed south to the country from where these migrants originated, starting his fieldwork in the town of Tepoztlán, close to Mexico City. In 1930 he published his monograph *Tepoztlán, A Mexican Village*. Around the same period, the University of Chicago created a Department of Anthropology separate from the Department of Sociology.[29]

The international scope of American anthropology developed through the 1940s at a pace matching the international expansion of U.S. power. The discipline started to change tack by contributing to the process of empire building, accompanied by the development of area studies.[30] As Neiburg and Goldman show, the involvement of figures such as Gregory Bateson, Ruth Benedict, Geoffrey Gorer, Clyde Kluckhohn, Ralph Linton, Margaret Mead, Rhoda Métraux, George P. Murdock, and many others in the North American war effort during World War II, comprised a crucial phase in the internationalization of this national anthropology.[31] The invention of a new theoretical object for the discipline—the national character studies—sanctioned the existence of a new field for its application: *external politics*. But the results of research on national character (of Americans themselves, the allied nations, and their enemies) were not just designed to pad out the dossiers of the armed forces' intelligence services or done simply to assist in the production of North American foreign policy. Rather, the results were also judged according to academic criteria presented in conferences, published in scientific journals, and transformed into books that keenly sought to establish national character as a full-fledged anthropological object.

At the risk of overstating the case, there are signs that French anthropology—for a long time active not only in its colonial backyard but also

in South and Central America and prominent in international debates—
might today be passing through a symmetrically inverse process of re-
nationalization. The gradual closure of some distant research fields during
the postcolonial period, the drying up of funding sources, and the stimulus
given to the study of the national ethnological heritage through the funding
of the French Ministry of Culture have all helped incite a growing number of
anthropologists to concentrate their attention on French territory.[32] In parallel the ever-increasing weight (in terms of both personnel and resources)
of the North American and, more generally, English-speaking academic
world, has tended to push French anthropology toward the margin of debates. While many researchers from Northern European countries write
directly in English for the international market, most French anthropologists still tend to publish in their own national language as their first choice
despite the fact that it no longer occupies the preeminent position it once
held in international intellectual exchanges.[33] It remains to be seen whether
French anthropology will expand again as part of a virtual European anthropology, which some hope might develop together with the political integration of Europe (Kuper 2004).

The close relationship between a state's zone of influence and the study
field of its anthropologists tells us much about the asymmetries existing
between the various national traditions in anthropology. Indeed, as Lomnitz
points out, anthropologists from the United States study Mexico, but the
reverse is generally not the case. The sphere of activity of Mexican anthropologists is usually confined to areas thought to be of strategic value to the
Mexican state itself. Thus, even those who have undertaken field research in
the United States have focused on Mexican immigrants.

The relationship between anthropology and the state develops within a
national context that itself never exists in isolation. The building of (national
and imperial) states must be comprehended as a process that is simultaneously internal and external—in a situation of interdependence between
political units that compete for status, prestige, and markets.

Various essays in this book suggest that a state's concern for self-legitimacy
vis-à-vis other international powers is decisive for its own internal politics,
since each state's policies toward its subaltern or minority populations are
subject to evaluation on the international stage. As the science of indigenous
populations par excellence, anthropology provides an expedient way of
demonstrating the state's interest in indigenous populations or ethnic minorities. Lomnitz and Souza Lima thus note that exporting the indigenist

model in which anthropology is linked with the state has been a vital part of Mexico's foreign policy, along with the display of the pre-Hispanic past unearthed by archaeology. Similarly, the development of anthropology as a science of native peoples in France and Portugal during the interwar period was connected to the need to demonstrate to an international audience the concern these powers felt for the natives living in their colonies. In the French case, ethnology established itself largely as a colonial science devoted to the identification and comprehension of indigenous populations, invested with the national mission of manifesting the universal values of both science and respect for the peoples under its rule (see L'Estoile 2003). Though with an undoubtedly different scope—and a clearly more nationalist agenda—this view, according to Thomaz, also appears to be the case in the relationship between anthropology of the nation and anthropology of the empire in Portugal. Even today, a concern for national prestige as well as the competition with other states in the study of native populations are driving forces in the support given by states to anthropological institutions or museums.[34]

Such a historical approach to relations of interdependence allows us to analyze the processes involved in the international circulation of individuals, theories, and political technologies, as well as the constitution of national schools (Crawford, Shinn, and Sörlin 1993), by looking both at the interests that support internationalization and those that reinforce the national frame (L'Estoile, in press). Internationalization may indeed prove to be a useful resource, opening up the possibility of creating new alliances; yet it also represents a potential threat to the extent that it encroaches on the interpretative monopoly held by national intellectuals. As Souza Lima shows, the association of some Brazilian anthropologists with Mexican indigenismo helped strengthen their position in the national context, as well as their presence in the development of policies targeted at native populations. Indigenism was not just an importation, but also a reappropriation, or even a nationalization, that found roots in the ways indigenous populations had been traditionally governed in Brazil since Portuguese colonization. A key element in the creation of a national Brazilian anthropology was precisely the desire to assume control over the study of indigenous peoples located within national borders, a task for a long time monopolized by foreign scholars (in particular German ethnologists). Exploring a more recent period, Pacheco shows how international pressure (mostly orchestrated by NGOs) was a crucial factor in forcing the Brazilian state to demarcate indigenous lands, a long-term project that itself opened up a new market for anthropological expertise.[35]

Finally, in South Africa, while Afrikaner anthropology—confronted by a mostly hostile international environment—became ever more inward looking in close alliance with the nationalist regime, English-speaking anthropologists, politically subordinate at a national level, moved toward internationalization. This denationalizing process can be illustrated by the fact that after leaving their home country some of these anthropologists gained international renown as members of the so-called British school rather than members of a South African school.[36]

Hence the close connection between the nation-centered character of national anthropologies and their involvement in internal policy does not imply that we are dealing with isolated or "authentically national" creations, as nationalist thinkers would have us believe. Instead, the notion of national anthropology can only make sense when placed in the context of international relations—both as a space where ideas and models circulate and as a system where political units exist in competitive interdependence.

Local Knowledge and Comparative Perspective

The authors of the essays in this book identify themselves in disciplinary terms as social or cultural anthropologists rather than as full-fledged historians. Most of the contributing chapters—even those dealing with a period of remote history—examine social processes that permit us to understand present-day situations, thereby contributing to what Foucault called a "history of the present." At the same time, all of the essays are located and dated: not only because they deal with situations and processes delimited in space and time but also because their authors are socially and historically situated by their professional and intellectual careers, by their positions within national and international academic space, and by the distinct concerns and rhetorical modes prevailing in the discursive universes to which they belong. Each of the authors is engaged in specific political, academic, and intellectual debates and conflicts. Even the most elementary intellectual sociology tells us that the authors' careers and their institutional and political positions are decisive factors in shaping the way in which their contributions were constructed—including, obviously, this introductory essay. In fact, all of the authors include a more or less explicit dimension of self-analysis, insofar as they involve a reflexive approach to the individual or collective experiences in which they have been embroiled.

Yet this does not mean that these essays are simply a compilation of subjective viewpoints. Instead, this book is an invitation to take part in a collective and comparative practice of reflexivity. Max Weber (1949: 59) urged social scientists to write for a "Chinese reader"—by which he meant that the writer should aim at developing an argument capable of being accepted as valid by someone sharing none of the commonsense assumptions of the writer's own particular social world. Although such a mode of writing is but an ideal, the comparison of cases often at some distance from each other in space and time allows us to relativize judgments that within each of the separate worlds take for granted the links between specific theoretical views on one hand, and particular political positions on the other.

Various situations studied in this book may serve here as examples. Taking the diversity of populations as a basis for policy cannot be labeled as intrinsically conservative or progressive, but each case acquires its meaning in a particular historical configuration. In other words, recognizing the uniqueness of a group's cultural tradition in relation to the other groups with which it interacts can be just as easily associated with a progressive political position, when the anthropologist supports the aspirations of the Kanak of New Caledonia, for example, or with a reactionary position, such as the case of anthropologists actively supporting the South African regime under apartheid.

Comparison therefore enables a temporary neutralization of normative value judgments. Placed in the context of a wider set of configurations, the engagement of anthropologists during World War II in the fight against the Axis powers, usually positively evaluated, or the involvement of others in the production of apartheid's classifications, negatively evaluated, can be observed within the same analytical framework, allowing us to address both similarities and differences. It should be stressed that our intention is not to invalidate ethical-political judgments concerning particular episodes of the discipline's history, but rather to provide grounds for a sociological understanding of these episodes.

This historical and comparative approach allows for a radical shift in perspective. Instead of assuming that the relationship between the production of knowledge and the construction of policies is based on a separation of science from the state, we can model a shared space where sets of knowledge practices and sets of policies progressively take shape. In turn, this approach allows us to observe a process of mutual construction among states (conceived as institutions/fields of struggle for governing social groups perceived to be different, and as instruments of national unification), anthropological knowledge, and population groups themselves.

Clearly not just anthropology is implicated here. Similar processes characterize the other social sciences.[37] Indeed, in this volume we also hope to provide other social scientists with analytical principles that allow a deeper reflection on the connections between academic and political practices, and to shift beyond the example of reflexive inquiries based on an unexamined naturalization of the current state of relations between researchers, public debates, and patrons of research into trendy issues.

Furthermore, the involvement of the social sciences in the formation of state policies enables a deeper understanding of the emergence of different national academic traditions. Beyond an analysis of the varying place occupied by anthropology in the different systems of disciplines, teaching, and research (here close ties with philosophy or prehistory; there alliances with archaeology, sociology, or linguistics), the multiple forms of interdependence with the state as analyzed here are key factors in bringing about national specificities.[38] Such a reflexive analysis can open up new critical horizons, contributing to the anthropology of knowledge and of identification processes, as well as to a comparative historical sociology of the state.

Notes

1 Among others, see Asad 1973; Copans 1975; Horowitz 1974; Leclerc 1972; Leiris 1950; Stauder 1980; and Weaver 1973.

2 It is worth remembering that in the United States the critique of anthropology as a form of domination (see for example Marcus and Fischer 1986) was linked to the redefinition of the discipline's frontiers, assailed at the time by the rapid growth of cultural studies in the country's universities.

3 We are certainly not the first to propose swapping denunciation for analysis. See, among others, Asad 1991; and Pels 1997.

4 Raymond Aron—himself a political journalist for the conservative daily *Le Figaro* and professor of sociology at the Sorbonne from 1955 onward—explicitly used Max Weber's lectures to raise the problem of the relations between "the scientist and the politician" as a practical dilemma: "For the professor of social sciences who wishes to be politically active, the outcome of all this is a permanent tension. . . . Each of us finds his or her own response to this personal problem concerning the relations between science and politics" (Aron 1959: 28).

5 The importance of the large U.S. foundations (Rockefeller, Carnegie, Ford, Wenner-Gren) in the development of anthropological knowledge, whether in Great Britain during the interwar period, or in Brazil from the 1970s onward, is well known.

6 We should also mention here hybrid publications situated on the borders between different worlds, such as journals with academic contributions published by NGOs and those linked to social movements, parties, or state bodies.

7 Colonial administration seminar, May 1933, in Malinowski Papers, Mal. 588, London School of Economics and Political Science.

8 This was the case of Iberic monarchies of the early modern period where the monarch controlled the ecclesiastical establishment through the intermediation of royal patronage. In imperial Brazil this model lasted until the separation of church and state in 1890.

9 Also see, among others, Bourdieu 1994; Elias 1972; and Tilly 1975.

10 Souza Lima's analysis (1995) of the conflicts in the Brazilian administration over indigenous policies is a case in point.

11 See, for example, Sen 1989 and Whitley 1984.

12 An identical point is made in a stimulating essay by Pels and Salemink (1999). Also see Thomas 1994 and Fabian 2000.

13 Arthur Ramos (1903–1949) was among the most prominent Brazilian intellectuals in the 1930s and 1940s, publishing works in a number of fields such as psychiatry, physical and cultural anthropology, social psychology, education, hygiene, and psychoanalysis. He founded the Brazilian Society of Anthropology and Ethnology. See Dias Duarte 2000; Seyferth 1989; Corrêa 1982.

14 Beyond this exceptional case, career shifts from university to administrative and political responsibilities, and vice versa, are far from rare. A recent case in Brazil is that of Fernando Henrique Cardoso, professor at the University of São Paulo in the 1960s, and a sociologist of international renown, who became president of the Republic (1994–2002). We could identify similar political and academic careers in other national contexts, involving other disciplines such as law, economics, or medicine.

15 This situation may be compared to that of bodies responsible for producing national statistics in various countries, such as the Institut National de la Statistique et des Études Économiques (INSEE) in France, the Instituto Brasileiro de Geografia e Estatística (IBGE) in Brazil, the Dirección General de Estadisticas in Mexico, or the Census Bureau in the United States.

16 Claiming the existence of a mutually constitutive relationship between anthropological knowledge, state policies, and the populations simultaneously constructed as the objects of such policies and knowledge does not imply a radical constructivism. It would be nonsensical to claim, for instance, that the populations who lived in what later became Brazilian territory were not different from the Europeans who conquered them; however, it is necessary to recognize that the conquest and the colonial and postcolonial state's implementation of legislation

unifying extremely heterogeneous groups under the generic category of Indians provided the groundwork for the much later development of an ethnological discipline specifically focused on the study of indigenous populations.

17 . In this sense, the process described by Kuper bears close resemblance to those examined in Cohn's pioneering studies (1990: 224–54) of the effects of colonial administration on the definition of native social groups in South Asia and, on another plane, those contemplated in Handler's analyses (1988) of the effects of anthropological production on the objectification of national cultures in Quebec.

18 This change began in the colonial period (see L'Estoile 1997a).

19 On Brazil, for example, see Albert 1997a and Ramos 1998.

20 Thus, the AAA Committee on Public Policy sets itself a double goal: "1. To advance the use of anthropological knowledge and expertise in policy making at the local, state, national and international levels; and 2. To increase the presence of anthropological expertise in the local and national media when policy issues are discussed."

21 Thus, the Associação Brasileira de Antropologia (ABA) possesses two commissions explicitly responsible for accompanying the evolution of policy-making issues: one commission on indigenous topics and another commission on human rights, monitoring "violation of the human rights of minority groups." Currently, ABA is represented on the National Indian Foundation's Indigenist Council, on the Inter-Sectorial Commission for Indigenous Health, on the Commission for Analysis of Projects in the Area of Indigenous School Education, as well as participating in the Indigenous Peoples Directive of the World Bank.

22 See, for example, Carneiro da Cunha 1987.

23 On the British case, see L'Estoile 1997b; and Mills, this volume.

24 In fact, similar situations may occur in nonstate contexts. Thus in those U.S. universities that are totally or partially dependent on private funds, academics whose chairs are endowed through profits accrued on Wall Street may nonetheless think of themselves as fighting against the system.

25 A clear example of this representation of anthropology can be found in the principle underlying the publication of a special issue of the journal Ethnos (Gerholm and Hannerz 1983) dedicated to national anthropologies. The case studies in the issue concentrate on the periphery (Brazil, India, Poland, Sweden, the Sudan, and Canada). The issue closes with a text expressing a "view from the centre," written by a member of the Anthropology Department at the University of Chicago (Stocking 1983; 2001).

26 The nation-centered orientation of thinking (natiozentrische Denkorientierung) is not exclusive to nationalist ideologies but rather pertains to all theories of culture or society whose horizon is defined by a descriptive and prescriptive ambition nurtured by ideas of high culture and good society relating to these social and cultural entities called nations (Elias 1989 [1968]).

27 As in Mexico, Brazilian anthropologists also focused on constructing images of nationhood (see Peirano 1981).

28 It is significant that when the Sub-Comandante Marcos organized the much-publicized Zapatista march from Chiapas to Mexico City in 2002, he chose the National School of Anthropology as a fitting place to stay on reaching the capital.

29 We thank Christian Topalov for calling our attention to these aspects of Redfield's career.

30 This transition process involved funding for research projects in strategic zones. The personal histories of two of the most famous of postwar American anthropologists, Clifford Geertz and David Schneider, are emblematic in this context: both of their careers reveal the opportunities opened up by the expansion of the American hegemony. On Geertz and his fieldwork in Indonesia, see Kuper 1999a: 77–81, and Geertz 2001: chapter 1. On Schneider in the U.S. Navy and in Micronesia, see Bashkov 1991: 171; and Schneider and Handler 1995: 61–67, 85–119.

31 Participation in the war effort also produced effects on the social sciences. See Schweber 2002, for instance, on the emergence of quantitative sociology.

32 See Carol Rogers 2001 and L'Estoile and Naepels, 2004.

33 French was the official language of the First International Congress of Anthropological and Ethnological Sciences, which was held in London in 1934. At the time, the texts of Durkheim, Mauss, and other authors from the French sociological school were often read in their original versions in both English and U.S. universities.

34 It may be speculated that one of the factors at play in the construction of the Kanak cultural center in the French domain of New Caledonia—a project handed over to one of the major names of contemporary architecture—was boosting France's profile in the Pacific region (see Bensa, this volume).

35 A number of nongovernmental organizations defending indigenous minorities—such as Survival International, created in 1969 to help defend the Yanomami—have anthropologists among their active members; these groups play an important role in mobilizing international public opinion. The Yanomami territory was officially delimited by the Brazilian state in 1992, in time for the opening of the Rio de Janeiro World Summit on the Environment.

36 Among others, this is the case of Isaac Schapera, Meyer Fortes, Hilda Kuper, and Max Gluckman. Adam Kuper (1999c) argues that this was an instance of the periphery transforming the center.

37 See, for example, Rueschmeyer and Skocpol 1996 and Whitley 1984.

38 See Elias 1982; Whitley 1984; and Wagner, Wittrock, and Wollmann 1991.

Benoît de L'Estoile

RATIONALIZING COLONIAL DOMINATION?

Anthropology and Native Policy in French-Ruled Africa

> Bureaucratic administration means fundamentally
> domination through knowledge. This is the feature that makes
> it specifically rational.—Max Weber, *Economy and Society*

> Science in the service of colonization always leads to Man,
> the people, and the native environment. The great colonial science is
> still ultimately the science of man.—Governor-General Jules Brévié,
> "Science et colonisation"

The bulk of the literature dealing with relations between the social sciences and the state assumes a fundamental contradiction between the two, which, although often concealed by unnatural alliances, eventually reemerges because scientific progress by its very nature tends toward increasing autonomy from institutionalized power. In particular, the relations between anthropological knowledge and policies of population management are usually treated as deviant practices to be condemned on ethical and epistemological grounds.

Here I wish to take a different approach, following the trail blazed by Bronislaw Malinowski in his formulation of a program for the "rationalization of anthropology and administration," in which he pointed out a potential affinity between administrative and scientific forms of rationality, founded on their common "interest in rationalization" (1930). Malinowski's program was intended both to reform colonial administration through what he called a "scientific control of colonial cooperation," and to catalyze a scientific revolution in anthropology, shifting from an antiquarian approach to a study of contemporary problems (see L'Estoile 1994). To explore this line of thought, I take a two-fold approach. At a theoretical level, my analysis makes use of Max Weber's idea that knowledge and rationality typify a specifically modern form of domination. At an empirical level, the same tools are deployed to study the highly complex relations between the growing body of knowledge concerning native peoples and the practices of French colonial authorities in Africa between 1920 and the 1950s.[1]

Attaining a clear understanding of this "elective affinity" means abandoning conceptions hampered by academic specialization and the division of labor between disciplines. This demands bringing together texts at present usually classified under different labels, whether as "history of ethnology,"[2] or as "colonial history." As a first example, we can consider the following text from 1925:

> When a colony includes peoples with a civilization inferior to, or very different from, our own, competent ethnologists may be just as urgently required as competent engineers, foresters or physicians. . . . It is generally accepted that more than capital is needed to improve our colonies as completely and economically as possible. Scientists and technicians are needed to provide a methodological inventory of the colony's wealth in natural resources (mines, forests, crops, etc.) and to identify the best means for harnessing them. Is the native population not the first among these natural resources—the resource without which the others remain largely unattainable, especially in equatorial or tropical areas? Is there not, therefore, a major interest in studying the population methodically, in having a precise, in-depth knowledge of its languages, religions and social forms, which it is unwise to rashly wreck? (Lévy-Bruhl 1925: 1)

This text includes ethnologists among the scientists and technicians who, by ordering the colonial world, were to help harness tropical resources in a rational way. The native population—classified as part of the "wealth of natural resources" and proposed as the means for tapping the others—required its own specialists. Along with the engineers and foresters who were to rationally control nature, and the doctors to take care of native bodies, ethnologists were to try to understand "native civilizations."

This declaration reads today as a blatant violation of the principle of scientific autonomy. Yet the author's prominent position in the French university establishment belies this interpretation. Close to the Durkheimian group, Lucien Lévy-Bruhl was professor of philosophy at the Sorbonne, editor of the prestigious journal *Revue Philosophique,* and internationally recognized for his scholarly work on "primitive mentality." The declaration comes from an article presenting the newly created Institute of Ethnology at the University of Paris, of which Lévy-Bruhl was secretary-general. His arguments were convincing enough for colonial governments to grant considerable amounts of funding. In 1929, for instance, the institute received 166,000 French francs in subsidies from the colonies as compared to 10,160 francs from its own sources (Lévy-Bruhl 1929: 421). The Institute of Ethnology depended for its very existence on colonial subsidies.

We can compare the quote above with an argument used a few years later in a text about science and colonization:

> Colonization has entered its scientific phase . . . Here too, knowledge is necessary for planning and taking actions. . . Black Africa's agricultural growth depends on detailed agronomic studies, sustained and impartial experiments, but also an equal investment in knowledge of the native environment, including African peasants and their mentality, methods and aptitudes. (Brévié 1936)

This assertion of the need for an impartial science as part of colonial policy was not mere rhetoric. The author, Jules Brévié, who served as governor general of French West Africa from 1931 to 1937, played a decisive role in founding research institutions in the colonies. In 1937 he set up the French Institute of Black Africa (Institut Français d'Afrique Noire; IFAN); and in 1942, when he was in the Ministry of the Colonies, he created the Office des Recherches Scientifiques Coloniales (Office for Colonial Scientific Research), later the Office des Recherches Scientifiques et Techniques Outre-Mer (Office for Scientific Research Overseas, ORSTOM).

How are we to explain the curious similarity between these two statements by authors holding quite dissimilar positions—the one among the academic elite and the other in the top ranks of the colonial administration? The debates on anthropology and colonialism have tended to provide a ready-made answer: ethnologists served as handmaidens of colonialism and provided the instruments for manipulating the colonized. Seen in such a way, this kind of similarity simply provides blatant evidence of an "objective complicity." Conversely, those working to counter this charge present it as little more than a tactical ruse; declarations such as Lévy-Bruhl's or Malinowski's are thought to have paid little more than lip service to colonial authorities, a necessary evil allowing academics to secure the material means to pursue their truly—and purely—scientific objectives (e.g., Goody 1995: 42–43). If, however, we refuse to accept the simplistic alternatives of condemnation or denial, we need to inquire further into this rapprochement between prestigious academics and colonial figures, both keen to advance the project of rational colonization grounded in the scientific study of native peoples.

Bureaucracy and the Rationalization of Domination

To investigate these affinities between administrative and scientific forms of rationality, we can borrow from Weber's ideas concerning the ways in which bureaucracy rationalizes domination.[3] Weber explicitly constructed his typology not out of the actual characteristics of specific forms of domination, but out of the principle underlying the legitimacy to which a particular form lays claim. Nonetheless, Weber also proposed a description of the formal characteristics of various types of domination, whose features were not necessarily determined by the principle of legitimation. The process of rationalizing domination can be analyzed by taking into account this quite productive ambiguity.

For Weber, bureaucratic domination comprises a specifically modern and rational form of domination; it is the final point in a process of rationalization, itself part of a broader trend specific to Western civilization. He states: "Experience tends universally to show that the purely bureaucratic type of administrative organization—that is, the monocratic variety of bureaucracy—is, from a purely technical point of view, capable of attaining the highest degree of efficiency and is in this sense formally the most rational known means of exercising authority over human beings" (1968 [1922]: 223).

What makes bureaucratic domination "specifically rational" is thus its being "domination through knowledge." This includes both "technical knowledge" and "knowledge growing out of experience in the service" (225). Bureaucratic organizations acquire "a special knowledge of facts, and have available a store of documentary material peculiar to themselves" (ibid.). Weber thus points out the mobilization of knowledge as a typical feature of bureaucratic domination.

Advances in bureaucratic domination, insofar as such domination is based on the technical qualifications of civil servants, call for specialized training.[4] For Weber, bureaucratic domination thus appears closely associated with two other characteristics: a process of rationalization; and the crucial role played by knowledge and expertise both in administrative practices and in the training of administrative staff. Rationalizing the instruments of knowledge within one's area of competence, fostered by bureaucratic activity, thus runs in harmony with rationalizing the systems for producing knowledge by scientific activity (999). At this first level of interpretation, rationality, as far as Weber is concerned, is a positive quality of this form of domination, in contrast to "irrational" forms (whether charismatic or traditional in type).

This "rational-legal" type of domination may also, however, be approached through the key Weberian concepts of legitimacy and belief. According to Weber, the legitimacy of traditional authority rests on the belief in the sacredness of tradition, while that of charismatic authority depends on a belief in the charismatic leader being "endowed with supernatural, superhuman or at least specifically exceptional powers or qualities" (241). Similarly, the legitimacy of legal domination is grounded in a belief in its rational character and "in the legality of enacted rules" (215). The reason we can describe this specifically modern form of domination as rational in this latter sense is that its legitimacy stems from the belief in its being founded on reason.

At issue then is not assessing how truly "rational" modern bureaucratic domination actually is (or how "traditional" traditional authority is, a question of little interest to Weber) but rather analyzing what is implied by asserting this form of domination in the name of reason. Weber thus calls for us to take seriously the arguments used to justify domination (rather than dismissing them out of hand as "ideological") because they affect the beliefs and practices of rulers, ruled, and bureaucrats alike.

Following Weber's steps, we can say that one of the characteristics of the modern state is its claim to rationality. Conformity to reason thus becomes a principle of legitimation—an essential criterion for assessing the legitimacy of domination, as well as an argument toward its justification. This may be dubbed the "Enlightened rule" paradigm, in reference to the alliance forged between the specialists of reason, philosophers and scientists, and modernizers of the monarchy in eighteenth-century Europe (Brian 1994). Science, the ultimate means of rationalization and progress, has gradually become a central factor in legitimizing state power, virtually replacing religion in this function (Elias 1982). Support for science provides evidence that the state is guided by the principle of rationality—that it has not only law but reason too on its side.

However, this convenient formulation in terms of state and science does not boil down to a confrontation between two self-contained and mutually exclusive entities. Indeed Weber himself insisted on taking into account the role played by administrative officials, who have a particular interest in formal rationalization because it shields them from the arbitrariness of rulers (1968 [1922]: 226). Rather than imagining two antagonistic monoliths, it makes more sense to see the state as a space where interdependent groups compete and where specialists in knowledge (who may or may not be administrative officials) intervene as both potential allies and rivals.[5] Likewise science should not be taken to refer to an eternal truth but to the set of practices recognized as "scientific" at any given time, the boundaries of this set itself being a crucial issue. Thus the notion of rational domination is open to a double interpretation along the lines of Weber's proposals. On the one hand, it refers to a process of formal rationalization of the methods of domination; on the other hand, it indicates the principle of legitimation— that is, the claim that a form of domination is rational.

In analyzing the uses of science by the state, two dimensions can be contrasted: first, science provides the state and its administrative officials with resources for rationalizing instruments of orientation and control; second, it can fit into legitimation strategies (L'Estoile 1997b: 348). Most analyses of the relations between scientific rationality (in the social sciences) and modern forms of domination overemphasize one dimension at the cost of the other by insisting on either legitimation or instrumentalization in the emergence of "political technology."[6] It is vital that we bear in mind this double aspect of rationalizing domination. In its favor, the concept of legitimation helps us escape from a narrow analysis in terms of instrumentality and move beyond the simplistic opposition, laden with value judgments, between a utilitarian know-how and a "useless" science presumed to be devoid of interests and, therefore, noble. For the purpose of legitimating domination, a disinterested science might turn out to be more effective than a technique too obviously aimed at practical goals.

These two aspects are ideal-typical: they should not be seen as mutually exclusive but rather as two poles between which actual colonial scientific practices were located. Claims to rationalize the study of populations in a colonial context can thus be analyzed not just as part of a wider effort to develop instruments for deciphering the colonized world but also in conjunction with arguments about the legitimacy of domination.

Identifying and Understanding Native Peoples

The endeavor to acquire a scientific understanding of the lands and peoples subjected to colonial domination has more usually been analyzed in terms of instrumentalization. For example, the considerable time and energy put into learning by explorers and soldiers before and during conquest has been interpreted as intelligence activity, as techniques for conquering populations and then controlling them once pacified (e.g., Nordman and Raison 1980). More generally speaking, administering conquered territories called for the establishment of a colonial order in both the cognitive and political senses of the word "order." Anthropological discourse in its various versions provided instruments for this ordering by offering both criteria for identifying native populations and interpretive frameworks for making sense of what was perceived as baffling and unintelligible behavior.

The French administration urged the study of natives because it needed to learn about the lands and peoples it ruled. The administrative hierarchy regularly recommended that reports (monographs) be written to synthesize what was known about each district. The repetitiveness of such recommendations is evidence that they often went unheeded. In 1920, however, the Commissaire de la République—head of the French administration in the Cameroons—insisted on the urgent need to know this territory, which had been taken away from Germany and entrusted to France as a mandate by the League of Nations following World War I. He asked for descriptive monographs that were to include ethnography under the following headings: "*Ethnography*—history—languages—customs—customary law—religion—grouping of populations and native authorities—racial characteristics—population—density—habitat—forms of family life—clothing."[7]

During the interwar period, a number of colonial officials, in public statements as well as in administrative correspondence, repeatedly insisted on the need to identify different human groups, usually called "races," and to adapt policies to them. The ethnic grid was thus to be a key for decoding the natives. The colonial bureaucracy sought to distinguish and localize "ethnic groups" (an academic term that would slowly replace the use of "race"). These categories for interpreting social differences informed both administrative practices and scholarly writings.[8]

Administrative and scientific objectification converged in the joint production of instruments for identifying and classifying native peoples. This process culminated in ethnology in the strict sense of the term—that is, a scholarly practice devoted to reconstituting the origins and migrations of ethnic groups. The colonial bureaucracy repeatedly asked for ethnic inventories, complete with population estimates for various groups as well as maps showing their geographical distribution (for a comparison with India, see Cohn 1990). While claiming to be guided by political aims, such inventories also followed scholarly principles. These products of administrative rationality could also travel to other spaces, as they might be published in scholarly journals or, alternatively, used for propaganda purposes.

A report from the Bureau of Political Affairs, dated 30 October 1933, thus gave an "account of the different linguistic groups in the Cameroons" with numerical estimates and an evaluation of the hegemonic tendencies of certain language groups, in particular Fang and Duala.[9] This document was prepared with practical purposes in mind, as the colonial government hoped to reduce the high number of African languages spoken (thought to hinder communication) by selecting and fostering those deemed the strongest, while simultaneously determining which of them should be learned by administrators.[10] The same report, under the title "Ethnic and Linguistic Inventory of the Cameroons under French Mandate," came out a few months later as a document in the *Journal de la Société des Africanistes,* the mouthpiece of the Society of Africanists founded in 1930 ("Inventaire ethnique" 1934).

Still, in the French Cameroons, one of the most acute political problems as identified by the government was that in the north, "pagan" peoples (known as Kirdi) were under the rule of Islamic (Fulani) groups. In 1923 and 1924, when the government decided to create ethnically homogeneous Kirdi cantons independent from the Fulani, administrators were urged to study native customs there.[11] Ten years later, Chauleur, head of the Political Affairs Bureau, wrote a long memorandum, "The Northern Region," as a preparatory guide for the commissary's tour through the area. He insisted on the importance of sorting out the ethnic problem: "The reason for placing special emphasis on the tribes in North Cameroon is that the political question primarily depends on the movements, relations and reactions of the various races peopling the area" (1934: 1). Chauleur devoted no fewer than twenty-six pages to these "races," with estimates of their ethnic distribution as well as locations on maps. In 1935 through 1937, he used the service's archives, German sources, and studies in physical anthropology by the colonial physician Dr. Poutrin to draft a "general study of the peopling of the Cameroons" with the aim of identifying the origins, migrations, and mixtures of the various groups (Dugast 1949: vi; 1948). Chauleur's study was published in the *Bulletin de la Société d'Études Camerounaises* in 1943 under the title "An Ethnological Sketch for the Study of the Principal Tribes of the Territories of the Cameroons under French Mandate."

This circulation between colonial files and academic publications tells us much about the overlap between administrative and scientific knowledge.

Significantly, the production and refinement of ethnic classifications continued to be a central concern for the research organizations that gradually came into being. In 1937, the Committee of Historical and Scientific Studies of Black Africa, an official learned society formally headed by the governor-general, was reorganized as IFAN (French Institute for Black Africa), a research center staffed with scholars sent from the mother country. In a sense, this can be seen as an instance of an institution dedicated to producing scientific knowledge acquiring an increasing degree of autonomy from the colonial administration. However, IFAN continued to fulfill its task of inventorying and identifying native peoples. Its local centers kept "ethnic files" for storing the data collected both by administrators and researchers. Thus the IFAN center for Cameroon produced an "Ethnic Inventory of South Cameroon," drawing on Chauleur's writings, updated from Political Affairs Bureau archives, and completed with census counts, as well as reports from tours of inspection, district officers, and members of the health service, and finally by the author's own research (Dugast 1949).[12]

The same applies to ethnic maps, an instrument used to identify and locate native peoples for both scholarly and administrative purposes.[13] In 1939, the *Journal de la Société des Africanistes* published a "schematic map of populations in the Cameroons" drawn up by P. H. Chombart de Lauwe (a young ethnologist and member of Griaule's fourth "Sahara-Cameroon" mission who would later pioneer urban research) and J. Deboudaud (a colonial administrator). In the text accompanying the map, the authors state their purpose in crafting this "temporary instrument" and how it affected their methodology: "The current interest of a distribution map is not to illustrate a more or less arbitrary classification but to note the major distinctions useful for the administration. Hence, all traits are useful for defining and delimiting an ethnic group, especially the material, political and religious customs, more so than the geographical and linguistic data mentioned previously" (Chombart de Lauwe and Deboudaud 1939: 197).

Ethnographic maps were thus designed as tools for the management of native populations as much as instruments for collecting and storing scientific knowledge about them. After 1945, the task of drawing such maps was gradually assigned to professional geographers and ethnologists within IFAN, who completed and systematized the work already accomplished by administrators in the colonial service.[14]

Beyond this concern for identification, ethnographic practice was also widely associated with a desire to understand peoples considered primitive or backward. One conspicuous feature of colonial knowledge includes the large part played by what Weber called "knowledge growing out of experience in the service." In the absence of watertight compartments characteristic of academic experience today, documentary material produced within the bureaucracy could turn into "scientific" evidence entering into scholarly discourse. A monograph by Felix Éboué provides a striking instance of this overlap between administrative and scientific knowledge, all the more so given both the author's exceptional career and the fact that this study was presented as exemplary during its day.

Félix Éboué (1884–1944), a man of African descent from French Guiana, obtained a diploma from the Colonial School in 1908. For many years he remained a local administrator in Ubangi-Shari, a colony at the bottom of the colonial hierarchy (now the Central African Republic). Éboué initially presented his study, titled "The peoples of Ubangi-Shari," to the ethnography section of the International Congress of Anthropology and Prehistorical Archeology, which was held during the 1931 Colonial Exhibition in Paris. It was then published as an "essay in ethnography, linguistics and social economics" in several colonial and scholarly journals, and finally edited as a separate pamphlet by the government-general.[15] Raphaël Antonetti, governor-general of French Equatorial Africa from 1924 to 1934, urged officials under his control to emulate Éboué's example in their districts: an official circular sent to all administrators and published in the *Journal Officiel de l'AÉF* cited Éboué's monograph as a model. A copy of the monograph was sent to every station, with the following comments:

> The remarkable study published by Mr Éboué raises, furthermore, a question of a more general interest to all those called to command in the bush. I shall not tire of repeating that good administration must be based on as complete a knowledge as possible of our natives. Nothing can replace this knowledge, and this is why I should like to see administrators make, insofar as possible, reports similar to Mr Éboué's, pursuing a deeper understanding of their natives not so much as an exercise in curiosity or an intellectual pastime, but as the means to avoid, thanks to it, many an error, while also discovering how to use these very customs in such a way that those they administer understand what we expect of them in their own language.[16]

Ethnographic reports were thus presented as a paragon to the whole colonial service.[17] The objective was to learn the code (i.e., customs) of the societies to be administered. Systematic knowledge and the effort to understand the natives provided instruments of communication and command that colonial administrators had to master in order to properly discharge their duties.

Antonetti also sent the monograph to scholars teaching at the Colonial School and at the Institute of Ethnology in France. Lévy-Bruhl thanked the governor-general for the pamphlet as well as for his support of the institute. His words are worth noting: "I read with much interest these observations about the peoples of Ubangi-Shari made by a man who has a talent for seeing and who apparently has a long experience of these populations. The light ethnology can shed on the mentality of the natives has never been more invaluable than today. Fortunately, our administrators are increasingly aware of the usefulness—one might even say the necessity—of such studies and lend them all the support they can."[18] Lévy-Bruhl's praise of Éboué's qualities as an observer is typical of the division of labor at the time, where metropolitan scholars were dependent on the quality of the data they received from those doing fieldwork, itself a consequence of government support (L'Estoile, in press).

In the 1930s the upper echelon of the colonial service became more actively involved in promoting studies by local officers about "their" natives, at least in some colonies. The emphasis on understanding was stirred by a new sense of insecurity about the empire. Following the Yen-Bay uprising in Indochina—interpreted as the outcome of a lack of contact between colonial officials and the natives—a 1930 circular from the Ministry of Colonies recommended to all administrators that they maintain closer contacts with the people under them by making more frequent tours and taking more personal interest in the natives.[19] Thus in French Equatorial Africa, for instance, official correspondence firmly encouraged inquiries into native customs.[20]

The quest for a "political technology" capable of controlling and transforming native societies thus emerges as a driving force behind the investment made by some colonial officials in understanding the natives. By providing both tools for identifying peoples and frameworks for interpreting their behavior, anthropology helped to create rational instruments for ordering the colonial world; instruments that helped to reassure the service that it could remain in control of a rather elusive situation. However this desire to establish a rational order had to contend with the strategies of the colonized—and the result was in many cases a mere semblance of order (Pels 1996).

Legitimating Domination: The Authority of Science

The new emphasis on acquiring knowledge and understanding of the natives may also have been related to a change in the conditions of colonial domination, in particular the new need to legitimate it on the international stage. The legitimizing component was already present in academic practices beyond the production of means of orientation. Insofar as it lent scientific credibility to evolutionist interpretations, anthropology since the nineteenth century had played a key role in formulating and justifying the colonial power's "civilizing mission." Even as late as 1930, in a statement reproduced in the *Bulletin de l'Afrique Française*, Governor-General Jules Carde declared to the General Council of French West Africa: "If we accept that there are evolved peoples and backward races and that the general interest lies in raising the latter to the level of the former, then the principle of colonialism is implicitly justified."

Within the gamut of academic colonial practices, ethnography, often in association with archeology, presented a sort of "ground zero" or "prehistory" documenting the state of native peoples before they entered history; the latter starting with conquest, the first act in a civilizing process propelled from the outside. This evolutionist narrative shaped most ethnographic displays in colonial or universal exhibitions (Greenhalgh 1987; Coombes 1994; L'Estoile 2003).

The need to find a new legitimacy for colonial domination formed the background for a growing interest in anthropology during the interwar period. During the 1931 International Colonial Exhibition in Paris, Albert Sarraut, a former minister of colonies and theoretician of colonization, did not refrain from talking about colonization's "moral crisis, crisis of domination, crisis of authority" (quoted in Hardy 1932). This feeling of crisis arose out of a series of new challenges: budding nationalist unrest in Asia (British India, the Dutch Indies, and French Indochina) and North Africa; demands being voiced by urban elites in Senegal and Dahomey; anticolonial propaganda being spread by the Komintern; and criticism issuing from the United States, Germany, and Italy—countries that had missed out on the colonial pie.

In 1932 Sarraut, once again minister of colonies at this time, addressed a group of Colonial School students in a speech that was reproduced in the journal *Outre-Mer* of that year: "The time when force alone could reign is over. . . We should not oppress, we should convince. Convince about what? About the supreme usefulness of our oversight, about our scientific and moral superiority, about the deep humanity of our intentions." These words echo Weber's analysis: domination does not just depend on a lineup of forces but also on a belief in its legitimacy. Sarraut clearly pointed to the need for a legitimacy based on a demonstration sufficient to convince French and, especially, international opinion. During his 1931 speech he described a new context of international competition: "A new international censorship pays closer attention to happenings in the colonies than it used to." This international pressure was especially strong in the case of the mandated territories, since the mandatory power had to report regularly to the League of Nations. As a study of "primitive" populations, ethnology could be used to explain the difficulties encountered by the colonizing powers in making changes and thus justify any delays or shortcomings in relation to proclaimed ideals.

Legitimating colonial domination through science was also directed at the colonized. According to Édouard de Martonne, a geographer who extolled the *savant colonial* (colonial scholar)—a category including both professional scientists and amateurs—science set up a barrier to demands from the newly schooled native elites: "At a time when, in nearly all colonies, demands are being voiced by native elites tipsy with their young knowledge as if with new wine, it is wise to moderate their overhasty presumption by demonstrating our scientific superiority, which alone might be capable of fettering their minds without constricting them: it is necessary to persuade these pupils of civilization that the degree of emancipation naturally grows with the degree of culture, and that nothing can replace the maturity brought about by science" (1930: 164). Regardless of the field of study, practicing science was thus construed as the justification for a position of domination. As spelled out in a school textbook published in 1916 for French West Africa, the French, "more advanced in civilization," were allowing Africans to share the benefits of science, "the White Man's work"; and blacks could study so as to profit from this situation (quoted in Conklin 1997:136). What was important here was not so much the direct utility of science but the fact that it served as a demonstration of the colonizing power's superiority and, therefore, of the legitimacy of its domination, since it had reason on its side.[21]

The legitimacy problem was addressed in different terms by reformers calling for more attention to be paid to native societies and for a more progressive policy. Maurice Delafosse (1870–1926), who after a long administrative career in West Africa had become a professor of ethnology and African languages at the Colonial School, proposed in 1921 a program for a "new orientation of native policy in Black Africa." His proposal opened with an "examination of conscience": "We actually feel the necessity of excusing, or at the very least justifying, actions that, to speak plainly, have consisted on our part of dispossessing peoples of their independence for the profit of our own country" (1921: 140). Objecting to the priority given to economic objectives and critically assessing colonial achievements, Delafosse argued that the effects on native populations should be the main criteria for the legitimacy of colonial policies: "It is absolutely necessary that, for them, our intervention be a cause of, and an element in, progress and happiness; otherwise, any attempt at colonizing would be doomed to failure" (147). This notion provided the touchstone for evaluating France's performance in discharging her duties as a colonial power: "We must ask ourselves whether the policy we have implemented up till now toward natives is really the one that ought to favor the rational evolution of black societies towards their well-being or, on the contrary, whether it does not risk disintegrating these societies and leading them to their ruin" (ibid.).

Delafosse's plea sheds light on another fundamental dimension of legitimation in modern states: the state is supposed to exercise domination for the well being and progress of its subjects (Foucault 1996). The colonial state was justified insofar as it brought progress to the lands and peoples under its rule; indeed, the word "development" began cropping up for the first time. Along with the prevailing argument justifying a European presence by the economic necessity of improving (*mise en valeur*) the colonies by harnessing the "natural wealth" (mining and farming) left untapped by their traditional inhabitants, colonization was now to be legitimated by a new concern for the natives.

Investing in the human sciences in order to acquire a rational knowledge of human behavior was thus in line with two concerns claimed by the colonial state: rational government and the welfare of colonial subjects. The scientific study of the natives offered, along with achievements in health and education, a convenient way to demonstrate simultaneously what Sarraut called the "deep humanity" and "scientific superiority" of the colonial power. What was new, therefore, was not the idea—already present in the nineteenth century—that colonial expansion had to be grounded in science. At that time, botany, geography, and geology were mobilized to help inventory the wealth of the tropics (Bonneuil 1999). In the early twentieth century, physical anthropology, which many colonial doctors practiced, was developing in conjunction with tropical medicine, oriented toward medical care. In contrast, the new interest in ethnology developed together with an emphasis on knowing about native peoples and their traditions. For Delafosse, respect for native traditions and institutions was to be the guiding principle of native policy. It is no accident that Delafosse, who argued for a recognition of "African civilizations" (1925), played, alongside Mauss, Lévy-Bruhl, and Rivet, a leading role in the foundation of both the Institute of Ethnology and in 1926 the International Institute of African Languages and Cultures.

The Stakes in Rationalization

This dual aspect of the process of rationalizing domination—the search for more effective instruments and a legitimation by "demonstrating scientific superiority"—can be detected in various projects for colonial rationalization that surfaced during the period. Reformers claimed that in order to meet the new challenges the phase of "improvisation" was over and colonial policy had to become "scientific." In an essay on "science and colonization," Brévié thus argued for rationalizing the methods of colonization, a process involving an alliance with science: "Improving the colonies raises general and technical problems of such a scope that, to tackle and solve them, we can no longer merely yield to solutions inspired by the circumstances, to the spirit of improvisation, or to empiricism's excessively liberal initiatives. Colonization is becoming a matter of method, calculation, prediction—of science, in a nutshell. It remains . . . a political and psychological art, but one to be guided and enlightened by exact scientific data" (1936: 42).

In this ideal combination of political and psychological qualities with scientific rationality, Brévié reserved a select place for the "science of man," a systematic study of the characteristics of native peoples. This theme also featured prominently in the foreword to the first issue of the journal *Outre-Mer*, where Ernest Roume, a retired governor-general, highlighted the urgency of studying the natives because they were now challenging colonial domination:

> New currents of ideas, feelings and passions are taking shape and reaching even the most backward and previously inert colonial populations. At the

same time, the relations arising out of contacts between such different civilizations have become significantly complicated. Whence, more imperatively than ever, it is necessary for the representatives of the race which has attained a higher degree of civilization to focus all their efforts on attentively studying the characteristics of the less evolved races, so as to anticipate as far as possible the often unforeseen reactions to the measures taken on their behalf: in short, to understand the native soul in the broadest sense of the word. (1929: n.p.)

Roume's formulation shows how the scientific endeavor to "understand the native soul" could in fact lend support to a belief in the evolutionary gap between "civilized" and "native."

A significant number of the individuals involved in these rationalizing schemes had strong links to the Colonial School, which provided a vocational training for colonial administrators (Cohen 1971; Dimier 1999). Brévié and Éboué were alumni of this school, while Roume was president of the board. Henri Labouret—who succeeded Delafosse at the Colonial School and the Institute of Ethnology when Delafosse died, and followed up on his call for a new native policy (Labouret 1931)—belonged to the same group. They took a leading role in stimulating interest in the study of native peoples and in drafting plans for colonial reform. Pursuing this double goal, Georges Hardy, director of the Colonial School, created a "general journal of colonization," *Outre-Mer*, in order to instill colonization with a "wholesome scientific spirit."

To understand the involvement of this group in reform projects, let us return to Weber's analysis of bureaucracy's interest in rationalization: "The specialized knowledge of the expert became more and more the foundation for the power of the officeholder" (1968 [1922]: 994). Possessing a specific knowledge enables officials in the administration to claim autonomy from the monarch or politician. Bureaucratic knowledge of the records forms the basis of their qualifications and legitimates their position. Qualifications certified by professional training are the means for both controlling access to positions (as opposed to the ruler's choice) and protecting oneself against the arbitrariness of political decisions.

Weber's approach sheds light on the lead taken by the Colonial School in promoting the scientific study of native peoples. This emphasis was set within a wider attempt to redefine the status of the key agent in overseas bureaucracy—the colonial administrator. These administrators often complained that they were seen as little more than adventurers. To counter this unflattering reputation, some of the Colonial School's alumni and staff adopted a "professionalization" strategy, based on legitimation through qualifications, so as to promote the occupation and vocation of colonial administrators. By emphasizing the specialized vocational training needed by these officials, the Colonial School gradually succeeded in monopolizing access to the Civil Service Corps of Colony Administrators: the title Administrator of the Colonies was reserved for members of this corps, who after 1912 had to hold a diploma from the Colonial School. Prior to this date, the school had trained no more than a quarter of these administrators.[22]

These administrators formed what Weber called a "status group," characterized by a strong sense of *esprit de corps* and by internalized heroic values. Various texts tried to define—and thus bring into being—an ethos for colonial administrators and a sort of charisma of office. These texts range from the minutes of the first Professional Congress of Colonial Administrators in 1931 to Robert Delavignette's book on the "Empire's true chiefs," a hymn to their glory. In a section on the "heroic organization of the world," Delavignette, who headed the Colonial School from 1937 to 1947, ascribed the "administrator's heroic superiority" to his personality as a leader—his character derived from constant self-improvement, while he possessed a superior form of knowledge that set him above both the colonized and his own compatriots: "The colonial [administrator] is a man who knows more things than the natives of the colonized land and who knows their value better than these other natives from the colonizing country" (1946: 53). These officials laid claim to the qualification of being specialists in natives. During the Congress of the Friendly Association of Colonial Administrators, held during the 1931 Colonial Exhibition, Hubert Deschamps (1900–1979), a young administrator at the time,[23] noted how important the "technical services" coordinated by the administrators had become, prompting a risk of their own work becoming purely bureaucratic. However, he commented, "the development of the various techniques leaves us one that is our own and that conditions all the others. The administrator is the specialist in native policy" (1931: 499). Further on, he added: "In order to carry out one's occupation well, one has to like it. And for us our occupation is the natives" (500).

Up until then the colonial administrator's qualifications had been based on mastering a purely administrative and supposedly universal type of knowledge: the law. Redefining these officials as specialists in natives entailed altering their training, which had mainly been in the law (Cohen 1971). Emphasizing knowledge about the native milieu, Georges Hardy reinforced the Colonial School's curriculum in human geography, ethnology, vernacular languages, and customary law. He also set up a course in "psychology applied to colonization." Under his leadership, the school began to work more closely with the Institute of Ethnology. As Rivet noted in 1931: "The largest number of students is provided by the Colonial School, and the Institute of Ethnology can be said to be an indispensable and accepted complement to the training of this School" (1931: n.p.).

The argument for rationalizing colonial policy was thus also a plea by these administrators for their own cause, since they claimed to be the best suited for this task. Claiming to be the specialist, or even the advocate, of the natives amounted to a call for the Colonial Service Corps to increase its control over determining colonial policy. This claim was used against anyone who threatened the administrators' autonomy: politicians back home (in particular members of Parliament), the minister of colonies (who was usually a politician rather than a colonial or a corps member),[24] specialists in colonial law (who saw administrators as mere executives applying universally valid rules), the representatives of major economic interests in the colonies, settlers, and, last but not least, the colonized elites.

As Hardy stated in his closing speech to the Native Society Congress in 1931, "It is necessary . . . to impose a scientific outlook on colonization, an *action based on reason* that it previously lacked and was inclined to scorn" (1932: n.p.). This formulation is evidence of the controversial, even polemical, nature of such a claim to rationality. Far from being an impersonal, self-driven process, as a superficial reading of Weber would have it, rationalization should be understood as a stake in the competition within colonial circles. In a relatively weak position before then, colonial administrators now appealed to science as an ally in the struggle for rationalization.

Division of Labor and Autonomization

The change both in the conditions of colonial domination and in the profession of colonial administrator during the interwar period formed the backdrop to the alliance struck by academics and promoters of a "rational" colonial reform, based on their common interest in rationalization. According to Brévié, this rationalization necessarily entailed a specialization and division of labor between "researchers" and "men of action": "Colonization thus has a growing need for scholars, impartial and disinterested researchers, who see far beyond emergencies and the stress of action. It needs better equipped laboratories and research institutes. It needs to base its action on a real colonial scientific culture, to take inspiration from the experimental method, to receive guidelines from an accurate, practical science" (1936: 42). Significantly, he stressed the need for impartiality and detachment, the very qualities to which academics laid claim. This program met the interests of academic entrepreneurs, in particular Paul Rivet, who was involved in a grand project for rationalizing and systematizing the "science of man" by unifying its diverse branches under the name of ethnology.[25] Whereas ethnography existed as a scholarly colonial practice, ethnology was still in effect at an incipient stage as an academic subject. Its development would depend on backing from colonial authorities.

This alliance brought about a series of institutional achievements. Besides the creation of the Institute of Ethnology, there was the founding of the Society of Africanists (1930), which would play a major role in the development of a distinctive French brand of African studies (*africanisme*), and official funding for the Dakar-Djibouti mission headed by Marcel Griaule in 1931–1933, which came to be regarded in official histories of the discipline as the beginnings of professional ethnography. Modeled on nineteenth-century naturalist expeditions, it symbolically linked French possessions in Africa from Dakar to Djibouti. Both of these initiatives were explicitly presented at the time as direct repercussions of the Paris International Colonial Exhibition (1931). Another outstanding institutional success was the creation of the Musée de l'Homme (Museum of Man) in 1937, which, as Rivet's request for the presence of colonial troops during the inauguration suggested, was intended to be a "great colonial museum"[26] (see L'Estoile 2003).

The need to demonstrate the state's scientific interest in colonial peoples was constantly cited as a justification for granting public funds to institutional initiatives in favor of ethnology. In 1930, for example, the minister of colonies wrote to the governor-general of French Equatorial Africa to ask him to support the Dakar-Djibouti mission: "As the 1931 Colonial Exhibition is drawing the attention of the general public and foreign scholars to France's colonial activities, it is indispensable to demonstrate to those elements informed about such questions that our public authorities have overlooked nothing in terms of learning about them [native populations] and to this end are employing modern methods on an equal par to those used by the institutes of other nations."[27]

Such a statement provides us with a key to understanding the considerable backing given to the program of scientific ethnology presented by Rivet. International competition and the need to demonstrate a scientific interest in the "natives" motivated investments in institutions such as the Institute of Ethnology or the Museum of Ethnography in Paris, which were best placed for upholding "French science" given their ability to mobilize a "scientific capital." The quest for international legitimacy thus appears as a driving force behind the delegation of the task of knowing the natives to "professional" specialists with institutional autonomy from the colonial service, rather than to colonial administrators temporarily seconded to undertake research.

The goading force of international competition became apparent during the 1937 Congress of Colonial Sciences. Highlighting the need to systematize the organization of research in French Oceania, Maurice Leenhardt declared: "The whole bibliography on these French possessions is in English or German. The most notable example is the New Hebrides. Compared to writings in English by Rivers, Deacan, etc., or in German by Speiser, French publications—I avoid using the word 'science'—fail to amount to a single volume, apart from P. Benoît's novel, *Eromango*. This does not suffice to persuade the English, who are keen to increase their influence in this archipelago, that we know the islands better than they do" (1938: 528). In this setting, scientific knowledge on a place thus becomes in effect a property deed. Obtaining it is a way to acquire a moral right to possess the land, a right useful for countering other nations' claims to it.

The support lent by colonial governments to scientific institutions in the mother country could be justified in two ways: first, as a means of training colonial staff, and second, as a way of organizing and stimulating research in the colonies. During the 1930s, the main aim of the scholars sent from the homeland institutions to local colonial centers was in effect to centralize and rationalize the production of knowledge. Scientific expeditions being few and expensive, colonial officials were still needed to collect field material. For instance, the Museum of Ethnography and the Institute of Ethnology used the colonial service's network to collect artifacts and data, whether of a linguistic or ethnographic kind (L'Estoile 1999).

Gradually, though, especially after 1945, a new division of labor took shape—that of a "functional specialization" that accorded increasingly distinct roles within state bureaucracy for the scientist and colonial administrator. This phenomenon, which entailed defining specific "spheres of competence," may be seen in line with Weber as a further step in the rational division of labor under bureaucratic domination; the "autonomization" of the machinery specialized in the production of knowledge pushed this process of functional specialization to its limits.

This transformation, leading eventually to the rise of a small group of professionals in ethnology employed by the state, set off a number of complex changes, more often blurred rather than clarified by terms such as professionalization and institutionalization. One of the first academic textbooks in ethnology—given the significant title *Ethnologie de l'Union Française*—formulated this new division of labor between research and administration in terms of specialization and complementarity. Published in 1953, it was the joint work of André Leroi-Gourhan, associate professor in colonial ethnology in Lyon, and Jean Poirier, professor at the National School for Overseas France (École Nationale de la France d'Outre-Mer), the Colonial School's new name. These two would become major figures within the discipline: Leroi-Gourhan would later dominate, in France, the areas of prehistory and anthropological studies of technology, whereas Poirier went on to become editor of the volume devoted to ethnology in the prestigious series *Encyclopédie de la Pléiade* (1968).

It is significant that a work specifically addressed to an academic audience raised the theme of ethnology as both an instrument of native policy and of legitimation. The introduction to the fourth section of the book, devoted to "French Union and Ethnology," is typically titled "National Interest and International Duty": "Ethnology alone can serve as the valid basis for a policy. It would be vain to claim to counsel and guide a native society without undertaking the study of its customs and mentality. Knowledge of its races, material culture, ways of life, languages, family and political structures, religious beliefs, the systematic study of psychology, are the very conditions for action" (Leroi-Gourhan and Poirier 1953: 897–98). Notice the continuity here with the arguments used by colonial administrators, who supported ethnography as the way to decode native peoples. The second argument is just as noteworthy:

> Although ethnological knowledge turns out to be indispensable in successfully conducting any actions overseas, we must also take note that this knowledge is now a response to *obligations of an international kind*. In effect, France has committed itself to taking all necessary measures for developing native cultures, and for respecting the originality of overseas societies. This implies continually improving our knowledge of the communities under our care. With regard to the former League of Nations mandates, even more definite

commitments have been made; here, responsible governments must periodically report on their actions. We can say that, in general, once French authorities take charge of an overseas population, they become responsible not just for the material improvement of the country but also for the improvement/ valorizing [*mise en valeur*] of the people. The study of customs, archeological and historical investigations, analyses of art, literature and philosophical thought—*all this ethnological research is part of the duty of authorities* exercising trusteeship. (897–98; emphasis added)

This twofold justification of ethnological research—based on national interest and international duty—was closely connected with both the objectives of colonial reform and the changes in the circumstances of colonial domination. To begin, the new 1946 constitution claimed to establish more equal relations between the mother country and the overseas territories: the name of the French Union was adopted, joining metropolitan France with its overseas territories, while French citizenship was extended (albeit with differences in status) to all inhabitants of the union. Furthermore, international pressure had grown since the interwar period. Evidence of this lies in the reference to France's obligations as a colonial power to justify its actions internationally, in particular in relation to the former mandates, the Cameroons and Togo, now United Nations trusteeships. Once again the need to legitimate colonial rule was foremost: ethnology was a pledge of good will, proving France's respect for native cultures. Presented as the counterpart of material improvement, the idea of a *mise en valeur* (improving/valorizing) of the native people echoes Lévy-Bruhl's arguments for supporting the Institute of Ethnology; however, it also recalls the emphasis placed by reform-minded colonial administrators on colonization's "human dimension."

Leroi-Gourhan and Poirier outlined a relationship of complementarity and mutual support between the colonial service and ethnology. The colonial service ought to base its actions on the work of ethnologists; the task of collecting knowledge was to be delegated by the state to professional scientists. Similarly, the program for a "sociology of dependent peoples" developed at IFAN in the 1940s by the young Georges Balandier and Paul Mercier (Mercier 1951) may be read as a translation into theoretical terms of the structural interdependence between two groups of civil servants, increasingly seen as distinct: academics and administrators. The research aims were to be worked out in talks between colonial administrators and researchers. However, this ideal of a social science in the service of enlightened colonial policy clashed ever more frequently with other requirements. By defining themselves as "specialists in native societies and mentalities," ethnologists entered into direct competition with these officials in the very field that the latter were trying to occupy. The relations between these two groups can be described as one of competitive interdependence, involving conflicts of interest and border clashes.

The conditions of this interdependence, however, were rapidly changing as new scientific institutions were brought into being in France: a section called Ethnology and Prehistory was organized in 1944 at the National Center of Scientific Research (Centre National de la Recherche Scientifique, or CNRS) and in 1947 the Rockefeller Foundation helped set up a new section at the École Pratique des Hautes Études, devoted to social sciences (which later became the École des Hautes Études en Sciences Sociales). In 1958 a chair of Social and Cultural Anthropology was created for Claude Lévi-Strauss at the prestigious Collège de France.

The competition thus shifted into academia, between individuals attached to colonial research institutions (IFAN or ORSTOM) and those who, established in academic or research positions in France, had to justify their status in Parisian intellectual circles. The claim to "scientific purity" was used as a weapon in these academic disputes, stigmatizing some research (mainly that conducted by the first group) as low-status "applied science" in contrast with the "pure," disinterested science (practiced mainly by the latter group). As ethnologists tried to obtain recognition from academia and, more broadly, the intellectual world back home, they endeavored to gain autonomy from the colonial bureaucracy (in Weberian terms, claiming a monopoly on the right to define the proper objects and procedures of research). This precipitated a conflict of values affecting the most scientifically ambitious among the colonial ethnologists, which is apparent in works by scholars such as Balandier or Mercier. Balandier, for example, had produced a number of "applied" studies on urban unrest, messianic political movements, and schemes for relocating populations in new villages, all at the administration's request. These studies were first published in local (colonial) journals (e.g., Balandier 1950b; Balandier and Pauvert, 1952) but later were transformed into articles in metropolitan academic journals such as the *Cahiers Internationaux de Sociologie* (Balandier 1950a, 1951, 1952) and then later into a doctoral dissertation and a book published by an academic press (Balandier 1955). In 1952 Balandier was recruited as a researcher for the CNRS and began teaching at the Institute of Ethnology; in 1957 he was elected to the École Pratique des Hautes Études, and later became professor of sociology and ethnology of black Africa at the Sorbonne. He failed, however, to be elected to the Collège de France because he lost the contest to Claude Lévi-Strauss— who was to argue that ethnology was more valuable when it was "pure" rather than "diluted" (Lévi-Strauss 1973 [1959]).

These developments led to a growing divergence between objects and forms of knowledge in scholarly and administrative circles. The requirements for a contribution to knowledge to be recognized as ethnological increasingly diverged from the kind of knowledge produced within the administration, which more and more was oriented towards new, and above all economic, issues (Cooper 1997).

Conclusion

The concept of a rationalization of domination enables us to move beyond the postulate of a radical, immutable antinomy between scientific reason and *raison d'état*. It offers a tool for analyzing similarities between forms of administrative and scientific rationality, provided it is understood as not only limited to a formal rationalization of the techniques of domination but also as including the recourse to a specific mode of legitimation, emphasizing the rational foundations of domination. The Weberian theme of domination through knowledge thus takes on a double meaning. The bureaucracy benefits, on the one hand, from the rationalization of its instruments of knowledge and, on the other, from the label of rationality conferred on it by science. The complex and occasionally paradoxical relations between scholarly knowledge about populations and the administration of populations are located on the continuum between these two poles. These are not independent, however, since using the "rational" instruments of science to order the natural and social world helps produce a belief in the possibility of mastering a complex situation—a belief legitimating domination in the very eyes of those who exercise it.

The notion of a rationalization of domination sheds light on another point. The relation between anthropology as an academic discipline and the colonial bureaucracy as an institution should not, as more frequently happens, be taken as the starting point for reflecting on these issues and then projected retrospectively onto the past. Instead, this relation must be seen as a special case: that is, as a unique historical configuration of the relations between the production of knowledge about native peoples and the practices for managing them.[28] The particularity of this relatively recent configuration is that distinct institutions and staff in Weber's sense implement these two sets of practices.

The colonial state's fostering of a scientific approach to native populations was not the outcome of an inexorable process of rationalization. Instead, this colonial project was "borne" (in the Weberian sense of a group bearing a religious message) by a combination of groups that shared an interest both in rationalization and in learning about native peoples. This "scientific" interest in learning about the natives and their customs, which came to be embodied in the discipline of anthropology, was both a key factor in, and a symbol of, a new political technology premised on acknowledging the differences between peoples and cultures. In a context of challenges to colonial domination and stronger international pressures, anthropology was apparently capable of bringing together three legitimating factors: exercise of a scientific activity, demonstration of a concern for the natives and of respect for their traditions.

During the interwar period, these shared interests laid the foundations for an alliance between the advocates of plans for rationalizing colonial domination (plans that redefined colonial administrators as specialists in natives) and academic scholars who relied on the backing of colonial authorities for the existence of their institutions and on its agents for collecting data. The relation between the colonial service and ethnology, such as it emerged during the institutionalization process, can be analyzed as a form of competitive interdependence between several groups linked to the state.

This alliance (based on a division of labor: the specialists in knowledge were to provide both information and interpretive frameworks to the specialists in action) provided the grounds for the development of research institutions. These in turn created the conditions for the emergence of a new group specialized in learning about native peoples, namely ethnologists, and helped this group obtain academic and intellectual recognition. As scientific institutions gained autonomy from colonial authorities (which explains why the discipline of anthropology has outlived colonialism), internal conflicts started to endanger the initially hoped-for complementarity between colonial and scholarly interests, and this led to a redefinition of the discipline. Meanwhile, intellectual circles in France were increasingly critical of colonial domination, making it ever harder to maintain that ethnology had a key role to play in developing the colonies, a role proudly claimed by Lévy-Bruhl and others during the interwar period. After the loss of (most of) the empire, the formative relation that connected this area of knowledge with the management of native populations vanished as the newly heralded "science of mankind" claimed to be the legitimate heir of the Enlightenment rather than the late child of colonialism.

Notes

I am grateful to Jean-Claude Combessie, Adam Kuper, Federico Neiburg, and Lygia Sigaud for their comments on a preliminary version of this chapter.

1 French Americanist ethnology developed in a different context of "internal colonization" conducted by independent nation-states (see the essays by Lomnitz and by Souza Lima in this volume).

2 In France, the term *ethnologie* was gradually adopted during this period to refer to the "science of man" as a whole, comprising linguistics, ethnography, physical anthropology, and prehistory. I shall not delve here into the complex uses of competing names (ethnology, anthropology, ethnography, folklore, etc.) applied to a field of study with unstable borders.

3 In particular, note Weber's writings "Types of Legitimate Domination" (1968 [1922]: 212–301), "Bureaucracy" (1968: 956–1005), and "Sociology of Religions" (1968 [1922]: 399–634). My purpose here is not to engage in a critical commentary of Weber's writings but to use them as a toolbox.

4 As Weber states: "Quite generally, one can only say that the bureaucratization of all domination very strongly furthers the development of 'rational matter-of-factness' and the personality type of the professional expert" (1968 [1922]: 998).

5 Weber's account of the relation between hierocratic and political domination offers a stimulating model (1968 [1922]: 1158–211; see also the volume's introduction).

6 The term "instrumentality" is preferred to "instrumentalization," the latter implying a strong sense of condemnation.

7 Commissaire de la République au Cameroun. Circular n° 43, 29/12/1920, Archives de l'Agence Économique du Cameroun (hereafter aéc), Aix-en-Provence, Centre des Archives d'Outre-Mer (hereafter caom).

8 See the studies edited by J. L. Amselle and E. M'Bokolo (1998 [1985]), in particular Jean Bazin's "A chacun son Bambara," which studies the process by which the fluid categories found in the precolonial period crystallized and reified into scholarly and administrative ethnic classifications.

9 "Etat des différents groupes linguistiques au Cameroun," a report of the Political Affairs Bureau, 30/10/1933, in "Population; recensement," aéc, caom, 353/168*bis*.

10 The very same year, the Commissaire de la République decided to grant

bonuses to administrators who decided to learn native languages as an incentive for them to "penetrate the mentality of those under their administration." *Arrêté* of 21/4/1933 reproduced in the *Journal Officiel des Colonies*, 1933, p. 244. The Commissaire may have been following what was by then a common practice in British colonies.

11 La region Nord. AÉC, CAOM, 928/2903, "Monographies," "Pacification Nord Cameroun," 1923 (see also «Rapport annuel du gouvernement français sur l'administration sous mandat des territoires du Cameroun pour 1924», 1925, p. 24).

12 This «Inventaire ethnique du Sud-Cameroun» opened a series, "Mémoires de l'Institut Français d'Afrique Noire" (Centre du Cameroun), devoted to "Populations." See in particular the introduction (Dugast 1949). The career of Idelette Dugast, who compiled the inventory, neatly illustrates the continuity between administrative knowledge and academic ethnology. Traveling to the Cameroons in the 1930s as a student at the Institute of Ethnology, she married there the administrateur-chef René Dugast. In 1943 Idelette Dugast became secretary-archivist for the official Société d'Études Camerounaises, created a few years before by the Commissaire de la République; in 1944, the Société was incorporated as a local center into IFAN. Dugast later contributed to the vast *Ethnographic Survey of Africa*, which was coordinated by the International African Institute (Dugast 1954), and wrote a monograph on the Ndiki tribe (Dugast 1955 and 1959).

13 *Togo-Cameroun*, a lavishly illustrated propaganda journal for the mandates, regularly published "ethnographic maps." Such maps also cropped up, year after year, in the *Annual Reports of the French Government on the Administration under Mandate of the Cameroons*.

14 In particular, they would produce a series of ethno-demographic maps of West Africa on a 1/100,000 scale published by IFAN's center in Dakar.

15 This paper was published in successive issues of *Renseignements coloniaux et documents*, a documentary supplement to the colonial *Bulletin de l'Afrique Française*; in the journal of a local learned society published by the General Government of French Equatorial Africa, *Bulletin de la Société des Recherches Congolaises*; and in *L'Ethnographie*, the journal of a learned society in the mother country.

16 Circular of Gouvernor-General Antonetti, 16/10/1933. Archives du Gouvernement Général de l'Afrique Équatoriale Française (henceforth GGAÉF), CAOM, 5D103.

17 Éboué's recognition as an ethnographer and hence as an administrator with a demonstrable understanding of the natives was instrumental in bringing him to the notice of his hierarchy, thus accelerating his career. Later, as Governor General of Chad, subsequently of French Equatorial Africa, he implemented a new 'native policy' based on respect for traditional political institutions and customs. He is the only member of the colonial service to be buried in the Pantheon.

18 Letter of 24/10/1933 from Lévy-Bruhl to the governor-general of French Equatorial Africa, GGAÉF, CAOM, 5D103.

19 Circular of 10/6/1930, *Bulletin Officiel des Colonies*, quoted in Cohen 1971: 191.

20 GGAÉF, CAOM, Political Affairs Bureau. However, according to Cohen (1971: 190), dedicating too much time to ethnographic research was not always well regarded in some administrative quarters.

21 This claim was not undisputed (see L'Estoile 1997a).

22 The term colonial administrator (*administrateur colonial*) is often incorrectly used for any administrative officer in the colonies. The *adjoints des services civils* were recruited locally and after 1912 had to undergo a year of training at the Colonial School before entering the corps.

23 Graduating at the top of his class in the Colonial School in 1924, Deschamps provides a typical instance of a double career, first as a colonial and after retirement as an academic. After becoming a colonial historian, he headed the Center of African Studies at the Sorbonne until 1970.

24 The single exception was Jules Brévié, minister of colonies from April 1942 until March 1943.

25 Paul Rivet, trained as a military physician, became professor at the Museum of Natural History in Paris, secretary-general of the Institute of Ethnology, director of the Museum of Ethnography, as well as a politician. He accumulated a series of scientific positions that allowed him to turn the Musée de l'Homme into the new center of French anthropology (L'Estoile 1997c).

26 Rivet to Daladier, 31/5/1938, in Rivet Correspondence, *Fonds Paul Rivet*, Library of the Musée de l'Homme.

27 GGAÉF, CAOM, Political Affairs Bureau.

28 Other chapters in this volume offer a panorama of the various forms taken by these configurations. See also Pels and Salemink 1999.

Omar Ribeiro Thomaz

"THE GOOD-HEARTED PORTUGUESE PEOPLE"

Anthropology of Nation, Anthropology of Empire

"For the Portuguese the heart is the measure of all things," stated Jorge Dias in the early 1960s, Coming from an author who later became Portugal's most renowned anthropologist, this bold assertion of the "Lusitanian character" raises a series of questions concerning the role of the discipline of anthropology in the country. Over the years, Portuguese anthropologists and ethnographers have frequently been asked to express their views on the Portuguese people or on the character of the nation—part of a process that can be fairly easily traced to the construction of national mythologies, a project that is also disputed in other academic and cultural domains such as history, sociology, literature, architecture, and music. As far as anthropology is concerned, the interest in discussing the Portuguese case stems from two fundamental and inextricably connected points: first, Portugal lived under an authoritarian regime for most of the twentieth century; and second, to a large extent the Portuguese colonial empire set the conditions for the (fairly limited) debate on the "national question," whether as a result of the existing institutional context (created to deal with the demands of the overseas territories) or as a consequence of the terms under which nation and empire could be debated. Indeed, this essay addresses an anthropological tradition that shifts between the discussion of empire and the discussion of nation. To start, I examine the works produced by two Portuguese anthropologists—Mendes Corrêa and Jorge Dias—that are rooted in specific historical and institutional contexts. Their cases provide support for my central hypothesis: namely, that starting from the discipline's formative period in Portugal and extending until 25 April 1974, it is impossible to draw any clear distinction between an anthropology that took the nation as its subject from one that primarily focused on the empire.

This conclusion arose from my observation of a recent tendency for Portuguese anthropologists looking back over their tradition to take into account only those works that deal with mainland Portugal and the nearby islands (Madeira and the Azores). This tendency reflects the widespread view that a poor and marginal empire failed to produce—with one or two exceptions—an anthropological tradition or body of knowledge on cultural diversity of sufficient depth to justify its exhumation by contemporary academics. This contrasts with the intense debates surrounding the Europeanness of Portugal. While this approach has proven useful in terms of stimulating a detailed analysis of a now long tradition of Portuguese ethnography, with a particular emphasis on the works of João Leal (2000), it fails to address a crucial point: the very peculiarities of Portugal as a European country that, in order to maintain itself as such, was forced to defend an imperial structure that gradually converged with the nation itself.

Anthropology of Nation, Anthropology of Empire

Among the elements specific to the production of knowledge in Portugal during the twentieth century, it is important to note the country's peripheral situation within Europe as a whole; the lengthy period the country spent under an authoritarian regime; and, above all, the deterritorialized perception of the nation, which is echoed in various institutions and areas of culture, such as literature, the arts, and the academic disciplines themselves. This idea of a deterritorialized nation refers to the existence of a community of meaning encompassing not just European Portugal and its adjacent archipelagos (Madeira and the Azores) but also Portugal's former colonial territories in Africa (Cape Verde, Portuguese Guinea, Sao Tomé and Principe, Angola, and Mozambique); enclaves such as São João Batista de Ajudá and Cabinda that are also located on the African continent; the former Portuguese State of India (Goa, Daman, Diu, Dadra, and Nagar Haveli); the city of Macao; East Timor; and the communities of Portuguese migrants spread across the world. Throughout Portugal's period of dictatorship (1926–1974), the aim was to incorporate the territories controlled by Portugal symbolically, and sometimes institutionally, under either the title of colonies or of overseas provinces. Within the limits imposed by a dictatorship, we can observe a fairly sustained attempt throughout different fields of knowledge to engage in a debate that assumed that the imperial reality was a translation of the nation: a singularly Lusitanian eschatology that looked to combine past, present, and future in a single temporal line and to reproduce the particularities of the nation over a vast geographic space.

However, the focus of this essay is not this eschatology or its expression in diverse fields of knowledge—a topic I have already discussed elsewhere (Thomaz, 2002)—but rather a specific kind of knowledge within which the ideas of nation and empire continuously overlap: anthropology. I aim to defend the notion that it is impossible to understand Portuguese scientific anthropology or ethnographic traditions without an analysis of "colonial knowledge": in other words, knowledge constituted in relation to the colonial territories, whether or not with applied aims. Notions such as culture or cultural diversity were conceived and interpreted in response to particular national contexts shaped by the dynamics of imperialism.[1]

Anthropology in Portugal constitutes an intriguing field of study.[2] Considered a marginal disciplinary tradition compared to the larger European centers, it certainly does not occupy the same position as its equivalents in France and Great Britain. Nevertheless, the Estado Novo (New State)[3] in Portugal did commit considerable resources toward the constitution of colonial knowledge and a series of studies on Portuguese culture in which anthropology came to perform a crucial role and where, most of the time, there was no clear separation between the notions of national, colonial, and imperial.

As a starting point, for example, take the meetings and congresses attended not only by individuals calling themselves "anthropologists" (in all their varieties) or "ethnographers,"[4] but also by historians, geographers, physicians, magistrates, colonial administrators, legal scholars, missionaries, and so on. At the 1934 Congresso de Antropologia Colonial (Colonial Anthropology Congress) as well as at the 1940 Congresso Colonial (Colonial Congress), the participants systematically emphasized the national aspect of the groups and territories that they endeavored to analyze and that constituted the human element of the colonial empire. Their national character was often interpreted as a "potentiality." With this in mind, I believe that a rigid classification of anthropology in Portugal perceived as a nation-building anthropology rather than an empire-building anthropology—as proposed by João Leal, in line with George Stocking's terminology—fails to translate the nature of the debate with any real precision: discussing the nation also meant discussing the empire (cf. Leal 1999a: 213; 2000). Those meetings that focused on the colonies and their people and lands mobilized a significant part of the Portuguese intelligentsia in the first decades of the Salazar regime. Some of these events accompanied the large exhibitions held in Portugal; for example, the Portuguese Colonial Anthropology Congress, which took place alongside the Exposição Colonial (Colonial Exhibition) of Porto in 1934, and the Colonial Congress, organized as part of the 1940 pluricentennial celebrations.[5] The organization of these large-scale events was only possible thanks to the combined efforts of the state, certain sectors of society, and a number of key figures from the Portuguese political and cultural world.[6] They also depended, of course, on a particular institutional setting favoring the production of colonial knowledge, which received significant input from anthropology—or at least from individuals describing themselves as anthropologists.

Portugal has been renowned for a long tradition of studies dedicated to folklore or popular culture, which in turn had a profound impact on the anthropology produced in the country over the course of the twentieth century (Pina Cabral 1991; Leal 2000). This tradition, I would suggest, fueled much of the discussion concerning the nature of the Portuguese people and their national identity, in addition to contributing to the formation of a particular state ideology. Here a number of questions arise. Given the increasing overlap between the notions of nation and empire, does it make sense to presume a hegemonic conception of the Portuguese people during the New State? To what extent can a political structure—the empire—hold together highly diverse cultural groups by means of the homogenizing concept of nation?[7] In what way did the studies on the "uses and customs" of native populations inform political practice and mold a global image of Portuguese culture? What is the relationship between anthropology and certain key categories in the New State architecture such as the *indigenato*—a legal framework constructed to deal with indigenous populations—and its potential parallel with corporativism?[8] Finally, in what way did colonial knowledge appropriate ideas initially formulated to account for the authenticity of the peoples of the peninsula and the adjacent archipelagos?

The significance of these questions becomes more apparent in light of the fact that one of the great traumas in contemporary Portuguese history concerns precisely the overlap between empire and nation, an illusion finally shattered by the violence of war. As Hannah Arendt has argued (1966), the transcontinental and openly multicultural empire is incompatible with national institutions: the nationalization of the empire inevitably leads to a crisis within the nation itself. In the Portuguese case, the process was more severe because it occurred in the context of an authoritarian regime that silenced all public debate on the empire or the nation.

To begin, I intend briefly to reconstruct the Portuguese institutional setting responsible for the production of colonial knowledge. Although I cannot explore the question in depth here, the increasingly central position
occupied by colonial knowledge in the first decades of the dictatorship
reveals the benefit of sketching a much more complex panorama of the
production of ideas in Portugal. Next, I turn to the work of Mendes Corrêa
who, although presently a neglected figure, was considered one of the most
prominent Portuguese anthropologists during the 1930s and 1940s. Finally,
taking Jorge Dias's work as a baseline, I discuss the idea of a "good-hearted
Portuguese people," a decisive element in reasserting the regime's paternalist
and authoritarian character and in defining its policies both in the colonies
and in the metropolis. Before reaching this conclusion, though, I briefly
explore the Portuguese political universe, since it seems obvious that in
Portugal the particular form taken by all of these questions owes much to the
dictatorship that held sway over the country for a large part of the twentieth
century.

Controlled Knowledge:
The Structures of Repression and the Colonial Act

In the 1930s, the concentration of power in the hands of Oliveira Salazar
and the institutionalization of the New State with the 1933 constitution
helped strengthen an authoritarian regime comparable in many ways to
other examples of European fascism.[9] Any public debate or scientific research on the colonial populations and dominions, or on living conditions
in Portugal, met obstructions and limits directly imposed by the regime, as
well as indirectly enforced through press censorship, the control of institutions, and the creation and expansion of the secret police. This repressive
system was extended to the colonies, and it remained in force until the 1974
Carnation Revolution. Although the system was mainly concerned with
political and military issues it also extended beyond these to penetrate the
moral and religious universe, cultural production, individual conduct, and
everyday behavior (Marques 1986: 426).

Given the way that the notions of motherland and nation were extended
to overseas territories—a process exemplified in the Ato Colonial (Colonial
Act) (1930) and in the Carta Orgânica do Império Colonial Português (Organic Charter of the Portuguese Colonial Empire) (1933)[10]—it is easy to

imagine how any debate on the colonies was stifled. Proposals such as the sale of the colonies, or even simply abandoning them and allowing the empire to shrink to peninsular Portugal—ideas put forward in the nineteenth century by renowned intellectuals such as Oliveira Martins and Eça de Queiroz—became unthinkable under the New State.[11] As a result, in contrast to the experience of other imperial powers during phases of democratic normalization, there was no real debate opposing colonialists and anti-colonialists in Portugal.[12] Contesting the colonial project amounted to contesting the nation. Censorship impeded access to the public sphere for the potential anti-colonialists who only later started to emerge, particularly after the war. The extension of the secret police (PIDE) to the colonial territories meant that the quotidian violence of colonialism was compounded by other forms of violence and institutional repression designed to prevent any display of nationalism or independence by native populations. The regime's structure and the importance of the Catholic Church in molding the state's ideology, including participation of its members in various institutions, had a significant effect on the course taken by anthropology (and anthropologists) in Portugal.[13]

Analyzing any field of knowledge on the colonies therefore requires a discussion of the legal framework that controlled it—in this case, the 1930 Colonial Act, which was drafted during the short period in which Salazar ran the Ministry of the Colonies while holding other offices in the Council of Ministers. Here I take legislation to be a representation par excellence, through which a particular society or group projects an image of itself. Although this image retains a dynamic relationship with the reality it intends to interpret, control, or even cover up, it also mirrors how the social group in question wishes to see and represent itself. As Manuela Carneiro da Cunha suggests (1992: 2), while the law should not be confused with a description of reality, reality cannot simply ignore its existence since the law transforms it. Law is a reality in itself insofar as it corresponds to the way in which groups from the dominant class represent the social order. It is therefore my assertion that we must locate the 1930 Colonial Act and its associated legal charters within the overall dynamic of the culture of empire. As the product of a specific ideology and a tradition of Portuguese colonial power, the act sought to define what the empire should be and the ways in which it should function within its territories, affect the lives of natives, and shape the mentality and activity of the Portuguese colonists.

The historian Fernando Rosas has drawn attention to the critical role played by the 1930 Colonial Act, given the function the empire came to assume in the Portuguese New State. Indeed, he argues that the "Colonial Act defines the general juridical-institutional framework of a new policy for the territories under Portuguese domination. An *imperial*, nationalist and centralizing phase takes root within the global colonialist policy pursued by the Portuguese state, the result of a new external and internal conjuncture, translated into a different overall set of directives for exploiting the colonies" (1994: 285). A series of legal devices was introduced to encourage political centralization within the movement. However, they also pushed to the limit the notion of a "difference in civilized state" between the native populations of the African continental colonies—including from 1946 onward Sao Tomé and Principe as well as Timor—and the metropolitan citizens and inhabitants of Cape Verde, the Portuguese State of India, and Macao.[14] These events took place at the same time as the introduction of the proposal for the nationalization of the colonial territories. This process was to be pursued at economic, political, and indeed cultural levels: the "natives" and the inhabitants of all of the Portuguese colonies would make up part of the body of the Portuguese nation, spread across the four corners of the world. Thus a legal structure was created for the empire, associating it with the idea of nation or even subsuming it under the latter.[15]

This legal formula dispelled (at first sight) the foreign threats menacing Portugal's overseas territories,[16] while implying the extension of metropolitan institutions to its colonial dominions. However paragraph 8 of decree 16.473—Political, Civil and Criminal Status of Natives—declared the inconsistency of such a proposal due to its "lack of practical significance" given the "state of their [the 'natives'] faculties" and "their primitive mentality."[17] The *indigenato* was therefore instituted, which legally embodied the differences in status between the inhabitants of the various colonies, defined by their "uses and customs." This represented a break with assimilationism, a tradition prized by certain metropolitan circles.[18]

Nevertheless, the "gradualism," which came to characterize the incorporation of natives into the political and spiritual body of the nation as outlined by the new legal code, resulted in a re-convergence with the assimilationist tradition. This gradual incorporation lent a messianic and temporal aspect to the Portuguese colonial project. The status of an assimilated person—an individual who could acquire a citizenship permit—was legally grounded in the adoption of Portuguese habits, culture, and language. The eventual aim of the indigenato was to incorporate Africans and Timorese into European civilization as full members of the Portuguese nation. It was the responsibility of the Portuguese authorities to codify the uses and customs of the empire's distinct ethnic groups without interfering radically in the existing social organization and common law.[19] This allowed a more efficient administration of native populations, respecting their cultural specificities, but without abandoning the aim of progressively incorporating them—a process to be accomplished through their "peaceful" coexistence with colonists (who should set a high moral example in all aspects) and the activity of religious missionaries.

An initial reading of the *Depoimento* (Testimony) of Marcelo Caetano,[20] and even some of the clauses from the Estatuto Indígena (Indigenous Statute) and the Colonial Act[21] suggest that the New State was institutionally respectful of native traditions, going so far as to protect the cultural specificity of the widely different groups and societies under its control. However, other clauses from the Colonial Act, and in particular sections of the Código do Trabalho dos Indígenas das Colônias Portuguesas de África (Labour Code for Indigenous Peoples from the Portuguese Colonies of Africa) issued in December 1929, reveal another dimension of a legislation that at first sight seemed to zealously protect native populations: the efficient control of human resources from the colonial territories, especially those in continental Africa.

The building of a modern colonial empire demanded efficient use of the colonies' physical resources, entailing their transformation into exporters of raw materials and tropical products, and importers of manufactured goods from the metropolis. This was obviously part of a more general process of contemporary imperialism. However, in Portugal's case this resulted in a fairly uncompetitive industry: the nationalization of colonial territories, as set out in the Colonial Act, involved as a counterpart the requirement to consume products from the Portuguese African colonies, very often at prices far above market value. The corollary of this process was the local employment of African labor, transformed into a cheap or even unpaid workforce. In fact, the Labour Code for Indigenous Peoples displays two fairly contradictory motivations. On one hand, it aimed at protecting Africans from the numerous mechanisms of forced labor (slavery) that continued into the twentieth century—thereby also responding to the constant denunciations of Portuguese policy made by other colonial powers harboring ambitions to take over its territories. On the other hand, the code responded to the need of ensuring the supply of (compulsory) African labor.

The New State's Labour Code ostensibly sought to protect native peoples from compulsory labor, as can be observed in its section titled "General Dispositions" or in article 18 of the Colonial Act. However, other clauses cast doubt on the state's real willingness to protect natives from the arbitrary processes that had come to characterize their recruitment; articles from the Colonial Act or the Labour Code referring to "obligatory work" allowed a number of divergent readings, meaning that compulsory labor in fact continued in the colonies until at least the 1960s.

The historian Gerald Bender (1980), as well as many African thinkers and leaders of national liberation movements, such as Amílcar Cabral (1978), have analyzed the ambiguity of Portuguese power enshrined in the notion of public good as inscribed in a clause enabling natives to be forced into work against their will. Various articles from the Labour Code left native children, adults, and elders at the mercy of the local public authorities, usually in connivance with the private projects of metropolitan colonists and colonial exploration companies.

In sum, the Colonial Act and the charters associated with it, all of which remained in force until the beginning of the 1960s, resulted in fixing a notion of uses and customs remarkably similar to ideas used by Portuguese anthropologists of the time. Cultural diversity, coupled with the idea of stages of development, legally protected the empire's structural inequality and assigned the state both a tutelary role and the coordination of the progressive assimilation of native populations into the political and spiritual body of the nation. Moreover, possessing, managing, governing, and colonizing the colonial territories became part of the nation's essence. Clearly, this endeavor must have been accompanied by some consideration of the reality experienced in these territories, albeit strictly supervised by the structures of the New State.

Colonial Knowledge: Institutions, High Culture, and Bureaucracy

During the first decades of the twentieth century certain sectors of the Portuguese intelligentsia—specifically those linked to the Sociedade de Geografia de Lisboa (Lisbon Geographical Society) and the Instituto de Medicina Tropical (Institute of Tropical Medicine)—made considerable efforts to provide the country with institutions capable of producing a body of colonial knowledge. This, in turn, was to meet the need for a "high colonial culture" (linking the present with the glorious years of seaward exploration) and train an efficient bureaucratic workforce capable of running the empire's lands and peoples. Even a cursory glance at Portuguese intellectual production concerning the colonial regions and their peoples reveals that its output extended well beyond the bounds of academia. Journal and magazine articles and even lectures, presented in congresses during the early years of the New State, suggest that the country's intelligentsia keenly pursued the creation of an institutional field focused on the immense problems posed by the empire. They also show that much of this debate took place outside formal institutions. This was the case with literary production, which is noninstitutional by nature. Nonetheless, such institutions did exist at the time, even if some scholars criticized their production (see, among others, Pélissier 1979; Margarido 1975; Gallo 1988).

The historian René Péllissier (1979) notes the existence of the following institutions in the metropolis: the Instituto Superior de Ciências Sociais e Política Ultramarina (Higher Institute of Social Sciences and Overseas Policy)—the former Escola Superior Colonial (Colonial Higher School)— the Museu de Etnologia do Ultramar de Lisboa (Lisbon Museum of Overseas Ethnology), which, in conjunction with the small ethnological museum in Oporto along with another museum in Coimbra and its sections in Lisbon, possessed some real ethnological treasures (although badly catalogued and relatively inaccessible to the public); the Missão de Pesquisas Agrônomas (Agricultural Research Mission), also known as Tapada da Ajudá; and the Laboratório Nacional de Engenharia Civil (National Laboratory of Civil Engineering). The latter two institutions were of a technical nature, with their work specifically focused on improving the means of exploration for the African colonies' natural resources. In Angola, Péllissier lists the Instituto Angolano de Pesquisa Científicas (Angolan Institute of Scientific Research) and the Museum of Angola, both in Luanda, as well as the Museum of the Congo, located in the ancient town of Carmona; the Museum of Uíla, in the ancient town of Sá da Bandeira; and the Museum of Dundo.[22]

A number of other institutions linked to the production of colonial knowledge also existed: the pioneering Sociedade de Geografia de Lisboa, responsible for a respectable series of studies focused especially on the African colonies; the Junta de Investigações Científicas do Ultramar (Board of Overseas Scientific Investigations), founded in 1883; the Instituto de Medicina Tropical (Institute for Tropical Medicine); and the Medical and Scientific Schools of

Lisbon and, particularly, of Oporto.[23] Overseas, it is important to note both the Escola Médica de Nova Goa (New Goa Medical School), responsible for important studies on natives, mestizos, and even Europeans of different colonies, and the Centro de Estudos da Guiné (Guinea Studies Center). An especially important institution, the Centro de Estudos da Guiné begs a set of interesting questions. Thought by many to be where research studies into historical, ethnographical, and anthropological topics acquired a systematically higher quality (the texts remain fundamental today), the works produced at the Centro de Estudos da Guiné concern the most marginal territory of the African empire. Alfredo Margarido (1975: 342) suggests that the research of this study center achieved its level of quality precisely because white colonists were virtually absent from the small West African colony of Guinea. Hence it is necessary to avoid imputing any strict correlation between anthropological production and concrete instruments of colonial domination. In the case of Portuguese Guinea, most of the native structures were maintained, exploration took place indirectly, and there was never any significant input from white colonists. Indeed, from the viewpoint of modern capitalist exploration during the colonial period, Guinea was considered one of the least interesting territories, especially when compared to Angola and Mozambique. Despite this fact, it was in Guinea that anthropology and ethnology—not to mention the classic studies of the common law of Fulahs, Felupes, and Mandingos—attained the highest quality.

The founding of the Lisbon Geographical Society in December 1875, fronted by the publicist, politician, and writer Luciano Cordeiro, can be seen as a landmark in the production of a body of colonial knowledge in Portugal. Its creation reflected a tide of modern Portuguese colonialist thinking eager to see Portugal assume once again a competitive place in the international world. It looked to encourage this revival not only by taking part in debates on knowledge of tropical territories but also by supplying the state with information that would enable its participation in the "rush for Africa." Ensuring a demarcation of borders favorable to Portuguese interests required more than a discourse proclaiming the country's historical rights: indeed, it was necessary to prove a real knowledge and mastery of the overseas dominions. With this in mind, the Geographical Society pressured the state to allocate funds that were used for trips to Africa and for publications and so forth.[24]

From its outset the Geographical Society envisioned the creation of a Colonial School, a project realized at the start of the twentieth century.[25]

Although the school's capacity to provide adequate training for bureaucratic and academic personnel in high colonial culture has been seriously questioned, the existence of a colonial project can be clearly perceived both in the design of the school and in the output of students and teachers. This project was also evidently influenced by the procolonialist faction of the Lisbon Geographical Society, as well as by the upheaval resulting from the 1891 British ultimatum (when the United Kingdom demanded that Portugal abandon its supposed interests in the territories linking Angola and Mozambique). Additionally, it was heavily swayed by the "1895 generation"—the group of colonialists responsible for studying the best ways to occupy and exploit the African colonies.[26]

Designed as a center with the double function of training the empire's administrative personnel and producing a body of high-quality colonial knowledge, the Colonial School underwent a series of reforms over the years, the most radical of which were carried out between the start of the 1950s and 1961. This was a direct consequence of the overseas territories' change in legal status, as well as that of the native populations themselves.[27] Its objectives, put forth in its founding statutes, were to provide "the most universally acclaimed training necessary for overseas officials," as well as a general colonial (higher) education system. It also sought to guarantee preference to diplomats in appointments to colonial administration posts.[28]

It is important to note that the demand for the creation of a Colonial School arose from an intellectual movement—also present in the other colonizing powers—that extolled a "scientific occupation" of the overseas territories. This idea of occupation not only presumed that knowledge was necessary in order to dominate more effectively, but it also assumed above all that the colonizing process should be guided by genuine scientific principles in the form of a colonial science. Colonial knowledge, domination, and exploitation were, in the perception of the colonial intellectuals themselves,[29] completely intertwined. The control of natives (their productive labor) and the colonial territories (the exploitation of their physical resources) could only be adequately accomplished when guided by scientific principles. The eventual aim was the complete incorporation of native peoples into the political and spiritual body of the nation.

Although funding problems were chronic, ideal conditions for the Colonial School's development existed during the first decades of the New State. The Colonial Act and the constitution created such an organic relationship between the colonies and the metropolis that the training of officials to run the empire became a state necessity. Adding to this homegrown demand, the "colonial issue" soon reached its boiling point not just in Portugal but also in other colonial metropolises. Colonial and ethnographic pavilions gained an unusually high profile in all of the universal exhibitions held during the interwar years, particularly in Paris in 1931 when the city hosted the most spectacular colonial exhibition of all time, which was attended by many of the Colonial School's students. This surge of interest meant that the new generation of Portuguese colonialists had access to a more detailed picture of the processes involved in the incorporation (or otherwise) of native peoples, as well as of the progress achieved by other colonial powers.

An examination of the Colonial School's yearbooks reveals that during the 1930s and 1940s members of its academic staff were constantly present at national colonial congresses as well as at numerous international meetings. The Ministry of the Colonies in conjunction with the school sponsored large events such as the Semanas de Arte Negra (Negro Art Weeks)[30] and even international meetings such as the II Conferência Internacional de Africanistas Ocidentais (Second International Conference of West Africanists), which was organized by Mendes Corrêa in Bissau in 1948[31] and supported by such figures as Darryl Forde, Theodore Monod, and Paul Rivet, as well as the meeting of the Instituto Internacional Africano (African International Institute) in 1952.[32] The aim of these efforts was to deepen the involvement of Portuguese intellectuals in international debate and to ensure the dissemination of their research, highlighting the particular directions taken by Lusitanian colonialism.[33]

Mendes Corrêa and the "Uses and Customs" at Home and Abroad

The 1946 reform, pushed forward by the minister of the colonies at the time, Marcelo Caetano, was undertaken during the Colonial School's fortieth anniversary celebration. But it also occurred in a rapidly shifting international context characterized once again by the uncertain future of the colonies. Further, there was another important change. Following the minister's suggestion, directorship of the school was taken over by a renowned intellectual, the anthropologist António Augusto Esteves Mendes Corrêa, who had studied at length the native groups in the Portuguese colonial regions.[34]

Trained in medicine at the University of Porto, Mendes Corrêa would later come to be known as the "first Portuguese anthropologist."[35] He is most noted for the development of studies that at first centered on physical and criminal anthropology then increasingly acquired an alternately ethno-psychological, historical, and cultural focus, though Mendes Corrêa never fully abandoned his earlier grounding in biology.[36] He also achieved a high profile as sponsor of the I Congresso de Antropologia Colonial Nacional (First National Colonial Anthropology Congress), which took place in Porto in 1934, alongside the I Exposição Colonial Portuguesa (First Portuguese Colonial Exhibition). At this exhibition, academic staff and students under the coordination of Mendes Corrêa carried out anthropometric studies and other surveys of the native peoples originating from the African colonies, India, Macao, and Timor.[37] The studies undertaken in Porto provided the basis for an overview of the peoples making up the Portuguese colonial empire, later systematically compiled by Mendes Corrêa in a work published toward the end of his career in 1945, *Raças do Império* (Races of the Empire).

In this work, Mendes Corrêa synthesized a body of information ranging from the "racial" composition to the "exotic" or "quaint" customs of each of the social and ethnic groups from the metropolis and the colonies. The work is written for both the scientific community and the general public, richly illustrated with photographs and drawings. Reading *Raças do Imperio* produces the impression of grasping the empire in its full gamut of human types: the empire not only appears as a political entity, it also emerges as an organic and unified whole, vividly expressed in its racial and cultural diversity. In the words of Mendes Corrêa: "Twenty million Portuguese add up to a multitude whose great diversity fails to impede an essential unity of hopes and interests, a brotherly solidarity, the existence of a wide and perfect national community, based simultaneously on history, politics and a profound feeling of universal sympathy and understanding" (1945: 604).

From the very outset of *Raças do Império*, Mendes Corrêa emphasizes the need to avoid abandoning the concept of race in favor of culture since both are irrevocably related. Along this line of reasoning, the Portuguese anthropologist not only summarized his career, he also opposed contemporary trends in modern anthropology that interrogated the excessive importance given by nineteenth-century anthropological schools to the notion of race, proposing instead to substitute it for culture as anthropology's main object of study. Mendes Corrêa made clear his preference for studies that considered the biological and hereditary aspects of each human group, as well as their psychosocial behaviors, their differing aptitudes for work, and their cultural production. His theoretical and methodological choices make more sense when taking into account his guiding objective: to explain the totality of races living within a particular political structure, the empire, which ultimately translated an extremely heterogeneous nation into the enormous variety of peoples inhabiting it—a multiplicity that nevertheless retained a unity of spirit.

After examining the "head" of the empire and adjoining islands (to which he devotes more than half the book), Mendes Corrêa turns to the overseas colonies: Cape Verde, Sao Tomé and Principe, São João Batista de Ajudá, Angola, Mozambique, India, Macao, and Timor. The Atlantic archipelagos and the fort of São João Batista de Ajudá are depicted as exclusively Portuguese creations. In contrast, the remaining territories are assigned their own prehistory, but it is the Portuguese presence that relocated them within the same evolutionary time flow. The author draws his conclusions from a combination of archaeological data sets and Portuguese historical sources along with ethnographic information collected in the field or from the native peoples who visited the Colonial Exhibition of Porto in 1934. From the extreme ethnic and cultural diversity of the peoples of these territories, the work turns to generic information on then-current socio-demographic trends, uses and customs, sorcery, beliefs and religion, and differing capacities for manual or intellectual work.[38] Finally, the author arrives at the modern conditions of colonization, the situation of white colonists, and the problems arising from miscegenation.[39]

In tackling this last topic, Mendes Corrêa adopts a curious stance. Although miscegenation was a reality in some Portuguese colonies such as Cape Verde, and despite the fact that it had provided the nation with a rich variety of benefits, the author opposes miscegenation in any intense form or across the whole of the empire so as to avoid the risk of diluting the singular qualities of the Portuguese people among the strange lands and peoples far from the empire's center.[40] Discussing "the Empire's population policy," Mendes Corrêa concludes that although miscegenation is almost "inevitable and fatal" in the absence of the white woman, its adoption throughout the empire would provoke the "rupture of the [Portuguese people's] historical continuity." The question of the *mestiço* goes far beyond "native policy": he should be treated justly and humanely, and when he displays "perfect identification" with the "feelings, tendencies and hopes of the Portuguese people," he may even be incorporated into the general political and administrative framework of the country (1945: 620). Here the anthropologist diluted his own assessment at the time of the 1934 congress, where he had announced his deep preoccupation with miscegenation:

> The biological and social problems of miscegenation, in all their unsettling and dramatic intensity, still do not worry our investigators enough, for example. These problems will be—and indeed cannot fail to be—debated at this Congress. In a sense they have been forgotten ever since the golden era when the great Afonso de Albuquerque favoured the crossing of Portuguese men with native women, and tried to juridically and religiously legalize unions contracted with such ease that, as the chronicles tell us, banquets in which several marriages were celebrated at once often ended up with the couples mingling in a tremendous pagan orgy.[41]

Mendes Corrêa attempts to do justice to the principles set out in the Colonial Act and the indigenato. These included recognizing the natural diversity of the empire's peoples while adhering to the traditional Christian fraternity that had characterized Lusitanian expansion from its outset (1945: 621); maintaining hierarchy through the strict regulation of the relations between the different cultural groups living in the colonies (basically colonists and natives); and controlling the processes of assimilation. Basing his argument on anthropological findings, Mendes Corrêa proclaimed the superiority of the metropolitan populations, the need for assimilation—as long as this preserved (eugenically) the historical and anthropological continuity of the Portuguese people—and a policy of inclusion that took into account the diversity (and inequality) inherent to the natives from the different colonies. Politics and anthropology joined forces, therefore, in preserving the Portuguese colonial tradition and the uses and customs of the native peoples. Moreover, this political assurance of the preservation of difference, combined with Mendes Corrêa's study based on anthropological methods, results in the hierarchical reproduction of inequality and the perpetuation of the empire.

Mendes Corrêa's stance differs little, then, from the opinions presented in the 1940 Colonial Congress, when among other themes he spoke about an anthropology of miscegenation. At that time the discipline was perceived as belonging to the natural sciences, and studies in the area emphasized the "biological" and "psychic" characteristics of individuals and groups. The aim was to analyze a particular "reality," the mestiço, in order to determine the possibility (or impossibility) of using such an individual in the colonial project orchestrated by the Portuguese New State. A number of questions thus surfaced: How do the hereditary traits from parents of different races combine in mixed offspring? Would the latter be more or less fertile than their progenitors? (a question quickly discarded by Mendes Corrêa). How does the inheritance of inferior and superior traits take place? While it was obvious to Mendes Corrêa that the colonization and formation of Brazil had only been possible thanks to miscegenation, he still attributed this success to the political, mental, and economic hegemony of the white element, despite the high proportion of mestiços, blacks, and Indians making up the Brazilian population.[42]

In any case, Brazil did not constitute an example to be copied by the new Lusitanian collectivities taking shape, especially in the African colonies.[43] For Mendes Corrêa this was a matter of colonial policy—a line adopted by many of those in attendance at the congress—which opposed the Portuguese attitude to the policies promoted by the other imperial metropolises. Mendes Corrêa also recalled an interesting discussion that had taken place in Rome during a session of the International Colonial Institute, when the Portuguese representative expounded on the tendency of the Portuguese to promote juridical equality among the races, as well as their "interpenetration," largely inspired by a true "Christian spirit." He cited Brazil as an example. This assertion was apparently ill received by the other national delegations. General Teruzzi, representing Italy, rushed to condemn the premises of the indigenato contained in Salazar's Colonial Act, which conceded juridical equality to assimilated natives while at the same time respecting their uses and customs so long as they caused no offense to the colonizer's morals. The Italian general reiterated that fascist Italy was hostile to any kind of miscegenation in its colonies, and he cited the Arab saying "God created the whites, a goddess the blacks and the devil the mestizos." In conclusion he remarked: "We want to raise the natives to the highest degree of civilization, we have created schools for them, some of which involve very advanced teaching, but we wish the native to keep his native spirit, rather than become a bad copy of the European spirit . . . There should be no mixing between natives and Europeans."[44]

Although fascism did not go so far as to ban marriages between Italians and natives, it did take measures to impede such "illegitimate unions." The evocation of Brazilian miscegenation also provoked a vivid display of repudiation on the part of the Belgian representatives, who stressed the measures taken by the government of the Congo concerning mulattos.[45] These measures included the obligation of a Belgian father to recognize an illegitimate child as legitimate; severe penalties for Europeans who showed a lack of respect to a mulatta or who had extraconjugal relations with her; and adoption of a policy of assimilating mulattos, while preventing the formation of associations for or by them and simultaneously placing limits on the participation of mulattos in Belgian organizations.[46] As a result, it seems that mulattos in the Congo were left stranded. Their assimilation was officially promoted, yet at the same time they were banned from forming associations or actively participating in Belgian associations.

But what did the Portuguese anthropologist think? As a follower of science, he was still unable to arrive at a clear position on miscegenation. The combinations were such that the influence of mestiços could appear good or bad, depending on the traits of their progenitors and the effects of time and environment. Yet in the name of the fatherland, Mendes Corrêa erred toward discouraging miscegenation: the vigor of the race could be lost, leading inevitably to "the dissolution of multisecular Portugal, the end of an uninterrupted and glorious living chain."[47] As we have seen, this was an issue he returned to in *Races of the Empire*.

In light of this, I agree with the view expressed by Mário Moutinho in a recently published work: miscegenation was politically and anthropologically unacceptable throughout much of the New State. In this sense, Mendes Corrêa was fully in tune with the colonialist policies advocated by Marcelo Caetano who, in a text titled "Mozambique," published in the second issue of the *Revista do Ultramar*, claims:

> On one point we must be uncompromising in terms of racial separation: namely, family-based or sporadic interbreeding between blacks and whites, a source of serious disturbances in the social life of Europeans and natives, and the origin of the grave problem of miscegenation. I say grave if not from the biological viewpoint—which remains controversial and is too complex for me to take any firm position—then at least from the sociological viewpoint. But while it is appropriate to avoid or suppress such racial interbreeding, there is no justification for any hostility towards mestiços just for being who they are: it is not their fault they were born, nor is it fair they should pay for any paternal error as innocent victims.
>
> Parents who abandon mestiço children to an uncertain future must be held responsible. Society cannot ignore the fate of these members who, once educated, can be useful elements in the work of colonization, just as when abandoned and miserable they are liable to turn into dangerous and disruptive agents. (cited in Moutinho 2000: 75)

Indeed, we can say that the anthropologist Mendes Corrêa was one of the leading producers of Portuguese colonial knowledge between the 1930s and 1940s, and that his intellectual production was absolutely consistent with the principles of the Colonial Act and Portuguese colonial policy. It was this consistency that eventually exposed the actual contradictions and paradoxes of the system: the imperative for assimilation combined with the rigid system of indigenato (which meant that those assimilated ended up representing a minimal percentage of the African colonies' population); the claim that the cultural diversity of the empire was the result of the state's tutelary strength, at the same time that the supremacy of the white element was ensured; an ambiguous stance in relation to mestiços (demographically insignificant in the colonial societies), simultaneously seen as examples of the "Christian humanism" that traditionally accompanied the Lusitanian colonizer and as living images of the latter's own potential degeneration in tropical lands. Finally, the aim was to foster a rigorously controlled process of assimilation that would ensure the hierarchy of the empire itself and the continuity of the nation in the colonies. This would be an enormous contradiction, indeed, if one did not take into account the fact that the metropolis's viability was seen throughout the New State as depending on the reproduction of the state's hierarchy and tutelary force over the people. *Empire* and *Nation* overlapped in the anthropologist's work. His vision of the empire's peoples was strictly in accordance with the policy promoted by the New State: corporativism in the metropolis, indigenato in the colonies. The paternalist corporativism fit perfectly with the vision cultivated of the Portuguese people, which found its fullest materialization in the Secretariado de Propaganda Nacional (National Propaganda Secretariat) coordinated by Antônio Ferro.[48] Mendes Corrêa's study *Races of the Empire* thus managed to satisfy one of the most important aims of the New State: it succeeded in integrating the hierarchical structure of the empire within a national whole.

"The Good-Hearted Portuguese People"

Reflections on the Portuguese people, their ethnic psychology and national identity, constitute an important tradition in Portugal. João Leal (1999b; 2000) identifies the intellectuals of the latter third of the nineteenth century as those responsible for the initial debate surrounding the "ethnic psychology of the Portuguese people." He then reconstructs an intellectual tradition that, traversing a good part of the twentieth century, eventually gave rise to the studies of "national character," whose main exponent in Portugal was the anthropologist Jorge Dias (see, e.g., Dias 1953).[49] What were the consequences of this systematic reflection on Portuguese identity in terms of the populations of the colonial territories? And, furthermore, how relevant was it to the functioning of the authoritarian state?

Taking the works of Mendes Corrêa and Jorge Dias as a guideline, it is possible to establish a link between the studies of the metropolis and those of the colonies. Mendes Corrêa evokes an empire wishing to be a nation, while its populations, racially and culturally so different, only form one in appearance: the imperative for assimilation and the hierarchical structure of the nation make everyone Portuguese. And while the empire is reproduced by maintaining hierarchy and difference, the nation too is reproduced in the same way. Such a process depended entirely on the notion of a "good-hearted Portuguese people," present in the ideology of the Salazar regime, in the songs of Amália Rodrigues, in the large public rituals—such as the 1940 Exhibition of the Portuguese World—and undoubtedly in the work of Portuguese anthropologists linked to the Salazarist institutions. Here we arrive at the work of Jorge Dias, part of which focuses on the definition of a "base-personality" of the Portuguese people, which took the natives from different colonies as an inalienable element of the "Portuguese being."

Jorge Dias's work constitutes a unique case within the anthropology produced in Portugal.[50] Linked from the 1950s onward to the Colonial School—renamed the Instituto Superior de Ciências Sociais e Políticas Ultramarinas (Higher Institute of Social Sciences and Overseas Policy) in the 1960s—Dias evidently followed the progression of the various modern anthropological approaches since the 1940s, in particular those developed by the North American culture and personality school (Leal 1999b: 15). However, as João de Pina Cabral (1991) emphasizes, although Jorge Dias cites contemporary anthropologists in his research on some of the peninsula's peasant communities and in his studies of the Maconde of Mozambique, his work's lack of theoretical sophistication reveals a great deal about the discipline's situation in the country. Without entering into the debate on the history of anthropology in Portugal, here I trace some parallels between the works of Mendes Corrêa and those of Jorge Dias—authors who appear to converge in their belief in the existence of a "good-hearted Portuguese people" both at home and abroad. Much cherished by the regime, this notion would be destroyed with the impending violence of war.

Regarded as one of the key figures in the revitalization of anthropology in Portugal (Pina Cabral 1991: 28), Jorge Dias defended his doctoral thesis on the village community of Vilarinho da Furna at the University of Munich during the harsh years of World War II. In 1944 he moved to Santiago de Compostela where he remained until 1947. Although his commentators fail to link him with any totalitarian ideology, his journey through Nazi Germany and Franco's Spain suggests a career path that was at the very least ambiguous.

Following the intervention of Mendes Corrêa—from whom he later looked to distance himself—Jorge Dias returned to Portugal, where he initially worked at the Centro de Estudos e Etnografia Peninsular (Center of Peninsular Studies and Ethnography), which was linked to the Institute of Anthropology at the University of Porto's Faculty of Sciences. Then in the 1950s, Jorge Dias and his disciples—clearly influenced by North American anthropology—produced a series of "community studies" and, in 1957, he was invited by the Overseas Ministry to direct the Missões de Estudos das Minorias Étnicas do Ultramar Português (Study Missions of Portuguese Overseas Ethnic Minorities). Working alongside his team, he carried out studies on the Chopes of southern Mozambique, the Boers and Bushmen from the south of Angola, and especially the Maconde populations of northern Mozambique.[51]

Dias's comfortable adaptation to authoritarian settings should not be overlooked. From the conceptual viewpoint, the "culturalist" vision, which acquired substance throughout his work, also helped promote Salazarist ideology. Likewise his later collaboration with Salazarist colonialism is clearly evident in his willingness to send reports to the Overseas Ministry, which were filled with details on the social and political conditions of the peoples he visited.[52] While it is true, as João de Pina Cabral has pointed out, that Dias's reports are honest and far from laudatory of the Portuguese colonial regime, the fact remains that he saw his collaboration as a way of correcting an accident, without ever questioning colonialism or authoritarianism per se. Dias never ceased to be a man of the regime who continually praised the inherent qualities of Portuguese colonialism (see, e.g., Dias 1961a; 1961b). His admiration, cited by João de Pina Cabral, for the United States and for the American academy does not necessarily imply any real fondness for democratic systems: what worked for the United States was unsuited to Portugal and its overseas territories due to the particular culture of the Portuguese people.

It is not my intention here to produce an in-depth discussion of the role played by Jorge Dias's work in the debate on Portuguese identity. My present interest is to highlight this intellectual's fixed conception of two basic questions: the character of the Portuguese people, and the importance of this character in defining the course taken by their expansionist and imperial history. In his approach to culturalism, Dias reaches very similar conclusions to those of Mendes Corrêa. This was in complete accordance, I should stress, with the official ideology expounded by the regime: while Mendes Corrêa took race to imply a series of constants revealing a Portuguese spirit, Jorge Dias believed these constants were instead expressed in culture, which defined a Portuguese identity distinct from those of other Latin peoples.

Obviously the shift from the concept of race to the concept of culture marks a crucial step in the history of anthropology in Portugal. Yet from the political viewpoint, the readings to which this notion of culture lent itself were entirely conservative: Portuguese culture defined a pattern that tended to reproduce itself over time (history) and space (the empire's geography). In Dias's view, the political structure of the New State and the Portuguese colonial empire should reflect the reality of the nation's spirit. Any deviation from the "base-personality" of the "good-hearted Portuguese people," such as the violence displayed by the colonial system, or the forced labor promoted by the Portuguese administration and colonists—all carefully observed and described by Jorge Dias in his field reports—should be immediately dismissed as an anomaly, foreign to the true Portuguese being, which was naturally affable in its treatment of exotic peoples.

Identifying a cultural pattern shaping the Portuguese people in all their diversity was also Dias's main aim in an essay published in 1953 (a later version of a work first drafted in 1942) titled *Os Elementos Fundamentais da Cultura Portuguesa* (The Fundamental Elements of Portuguese Culture). These elements were meant to help reveal the "base-personality" of the nation. Here the Portuguese emerge as a deeply contradictory people: although intrinsically good, they could be extremely violent when their pride was hurt. They alternated between periods of glory and periods of complete decadence. They were at once introverted (in contrast to other Latin colonizers) and socially minded. Finally, they had a tolerant attitude that made them unique as a colonizing people since they based assimilation on adaptation. Assimilation of native peoples, adaptation to the environment: these processes were only conceivable thanks to the same universalist conception asserted by Mendes Corrêa and the plasticity defended in the 1940s by Gilberto Freyre (1940).

João Leal (1999b: 20) argues that for Jorge Dias, "the Portuguese national character is always seen as a mixture of one quality and its opposite": gentle and violent, solitary and socially caring . . . All qualities converging in a particular interpretation of the "Portuguese being," a set of sentiments that clearly culminate in the idea of *saudade*: a sense of longing and nostalgia.[53] And as "the contradictory qualities upon which the Portuguese national character was based were qualities situated in the universe of emotions and feelings" (17), the country obviously required a strong, authoritarian state to control its emotional excesses, while simultaneously giving them a voice. Just like the primitive natives from the different colonies under Portuguese administration, this deeply emotional being needed a strong political structure: indigenato in the colonies, corporativism in the metropolis—institutions created with the aim of controlling the wilder extremes of the Lusitanian spirit. It can be seen therefore that although the "politics of the spirit" defended by Antônio Ferro were already showing signs of terminal decline in the 1950s, the very idea of a Portuguese spirit, as the expression of a race or culture, is once more adopted. Now, however, it can only be defined by appropriating the image of the native, transformed into a passive agent of the loving and loveable process of assimilation (with the native being conceived as Portuguese from the onset).

In his analysis of the relations between ethnological production and colonialism, Mário Moutinho (1982) considers the role of anthropology in legitimizing the New State both in the metropolis and in the colonies. This was more a question, perhaps, of supplying an ideological perspective rather than actually providing information for state action. His work is surprising in the way it reveals the political aims behind the thinking of renowned and sophisticated intellectuals like Jorge Dias—thinkers who gave a messianic cast to the Portuguese cultural mission in the world, saluting its uniqueness when compared to the actions pursued by other colonizing powers.[54]

Fully committed to the imperial ideology of the time—which shortly after mutated into Luso-Tropicalism[55]—Mendes Corrêa, Jorge Dias, and other professionals linked to the Colonial School sought to produce a body of colonial knowledge (and particularly an anthropology) on par with the other colonial powers, while preserving the particularities of Portuguese colonization. This process became vividly apparent in the course taken by the research of the school's students and teaching staff, especially from the 1950s onward. A number of events announced profound changes in the Portuguese overseas domain, particularly the organization of groups, which later turned into movements for national liberation; the proliferation of messianic outbreaks, especially in Angola and Mozambique; the massacre of the Batepá in Sao Tomé and Principe (February 1953); the pressures from the Indian Union and the occupation of Dadra and Nagar Haveli (August 1954); and the massacre of the Pinjiguiti in Bissau (August 1959). In response, the studies developed under the school's auspices tried to explain the native dynamic, at the same time as they sought to prove to the world that Portugal possessed detailed knowledge of its peoples and the cultural manifestations of the Portuguese from the four corners of the world.

Significantly, it was the uprisings of native peoples in the colonies that finally overturned the image of the good-hearted Portuguese people. Both at home and abroad, itemizing the uses and customs of different peoples ended up crystallizing an eschatological relationship between nation and empire within which origin and destiny became inseparable. Faced by these lists of uses and customs, war was the only option in a struggle for freedom that ended up exposing the fallacy of both the notion of a good-hearted Portuguese people and the substantive cultural identities that the empire's hierarchy aimed to preserve. On both sides of the trenches, what could be observed was far from the idyllic world that many believed to exist in Portugal and its "overseas provinces." A few years before the start of the war, Jorge Dias had extolled the "intrinsic kindness" of the Portuguese who based their actions on their emotions and hearts. However, it would be left to the ironic words in the poetry of the Mozambican Rui Guerra to reveal the violence giving impetus to the Portuguese colonial system: "Even while my hands are crushing, culling and killing, my heart shuts its eyes and, in all sincerity, weeps" (Mesmo quando as minhas mãos estão a triturar, trucidar, matar, meu coração fecha os olhos e, sinceramente, chora).

Notes

1 The building of contemporary nation-states in Western Europe exists in a complex relationship with the modern colonial empires. They are by no means independent phenomena, and nationalism and imperialism could be found in numerous political and cultural contexts (cf. Calvet 1981; Anderson 1991; Arendt 1990; Thomaz 2002).

2 Recognizing the discipline's particularities in different national contexts does not imply assuming a specifically national approach. I therefore concur with João de Pina Cabral and prefer the designation "anthropology in Portugal" instead

of "Portuguese anthropology" (cf. Pina Cabral 1991). Although the work of these anthropologists often took the colonial territories as its universe of observation, its point of reference remained the metropolis. On anthropology in Portugal and its relationship with colonialism, see, among others, Margarido 1975; Moutinho 1982; Gallo 1988; and Pina Cabral 1991.

3 This is the self-designation used by the authoritarian regime institutionalized by the 1933 constitution. The New State came to an end on 25 April 1974.

4 The quotation marks here do not imply any kind of irony but rather correspond to the fact that there was no institutionalized anthropological field in Portugal at the time. Those who defined themselves as anthropologists or ethnographers were mostly so as an adjunct to another occupation such as physician, biologist, missionary, administrator, or even a member of the military. Indeed, the fragile state of anthropology in Portugal was stressed by the intellectuals of the period.

5 The bicentennial of the Foundation and Restoration was celebrated in 1940. The Exhibition of the Portuguese World was organized alongside a series of congresses. The structure of the former was ostensibly based on the grand Universal Exhibitions; however it was very particular in terms of its content due to its objective of translating the spirit of nationality. The centrality of the empire during the 1940 events also revealed much about its national meaning (cf. Thomaz 2002).

6 I refer to the dictator himself as well as to personalities such as Antônio Ferro, Cardinal Cerejeira, Henrique Galvão, and Armindo Monteiro, among others.

7 "Nation" here is understood as an "imagined community" in Anderson's sense (1991).

8 The indigenato regime lasted until 1961 and imposed the creation of a dualism in terms of personal status, resting on the fundamental distinction between natives and citizens. Yet while political status was dual, everyone was Portuguese—that is, they made up part of the (hierarchical) body of the nation. In any event, it is useful to stress that the virtual limit of this duality was progressive and gradual assimilation. The indigenato was not present in all the colonial territories: Cape Verde, the Portuguese State of India, and Macao were never subject to this regime, in contrast to Guinea, Angola, and Mozambique. The indigenato was introduced in Sao Tomé and Principe and Timor only after World War II. The corporative structure proposed by the regime for the peninsular population was, like the indigenato, paternalist and based on the state's intervention. In both cases, "natives" and "people" are represented as groups lacking initiative and requiring protection from the state, which seeks to ensure immobility and avoid transformation (cf. Rosas 1994).

9 All the literature focusing on this period has been compelled, in some form or other, to discuss the specificities of Portuguese "fascism," the nature of its corporative structure, Salazar's relation to the church, the metropolitan bourgeoisie and the rural sectors, the centrality of the empire, and so on.

10 Agência Geral das Colônias, Coletânea de Legislação Colonial, *Carta Orgânica do Império Colonial Português—Ato Colonial—Estatuto Político, Civil e*

Criminal dos Indígenas das Colônias Portuguesas de África (disposições fundamentais)–Regimento do Conselho do Império Colonial, Lisbon, 1948 (hereafter referred to as AGDC).

11 Concerning Oliveira Martins's conception of the nation and its relationship to the colonial empire, see Alexandre 2000a. Oliveira Martins believed in the sale of a good portion of the colonies in order to create a new colonial territory in Angola, which would not be the result of assimilationist or integrationist ideas defended by humanists and philanthropists of the period. The nation, he felt, was essentially different from the colony, and seeking to apply to it the same institutional and legal principles prescribed for the metropolis amounted to an aberration.

12 The French case is highly instructive in terms of the public debate surrounding the colonies (see, among others, Girardet 1972; Arendt 1990; Biondi and Morin 1992).

13 The power of certain conservative sections of the Catholic Church became more apparent following the concordat signed with the Vatican in 1940, along with the missionary accord of the same year.

14 The inhabitants of Cape Verde, Macao, and the Portuguese State of India were never subject to the rigors of indigenato, although they were normally referred to as natives.

15 Article 1 of the *Carta Orgânica do Império Colonial Português* (Organic Charter of the Portuguese Colonial Empire) defines the colonies as "an integral part of the nation's territory"; article 2 of the Colonial Act states that it is "of the organic essence of the Portuguese nation to fulfil the historical function of possessing and colonizing overseas dominions and civilizing the native populations included within them, as well as exercising the moral influence which is recorded in the Patronate of the Orient" (AGDC 1948).

16 One must not forget the expansionist and bellicose nature of imperialism at the time—an issue from which the Portuguese empire distanced itself through its adoption of a more defensive stance (cf. Arendt 1990; Hobsbawm 1987).

17 Estatuto Político, Civil e Criminal dos Indígenas das Colônias Portuguesas de África. AGDC 1948.

18 Albeit only formally, the natives of the different Portuguese dominions were classified with the same political status as the metropolitan populations throughout long periods of the nineteenth century and the early twentieth. It may be argued that the origin of the modern Portuguese indigenato can be largely attributed to the men of thought and action who planned the modern Portuguese colonial empire, especially those linked to the generation of 1895 in Mozambique, such as Antônio Enes and Mouzinho de Albuquerque. As products of their time, they allied their military experience in the "wars of pacification" against the natives with the evolutionist and Darwinist thinking popular at the end of the nineteenth century, according to which the political incorporation of "inferior" and "backward" masses was an absurdity (cf. Alexandre 2000b).

19 It should be noted that although the inhabitants of Macao and the Por-

tuguese State of India were considered Portuguese citizens, a fact that could perhaps be put down to the level of development of "orientals" or the impotence of Portuguese power, common law was to a large extent respected and sometimes even underwent a process of codification.

20 Marcelo Caetano, the last head of government during the dictatorship, was a prominent figure throughout the entire period of the New State's existence and one of the ideologists of the indigenato. On his thinking, see Caetano 1974.

21 Estatuto Político, Civil e Criminal dos Indígenas das Colônias Portuguesas de África. AGDC 1948.

22 On the Museum of Dundo, see Porto 1999.

23 As Alfredo Margarido (1975: 327) stresses, the Congress of Tropical Medicine in Luanda in August 1923 included a set of proposals arguing for the need to promote anthropological studies as the only means of "achieving flawless colonization."

24 Portuguese intellectuals thereby aligned themselves with sectors of the bourgeoisie who pressured the state in order to assert their interests in the overseas territories. It is worth highlighting the fear of an "Iberian Union" that tormented a large portion of the Lusitanian bourgeoisie and intelligentsia in the face of European irredentism: a colonial empire seemed to be the best way of escaping the possibility of being transformed into a Spanish province.

25 According to information provided by Gallo (1988: 173), the first proposal for the creation of the Colonial School was made in 1878 by the Geographical Society. The school was founded a few years later in 1883, but only acquired formal existence with the decree of 18 January 1906.

26 The nationalist currents at the end of the nineteenth century were especially successful in catalyzing the enthusiasm of petit bourgeois urban groups, which were generally linked to the commercial bourgeoisie that regarded protectionist policies in the colonies with approval. The school's intake was mostly drawn from the shrunken metropolitan middle class and from bureaucrats already working in the colonies who wished to improve their social standing.

27 In the 1950s the Colonial School was transformed into the Higher Institute of Social Sciences and Overseas Policy, while the Colonial Act underwent a (small) number of modifications such as abandoning the term "colonies" in favor of "overseas provinces." The end of indigenato in 1961 corresponded to a deeper transformation, a moment during which the natives came to be categorized as citizens. It can be inferred that the successive reforms undergone by the school were profoundly related to transformations in the international setting.

28 Legal decree 35.885, *Anuário da Escola Superior Colonial*, year XXIX, 1947–1948: 5; hereafter referred to as AESC.

29 I refer the reader to the acts of the Congress of Colonial Anthropology (*Trabalhos do I Congresso de Antropologia Colonial Portuguesa*, Porto, 1934), the Meeting for Colonial High Culture (*Alta Cultura Colonial*, Lisbon, 1936), and the Colonial Congress (*Congresso do Mundo Português*: vol. XIV–Congresso Colonial, Lisbon, 1940).

30 Despite the organization of the Negro Art Weeks, African art had little impact on the arts in Portugal in contrast to the influence it later exerted in other European metropolitan centers. The peripheral location of Portugal and above all the authoritarian and regressive regime installed in the country hindered the emergence of a more daring modern art movement (França 1985).

31 The Second International Conference in Bissau was promoted as part of the commemorations of the Fifth Centenary of the Discovery of Guinea, celebrated in 1946. The First International Conference had been held in Dakar in January 1945 (AESC, year XXIX, 1947–1948: 93). Supports are listed in AESC, year XXIX, 1947–1948: 94.

32 AESC, year XXXIV, 1952–1953: 46.

33 The successive reforms of the school reveal this concern insofar as they were accompanied by discussions that sought to compare it with training institutes for overseas personnel in other imperial metropolises, such as France and Belgium. At the time of the 1946 reform, the range of disciplines in the French and Belgian schools was widely discussed as a way of making the deficiencies of the Portuguese institution explicit. The French National Overseas School offered a much higher number of disciplines, as well as various special courses dedicated to the student's destination country. Belgium in fact possessed a Colonial University, located in the city of Antwerp, which prompted the Portuguese intellectuals to discreetly drop the project of transforming the school into a university.

34 Space limitations prevent me from undertaking any analysis of the scientific quality of Mendes Corrêa's works: his anachronism in relation to international trends in the discipline during the period has already been pointed out by Pina Cabral (1991). I would only stress the lack of rigor that sometimes characterizes his work. This, however, does not negate his immense importance during the period.

35 AESC, year XXVIII, 1946–1947: 8.

36 João Leal (1999b: 14) reminds us that Mendes Corrêa later tackled the theme of "Portuguese ethnic psychology" from the viewpoints of physical and criminal anthropology, in texts published in 1913 and 1919. However, these studies had relatively little impact on a debate dominated by the narrative of nostalgia.

37 *O Instituto de Antropologia da Universidade do Porto na Primeira Exposição Colonial Portuguesa*, Porto, 1934, p. 15. The observations in Porto were based on a sample of 305 adults and 19 children, and involved a total of 59 anthropometric measurements (p. 17). It is worth noting that during the International Colonial Exhibition of Paris in 1931, French scientists were not authorized to study any of the individuals present there: a fact Mendes Corrêa stresses, and laments, in the inaugural session of the 1934 Colonial Congress (*Trabalhos do I Congresso de Antropologia Colonial Portuguesa*, Porto, 1934).

38 It should be remembered that the dictatorial regime encouraged the study of the colonies as a way of improving the exploitation of native labor. This dimension was underlined by Mário Moutinho in drafting one of the recommendations for the acts of the Congress of Colonial Anthropology held in Porto in 1934: "Not

all the natives are suitable for military service, just as others are incapable of manual work in factories. The aim is therefore to organize a pre-selection process in order to avoid the ineffective employment of people and consequent economic failures. Calculation of the degree of physical development is based on simple anthropometric observations whose results or practical formulas are expressed by indexes or coefficients of robustness which can be easily applied in practice. Functional selection, even in military circles, should be effected through the use of ergographic and motor reflex measurements, and so on" (Moutinho 1982: 427–28; also cited in Pina Cabral 1991: 31).

39 The author calls "miscegenation" the result of the sexual relations between Portuguese men and African women.

40 This seems to be a paradox: were they not all Portuguese? The paradox is only superficial. "Portuguese being" is defined in terms of its capacity for assimilating natives: in turn, the natives would become Portuguese insofar as they displayed nationality, while the active role in this process of revelation fell to metropolitans (the head of the empire).

41 *Trabalhos do I Congresso de Antropologia Colonial Portuguesa*, Porto, 1934, p. 28.

42 Here, one may note the intense dialogue between Mendes Corrêa and Brazilian thinkers such as Roquette-Pinto and in particular Oliveira Vianna. Based on Oliveira Vianna's work, Corrêa proclaimed the supremacy of Aryans in Brazil, despite the high number of mestiços.

43 The idea of the mestiço as a symbol of Brazil or the negro as a participant of Brazilian culture was far from being fully accepted in many Brazilian intellectual and political circles—a fact testified to by the strong reaction to the presentation of artifacts linked to the African heritage in the Pavilion of Brazil at the Exhibition of the Portuguese World (cf. Thomaz, 2002). The potential universalization of Freyre's theses to the whole of the Portuguese world would have to wait until the 1950s, although even then it still met strong resistance from various sectors of Portuguese society (cf. Castelo 1999).

44 *Congresso do Mundo Português*, vol. XVI—Congresso Colonial, Lisbon, 1940, p. 128.

45 This refers to the result of the mixture between Europeans and Africans.

46 The association between colonizers and natives is always seen as an illegitimate union, and therefore a result of an illegal union, between the white man and the native woman.

47 *Congresso do Mundo Português*, vol. XVI—Congresso Colonial, Lisbon, 1940, p. 121.

48 The Secretariado de Propaganda Nacional later changed its name to the National Information, Popular Culture and Tourism Secretariat and later still to the State Secretariat for Information and Tourism.

49 Among others, see Dias 1953. These kinds of works were produced by summarizing elements already present in the work of anthropologists such as

Mendes Corrêa and the output of the North American culture and personality school. On the latter body of work, see Goldman and Neiburg, this volume.

50 Current studies of the work of Jorge Dias are largely indebted to the work of Pina Cabral (1991), Leal (1999a; 1999b; 2000), and Moutinho (2000). The connections between his reflections concerning peninsular Portugal and the empire are my own.

51 Pursuing research in the African colonies under the patronage of the Overseas Ministry was clearly not an ingenuous undertaking. Concerning Jorge Dias's work on the Maconde, see Leal 1999a.

52 For a discussion of these reports, see Pereira 1988.

53 I would highlight the fact that the idea of *saudade* (nostalgia) as a particular sentiment of the Portuguese is deeply imperialist. After all, *saudade* of what? That of the immigrants who found themselves far from home, without doubt, but also that of the adventurers and colonists, those who for centuries dedicated themselves to "giving new worlds to the world," feeding the imperialist enterprise that reached its end in 1974; or even nostalgia for the empire, moment, and territory where Portugal had revealed its national greatness.

54 Moutinho's essay is interesting in that it delineates a colonial ethnology that skirted the grotesque in the work of anthropologists who, in a more sophisticated way, helped to provide the ideological bases of the New State.

55 A detailed analysis of the absorption of Luso-Tropicalism in Portugal may be found in Castelo 1999. The analytical perspective adopted by the author reveals that Luso-Tropicalism was far from configuring a social theory, as proposed by Moreira and Venâncio (1999). I have discussed the premises of Luso-Tropicalism in Thomaz 2002, wherein I disqualify it as either method or theory because by adopting the concept the researcher already knows beforehand what will be found in the tropical territories under study, without any concern for systematic observation or description of the realities encountered.

Florence Weber

VICHY FRANCE AND THE END OF
SCIENTIFIC FOLKLORE (1937 – 1954)

More than sixty years after the end of World War II, the history of French ethnology is still held hostage to the political divisions and social myths of the occupation period. While Robert Paxton's (1972) groundbreaking study of Vichy France revolutionized the historiography of the era by calling attention to the occupation's "gray areas,"[1] the history of the social sciences continues to be written in black and white. Prominent historians continue to interrogate individual social scientists for their "guilt" or "innocence," their status as collaborators or as members of the Resistance. Similarly, the shifts in institutional structures and disciplinary boundaries that occurred during the war are often attributed to social scientists' collective post-Vichy "shame" (c.f. Fabre 1998; Velay Vallantin 1999).[2] In this ongoing historiographical prosecution, the "choice" of continuing to work under Vichy is read as a sign of anti-republicanism or (worse) closeted Nazi sympathizing. Rather than continue this perpetual prosecution, I propose a retelling of the French social sciences' wartime history that escapes Manichaean dualities. Using the historiographical tools introduced by Paxton, I offer here an account that emphasizes two related sociological axes that are too often lost to stereotype and myth: first, the historical and institutional conditions under which French social scientists made "choices" about the form and content of French ethnology; and second, the role played by prewar scientific and ideological trends in the postwar emergence of an anthropology of France defined against "exotic" anthropology, art, history, folklore, and social geography.

The Unending Trial of Vichy-era Science

The history of the social sciences in postwar France begins with a trial born out of the political fissures and personal rivalries of the occupation. On

29 August 1944, just after liberation, an anonymous informant accused Georges-Henri Rivière of collaboration. Rivière was, at the time, director of the Museum of Folk Art and Tradition (Musée des Arts et Traditions Populaires, hereafter ATP), the governmental body dedicated to the construction and institutionalization of what would become French ethnology.[3] The anonymous informant was, most likely, Rivière's assistant, André Varagnac. The accusation and the reactions it provoked led to an investigation by the Commission d'Épuration, a legal body established at the close of the war to investigate and punish Nazi sympathizers.[4] For a short period, control of the ATP was given to Marcel Maget, who had been a colleague of Varagnac's since their work together in 1935 on one of the ATP's intellectual antecedents, the Commission for Collective Research (Commission des Recherches Collectives, hereafter CRC). Ultimately, with the aid of testimony from friends and colleagues, Rivière was cleared of all charges and returned to the ATP in April 1945. Varagnac also eventually reentered public academic life: on 1 January 1946 he was appointed to the Museum of National Antiquities in Saint-Germain-en-Laye. These de facto acquittals, like the accusations themselves, hinged on classic postwar politics: the fabrication of eleventh-hour resistance fighters, anonymous denunciations, endemic distrust, and professional tensions.

But while the investigation into Rivière and Varagnac's behavior had ended by 1946, the question of their guilt and (by extension) that of the ATP itself continued to shape the historiography of the French social sciences. A few facts mobilized by Rivière's accusers have been recycled repeatedly as proof of the ATP's collaboration. As was noted during the investigation, the ATP did have ties to the National Peasant Corporation (Corporation Nationale Paysanne), Vichy's replacement for the Permanent Assembly of the Presidents of the Chambers of Agriculture (Assemblée Permanente des Présidents de Chambres d'Agriculture). In addition, the ATP was linked to the National Folklore Propaganda Committee (Comité National de Propagande par le Folklore) created in 1939. Rivière had even made reference to this committee in a 1942 article, noting his hope that it would provide the foundation for a "true national folklore corporation" (1942: 316). But beyond these few facts, many of which are complicated by prewar institutional genealogies,[5] postwar social science historians condemn the ATP largely for its occupation-period popularity. The ATP's critics attribute its success to an imagined ideological harmony between the institution's mission (the promotion of folk arts and traditions) and Vichy's valorization of the notion of local roots and an immutable agricultural past.

This ongoing historiographical indictment has inspired a defense that perpetuates the cycle of recriminations and justifications. In 1973, Rivière wrote an article defending the ATP against continued rumors of collaboration; in 1993, Maget penned a similarly inspired piece.[6] Both men argued that the four intellectual camps (*chantiers intellectuels*) created by the government and run by the ATP after October 1941 proved the organization's innocence. Despite having been organized by Vichy and approved by the German occupiers as part of a propaganda and employment campaign, these camps (like their separately administered youth-camp counterparts)[7] often protected Jews and Resistance fighters.[8] Thus, according to Rivière and Maget, the case should be closed and the ATP cleared of any suspicion of collaboration. But historical anthropologists like Daniel Fabre (1998: 378) view these repeated attempts to clear the record (what he calls French ethnology's "unrelenting and ubiquitous denial") as evidence of the French social sciences' collective guilt. As he writes: "A whole generation of French anthropologists, in the broad sense, has spent much energy denying and attempting to erase Occupation-era missteps and frailties" (378). And thus the cycle begins again, leaving largely unexplored some serious questions about the scientific purchase, institutional organization, and political implications of the French social sciences.

However, if we transcend this attempt to clearly categorize individuals and institutions as "Resistance fighters," "collaborators," or "opportunists," we are confronted with historical and political ambiguity on the order of Primo Levi's famous statement, "neither white nor black." This does not mean that there were no individual "bad guys." The physical anthropologist Montandon helped Vichy establish the legal definition of a "Jew" and served as the only French expert on the lethal Department for the Jewish Question (Commissariat Général aux Questions Juives). His anthropology—beginning with his definition of an *ethnie française*—was without question informed largely by his unapologetically racist politics. In contrast, an institution like the ATP (which never employed Montandon) certainly did not have a uniform politics. Fabre himself notes that whereas Varagnac was in "full and complete" agreement with Vichy, Rivière hid political skepticism beneath superficial deference to war-period authorities, and Maget remained obsessed with the integrity of "science" (1998: 374–75). Indeed, the case of the "good guys" is not clear-cut. The Musée de l'Homme (Museum of Man), the ethnographic museum established in 1937, is rightly heralded as one of the first bastions of resistance in France.[9] But despite this reputation, a number of the museum's anthropologists largely ignored the war period's changed political context and pursued their research as usual.

Rather than renew a fruitless attempt to impose rigid categories on social complexity, I propose here a preliminary exploration of the scientific, institutional, social, and political constraints that shaped the kinds of professional and political choices made by the social scientists of the ATP during the occupation. Such an approach not only reframes current debates about war-period social science, it also helps to shed new light on contemporary disciplinary configurations. While partisans of the "trial approach" often attribute postwar French ethnology's dedication to "pure science" and its hostility to "folklore" and other "applied sciences" to a collective disciplinary guilt (cf. Fabre 1998), I would argue that these disciplinary developments were rooted in republican ideological and institutional formations that predate Vichy.

Social Scientists under Vichy:
Republican and Passionate about Science

In a book published in 1999, Gérard Noiriel offers a hypothesis that provides the foundation for understanding the relations between the French state and the social sciences. He suggests that the Vichy government forced French academic social scientists (mainly historians and sociologists) to separate scientific and republican ideals. This divorce represented an almost unprecedented shift. As Noiriel reminds us, from 1871 until the interwar period, positivist historians, Durkheimian sociologists, and Vidalian geographers constructed the French social sciences as a tool for republican nation-building.[10] Vichy, however, forced republican academics to choose between their scientific commitment to research and their political abhorrence for their new masters. While the men and women deprived of their positions—deported and/or killed under Vichy's new laws (Jews, political prisoners, foreigners)—never faced this choice, most other scientists did.[11] Maget, for example, wrote of his own dilemma: "What to do? Should one be resigned to doing folklore in an easy-chair and mulling over theory in the shadow of inaccessible libraries? Or should one reluctantly and grudgingly agree to the terms under which desperately needed ethnological work can at least partially be accomplished? The ATP's director [Rivière], several of whose assistants are war prisoners, is taking the risks that accompany the latter option" (1993: 95). Rivière revealed his view on his own war-period choices in an October 1944 letter to Rivet, then director of the Musée de l'Homme. He wrote: "I followed, I think, your main advice: to do science."[12] Science also motivated Lucien Febvre's notorious decision to continue publishing the journal *Annales* during the war years. In summarizing the controversy surrounding this choice, Schöttler remarked: "Should/could the *Annales* continue in 1940/41—or was the price too high to pay?" (1995: 95).

Rather than condemn Maget and Rivière of political or professional opportunism, we must take seriously their insistence that a "passion for science" motivated their Hobbesian choices. But what did this mean in the context of the dying Third Republic? Further, how were the social sciences then conceived, and how might this help us understand why so many members of the ATP continued their scientific endeavors under Vichy?

In 1935, in the wake of the organization and publication of the *Encyclopédie française*,[13] Febvre, Varagnac, and Maget established the Commission des Recherches Collectives (CRC) to undertake large-scale scientific projects on the history of everyday life (Weber and Müller 1999). Following a method similar to that used by Van Gennep in his *Manuel de folklore français contemporain*, the CRC analyzed, indexed, and categorized open-ended surveys sent to a thousand unpaid volunteers, mostly primary and secondary schoolteachers, who responded through letters.[14] This correspondence approach had roots in an older French intellectual tradition, namely that of learned-society journals. Propelled by close relations between state-trained schoolteachers and republican social scientists, these journals reappeared during the Third Republic. Varagnac, for example, created the *Revue du folkore français et du folklore colonial* in 1928,[15] just before joining the CRC. But unlike this older form of publication, the CRC institutionalized the division of labor between "informants" and "analysts" favored by Van Gennep. While the learned-society journals published a selection of unedited correspondent monographs, the CRC viewed correspondent responses as "raw data" for future scientific study. Rather than present completed analyses, the CRC intended to archive the material it gathered, thereby making it available for later systematic research and analysis.

The CRC's focus on folkloric practices, its new division of scientific labor, and its close relationship to French republican nationalism, made it the ideological and material foundation for the later ATP. An impassioned 1938 radio address delivered by Febvre on the newly formed ATP illustrates the still firmly republican vision of "scientific folklore" that underwrote both institutions. Febvre pleaded:

The past is slipping away. The past is leaving us at break-neck speed. We must all start to work even to save the memories! You who are listening to me, you who are out there in the dark, I pray that this appeal, this appeal that you will hear repeated eleven times and that you will hear every Tuesday, will rattle you, will awaken in you your filial devotion to those ancestors who live in and through us, without our even knowing it! Help us! Help, and I will close with these words, those who are forming the ATP Museum, *those whose folkloric studies are saving both our country's and humanity's crowning glories.* (quoted in Velay Vallantin 1999: 506; emphasis added)

As Febvre's desperate words suggest, the ATP's founders shared with their CRC counterparts a fervor for a "science" formed and fueled by fears of a disappearing past and by a naive belief in the possibility of exhaustive collection, of objectively capturing and preserving the past through decontextualized artifacts. For Febvre, this science had clear links to a set of social interests, in particular a commitment to regional cultural integrity, the republican French nation-state, and universalistic humanism. This surprising series of concatenations suggests that in 1938 the postwar boundaries between "applied" and "pure" science, between "regionalism" and "republicanism," and between "nationalism" and "universal humanism" were not yet firmly constructed. In fact, the roots of these contemporary dichotomies were just beginning to be laid at the end of the Third Republic.[16]

During the interwar period, a form of "consensual regionalism" linked local intellectuals (provincial academics, schoolteachers, doctors, and priests) to local elites (entrepreneurs, politicians) interested in using regional distinctiveness to promote tourism and economic growth. This form of nationalist regionalism permeated everything from school programs (Chanet 1996; Oulmont 1999) to economic policies and marketing strategies for local products. However, this harmony of academic and commercial interests began to disintegrate in the 1930s. Concerns about scientific accuracy and authenticity alienated academics and local intellectuals from increasingly spectacular displays of local culture and folklore (Laferté 2002, 2001). Although some French historians have argued otherwise (c.f. Velay Vallantin 1999: 491), these concerns suggest that the preoccupation with a certain form of sociologically oriented "pure science" was not a postwar invention born of Vichy-inspired guilt. In fact, the growing tension between a commercialized, regional folklore and a "pure" descriptive science accounts for the way that the ATP organized its 1937 International Folklore Congress (Congrès International de Folklore). In order to distinguish the emerging "science" of folklore from the popular folkloric movements authorized by the prior regionalist consensus, "descriptive folklore" and "applied folklore" sections were created. The ATP organizers imagined the "descriptive" section as a forum for the exposition of "pure" science. In contrast, the "applied" section handled the contemporary question of "leisure politics" raised by movements that, though ideologically opposed, all took part in "reviving" folklore and reinventing tradition.[17]

The descriptive folklore section of the congress was animated primarily by staunchly republican academics with historical or sociological training, among them seasoned veterans like Lucien Febvre, March Bloch, and René Maunier (a colonial specialist) as well as younger social scientists like Georges Dumézil and André Varagnac.[18] The section's heated debates about the historicity of folklore highlight the disciplinary tensions and alliances that cross-cut the developing "science of folklore." In the early 1930s, Bloch and Febvre began railing against a-historical approaches to folklore studies. Bloch wrote of the urgent need to "reject at all cost" any illusions about the "unitary, egalitarian nature of the 'people,' especially of country people" (quoted in Weber and Barthelemy 1989: 131). Both men denounced the "insufferable myth of the unchanging peasant" and the essentialist arguments proffered by colleagues less interested in actual workings of society (131). Their conception of a "history of the present"—history as a science not of the past but of people in society through time—separated them epistemologically and politically from a rural geography focused on "physical" rather than social factors and from an antiquarian folklore dedicated to the study of origins. Neither Bloch nor Febvre hid their criticism of scholars who downplayed social and cultural factors. They took to task Albert Demangeon, a geographer, for constructing highly stylized "regional types" by overemphasizing physical geography and ignoring history, particularly that of social class. They did not even spare folklorists like Van Gennep, whom they accused of constructing sociological artifacts like "people" and "nation," of not properly using the "historical method," and of overlooking the state's role in constructing "folk cultures."

These very tensions over the nature and definition of "scientific folklore" shaped the war-period choices of French social scientists. Febvre may have articulated the views of many republican ATP scientists when he wrote:

> Until the present day, folklore studies in France have been the work of isolated individuals. This work is just starting to be organized on a solid, *scientific* basis. Folklore is forced to accept help from people who come from a wide-range of different academic and social backgrounds, people who do not and cannot easily forget their diverse disciplinary formations when they begin their new studies. [But] little by little, everything will clear up. And the young

people who are starting to be educated within the somewhat improvised disciplinary structure we, men of good will, are constructing for them, will know, *perhaps in spite of us,* how to make necessary distinctions. (quoted in Velay Vallantin 1999: 500; emphasis added)

This allusion to an emergent "disciplinary structure" not only signals the ATP's diverse intellectual roots but also helps to explain why republican ATP scientists continued to work under Vichy. If those beginning to be trained as "folklorists" continued the work of maintaining the ATP, gathering material, and pursuing prewar research tasks, developing disciplinary standards would not be lost or undermined. Alternatively, if these "scientists" withdrew from central research institutions, their retreat would potentially politically empower unscrupulous "amateurs." These amateurs would then be free to take over official institutions and manufacture a "science" that suited the contemporary political moment.

This version of French folklore's prewar history breaks with classic French accounts in several ways. In contrast to historians like Velay Vallantin (1999) and Fabre (1998), I would argue that the ATP's "science of folklore" was always already historically oriented and therefore in opposition to the often biological presentism of other contemporary disciplines.[19] If the ATP owed its material existence to Rivet's political connections with the Front Populaire, its intellectual life had been inspired by the heavily historical CRC and the *Encyclopédie française*. In addition, while contemporary historiographers tend to dismiss war-period French ethnologists' preoccupation with "pure science" as post-Vichy political remorse, a growing gap between "pure" and "applied" work existed prior to the occupation. This intellectual distinction motivated the work undertaken by the CRC in 1935, the 1937 congress' division of labor, and widespread republican commitment to scientific institutions during the occupation.

Regional Republicanism and Avant-Garde Folklore

But two postwar stereotypes still remain to be deconstructed. As we shall see, the ATP's focus on the documentation and preservation of regional cultures and traditions did not, as later scholars would have it, imply antirepublican tendencies. Similarly, no inherent opposition existed between the ATP's scientific folklore and modernist sensibilities.

If Febvre refused a distinction between homeland and humanity, many of his contemporaries did not separate love of their region (*petite patrie*) from love of the nation-state. As Anne-Marie Thiesse's work (1991 and 1997a) on regionalist literature demonstrates, an identification with a particular French locality was a means of attaching oneself to the French nation. According to Thiesse, in 1937 regionalism was still an "omnipresent theme of the Third Republic, an expression of consensual reformism" (1997b: 121)—a conclusion also reached by Jean François Chanet (1996) and Philippe Oulmont (1999) in their work on schooling. Thus Rivière's decision to use a series of regional home interiors to represent France at the 1939 New York World's Exposition was hardly anti-republican. The glorification of what he called, in a *La Renaissance* article, "but a few of France's countless aspects" (1939: 37) grew directly out of a republican academic, representational, and commercial tradition.

During the 1930s, a similarly "paradoxical" consensus over the modernity of folklore emerged among certain ethnologists, artists, politicians, and entrepreneurs. Rivière's 1939 article again encapsulates this ideological position. Describing the French folklore on display at the exposition, which tellingly had been classified as cultural patrimony on par with French literature, fine arts, and decorative arts, Rivière began: "Barbentane, the name jingles like a tambourine from Provence; Barbentane, a laborious and joyous commune in the Bouches-du-Rhône department; Barbentane, famous for its agricultural futures market [*primeurs*] and its farandoles, represents rural France at the 1939 New York World's Fair" (33). Later in the article, he returns to his description of Barbentane, noting: "Thus Barbentane, which could have become a suburb, remained a village. The virtue of traditions produced this miracle—traditions that some represent, incorrectly in our estimation, as survivals, as debris, as the residue of a vanished past!" (35).

In addition to the elegy to Barbentane as represented in New York by the Musée du Terroir de Barbentane-en-Provence, Rivière went on to make comments about the New York reconstructions of four regional home interiors. Provence was represented by the collections and work of the Musée Arlaten and Fernand Benoît; Alsace by the Musée Alsacien de Strasbourg and Adolphe Riff; Brittany by the Musée des arts Décoratifs de Nantes and J.-S. Gauthier; and the Alps by M. J. Le Meme. Rivière noted that the Alps installation included a room from a Savoyard-style youth hostel and that its designer, M. J. Le Meme, was a "*young* and *brilliant* architect from Megève" (37; emphasis added). Farandole dances and *primeurs*, traditional home interiors and a youth hostel built by a young architect—these elements comprise a surprising list that suggests the compatibility between and among local popular traditions and the modernism of contemporary economic, architectural, and leisure practices. Rivière goes on to conclude the article by stating:

These are the displays entrusted by Governor General Olivier[20] to the Museum of Folk Arts and Traditions and to the *young* team *I have the pleasure* of directing with my assistant, M. A. Varagnac. I appreciate being given the opportunity to thank the pavilion's architects, Expert et Vermeil, our colleagues working at museums in the provinces, as well as all those who helped us in this *labor of love* [*passionnante entreprise*]: Guy Pison, who created the layout for the [Barbentane] museum and the Exposition interiors; Marcel Maget whose fieldwork enabled me to write this article; and, last but not least, the decorators Agnès Humbert and E. Margulies . . . . I can only hope that, in presenting *but a few of France's countless aspects*, we have helped Americans come to know and love her. (35; emphasis added)

Rivière's statements go beyond the required courtesy by insisting repeatedly on the passionate nature of the work and the youth of its executors. At the time, the oldest members in the ATP team were Varagnac and Humbert, both forty-five; Rivière himself was forty-two, and Pison and Maget barely thirty. Despite the team's relative youth, the ATP had already received its highest artistic and scientific accolades—not coincidentally during the same time period, 1937–1938. During that year, the ATP was praised for the artistry of its village museum at the 1937 Paris World's Fair and for the scientific achievement represented by the Congrès International de Folklore.

Only later did Vichy reappropriate and resignify folklore for propaganda purposes.[21] During the war, regionalist federations consolidated relations already established between folklorists and members of the local intelligentsia, many of whom had close ties with the cultural and economic elite. This elite often openly sided with Vichy or, at the very least, advocated a "folkloric revival." This meant that the survey network established by the CRC in the 1930s and reactivated during the war by Varagnac on behalf of the ATP shifted its purpose and significance drastically. According to the ATP's January 1944 activity report, the network's regional delegations formed a "powerful organization" enabling the museum to spread its methods and "develop its contacts with the *volk* [*pays folklorique*]."[22] This very phrasing (*pays folklorique*) suggests that the ATP's local informants were no longer simply associates in a scientific undertaking but also partners in political project dedicated to the glorification of Marshal Pétain. In contrast to the Third

Republic regional practice of using folklore to boost localities or local products, Vichy organized large-scale folkloric ceremonies designed to pay homage to Pétain. As this cult of Pétain developed, the firm distinction between applied and descriptive folklore reified in 1937 began to erode. Folklore thus became a tool for rallying crowds and political support.[23]

These wartime uses of applied folklore doomed its relationship with artistic folklore, which previously had been considered an expression of national republican genius.[24] But in 1937, this was not yet the case. The split between "pure" and "applied" folklore enshrined through the 1937 congress did not yet imply republican distrust of or distaste for applied work. In fact, the congress' exhibits suggested that with proper social, political, and scientific credentials, applied folklore could rise to the status of popular or national art. This possibility was most clearly illustrated in the musical world—in particular by composers like Bartok, Manuel de Falla, or Ravel—but it was equally true for the decorative arts, architecture, dance, and theater.[25]

As was the case with regionalism and republicanism, the war hastened a split between the avant-garde and scientific folklore. After 1939, international hostilities made hosting prestigious, international *expositions universelles* impossible, eliminating the preferred venue for both "descriptive folklorists" and artists. In addition, once Vichy propaganda linked folklore to reactionary politics and collaboration, effacing its republican past as a mediator between "local" and "national" sociopolitics, artistic folklore lost both its legitimacy and part of its attractiveness. By 1943, while scientists like Pison and Rivière continued to insist on the links between modernist art (notably architecture) and science (human geography, economic and social history, ethnographic folklore), they also had to acknowledge that pre-Vichy visions of scientific folklore were no longer tenable. In that year, the pair wrote an article for a professional architectural magazine (*Techniques et Architecture*) that was published in a volume dedicated to local architectural techniques.[26] In the article's conclusion, Pison wrote:

> Now you know why we, as *architects enlightened by the wisdom and experience of ethnographers*, must free ourselves from an *obselete regionalism*. We must turn our studies toward a bold functionalism. Following the lessons of our research, this functionalism must be humanistic, building-up rather than tearing-down the individual and the social being. Through working on our survey, our researchers have become rural architects convinced that a revolution in rural living conditions is overdue. In this enormous undertaking, they hope to collaborate with urbanists. (1943: 312; emphasis added)

Pison thus still maintained that a purely "scientific" folklore could be constructed. But he was also clearly anxious to separate a scientific interest in the past from a commitment to reviving naively conceived "traditions." While he continued the call for the former, he refused the suggestion that a past could or should live again. Rather, a "science" of the past would pave the way to an absolutely new future:

> Recognizing the humanity, beauty and unity exhibited by the ancient rural buildings that dot the French landscape, a number of theorists have turned to a set of quite debatable aesthetic principles to advocate the "return" to the local techniques used to erect these edifices. And, when these methods prove too expensive in relation to modern industrial equivalents or impossible to recreate due to a lack of qualified artisans, these theorists are perfectly satisfied to resurrect mere *forms*. They are satisfied with the recreation of the outward "picturesque" or "characteristic" appearance of a more or less distant past.
>
> The term "regionalism" seems *a priori* to conform to this tendency. Given its foundation in an erroneous interpretation of the word "tradition," we would argue that this version of "regionalism" is just as misguided as its opposite: the attempt to standardize and homogenize all new construction everywhere in deference to the theoretical unity of human needs and industrial capabilities. It is equally problematic to seek either to create or to avoid "regional" architecture. The "regional" character of a building has never been and never will be an end in and of itself; it is always the unintended consequence of a whole range of material and spiritual factors. (312; emphasis added)

As these passages powerfully illustrate, Vichy made the simple logic of the Barbentane Museum untenable. Traditional dances could no longer be paired unproblematically with modern market forces. The "regional" and the "traditional" were becoming inseparable from Vichy propaganda and from a reactionary and anti-republic politics. Thus the concatenation of folklore and avant-garde art was becoming an oxymoron. The citation above similarly illustrates the ATP scientists' growing discomfort with any form of "applied" social sciences. Pison's condemnation of "regional" and "nonregional" architecture implies that society cannot be changed by decree. He seems to be warning of the betrayal of the "scientific," fundamentally descriptive, aspect of the mission of those social scientists who seek to economically, culturally, or administratively apply their work. Ethnography's postwar configuration had already begun to emerge.

Liberation: The End of Scientific Folklore?

The late 1930s scientific and artistic fame of the ATP proved short-lived. After the ship carrying the ATP's contribution to the 1939 New York Exposition ominously sank, the new war-period intellectual context ruined the ATP's prospects while simultaneously seeming to favor them. While folkore had been politically mobilized throughout the 1930s, it was only in the context of Vichy that its propagandistic uses became evident and ultimately fatal. In addition, the war hastened the already nascent division between colonial ethnography and folklore. On 1 May 1937, one year after the massive May Day workers' strikes, the new Musée de l'Homme's "national folklore" department became independent.[27] This distinction between national and colonial ethnography was accentuated by the war itself as French colonies escaped Vichy rule and rejoined the Free French forces. In a metropolitan context, the ATP justified the distinction between the two "disciplines" by reference to a German-inspired theoretical distinction between general and national ethnology.[28] Eventually, even the term "folklore" fell out of scientific use. In 1944, the Durkheimian-oriented Maget became the first to give it up, replacing *ethnographie folklorique* with *ethnographie métropolitaine*.[29] His fellow ATP scientist, the die-hard folklorist Varagnac, continued using the term, but in 1947 he coined the term *archéocivilization*, which referred to his decontextualized collection methods. He then defended his dissertation, created an organization called the Institut International d'Archéocivilisation, and in 1948 organized the first international conference on archéocivilization's.[30] Needless to say, Varagnac's attempts to create and occupy a new discursive field failed.

Fabre thus rightly attributes the definitive rupture between "applied" and "descriptive" folklore[31] to postwar discomfort with the Vichy past, as well as the ultimate restriction of the term "folklore" to a special kind of second order artistic activity, born from "applied" folklore and culturally illegitimate. In 1950, an erudite Burgundian expressed the confusion this created within the French social sciences: "The lone provincial scientist feels lost among the adventurers and guides currently arguing over 'folklore' . . . He does not know whether he is the disciple of Van Gennep, of the so-called 'ethnographers' [an allusion to Maget], of A. Varagnac, of H. Donteville [a specialist in 'French mythology'] . . . The main paths are lost for him in confusion. He prefers to stay at home and satisfy himself with the little local 'learned society,' which does everything and in its own way" (Drouot 1950: 221).[32]

In the end, local scholars did just that—they retained the term "folklore" and cut themselves off from deeply divided, national scientific circles.

The memory of these prewar intellectual struggles and alliances lapsed quickly. This loss of memory may have been the price paid for saving the ATP, the ethnographic method elaborated by Maget and a number of personal careers. After liberation, *ethnographie métropolitaine* and museography became the orphaned, squabbling survivors of the artistic and scientific collaboration once called "folklore." The fate of volume 14 of the *Encyclopédie française* encapsulates some of the sea changes experienced by French ethnology during and after the war. The volume, originally scheduled to be published in 1937 but delayed until 1954, was titled *Well-being and Culture* [*Le bien-être et la culture*] and was to include a preface written by Lucien Febvre in 1940. In 1954, after reviewing his original preface, Febvre decided that it needed to be entirely rewritten. He noted: "It turn[ed] out that nothing from my 1940 text [could] be retained nowadays. No single line [could] be borrowed and inserted as such in this volume 14 . . . The whole climate for the book has suddenly changed, its whole spiritual and moral atmosphere. A cataclysm, a tidal wave, has swept away much more than the broken pieces of a material world that has fallen apart. A certain way of thinking and feeling life. A certain way of judging everyday civilization. I'd even say a certain style" (1954: 2–3). Maget echoed this sentiment in a 1983 interview: "The war was a dreadful rift, a break, a disaster . . . The *Annales* school, Bouglé, Febvre, Berr . . . everything collapsed. Not everything in sociology and social anthropology had to be reconstructed after the war, but French social scientists felt the need to start over from scratch."[33] Maget here suggests that, despite the ATP's postwar institutional survival, the intellectual accomplishments that lay behind it were destroyed. As a result, neither disciplinary continuity nor institutional "memory" was possible.

Conclusion: Writing Histories of the Social Sciences

The disintegration of the scientific and artistic alliances on which the ATP built "scientific folklore" significantly impacted postwar French social science. Despite the efforts of scholars like Georges Balandier, Roger Bastide, and Marcel Maget, the Durkheimian tradition that had flowered during the interwar period fragmented in the wake of Vichy. Postwar ethnology became resolutely antihistorical. In addition, it became internally divided between a social anthropology focused on the "exotic," "primitive," or "savage" and a sociology dedicated to European modernity. As a result of this fragmentation, the conditions of possibility for a folklore grounded simultaneously in history and sociology no longer existed. Folklore as an intellectual space became an uninhabited no-man's land that presupposed and entailed a double amnesia: the social sciences' wartime compromises and its prewar intellectual "advances" were forgotten. Even after the 1980s, when Vichy finally became an acceptable topic of French historiographical investigation, French ethnologists continued to analyze war-period French social sciences through the lens of German anti-Nazi critiques of "folklore" (Bausinger 1993 [1971]). This very optic obscured the intellectual differences between France and Germany that had made historically grounded, interdisciplinary French "folklore" possible in the first place. Thus, in some ways, the cure exacerbated the original malady. As part of this forgotten history, the exemplary work of ethnologists like Marcel Maget remains marginal even today.[34]

The silence surrounding the prewar and occupation period social sciences hides important successes and failures. This historical amnesia tacitly affirms a blanket condemnation of war-period ethnography as politically reactionary if not downright racist. And all too often this condemnation justifies a deep mistrust of any kind of "scientific ideal." The social sciences' empiricist rhetoric is admittedly dangerous in both its totalitarian (propaganda) and democratic (marketing) incarnations. But must we give up the ideals of an objective science *and* deny that the social sciences are of any use? Or, on the contrary, can we acknowledge a real "passion for science" while interrogating both the social conditions for the production of "scientific knowledge" and the social uses to which that knowledge is put?

It is in the context of that contemporary debate that attention to the history of the sciences becomes crucial. There are three very different interests embedded in the production of the history of the sciences. For scientists, the "advancement" of knowledge depends on a presentist reading of scientific "progress." Scientists sort their disciplinary past—studies, results and lines of inquiry—into two categories: those that have or may prove fruitful or successful and those that have failed or remain incomprehensible. Now and then, an "outsider" pursuing an abandoned trail comes up with a brilliant innovation that completely reorders perceptions of the scientific past and its potential future. As a result, a discipline's past is not only a subject of idle interest for its practitioners but also a set of potential resources for future inquiry and discovery. Historians of science look at the past of a discipline in a quite different way: they want to explain scientific knowledge by observing the social conditions underlying its production—a form of inquiry that may lead to attempts to socially engineer "optimal" institutional conditions for scientific inquiry. For social scientists, the past has yet a third significance. Here the past serves as a field for examining the political conditions of possibility for social scientific research and the social uses to which the results of that research are put. When social scientists turn toward the history of disciplines, they strive to understand how the international or national political contexts that frame social questions impact what counts as social science. In particular, they seek to elucidate the sociopolitical conditions of possibility undergirding certain objects of study, methods of inquiry, and publication-worthy results. The distance that comes from observing past knowledge makes the contemporary situation easier to analyze, thereby sharpening our critical awareness of the current assumptions and work conditions in anthropology, sociology, and history. Theoretically, this kind of historical work helps the social sciences avoid being instrumentalized, either by ruling powers or by "natives." It also facilitates the creation of institutional arrangements best suited for ensuring scholarly independence, and therefore the very conditions of existence for the social sciences.

Thus the history of the social sciences occupies, or should occupy, a special place. It is the perfect tool for revealing the embedded social and political positions of the supposedly autonomous "scholar." Done properly, it presupposes and entails a level of internal reflexivity and critique that can only benefit anthropology and its related disciplines.

Notes

This essay grew out of an extended literature review (Weber 2000). In this English version of the text, following the helpful and greatly appreciated suggestions of Benoît de L'Estoile, I integrated the principal ideas of three additional essays that were based on original archival research (Weber 2003b; Weber 2003c; Weber and Müller 2003). I would like to thank Kimberly Arkin, who not only translated the essay but also adapted it for an American audience—a process that raised useful questions about its content.

1 The term *zone grise* (gray zone) was first proposed by Primo Levi in *Les naufragés et les rescapés* (1989: 20), where he uses it to explain the complex reality of the relations between Nazi guards and victims in concentration camps. I intend to use the phrase to illuminate the somewhat less horrific context of Vichy France. Certain French bureaucrats, moved by the need to "save" something (institutions, science, Jewish individuals, resistance fighters, or just ordinary men), entered a gray zone between those who can be called "righteous" and those who have been identified as Nazi allies. As Levi notes: "In the face of such cases, we must forcefully insist on the imprudence of hastily issued moral judgements. We must instead clearly state a basic principle: in a totalitarian state, the greatest wrong rests with the system itself. As a result, it is always difficult to evaluate the role of individual collaboraters, whether major or minor players . . . Any right to moral judgement must be accorded only to those who have themselves experienced what it is like to act under conditions of structural constraint" (1989: 43).

2 One example strikingly sums up these shifts: in 1937 the Premier Congrès International de Folklore brought together ethnologists, historians, geographers, and sociologists, but by 1945 the ideological and institutional boundaries established between these discplines rendered the repetition of such a conference impossible.

3 The ATP and the Musée de l'Homme were created on 1 May 1937 by the then-sitting French socialist government (Front Populaire). The decree established an institutional segregation of the ethnographic collections contained in the defunct Trocadero Ethnographic Museum (Musée d'Ethnographie du Trocadero, hereafter MET). The MET's French collections were given to the ATP and those of colonial or foreign origin went to the Musée de l'Homme. From its creation, the ATP was administratively affiliated with the Department of National Museums (Musées Nationaux) and therefore with the Ministry of Culture. In contrast, the Musée de l'Homme, like the MET, was affiliated with the Museum d'Histoire Naturelle and therefore with the Ministry of National Education. This institutional separation reified a growing intellectual division between colonial ethnography based on a natural history of Man and national ethnography based on patriotism and a commitment to social history. Prior to this institutional division, the emergent science of "ethnography" included work on "primitive" and "popular European" cultures. Following the division, primitive customs became conflated with "nature" while popular European practices signified "culture," and perhaps even "national culture." While the German context favored an early, clear separation of *Völkerkunde* (primitive culture) and *Volkskunde* (folklore), this institutional separation ran counter to prevailing French ideology, including that of a French colonialism founded on intellectual principles of universalism.

After its creation, the ATP immediately integrated the personnel and collections of the Commission des Recherches Collectives (CRC), thereby giving it a double set of roots reflected by the individual histories of its first directors. Georges-Henri Rivière, the ATP's curator, hailed from MET while André Varagnac, his assistant, previously worked at the CRC. Although the ATP was slated to have a physical location—a true museum in the English sense of the word—as early as 1954, the first public hall did not open until 1972, almost forty years after the ATP's initial decree. Just over twenty years later, in 1999, the government decided to dismantle the museum's hard won physical infrastructure in the Bois du Boulogne, scheduling the ATP for transfer to Marseille.

4 Shanny Peer cites Lebovics (1992: 179–86) while discussing this episode: "After the war, Rivière was denounced as a collaborator by André Varagnac, though he was eventually cleared of charges" (1998: 171).

5 For example, in 1937 Maget headed the "Service de Folklore Paysan" for the Assemblée Permanente des Présidents de Chambres d'Agriculture—a service that was located within the ATP itself (Maget 1993: 97).

6 Rivière's account was published as "Le chantier 1425: un tour d'horizon, une gerbe de souvenirs"; Maget's article appeared as "A propos du Musée des ATP de sa création à la Libération (1935–1944)."

7 For one example, see Joseph Joffo's autobiographical account (2001: 231–49).

8 As evidence, Maget cited four individuals, including one by name. He explicitly mentioned Jean Amblard, a draughtsman for Chantier 1810 who was also a Communist and Resistance fighter in Auvergne. He also made reference to "three of our departed": a history professor (Albert Soboul) who lost his job in 1942 and took part in the camp in 1943; a Secret Army captain (Pierre-Louis Duchartre) who conducted surveys in Sologne and was an "ardent defender of folk arts and crafts," and an unidentifiable man who had moved to "Toulouse along with his wife because of the latter's affiliation with the persecuted religion" (1993: 105). In addition, Maget noted that "despite the diversity of 'persuasions,' the ATP environment never became a site for mutual incrimination" (105).

9 During the war, two museum employees, Boris Vildé and Anatole Lewitzky, were executed as Resistance fighters by the Nazis, and the museum's director, Paul Rivet, was forced to flee to South America.

10 Noiriel's (1999) work combines insights taken from the history of geography, sociology, and history. The sociological works of Chamboredon (1982) and Fabiani (1988) in particular have influenced Noiriel's work. Historians of ethnology have apparently failed to take notice of these studies.

Following the insight of Benoît de l'Estoile, I would take slight exception with Noiriel's otherwise well-taken point. Although often forgotten, the Colonial School (École Coloniale) and the Musée de l'Homme are both examples of successful interwar period relationship, between legitimate science and government.

11 This all too frequent occurrence can be illustrated by the case of Marcel Mauss, a Jew fired from his teaching positions at the Collège de France, the Institut d'Ethnologie, and the École Pratiques des Hautes Études. Although he survived the war, his horrific experiences left him mentally deranged. He died in 1950.

12 Rivet's 18 October 1944 letter was published in 1986 in *Gradhiva* (p. 27).

13 The *Encyclopédie française* was created in 1933 by Anatole de Monzie,

minister of national education. From 1933 to 1966, Lucien Febvre headed the project, which was similar in scope to the *Encyclopedia Britannica*. The undertaking was presented as a "national project" in the 1930s, and several of its volumes were enormously successful prior to the war. These successful volumes included volume 6 (*L'espèce humaine*, 1936), which was produced by a team of anthropologists with Paul Rivet as editor; and volume 8 (*La vie mentale*, 1938), which was produced by a group of psychologists with Henri Wallon as editor. Publication resumed after the war.

14 This method reaped a wealth of information in a variety of forms—everything from terse single-page answers to hundred-page manuscripts.

15 Varagnac's *Revue du folklore français et du folklore colonial* enjoyed the support of none other than England's Sir James Frazer.

16 Interpreting, as Velay Vallantin (1999) does, the debates of the 1937 International Folklore Congress in terms of an opposition between "Jacobinism" and anti-republican regionalism is anachronistic. As Velay Vallantin writes: "The Congress rang with calls for more regional museums, local museums; this led to tension with the Popular Front's secular, republican Jacobinism" (1999: 493).

17 These movements included Soviet cultural centers, Nazi Kraft durch Freude, French youth hostels, and various regionalist movements (Velay Vallantin 1999: 492).

18 While Varagnac has gained a reputation for having been always sympathetic to Vichy, his personal and intellectual history suggests otherwise. In the late 1930s, Varagnac was still a committed Durkheimian and his uncle (Marcel Sembat) had been a socialist minister.

19 Velay Vallantin, for example, has argued that Rivet assigned the 1937 congress' "descriptive folklore" section to historians in order to "legitimate the links established between historians and ethnologists" (1999: 491).

20 Olivier, along with Marshall Lyautey, headed the 1931 Colonial Exposition (L'Estoile 2003).

21 As early as 1925, these republican "spectacles" had begun to reap the scorn of local intellectuals, historians, and folklorists.

22 ATP Archives, Rapports d'activité, 1944–45.

23 It is possible that Vichy did not go as far in its instrumentalization of folklore as the Third Republic had done in its use of colonial ethnography. But in some sense this remains a question to be answered—and one that requires close readings of local Learned Society archives, the archives of the Corporation Paysanne, and the fieldwork journals kept by ATP staff during the war.

24 French republican scientists made this connection outside the Hexagon as well. *Art nègre* was considered the symbol of "primitive genius" and the various folkloric practices of other European countries were seen as expressions of "national" genius.

25 This part of this essay comes from a seminar lecture on the history of cultural policies. It has been published under the title "*L'ethnologie de l'état en France, des années trente aux années cinquante*" (Weber 2003a).

26 Rivière wrote the introduction of the article and claimed to share responsibility for the content.

27 From the moment it opened in 1878, the Musée d'Ethnographie du Trocadero (MET) had a room dedicated to local French culture and tradition—a clear indication that the disciplinary boundaries between "exotic" or colonial ethnography and "national" folklore had not yet been established. When the MET became affiliated with the Museum of Natural History under Paul Rivet's leadership (in 1928), this "French room" became a department. Just after the creation of the new Musée de l'Homme in 1936, the department became fully independent.

28 ATP Archives, Rapports d'activité, 1944–45. In this, the ATP founders followed the German model of the distinction between *Volkskunde* and *Völkerkunde*.

29 Maget made the shift during his inaugural lecture as chair of the History of Folk Arts and Traditions at the Louvre. Maget held this chair, created in 1938 for Varagnac, from 1944 to 1961, when Suzanne Tardieu took his place.

30 The ATP always manifested its diverse intellectual roots through Maget and Varagnac's diametrically opposed methods. Following Varagnac's archaeological methods, the museum ravenously collected objects with little regard for their social or historical context. But at the same time, the museum conducted ethnographic surveys and wrote deeply contextualized ethnographic monographs, a style of research pioneered by Marcel Maget and Louis Dumont to counter approaches like Varagnac's. Historians and ethnologists quickly forgot Varagnac's influence on the museum's methods. Partially as a result, the objects the museum collected in the 1940s were not exhibited until 1972.

31 "Descriptive folklore" became *ethnographie métropolitaine* while "applied folklore" got stuck with the belittling term "folkloric."

32 I would like to thank Gilles Laferté for alerting me to this quite telling passage.

33 Interview by the editor on 8 June 1983.

34 Despite the commotion and turmoil of the war period and the immediate postwar period, contemporary French social science produced a few enduring gems. In 1939, during an ATP survey in Sologne, Maget and Dumont "discovered" the Malinowskian method that they would use with success after the war. Dumont, an anthropologist best known for his work on India and his comparative analysis of Western modernity, first tested the "new" method through an analysis of a contemporary ceremony in Tarascon in southern France (Dumont 1951). Using the same method, Maget wrote a long study about the village of Villard d'Arêne in the French Alps. His slightly later *Guide d'étude directe des comportements culturels* (1953) helped diffuse the ethnographic method beyond his circle of colleagues. In addition, the Vichy period sharpened his critical senses, allowing him finally to exorcize the demons of "folkloristic populism" (cf. Maget 1968).

Federico Neiburg and Marcio Goldman

FROM NATION TO EMPIRE

War and National Character Studies

in the United States

> The devil doesn't have to exist for there to be one—
> when people know he doesn't exist, that's when he takes over.
> —Guimarães Rosa

The attack launched in December 1941 by the Japanese armed forces on the military base at Pearl Harbor is renowned for having led to the intervention by the United States in World War II. It is less well-known that this war between nation-states provided the background for the first chapter in the history of anthropology in which nations were explicitly taken as objects of analysis, for, at the same time as the United States entered the war, the "culture and personality" school began its studies of "national character."

The aim of this essay is to analyze certain dimensions of this chapter in the history of anthropology, which unfolded in the United States in the frame of the school of culture and personality in the period approximately between the beginning of World War II and the start of the cold war. Contrary to the current representation of studies of national character—which are limited to accusations of its theoretical "poverty" or its "ideological" meaning—we think that the examination of the conditions in which these studies were formulated, and of the content of their theoretical and methodological proposals, can serve as a contribution to some important debates in contemporary anthropology: the rise of nations and international relations as objects of anthropological study; the discussion of the possibilities and limitations on the anthropological knowledge of our own societies; and the debate about the place of the history of anthropological thought in the present-day framework of the discipline.

Such studies are a fertile site for the development of our contribution to these debates. The reasons for this are threefold: first, in analyzing national character, anthropologists were initiating an explicit discussion of "nations" as objects of study. Second, in so doing, it was necessary to reflect on the "methodological adjustments" required by an anthropological approach to these large-scale social forms. Finally, because it is our intention to show that we can see in such studies the formulation of theoretical problems whose origin we tend to attribute, at times too hastily, to features of supposedly new empirical objects—such as those implied in the processes of denationalization, localization, and transnationalization of social life.

An Anthropology Applied to International Relations

The U.S. intervention in World War II was the second time that the United States participated in an armed conflict where the major actors were European nation-states. The first, when war was declared on Germany and its allies in April 1917, was marked by varying reactions from American intellectuals, many of whom opposed entry into the conflict on neutralist grounds. Within anthropology, these disagreements reached their high point when, after the war, in 1919, a vote of censure removed Franz Boas from the presidency of the American Anthropological Association. The explicit reason for this act was Boas's public attack against the participation of anthropologists in federal intelligence and espionage agencies, but the association was also censuring him for his pacifist position against U.S. intervention in the war. As George Stocking has observed, the climate of heightened patriotism after 1918 could not tolerate the pacifist ideas of an author seen by some as a suspect German immigrant of Jewish extraction (Stocking 1976: 1–3).

By contrast, U.S. intervention in World War II was felt by anthropologists to demand an active engagement. This demand was largely promoted by a group of anthropologists formed, significantly enough, by various of Boas's former students, who by then held some of the most important positions in the university departments and funding bodies of the time. The group included Margaret Mead, who in 1939, along with Gregory Bateson and Geoffrey Gorer, took part in the first initiative to put anthropology at the service of the war effort by setting up the Committee for National Morale, with the object of producing a study of national culture that would lead to recommendations for keeping American morale high during the conflict.

After Pearl Harbor, members of the committee began to work directly with the Office of War Information, which was linked to the U.S. Navy. Also taking part in this initiative were Ruth Benedict, Clyde Kluckhohn, Ralph Linton, George P. Murdock, and Rhoda Métraux. Before Pearl Harbor the committee's attention had focused on the United States, but after the attack the project was expanded to seek to contribute to the better understanding of allied nations, especially enemy ones.[1] This work was not simply directed, however, toward the archives of the intelligence wings of the armed forces, nor was it restricted to furnishing directions for U.S. foreign policy. Indeed, the results of the research were also evaluated by academic criteria, presented at conferences, published as articles in specialized journals, and turned into books that sought to found a new object for anthropology: "national character."

The United States and the Americans, Japan and the Japanese, Germany and the Germans, Great Britain and the British—and, a little later, Russia and the Russians, and Poland and the Polish—all came to be treated as cultural worlds susceptible to analysis on the basis of the same categories used in the study of the so-called simple societies, those to which, until then, the majority of anthropologists had restricted their attention. The context of war and of conflict between nations demanded, however, the methodological "development" of "studies of culture at a distance." Anthropologists, prevented from carrying out the traditional task of prolonged participant observation in the field, would now interview immigrants, analyze novels or films made in other countries, or examine media productions in order to reach those cultural universes that were always qualified as national. The frontiers between countries were treated as cultural, and cultural frontiers were treated as national, thereby delimiting new objects of analysis.

The end of World War II provided what would be considered the best test of this anthropology. After the surrender of Japan, the U.S. government decided to keep the Japanese emperor in place—just as Geoffrey Gorer had recommended in a memorandum to the Office of War Information in 1942. Without access to U.S. government documents, it is clearly impossible for us to evaluate the real weight of that memorandum in the U.S. decision regarding the emperor—a decision that provided stability to postwar Japan and guaranteed that despite Hiroshima and Nagasaki a new equilibrium between the two countries could be found. However, the concurrence between U.S. foreign policy and the anthropological analysis of the place of the emperor in Japanese culture would serve, from then on, as a well-remembered example of the potential of the new kind of "applied anthropology" that studies of natural character allowed.

Obviously, the "application" of anthropology was not restricted to this type of study. Throughout the 1930s, attempts to socially legitimate American anthropology gained force, stressing its capacity to find solutions to problems defined as "practical." The main focus of attention had been the social and cultural diversity of the United States: "Indians," "Blacks," and "immigrants" of various national origins, small rural communities and big cities with highly diversified populations. Applied anthropology—and also other disciplines such as "applied" sociology and psychology—sought to respond to "practical problems" connected to the process of social and cultural homogenization characteristic of the composition of nation-states, and health, education, nutrition, and work were the principal areas in which this process took place. The center of attention was within the national frontiers, being primarily a problem of domestic policy,[2] while studies of national character had foreign policy as their field of application.[3] Despite this difference, all efforts for the social legitimation of anthropology as "applied anthropology" had a common element, which was that all the practical problems to which they sought to contribute solutions addressed social and cultural domains that were always defined as national.

In fact, this was not the first time that the boundary between social and sociological problems had been blurred in the discipline's history (the most obvious example being British anthropology and its contributions to the ideological legitimation of colonial conquest and the administration of the colonies). An important difference, however, marks this new episode in the history of anthropology, happening now in North America rather than Europe.[4] By identifying national frontiers as the boundaries of the objects of analysis, it became possible not simply to constitute other nations as objects of study, but, simultaneously, to turn the anthropologists' own society and national culture into a legitimate object of analysis.

In the U.S. context, research projects undertaken by some anthropologists from the 1920s and 1930s onward are generally held to be the precursors of an "urban anthropology" or an "anthropology of complex societies" turned back to our own societies. However, although the studies done by anthropologists such as Lloyd Warner had taken American society as a reference point, they engaged in no systematic reflection on the status of nations as objects of investigation. That is, this was an anthropology (or rather, a sociology)[5] turned inward from national frontiers, with the practical intention of contributing to the resolution of problems internal to the United States. National character studies, by contrast, originated in international relations (in their extreme form: war between nations) and their practical intentions focused not on a nation but on nations, in the plural.

The density and complexity of this episode in the history of anthropology contrasts with the scant attention paid to it in the literature as well as with current representations of it.[6] On the part of some of its major protagonists, such as Margaret Mead (1962 [1953]: 396), it is treated as little more than a particular "application" of the theory and methods of the culture and personality school. On the part of its critics, all detailed theoretical examination gets trapped in the convergence of a theoretical argument about the supposed conceptual poverty and poor results of the enterprise, and a charge of complicity with U.S. foreign policy (see, for example, Harris 1968; Kaplan and Manners 1972; Suzuki 1980).[7]

An analysis of the social conditions that made this chapter in the history of American anthropology possible is beyond the limits of this essay. That social and cultural history is, without doubt, still to be written, and it would have to consider the relations between the social and cultural milieu of the anthropologists and of the surrounding society and culture, specifically exploring the relations between the university and academic world on the one side, and those of politics and state agencies of social intervention on the other. In particular, it would have to consider the mediation between these spheres that was affected by the private and state agencies for the funding of scientific activity. Only in this form would it be possible to understand not only the singularity of the relations between the political field and the process of social legitimation of a discipline defined as "academic," but also the interlacing of problems considered "anthropological" and problems thought of as "practical"—interlacings on which anthropology was built in the postwar United States.[8]

In this essay we limit ourselves to the analysis of this moment in the history of American anthropology to show how its density and complexity can turn it—to use an expression of Marcel Mauss—into a "privileged case" for the examination of the process of formation of certain theoretical and ethico-political questions debated in contemporary anthropology, as well as many of the theoretical and methodological problems involved in any study that takes as its object national or international cultures, societies, identities, or stereotypes. This chapter in the history of anthropology saw the development and legitimation of questions that today we tend, significantly, to take as familiar.

Cultural Critique and Social Engineering:
The Paradoxes of a Constructed Polarity

The following text written by Margaret Mead in 1953 is notable for the way it brings together the most significant features of anthropological studies of national character.

> National Character studies are a recent development in anthropological research on problems of personality and culture. They take both their form and methods from the exigencies of the post-1939 world political situation. Although the national-character approach utilizes the premises and methods of the personality and culture field, historically it has had two distinguishing features: the group of persons with a shared social tradition whose culture is studied is selected because they are the citizens or subjects—the "nationals"—of a sovereign political state, and the society *may* be so inaccessible to direct field observation that less direct methods of research have to be used. These contemporary national-character studies of culture at a distance resemble attempt to reconstruct the cultural character of societies of the past . . . in which the study of documents and monuments has to be substituted for the direct study of individuals interacting in observable social situations. However, they differ from historical reconstruction in that, whether they are done at a distance or through field work in the given nation, they are based primarily on interviews with and observation of living human beings. (1962 [1953]: 396)

Here Mead situates the origins of the problem in the context of the history of anthropology, and she explicitly claims that it was the war situation that led to, or at least favored, the development of these studies. Further, she takes "nations" as the analytical units of these studies, and she proposes "the study of culture at a distance" as the method. The apparent objectivity and simplicity of these points hides, for all that, a complexity we would like to explore here.

As is well known, the history of anthropological thought can be read, in part at least, as a constant oscillation between the two principles that constituted the discipline at the end of the nineteenth century—the emphasis on cultural diversity versus the emphasis on the similarities between human societies. The issues raised by the notion of national character tended to appear more in the currents following the former principle than in those following the latter. While obviously not a necessary property of this field of issues, the notion of national character also functions as a way of referring to—and constructing—the unity of large and embracing social and cultural wholes. It is standard now to attribute the origins of this category to Romantic thought that, in supposed opposition to Enlightenment universalism, would tend to emphasize exactly the originality of each people or nation.[9]

This is, of course, a rather simplistic vision, insofar as terms such as Romanticism and the Enlightenment—along with the various schools through which we traditionally teach the history of anthropology—always designate ambiguous categories, present in differing proportions in all theoretical formulations. Thus, and this is a point of some importance in our argument, the theorists of national character commonly attribute an almost spontaneous origin to the notion: all societies, at all times, tend to perceive and set up differences between their modes of being and doing and those of their neighbors (cf., among others, Gorer 1948: 11; Stoetzel 1955 [1954]: 15). The naturalization and universalization of the notion of national character—which invokes, reinforces, and transforms the everyday meanings of the term—produces two effects: on the one hand, the mechanisms whereby social and cultural boundaries are made in nonnational societies become identical to those that serve to sanction the existence of national frontiers; on the other hand, the specificity of the processes of the creation of social and cultural boundaries within societies that see themselves as national is annulled.

There seems to be nothing odd, then, in the fact that in anthropology as an academic discipline it should have been exactly in the relativist context of American culturalism that the key ideas on national character should have been developed. However, this development was hardly inevitable, for it is hard to see how this notion could have found a place in the thought of Franz Boas. As is well known, the first studies of national character invoked a "Boasian" legacy as one of its sources of legitimacy. It is possible to discover, through a view of the debates that stirred American anthropology in the 1930s, that what later tended to be considered the "orthodox" Boasian line—formed by some of the exponents of the culture and personality school within which the studies of national character started—was simply one among many perspectives claiming the same inheritance. An analysis of the ambiguities and potentialities of Boas's thought, and the invention of an "authentically Boasian" tradition is the first step in clarifying the content of the dilemmas and paradoxes revealed by studies of national character.

The first point to note here is that Boas's work is marked by a constant shifting between the presupposition that each specific culture is a fragmented ensemble that can only be studied historically, and the postulate that despite this a whole exists at some level and it can be apprehended by anthropologists. If the principle of fragmentation makes the development of concepts such as national character difficult, it is important to remember that the Boasian perspective recognizes wholeness. Such a whole could be found in the relations between individual and culture, given that the former must synthesize in some way a cultural and historically fragmented experience—it was only in such individual experience that the anthropologist could discover some form of whole (cf. Boas 1966 [1932]: 268–69; Stocking 1968: chapters 7 and 9; 1976: 3–7; 1986: 5–9).[10]

Boas's shifts and ambiguities do not show up simply in his theoretical writings, but rather also appear in his ethical and political stands and in the way in which his students took on and developed his thought. As stated above, his distrust of direct political involvement by anthropologists, undoubtedly along with his German origins, made Boas take up a pacifist stance during World War I. He opposed U.S. intervention and criticized the position of the interventionists, who confused values that were historically specific to the United States with supposedly universal democratic values. Obviously, World War II made this position much harder to sustain, to the point where Boas began to think of abandoning his anthropological career to dedicate himself, as a layman, to fighting Nazism (Yans-McLaughlin 1986: 185–87). Further, the experiences and difficulties that Boas faced as a German Jewish immigrant in the United States of the early twentieth century aid the understanding of some of the social dispositions that led him to formulate, in the words of Stocking (1976: 3), "an experiential standpoint from which a systematic critique could be developed"—a critique that confronted on the theoretical plane social evolutionism, and on the ethico-political plane confronted certain aspects of American society. Beyond this, the meeting of an author from the German intellectual tradition and a national society that seemed to need immediate responses to its "integration problems" could not but produce serious effects on Boas's own work. This set of variables explains, in part, the apparent contradiction between, on the one hand, Boas's "puritanical methodological posture" (Stocking 1976: 4) and his ideal of scientific objectivity, and, on the other hand, his cultural and political influence, be it direct, in the critique of racism and ethnocentrism, or be it indirect, through the activities of his students.[11] It cannot be denied, however, that "Boas never confronted the contradiction between his universalism and his commitment to respect minority cultures" (Jackson 1986: 95).

This contradiction appears clearly, for example, in the distance that separates the practical aims of Boas's works in physical anthropology—which, as is well known, were explicitly intended to influence U.S. immigration laws—from the refusal, equally explicit, to put cultural anthropology at the service of practical programs.

Boas's students did not stop dealing with the same problems as their teacher, although from the first moment it was precisely the ambiguities of his thought that allowed for different forms of development. The personality and culture school set itself up, without doubt, to oppose the historicist interpretation of Boasian thought, represented by writers like Alfred Kroeber (in his early period) and Robert Lowie.[12] The central theses of Ruth Benedict's *Patterns of Culture* are well known: each culture, despite being formed by fragments of different origins, would develop a specific "style," capable of unifying it as a synthetic whole and, at the same time, distinguishing it from other cultural units. The notion of "cultural pattern"—beyond the vicissitudes of history that almost always escape the observer—confirms the existence of these great configurations and allows for the description and differentiation of human cultures through the use of categories borrowed from psychiatry and the philosophy of history: the "Apollonian" Pueblo, the "Dionysian" Plains Indians, the "paranoid" Kwakiutl. And while it might be true that the Boasian idea of the individual as the unique unifying locus of culture can only with difficulty be assimilated to a transcendent and totalizing pattern, Benedict's referencing of Dilthey, Spengler, and the notions of gestalt and zeitgeist (cf. Benedict 1934: 50–55), undoubtedly refer to the German origins of Boasian thought, to "the genius of a people." Moreover, it should be recalled that a large part of the theoretical work of the culture and personality school was published during Boas's lifetime—at the same time as his own work—and that he never claimed any incompatibility between those models and his own.[13]

The expression "culture and personality" crystallized around and was legitimated by the seminar conducted by Edward Sapir at Yale, from 1931 on. Sapir, however, remained far from the configurationist model that was to become dominant in the field of American anthropology. His critique of all forms of reification of culture, and his presupposition that, in the last instance, the only reality is individual personalities in interaction (cf. Sapir 1985a [1924]; 1985b [1934]), are much closer to Boas's position than to Benedict's cultural patterns model—which did not stop him feeling marginalized by Boas or prevent references to his work becoming increasingly scarce on the part of authors later recognized as belonging to the Boasian orthodoxy (cf. Darnell 1986; Handler 1986, 1989; Manson 1986). Further, from very early on, Sapir expressed profound doubts about the possibility of an easy application of anthropological knowledge to sociocultural problems, and, contrary to those of his colleagues who openly defended the use of anthropology in the formation of "social engineering," he remained loyal to the tradition of "cultural critique" that developed in the United States in the 1920s.[14]

For all that he was outside of the mainstream of American cultural anthropology, Sapir was not alone in this distanced and critical attitude. Melville Herskovits (1941), too, expressed his doubts on the practical applicability of anthropology, which cost him strong criticisms from Benedict (Jackson 1986: 114–15, 121–22). Abraham Kardiner (1939) also, although on a lesser scale, remained on the margins of this involvement of anthropology with wider sociocultural issues.[15]

To be more precise, and as Alfred Lindesmith and Anselm Strauss (1950: 587) show, the theoretical system of the culture and personality school was based on two key points: the description and psychological characterization of cultural configurations and the personality types associated with them; and the attempt to explain the relations between types of cultures and types of personalities on the basis of early childhood experiences. These two points may or may not appear at the same time, and their relative weight tends to vary from author to author. Mead, for example, described her own theoretical trajectory as a passage starting from an exclusive emphasis on the processes of standardization of personalities then moving to a greater attention to cultural patterns properly speaking (1978: 173–74), explaining that the catalysts for this change had been, first, reading the manuscript for *Patterns of Culture* and, later on, "the wartime problems of cross-cultural understanding and morale building" (178).

Benedict's model, claiming that cultural patterns correspond to arbitrarily selected and imposed human psychological potentials, perfectly synthesized the two constitutive aspects of the culture and personality school, emphasizing the constant oscillation between the affirmation of an absolute human plasticity and a certain belief in a precultural biological base. The function of this oscillation is more profound than it appears: we are dealing with a fundamental operator that allows for an explanation of deviations from the global norm, behaviors that do not seem to be adapted to the supposed local pattern, differences between distinct groups of the population, and, in the last instance, providing the foundations for social engineering. In other words, and for all that this had remained in the background for some time,[16] culturalism always tried to distinguish itself from racism, on one side, and behaviorism, on the other, claiming simultaneously the existence of innate individual differences, and the work of culture in the formation of character through education—a process that would follow certain natural and universal lines (cf. Mead 1965 [1942]: 328–30). This position simultaneously provided the legitimacy for efforts to know human nature and for attempts at intervention to mold and domesticate it.

It can be seen that, as with so many other dichotomies that have haunted anthropology and other social sciences from their beginnings, "social engineering" and "cultural critique" are constitutive dimensions of the same complex of representations far more than they are mutually exclusive alternatives. That which on one level can be viewed as theoretical oscillations or ambiguities, on another level translates itself into alternatives of a discourse at once positive and normative. In this sense, the passage from culture and personality studies, undertaken in "other" societies, to those of national character, undertaken in "our own," has an important function: hiding the dialectical relationship between "cultural critique" and "social engineering."

It is thus significant and paradoxical that when George Marcus and Michael Fischer (1986:158–61) search in culture and personality studies for a legitimation of their theoretical and ethico-political positions, they avoid any mention of the fact that these were also studies working on the foundations of a politics of social intervention. And that Margaret Mead—whose work is presented as the best example of "cultural critique"—had also been one of the inventors of "applied anthropology." To be sure, the works of Mead to which Marcus and Fischer refer were from before her interest in studies of national character. However, as the authors themselves note, even when she is speaking about adolescence and the family in Samoa and New Guinea, Mead mentions that her central preoccupation was with American adolescents and the American family. What the content of "social engineering" and "cultural critique" might be are different for Mead and for those who today claim her legacy. Nevertheless, in the one case as much as in the other, "engineering" and "critique" are much more than the terms of simple dichotomy. To study other (nonnational) cultures and to "criticize" one's own (national) culture allows for the complicity between these positions to be hidden, a complicity that the study of national cultures (and national character) can but reveal.

The Consequences of the Wartime Shift
to National Character

It is undeniable that one effect of the war was the reinforcing of the configurationist tendencies and of the emphasis on social engineering (Manson 1986: 86). This, we should note, is the second point given in Mead's definition of national character studies quoted above: the pressure of the "exigencies of the post-1939 world political situation." These exigencies led to three complementary preoccupations. At the beginning of 1942, the memorandum written by Gorer for the State Department, beyond the recommendation that "the United States refrain from attacking the Japanese emperor as he would be needed at the end of the war"—a prophetic recommendation which events proved correct—suggested that "a firm fatherly tone" be adopted in war propaganda directed at the Japanese. Gorer was shocked, however, when he learned that the radio broadcasts said, literally, "the United States is your father." Following Mead, this gap in understanding between the English anthropologist's vision and the U.S. army propaganda was the product of a profound difference between the national characters involved: in the American case there is none of the strong respect for father figures found in English culture. That is, and still following Mead, Gorer should have written "talk to the Japanese as if they are fourth graders and you are fifth" (Mead 1978: 181).[17] In short, the war effort required a knowledge of the enemy in order to beat him; a knowledge of the ally to be able to fight alongside him; and a knowledge of oneself in order to know how to use one's own strengths.

The two texts most representative of this preoccupation with the enemy are, without doubt, Gorer's essay "Themes in Japanese Culture" (1943) and Benedict's *The Chrysanthemum and the Sword* (1946). The origin of the first work was in a text, written in 1942, that was restricted in its circulation—a text that in turn developed out of the famous memorandum sent, at the beginning of the same year, to the U.S. State Department. Benedict's book, for its part, was originally written as a report for the Office of War Information. From the theoretical point of view, Gorer's analysis focuses on Japanese pedagogical techniques, trying to explain the formation of those aspects of Japanese character that appear odd or paradoxical to Westerners. *The Chrysanthemum and the Sword*, on the other hand, attempts to sketch a general picture of Japanese cultural patterns through an investigation of the rules and values that configure these patterns.[18]

The preoccupation with allies and "national morale" makes its appearance most clearly in Mead's *And Keep Your Powder Dry* (1965 [1942]) and Bateson's "Morale and the National Character" (1942). As Mead wrote in her preface to the 1943 edition of her book (which had the significant subtitle, *An Anthropologist Looks at America*) her objective was to offer "a social scientist's contribution to winning the war and establishing a just and lasting peace" (xi). The book was, as Mead further explained in a new prologue to the 1965 edition, about "giving Americans a sense of their particular strengths as a people and of the part they may play in the world" (xxx). In other words, this was an attempt to study one's own society anthropologically (for the first time in the history of the discipline), with a view to allowing that society to know itself better, and hence using that knowledge for raising morale in a war situation.

Bateson's text, also written in 1942, had the same objectives as Mead's: to know one's self, but also to know the allies and the enemy, and to establish strategies for the raising of "national morale" for the war. Despite this, and unlike Mead, Bateson addresses theoretical issues, producing the most sophisticated account of the presuppositions that underlie the transformation of national character into an anthropological object. He organizes his argument around a discussion of the obstacles and possible objections raised to "any concept of 'national character.'" His intention is to specify under what conditions it is possible to speak of national character, and to establish the kinds of cultural processes in which this notion can be used positively. Two points of his formulation deserve special mention. The first addresses the criticism of a certain cultural essentialism that might be present in studies of national character. Bateson responds by saying that the fact of "national characters"—with the use of the plural being an important distinguishing mark of his argument—being "constructed" (as we would now put it) does not mean that they do not exist or that they cannot act as markers of cultural difference. The second point replies to accusations against the excessive emphasis on cultural homogeneity in formulations of national character. Bateson argues that to speak of national character does not imply the assumption of cultural uniformity but rather the recognition of a system of differences organized by a pattern—a set of stereotypes—seen as dominant. To speak of difference, or even of deviation, only makes sense in relation to a norm (74–79).

In more general terms, Bateson approaches the problem of national characters from a theoretical perspective foreign to the discussions of the period.

From his point of view, the central issue in the debates about national character concerned—in words that are not his—the false opposition between "reality" and the "representation of reality." The circularity involved in any argument that is hostage to this opposition becomes particularly clear when the consequences of the invention of national frontiers are considered. These are good examples of things that, socially produced, generate effects by acting on the self-perceptions of the communities they divide, and cause the formation, as time passes, of ways of being and feeling, ways of life and moral patterns.[19] Bateson's approach has another effect: it explicitly raises the possibility of defining nations and national characters as units of analysis, arguing that if these entities exist culturally—as representations and as reality, we would say—it is legitimate to try to understand them from an anthropological point of view. Bateson thus shows the dual existence of national character, at once a folk category and a theoretical concept.

Compared to Bateson's sophisticated argument, his colleagues' formulations, which naturalize the nation as a unit of analysis, seem, to say the least, simplistic. In the case of Mead's programmatic statement quoted above, mention of the units of analysis gives way to the definition of a "methodological" problem and a "technical" solution. This is the last of the traits invoked in the definition of the field of studies of national character: the use of special techniques of investigation—"studies of culture at a distance." This was the name of the "manual" edited in 1953 by Margaret Mead and Rhoda Métraux, which brought together a series of papers by researchers who had worked for the project called Research in Contemporary Cultures that was directed by Ruth Benedict at Columbia University starting in 1947—with the book being, in fact, "a very much condensed version of a preliminary draft presented to the Office of Naval Research in the autumn of 1951" (v).[20]

In his contribution to the book, Gorer denied any privileged relationship between studies of character and nations as units of analysis, preferring instead to attribute this connection to the necessities of war and proposing the more general term, "studies of cultural character" for this kind of investigation (1953: 57). Mead's own position, as presented in the introduction to the volume, seems to be different from the text quoted above, for she adopts the hypothesis that nations only became the preferred object of these kinds of analyses as a result of World War II, and that work on the major configurations of character could be carried out in any kind of society—witnessed by the fact that Mead herself, along with Bateson, had produced before the war an analysis of "Balinese character" (Bateson and Mead 1942).

The proposal of "studies of culture at a distance" as the privileged method for anthropological work with "nations" contains a paradox, insofar as anthropologists are always members of national states and thus are much "closer" to the nation as an object than had been the case with the societies and cultures on which they traditionally worked. Everything suggests, therefore, that the "studies of culture at a distance" have no privileged relationship with distance. A proof of this is that the first book to use this methodology—obviously without calling it by that name—was precisely Mead's work on the United States. Further, already in 1950 Gorer had started his work for *Exploring English Character*, following a request from the editors of the newspaper *People*.[21] More significant than these examples, however, is the fact that the techniques proposed for this kind of research are exactly those used by contemporary anthropology in investigations of "national" (or "modern" or "complex") societies, especially when the anthropologist is part of the society under study.[22]

An article published in the *Annual Review of Anthropology* of 1983, titled "Anthropologists View American Culture," shows this point clearly. Noting first that "though one rarely hears talk of cultural values . . . or national character today, some anthropologists are still trying to capture the essence of the whole" (Spindler and Spindler 1983: 52), the authors conclude that the means used in these attempts are very similar to those used in the analysis of national character and studies of culture at a distance. In other words, the nonutilization of participant observation seems to be much more closely connected to the properties of the object chosen as the unit of analysis—or the relations between the object and the investigator, which are precisely characterized by their proximity—than any supposed impossibility of access to that object.[23]

This point allows us to see a certain partiality hidden beneath the apparent objectivity with which Mead isolates the formative traits of national character studies. It is not just that distance does not define such studies, but the rest of the characteristics that she alludes to are more problematic than they seem. In the first place, to claim that studies of national character grew out of work on personality and culture is a mere historical fact—and we saw, however briefly, that the process was a great deal more complicated than this claim would suggest. Second, to hold that "the exigencies of the post-1939 world political situation" were the only factors responsible for anthropology's inclination toward national societies is doubtful. As Roger Bastide noted (1974: 168), Mead's own point of departure was "the adolescent troubles of young Americans, leading her to find out if these troubles had physiological or sociological causes," and this made her go to Samoa.[24] Third, to postulate a privileged relationship between studies of national character and a certain kind of society (national societies) is to offer implications that go far beyond Mead's aims. It was not necessary, therefore, to wait for "culture and personality" to turn into "national character" for the anthropologists' main focus of interest to become their own societies. Further, Mead and Bateson's work on Bali, as much as the "cultural patterns" isolated by Benedict, show that the model of national culture does not need nations, any more than it needs distance, to be applied.

The Limits of Critique and the Fact of Ideology

The criticisms leveled against the studies of national character form the beginning—or even *avant la lettre*, if we note the care with which, as we saw, even in 1942, Bateson respond to possible objections—do not seem, then, to have taken into account the real complexity and the real problems they contained. To this can be added the ambiguity mentioned above that surrounds perspectives on studies of national character in American anthropology, which might explain why the most interesting interpretation to date, as well as one of the most interesting critiques of theories of national character, is by neither an American nor an anthropologist.

In 1954, Dante Moreira Leite presented to the University of São Paulo his doctoral thesis in social psychology: "O caráter nacional brasileiro" (Brazilian National Character), with the significant subtitle "The History of an Ideology." Published immediately in book form, the work was never translated into English—which undoubtedly explains why it has remained totally unknown in the English-speaking world. In his book, Leite describes in detail the origins of the notion of national character (starting from Romanticism and extending to the culture and personality school), after which he analyses the various authors who have tried to apply it to Brazilian society. In the process, he develops a critique with three main aspects. First, from an epistemological point of view, theories of national character, and culture and personality studies, failed to escape from a vicious circle: starting from empirically observed behavior in a society, they go on to deduce the general pattern for this society, which is reproduced in the personalities or characters of its members. This pattern is then used to "explain" any behavior observed among them.

Second, from a methodological point of view, these theories are inevitably marked by confusion between the supposed deep character of a society being analyzed and the observable behavior of a small section of that society. Thus, they imagine that they are studying German national character when in fact they are talking only about Nazis; they imagine that they are getting at the deepest parts of being Japanese when in fact they refer only to members of the military who dominated Japanese politics for a certain period; they believe they have grasped the "Brazilian" when they only have described some rural elite.

Finally—and this is the most important point for Leite—from a political point of view theories of national character are no more than ideologies, in the traditional marxist sense of the word: that is, discourses destined to disguise reality, whether through ethnocentrism, fully compatible with the replacement of European colonialism by U.S. imperialism, or through the omission of politics, economics, or history as the genuine reasons for the differences and inequalities between societies. The result of this process is a kind of substantialization of differences, located in a tradition and at a psychological level so deep that they become almost indistinguishable from the biological rootedness of diversity that racialism promoted, and from which culturalism is supposed to have distinguished itself so clearly (Leite 1969 [1954]: 44–45, 65–66, 100–125).

The most interesting aspect of Leite's book—aside from the radical aspects of his critique of theories of national character, which proposes, in the end, simply the substitution of ideology with "scientific theories" capable of accounting for concrete social, political, and economic situations—is that the author is forced to raise, albeit in passing, a fundamental issue: How can one explain the popularity of these theories, given that their explanatory value is nil? That is, what can one do with the fact that, from the point of view of social agents, national character actually seems to exist, promoting mutual identification with some people and differentiation with regard to others? (26–27, 103).[25]

In a recently published autobiographical account, David Schneider—whose anthropological training took place precisely during the apogee of culture and personality studies—related that:

> I had early noticed how academics, scientists one and all, took simple folk notions and elevated them to the stratospheric position of scientific theory. This was early made most vivid to me at Yale where Clark Hull held sway. With Geoffrey Gorer in the background pushing Freudian ideas, it didn't take me long to observe that learning theory's punishment and reward scheme was very much like my mother's, and she was certainly no high-flown scientist, but

she could give a good slap when she felt a reward was not indicated. (Schneider and Handler 1995: 222–23).

Obviously, in this context, Schneider has no reason to point out that the same words operate in a completely different way when they are spoken by one's mother or by a "high-flown scientist." In other words, the possible theoretical problems in studies of culture and personality and national character must not allow us to forget that, from the point of view of social and cultural analysis, confusion between ordinary language and scientific discourse is rather more than an epistemological mistake. We are dealing, instead, with taking seriously the discursive differences hidden behind the apparent similarity of words, and with showing how that discourse contributed to the production and objectification of the very things that go beyond it.

The opposition between "fiction" (or representation) and "reality" is far from being an exclusive characteristic of analyses based on the notion of ideology. The traps awaiting analyses of ideology—so well represented by Leite—are shared by all theories that are based on any dichotomy of facts and concepts, behaviors and representations. If theories of national character are certainly not the direct expression of "reality," neither are they its deformation or falsification. We are dealing here with discourses that are simultaneously descriptive and normative, and which through their social circulation tend to act as performative structures synthesizing, diffusing, and, in the extreme case, creating their own referents. In other words, it would be more interesting to investigate this kind of discourse as part of a *dispositif*, in the Foucauldian sense of the term. This dispositif would not simply contain "theories" of national character but also the various nationalist discourses and practices, the programs put in place to reconcile citizens to their nationhood, the behavior of agents in specific situations where traits of "national character" are used as an explanation, justification, or rationalization, and even our quiet satisfaction when we come upon apparently satisfying descriptions of our ways of being and acting.[26] In sum, if Leite was correct to insist on the persistence of substantialism in the passage from racist models to culturalist ones, it is then necessary to go a step further: the adoption of a resolutely processualist perspective capable of taking into account not just the "history" of national character and its theories but also what we might call its profound historicity, how it is continually being constructed in history and in social, political, and cultural relations.

Does National Character Exist?

If Stocking's doubts about the repeated announcements of the "death" of studies of national character or culture and personality seem to be more than justified (1986: 9), the survival of models that are the foundation of these studies is greater than he suspected—and not simply in the form of the "psychological anthropology" that continues to operate.[27] When Clifford Geertz (1995: 23) suggests that the differences between the "countries" he has studied throughout his career would be translatable into distinct "historical operas," we can reasonably ask how far we are from theories of national character. In the same way, Louis Dumont's macrodichotomy between an individualistic "West" and a holistic "Rest" (1980 [1966]), is not that far, save in its magnitude, from the distinction between Apollonians and Dionysians proposed by Benedict.[28] The difference clearly lies in the fact that culturalist models try to articulate the values seen as dominant with their means of transmission, and make the process of socialization the concrete ground on which are founded entities that would otherwise seem rather ethereal. By contrast, more-recent authors (along with thinkers on national culture and identity in general) tend to leave implicit a series of presuppositions—which refer, without acknowledgment, to the models developed by the school of culture and personality and studies of national character—without which their analyses would make little sense. What is this odd continuity about?

Already in 1921, Marcel Mauss called attention to the close connection between the notion of psychological character and of the nation: "A character is the integrated ensemble of the diverse faculties of an individual, some being more or less sensory, others more or less intellectual, or volitional. . . . A complete nation is an adequately integrated society with a central power which is in some degree democratic, in all instances possessing the notion of national sovereignty and determined by frontiers which are, in general, those of a race, a civilization, a language, a morale, in a word, of a national character" (1969 [1921]: 603–4). For his part, Norbert Elias, in a text originally written in 1968, pointed out the affinity between the genesis of national states and a particular "natiocentric" intellectual orientation that would be responsible for the transposition of the idea of the "good society," proper to bourgeois national society, into the categories of the social sciences(1989 [1968]: 26–27).[29]

In this sense, we can see that anthropology's contribution to the construction of national societies was not limited to the "invention of primitive society," of which they were simply an inverted image (Kuper 1988). The studies of national character show an explicit intervention by anthropological thought in the objectification of things national. As stated above, there is a close connection between nationalist models and many of those used, inadvertently or not, by social scientists. In fact, treating any human group as a "society" or "culture," clearly bounded and relatively closed, is the same as treating it as a nation. Further, if nationalism really is linked to possessive individualism, through conceiving the nation as simultaneously a collective individual and collection of individuals,[30] then studies of culture and personality and of national character—with their attempts to delimit a psychological pattern common to all members of a society, which simultaneously makes this society stand out from all others—are perhaps among the clearest examples of natiocentrism in the social sciences. Therefore, we can only conclude that the concept of national character may only be applied to nations because it was created from a model that—transcending all "theories" and forming part of all national cultures—treats all societies and cultures as if they were national societies or cultures and treats the relations between them as international relations.

Once we have recognized this complicity and the paradoxes it leads to in all attempts to comprehend it, what is to be done? Accept that "character" and "national" and the connection between them actually exist, thus following the work of the theorists of the 1940s and 1950s? Or reject the existence of the concepts and their connections by denouncing the ideological bias and theoretical poverty of this work, and then simply abandon it? From our point of view, it is necessary to free ourselves from these false alternatives: if "national character" is the result of a process of production and objectification that involves, at the same time, social relations, political strategies, and theoretical discourses, this does not mean—quite the opposite—that it is nothing. What must be done is to map out, in its various foci of production and propagation, the mechanisms of constitution and diffusion of the categories related to this notion, showing how apparently self-evident concepts and facts, as well as the most commonplace of words and things, come to acquire, throughout history and in social usage, the density that is attributed to them as if it were a second nature.

Over twenty years ago, François Châtelet, pondering on "the question of the history of philosophy today" (1976: 36), concluded that reference to the "authors of the past" has meaning and worth only insofar as below every "history" there is a "geography." That is, ideas and practices do not simply come into being, grow, and die but rather they are always "alive" and they "migrate" incessantly from one author and from one system to another. To investigate the "past" is, therefore, simultaneously to question the present and to sketch out the future (1976: 40). History and, obviously, the history of anthropology take on meaning insofar as they are situated in contemporaneity.

Questioning the status of nations as objects of analysis is, certainly, at the heart of some contemporary anthropological debates. Some tend to attribute the need for such questioning to the properties of certain empirical phenomena—those linked to the denationalizing, localizing, and transnationalizing of social and cultural life—the existence of which, independent of any theoretical representation, is thought of as a historical novelty. Others prefer to point to the limitations of theoretical models that are a reflex of the very world of nation- states that these models seek to describe. Beyond these alternatives—that which attributes to history the responsibility for constituting new phenomena, and that which blames theory for the incapacity of perceiving the disappearance of the old—we choose to follow the history of theory as a means to point toward a more comprehensive way to reflect on the status of nations and of international relations as an object of anthropological knowledge.

Analyses of national character reveal that any account of "national phenomena" (national cultures, identities, societies, characters, stereotypes) implicates, in its very formulation, statements endowed with some level of performative efficacy: any description that gains recognition will be destined to form part of the thing it describes (cf. Bourdieu 1981). And the same seems to happen with much more recent notions: in speaking of modernity, complexity, national identity, national culture, internationalization, and globalization, do we not run the risk of falling into the same analytical short-circuits as in the studies of national character, contributing to the existence of the very thing that we supposedly are taking as a pure object?

In order to avoid overly easy solutions, it must be recognized that none of these notions exist only in academic discourse, for they are also present, in one form or another, in ordinary language and discourses such as the journalistic or political. We are dealing here not simply with notions and discourses but also with objects and practices. This immediately raises a question that has always, directly or not, haunted anthropological thought: the problem of the applicability of anthropology and its correlates—the well-known dilemmas of the debates between universalism and particularism, and the recurrent paradoxes of absolutism and relativism. All this points toward a greater convergence and interpenetration than might have been thought between anthropology and certain central issues in the societies in which it is produced, more specifically, in the case at hand, to a clear correspondence between nationalist models and those of the social sciences. The refusal to explore these juxtapositions threatens to turn sociological and anthropological theories into simple rationalizations of dominant native theories.

Therefore, the critique of the impasses into which the use of notions such as national character can lead must go beyond the denunciation of their purely imaginary and ideological elements, and beyond simply abandoning them. The examination of the field in which such notions are enveloped reveals that national character studies can function as an example of anthropology's potential to address central themes of our societies, while avoiding two symmetrical risks: unreflexively converting itself into just one more focus for the production and dissemination of collective representations, or, on the pretext of remaining free of all ideological contamination, losing contact with the very representations that circulate in those societies.

Notes

We would like to thank Mariza Peirano, Enrique Rodriguez Larreta, and Eduardo Viveiros de Castro who, at different times and in various ways, contributed to the formulation of this work. We would also like to thank Peter Gow for his careful translation of the Portuguese original.

1 Other important initiatives for participation in the "war effort" included the activities of several anthropologists in the National Research Committee on Food Habits, organized by the National Research Council with the intention of preparing the U.S. population for the changes in food habits that the war would require, and in the War Relocation Authority, which was created for the management and control of the relocation camps in which, after Pearl Harbor, approximately one hundred thousand Japanese Americans were interned on U.S. territory (cf. Stocking 1976; Partridge and Eddy 1978: 28–32; Suzuki 1981; Yans-McLaughlin 1986; Starn 1986).

2 Stocking (1976: 33–34) makes special mention of two projects of the "application" of anthropology that were linked to social policies that the U.S. government implemented during and after the New Deal—one in the Department of Agriculture and the other in the Applied Anthropology Unit of the Bureau of Indian Affairs (later known as the Indian Service). The first meeting of the Society

for Applied Anthropology took place at Harvard in May 1941. Anthropologists connected to the society took part not only in the Office of War Information and the Committee for National Morale, but also in other government bodies like the United States Trust Territory of the Pacific Islands (Partridge 1978: 31–40). On the other hand, articles on the application of anthropology were not only published in *Applied Anthropology* (established in 1941), but increasingly appeared in other publications, especially *American Anthropologist.*

3   In the manual for the study of "cultures at a distance" presented by Margaret Mead and Rhoda Métraux to Columbia University Research in Contemporary Cultures (founded by Ruth Benedict two years before thanks to a grant from the Human Research Division of the Office of Naval Research), Mead defined the possible "political applications" of her results in the following manner: "The approach described in this Manual has been used for a variety of political purposes: to implement particular governmental programs within a country, to facilitate relationships with allies, to guide relationships with partisan groups in countries under enemy control, to assist in estimating enemy strengths and weaknesses, and to provide a rationale for the preparation of documents at the international level. All these uses involve diagnosing the cultural regularities . . . The diagnosis is made for the purpose of facilitating some specific plan or policy, and at least implicitly, includes predictions of expected behavior that may make such a plan or policy successful or unsuccessful" (1962 [1953]: 397).

4   Margaret Mead, in the prologue to the book in which, in 1942, she analyzed "American national character," noted that the English deserved the credit for inventing the use of anthropologists as "advisers to the government"; she stressed, however, that the real difference between British anthropology's involvement in colonial administration and that of American anthropology in the war effort lay in the fact that, in the latter case, anthropologists explicitly focused on their own society as well as on others (1965 [1942]: 8–9).

5   Further, it is worth noting that the works undertaken by Warner—or those of the Lynds and the Chicago school—were only recognized as "anthropological" after the "anthropology of national character." In the *Handbook of Social and Cultural Anthropology*, published in 1973, Gulick (1973: 981) has no doubts about maintaining that *Yankee City* "became part of the corpus of American sociology— not anthropology" and that "Warner became, in effect, a sociologist. Margaret Mead, in contrast, became in the ensuing forty years the epitome of anthropology for many people in the United States and elsewhere in the world."

6   Speaking about "psychological anthropology" in general, Stocking (1986: 9) called attention to the fact that, for all that it might be the subdiscipline of American anthropology that deserves the most study, the works devoted to it remain to date limited to internal analyses and never external or sociohistorical analyses.

7   It should be noted, however, that there seems to be a tacit agreement to restrict such charges to illegitimate applications of anthropology to the period after World War II, which corresponds to the cold war. They are never applied to the use of studies of national character at the beginning of the war.

8   As Michael Pollak has shown, the genesis of the articulation between the design and implementation of a type of policy (policy making) and the constitution of a type of science (policy sciences) in the United States goes back to the New Deal and to the expansion of the welfare state. The parallel invention of (applied) social sciences and psychology, and of techniques of research and measurement, counting on the help of mathematics (survey research), was completed during and after World War II by institutions such as the Office of Strategic Studies (oss, forerunner of the cia) and the Bureau of Applied Social Research. It is interesting to note that this bureau—directed, among others, by Paul Lazarfeld, Richard Merton, and Samuel Stouffer (organizer of one of the principle studies produced by the institution, *The American Soldier*)—had as its base, after 1939, Columbia University, the same institution in which Ruth Benedict set up the Research in Contemporary Studies (cf. Pollak 1979). On the other hand, it must be remembered that these processes were also connected to the growth of the universities and the provision of jobs by the administration and foundations, which new graduates entered in great numbers (cf. Partridge and Eddy 1978).

9   It should be remembered that the genesis of notions like *Volkgeist* and *Zeitgeist*, produced in the context of German Romanticism and pre-Romanticism, were associated with the genesis of specialities and specialists (folklorists, poets, men of letters) whose activities were also understood as "applications" or practical intent—the theory and practice of German "nationalism" (cf. Elias 2000 [1939]: 57–82).

10   Note here that similar formulations were common in the first half of the century among Portuguese, Spanish, and Latin American intellectuals, who were also influenced by German thought. In the case of Spain there are the influential works of José Ortega y Gasset, and in Latin America there are the ideas about Brazilian national character of Gilberto Freyre, or about the place of the mestizo in postrevolutionary Mexican culture of Manuel Gamio. Both Freyre and Gamio were students of Boas in the 1920s.

11   It should be observed that this influence was also exercised through a series of books destined for the general reader; for example, Herskovits 1948; Kardiner and Preble 1961; Klukhohn 1949; and Linton 1936.

12   Lowie published in 1945 a little book in which, with the explicit object of aiding the understanding of Nazism and the war, he rejected "fatalistic" interpretations of these phenomena, preferring to attribute them to historical accidents that he attempted to reconstruct (1980 [1945]: vii, 111–14).

13   From this point of view, the introduction written by Boas for Benedict's *Patterns of Culture* is especially significant. After reaffirming the importance of the historical method, Boas holds that the method is not foreign to a notion of the whole and, further, that an interest in "socio-psychological problems is not in any way opposed to the historical approach . . . Dr. Benedict calls the genius of culture its configuration" (xvi–xvii).

14   Cf. Benedict's hope for "what may one day come to be a true social engineering" (quoted in Handler 1986: 150). See also, among others, Mead 1965 [1945]: 169–71, 248; and Handler 1989: 1–2, 11–12 n.1.

15 Kardiner, having studied with Boas at Columbia and simultaneously entered psychoanalysis—later being analyzed by Freud (Manson 1986: 74–75)—developed in the years immediately before World War II the theory of modal personality, the emphasis of which is on the fact that psychological processes that make up individual characters in specific cultures is opposed, in many ways, to the then dominant configurationism.

16 This may be due to a resistance to publicize the thesis on the existence of more or less innate temperaments differently developed in different cultures due to the political implications of the idea in the context of World War II (cf. Yans-McLaughlin 1986: 204–5) or to Mead's theoretical position, which claimed that "we could not begin to discuss what types of behavior were innate, linked to the biologically given rather than to the socially or situationally given, until we had explored the extent to which cultural expectations stylized behavior" (1978: 174).

17 This misunderstanding would also seem to attest, at least in part, to the fact that anthropological advice was actually followed by the military.

18 If Gorer's article was directly motivated by the attack on Pearl Harbor, Benedict's report also derived from exigencies of the same type. After the entry of the United States into the war, the problems caused by the implementation of the policy of displacing approximately one hundred thousand Japanese Americans to internment camps, led to the setting up of the Bureau of Sociological Research. At the end of 1942, a series of rebellions in the camps led to the creation of the Community Analysis Section—inspired by previous studies done on Indian reservations—the intention of which was to clarify "cultural aspects of Japanese behavior." Twenty-seven social scientists took part in this organization, twenty of whom were anthropologists (among them, Robert Redfield, Elizabeth Colson, Solon T. Kimball, Weston LaBarre, and Conrad M. Arensberg) (Partridge and Eddy 1978: 29–30; Suzuki 1981).

19 Although in this sense Bateson seems very close to Elias's approach—which proposes the study of the genesis of *national habitus* (Elias 2000 [1939]; 1996)—it must be noted that his text is fundamentally ambiguous. The first part, devoted to theoretical discussion, is undoubtedly richer than the second, which develops a formal model for the isolation and comparison of national characters (Russian, German, English, American, and Balinese), in which, oddly enough, the earlier theoretical considerations are abandoned. Finally, the last part of the text is devoted to the "practical" realization of the model in the task of raising American "morale" in the context of war (1942: 89–91).

20 It must be noted here that the project that Benedict directed continued, on the one hand, with the "Studies in Soviet Culture" undertaken for the Rand Corporation, and, on the other hand with the "Studies in Contemporary Culture" undertaken for the Office of Naval Research and for the Center for International Studies at MIT (Mead and Métraux 1953: v).

21 This was a Sunday newspaper with twelve million readers, the second-largest circulation in Great Britain at the time (Gorer 1955: 3–4). To write the book

Gorer developed a questionnaire, which was sent to 14,605 readers who had responded to a coupon that accompanied an article by Gorer explaining the research. Of the total sent, 10,524 questionnaires were returned filled in, then codified and analyzed. Analysis of the material was published in the newspaper and later integrated into Gorer's book (1955: 7–10).

22 Some of the works brought together in the manual take as their material the most remarkable range of cultural products: not simply the use of projective tests (widely used by some anthropologists from the 1930s on), but literary works and autobiographies, popular stories, national rituals and festivals, letters from immigrants, films, schoolbooks, and handbooks for teaching chess strategies. Studying cultures at a distance—or rather, studying national cultures—seems to have demanded tremendous creativity on the part of anthropologists, which makes the studies presented by Mead and Métraux the forerunners of contemporary studies of national and transnational cultures and identities. It seems to us that the unevenness of the results of the research, which go from the brilliant (in the case of Bateson on the Nazi propaganda film *Hitlerjunge*) to the mere naturalization of national stereotypes (in the case of the majority of texts on the study of Russian national character) is less an oddity of the book than a demonstration of the extremes within which all the possibilities of studies of national cultures are contained.

23 Perhaps this point was responsible, at least in part, for the development of the intense institutional cooperation between anthropologists studying national character and the many scholars who—especially from the beginning of the 1950s—dealt with the same themes in other disciplines, especially social psychology and political science (cf. for example, Inkeles 1972 [1961]).

24 Margaret Mead herself is explicit on this point, claiming in *And Keep Your Powder Dry* that after six fieldtrips to other cultures she "came home to a world on the brink of war, convinced that the next task was to apply what we knew, as best we could, to the problems of our own society" (1965 [1942]: 3). In the introduction to the 1965 edition, the issue is made even clearer: "My own interests had always turned on the relevance of the study of primitive peoples to our understanding of our own customary behavior and our attempts to modify it" (xxvii). For all that, it is worth noting that the final chapters of *Coming of Age in Samoa* (1969 [1928])—which deal with the relation between Mead's field data and the problems of American adolescence, and which probably were responsible for turning the book into a best-seller—were only included in the book at her publisher's insistence (Marcus and Fischer 1986: 158).

25 It is always difficult to decide if the argument of "psychological validity"—the verisimilitude of a theory "from the native's point of view"—testifies for or against any given formulation. Benedict's *The Chrysanthemum and the Sword* was translated into Japanese in 1948, and by 1952 it had already been through eight editions. In 1953, a group of fifteen Japanese intellectuals came together to discuss the book. The general tone of their response was of complete acceptance of the

book, and the criticisms they made were in no way different from those made by Western anthropologists (cf. Bennett and Nagai 1953).

26   Cf. the suggestions of Michael Herzfeld (1993: 71–97) on the value of analyzing the production and reproduction of national stereotypes in the context of everyday interactions. For his part, Gérard Noiriel (1988: 69–123) has shown, through a fine historical analysis, the complex articulations between common sense and the knowledge that underlies the invention of national stereotypes.

27   Francis Hsu remembered in an article published in 1972 that he suggested in 1961 a new title to refer to studies of culture and personality: "psychological anthropology" (Hsu 1972: 6–7). This attempt at relegitimation seems to have been successful given the great number of works that place themselves under this rubric as well as the notable number of journals that devote themselves, wholly or in part, to this field. For a reevaluation of the theory of culture and personality, see Shweder 1979.

28   From this point of view, it is interesting to note that a series of Benedict's considerations on the contrast between Japanese and Western cultures come very close, in their substance, to Dumont's points: the feelings of debt and dependency (chapter 7), of honor and shame (chapters 8 and 10), and self-discipline and conformity (chapter 11) are all globally opposed to the individualism and equality of American society: "We uphold the virtue of equality even when we violate it and we fight hierarchy with a righteous indignation. . . . Inequality has been for centuries the rule of their organized life at just those points where it is most predictable and most accepted. Behavior that recognizes hierarchy is as natural to them as breathing" (Benedict 1989 [1946]: 45–47).

29   According to Elias, the model for the fulfillment of this nationcentric orientation in sociological theory would be Talcott Parsons concept of the "social system" (Elias 1989 [1968]: 28).

30   The nation, Handler states in his study of Quebec (1988: 179), is conceived of "as a collection of collective individuals."

David Mills

ANTHROPOLOGY AT THE END OF EMPIRE

The Rise and Fall of the Colonial Social Science

Research Council, 1944–1962

The histories of organizations are not generally seen as glamorous affairs. Novelty and innovation are often buried amid the day-to-day bureaucratic paper trail. At first glance the British Colonial Social Science Research Council (CSSRC) is precisely such a bureaucracy: a civil service committee dedicated to lubricating the administrative wheels of social science research in the "dominions." This essay tells the story of this first significant government attempt to plan and fund social science research; the influence of a few key anthropologists in shaping these plans; and the implications for British social anthropology's intellectual and institutional status. As the discipline benefited from the CSSRC's political and financial patronage, it increasingly articulated its own metropolitan intellectual agenda, which was rather different from the council's pragmatic focus on colonial social problems. Ironically, the growth and reproduction of social anthropology as a primarily British-based university discipline depended on this colonial research base, and in this tension lay both the seeds of future conflict and gradual marginalization of the discipline.

The story begins laden with high moral purpose: an ambitious Colonial Office blueprint produced during World War II for a new "developmental" empire to complement plans for a fledgling welfare state in Britain. Known as the Colonial Development and Welfare Act, this major piece of legislation recognized for the first time that rational development planning and spending required careful preparatory research. As a result, £500,000 annually was earmarked for research. Only a small proportion of this went to the social sciences, yet this amount was enough to provide a major multidisciplinary research agenda and a large number of research fellowships, all crowned with four high-profile regional research institutes in Africa and in the Caribbean.

The selection, training, supervision, and support of younger scholars at these institutes was a central concern of the new research council, and a concomitant influence on the reproduction and growth of the respective disciplines.

The problem-focused agenda of the cssrc still resonates today in the concerns of its successor, the United Kingdom's Economic and Social Research Council, which funds most social science research. In a contemporary academic economy ever more anxious to demonstrate its "national" competitiveness, the British Government's patronage of social science research remains conditional on the latter making explicit its "relevance" and "application" for users. Rather than presume such an a priori tension between "pure" and "applied" anthropological work during this late-colonial period, I take up here Benoît de l'Estoile's argument that both derive from the same original matrix: "An effort to build a science of social phenomena that could serve as a basis for the resolution of colonial 'social problems'" (1997b: 366). As he further notes, "social anthropology's strategic importance for the colonial project of social transformation thus appears to have been an essential factor in the autonomisation of the discipline" (366). In this essay, I explore this unfolding dynamic.[1]

An Empire of Moral Purpose

Prior to 1940, there had been virtually no government funding for British social science research in Africa. A Colonial Research Committee was established in 1919, but its main focus was on small projects in botany and geology (Jeffries 1964). The first Colonial Development Act of 1929 was primarily concerned with reducing unemployment in the United Kingdom. Money was channeled solely into research on suitable export commodities, through grants to the Imperial Marketing Board. For this reason the American philanthropic organizations such as the Rockefeller and Carnegie foundations played the key role in supporting British social research in the 1930s and in founding the International African Institute (originally the International Bureau of African Languages and Cultures). This effort contrasts with the Australian National Research Council, which sponsored many of its doctoral students, including the first fieldwork trips of Raymond Firth, Phyllis Kaberry, and Ralph Piddington, all of whom went on to play an influential role in British anthropology.

This lack of funding for research in the colonies was indicative of the larger context in which the empire was viewed. Something that began to change in the 1930s, as an increasing number of intellectuals wrote about the "colonial question." As Ronald Hyam comments: "From the 1930s the Colonial Empire gradually began to be seen more as a whole, and as a stage upon which more interventionist and generally applicable policies might be evolved, beginning with Colonial Development and Welfare" (1999: n.p.).

The story begins with a now famous meeting in Whitehall at the Carlton Hotel on 6 October 1939. The war had just begun. Called by then Secretary of State Malcolm MacDonald, the meeting was attended by a key set of thinkers and writers linked with the Fabians and influential in the colonial reform movement. Present too were the two larger-than-life defenders of British imperialism, both old (Lord Lugard) and new (Lord Hailey).

The secretary of state briefed the meeting. Dampening the expectations that some major new policy shift was to be announced, instead he raised three topics for discussion, of which "the policy with regard to land is fundamental to everything else." As with political development, he pointed out that "we need more knowledge on this subject." The best way forward, he suggested, would "be a series of local inquiries" rather than a royal commission. Opening the discussions, Lugard and Hailey presented their views. Hailey rather characteristically pointed out that the object of the meeting was "not to decide what policy ought to adopted, but to explore what investigations it might be useful to initiate with a view to arriving at a policy." The emphasis on careful planning and research was taken up by Margery Perham, who commented that "land could not be studied in isolation. Subjects such as these should be studied in groups" and "a new technique of study was needed. There might be three or four experts, each knowledgeable in a different subject, investigating the whole range of these subjects co-operatively."[2] The stress laid on the importance of a multidisciplinary research model echoed Hailey's own views in *The African Survey* (1938). The conversation went on to discuss the economics of this new colonial settlement and the major investment it would need from Britain.

This meeting is largely remembered for its political ramifications, influencing the shape of the legislation a year later. Yet the priority given to strategic planning and careful research is also telling. Key to the success of this postwar settlement was to be the new science of "national planning," a science described in a speech by Member of Parliament Herbert Morrison as "constructively revolutionary . . . a contribution to civilisation as vital and as distinctively British as parliamentary democracy and the rule of law."[3] This speech was read and discussed with interest in the Colonial Office in the early 1940s and led to repeated calls for priority setting in colonial research spending.

What led to this new sense of financial and political largesse by the imperial power? A good-sized portion was motivated by self-interest and self-image: the recognition that defending colonialism as a moral project to the Americans during the war might be difficult. As Hyam notes, MacDonald was anxious to make the colonial position in wartime unassailable. It was " 'essential to get away from the old principle that Colonies can only have what they themselves can afford to pay for' " (1999: 275). A second factor was the influential Moyne report, compiled on economic and social conditions in the British Caribbean Islands after a period of anticolonial protest that the Colonial Office euphemistically called "disturbances." Lord Moyne recommended that a "West Indian Welfare Fund" be established to finance colonial development in those particular colonies.

The final piece in this new modernist jigsaw was Lord Hailey's voluminous *African Survey* (1938), a multiauthored Carnegie-sponsored report on "economic and social conditions in Africa." A highly influential survey, it became the Urtext for British colonial reformers and social scientists. E. M. Chilver notes that within weeks of its publication it was "as familiar an object on the desks in the Colonial Office as . . . the Imperial Calendar" and that "there can have been few books that have exercised such a direct influence on policy" (1957: n.p.). The key to its significance was its proposal for the wholesale reorganization of colonial research and enquiry. Together these factors convinced MacDonald of the importance of including a special research fund within the planned Colonial Development and Welfare Act. In a handwritten note in the margin of his copy of the official history of colonial research (Jeffries 1964: 23), Hailey wrote "He [MacDonald] and I paid a joint visit to the Chancellor." The treasury was clearly amenable, for the new act was passed in July 1940, at one of most difficult moments of the war. It allowed for the spending of £5 million annually for ten years and, more significantly, for another £500,000 for research each year. It was an impressive sum of money, and it was the first time that the British Government had seriously funded academic research in its colonial territories.

The Hailey Effect

With the publication of *The African Survey* Lord Hailey had come to be regarded as a principal spokesman for colonial reform and development, ensuring his close influence on the shaping of the postwar funding and structures of British social science. Hailey's achievement is all the more impressive when one realizes that this was a postretirement project carried out after a long career in the Indian Civil Service. Hailey was never an academic, and he had been chosen to lead the survey precisely because of his lack of African experience—that is, he would bring a "fresh eye" to the task. A more cynical interpretation, offered by Paul Rich, is that this was no fortuitous choice, for "one of the central objectives behind the survey was the promotion of a common pattern of Western control over the separate African territories, as had been produced in the Indian Raj" (1986).

Hailey was first offered the opportunity to carry out the survey in 1933, but he had no idea that the task was so enormous, and it would almost overwhelm him. The survey's value and its limitation both lie in its rather ponderous compendiousness. It provides what now might be described as a baseline survey of colonial and African systems of governance in sub-Saharan Africa. It was written by a team of scholars, including two students of Bronislaw Malinoswki, Lucy Mair and Audrey Richards, who were seconded to the Colonial Office during the war and went on to influential positions within British anthropology. The report's emphasis is determinedly administrative, with chapters on "native administration," "the problems of labour," and "African economic development." In some ways the most influential part of the text turned out to be the conclusion. It was there that Hailey recommended a broad program of research, a term he carefully gave a wide connotation by describing it as "studies either of an abstract or (to use a convenient term) of a practical nature" (1938: 1611). He demonstrated how previous research had been "in response to an unrelated series of demands rather than as the outcome of comprehensive planning," and so made a strong case for "liberal assistance from the British Treasury" (1629) for a new fund. Hailey's ideas were taken seriously, and plans began for the coordination and funding of research as part of the new Colonial Development and Welfare Act.

The Founding of the Colonial Research Committee and the CSSRC

After the Colonial Development and Welfare Act was published on 20 February 1940, MacDonald wrote to Hailey congratulating him on his role in its creation and expressing the hope that he had taken "particular pleasure in the knowledge that effect is now to be given to your own proposals for research." Anxious to keep the preparations going as fast as possible, Mac-Donald went on to ask Hailey to be chair of the new Colonial Research Advisory Committee, for "the general scheme for colonial research is so much your own project, and one which I know you have so deeply at heart."[4]

A month later, another lengthy letter from the secretary of state suggested an outline committee to Hailey, which is revealing both in its perceived scientific division of labor and in the ambiguous status accorded the social sciences. MacDonald proposed a committee of up to fifteen scientists with representatives from the Medical Research Council, the Royal College of Physicians, "someone from the Royal Society," and even "a business man connected with one of the big companies, such as Imperial Chemicals." He went on to write that "the selection of members to represent the somewhat wide field of sociological research may perhaps be a matter of greater diffi-culty." The situation became even more complicated when he added, "one special point on which I shall wish to consult you on your return is whether an anthropologist should be included on the committee. I felt that I shall be pressed later on to include an anthropologist, but I gather that it will be rather difficult to find one who has not his own personal axe to grind, and I am told that in any case anthropologists, as a class, are rather difficult folk to deal with."[5] The anthropologists' own self-flattery that they had the willing ear of colonial civil servants was thus not necessarily accurate. Indeed, there were strong Colonial Office prejudices about the limited practical utility of "professional" anthropologists (Kuklick 1992: 201).

Secretary of State MacDonald goes further to suggest that the existing scientific advisory committees should be used wherever possible for prelimi-nary examination of the schemes, but then recognizes that there is "no similar body in existence which could do this preliminary work on schemes of sociological research, and we may have to set up an advisory committee for the express purpose of undertaking this." Again, this is a moment he uses to express his reservations about these new sciences. "The trouble of course, is that sociological research covers such a very wide and divergent field, and it will be very difficult indeed to get together a really representative and harmonious committee to tackle this work."

Hailey duly responded to these thoughts. Diplomatically ignoring the implied criticisms of the social sciences, he went on to suggest a further set of academic disciplines that he thought MacDonald's proposed representa-tives might not be able to cover. Of these, he felt that geology and anthropol-ogy particularly deserved attention. Agreeing that "it is true that anthropologists are difficult folk to deal with," Hailey pointed out that "there are many people, not themselves professional anthropologists, who will constantly make it their business to remind you, that it is useless to provide for enquiry into the physical sciences, unless you consider also the human elements to which the result of these enquiries must be applied." He went on to suggest that "some of the colonial governments would feel the committee to be incomplete, unless this side of the enquiry were represented." In a veiled reference to nascent anticolonial movements, he noted that both the Gold Coast and Kenya had recently admitted to "grave gaps in their knowledge of the native social organisations with which they have to deal." However Hailey acknowledged MacDonald's concern regarding the "limits within which support should be given to anthropological studies by a body such as that which you are establishing." He then went on to state that "its aim is not primarily to encourage academic study . . . it is limited to discovering those things which our administration must know if it is to make the best use of its resources for the development of the people in the colonies. In looking for an anthropologist therefore, our main object should be to seek someone whose experiences enable him to help in estimating the social factors which must be taken into account if our technical or administrative agencies for development are to operate with success."[6]

Hailey's strategic manipulation of the "pure/applied" dichotomy is visible during this period, and indeed throughout the history of the CSSRC. Insisting that its focus should be on the social factors to take into account whether "our technical or administrative agencies for development are to operate with success," he put forward two "very suitable" names: Edwin Smith (an ex-missionary and one of the founders of what became the International African Institute) and "Dr Raymond Firth, now secretary of the Royal Anthropological Institute, and he would perhaps be more acceptable to the younger school of anthropologists."

Firth, one of Malinowski's protégés, published *We, the Tikopia* in 1936. He was shortly to be made professor of anthropology at the London School of Economics, and more than anyone else he ensured the institutionalization of the discipline within British universities over the subsequent two decades.

Despite the fanfare with which the Colonial Development and Welfare Act and its research component was launched, very little of the funding was spent in the first years of its existence. Indeed, a month before the act was finally passed in July 1940, it was announced in the House of Commons that it was not felt appropriate to set up the advisory committees in the present circumstances. It was a further two years before the matter was raised again, which was done by the new secretary of state, Lord Cranborne, in June 1942. This time a smaller nucleus committee of four or five was proposed, again with the emphasis on medicine and agriculture that "between them have more to contribute to the welfare of colonial peoples than most other sciences." Ironically, given the lack of social science representatives, one of the factors influencing Lord Cranborne's decision to resurrect the plans were a number of applications from the social sciences for funding. Without quick decisions, he foresaw the "danger that the academic bodies concerned might feel obliged to proceed with their individual plans and that this might lead to uneconomical and inconvenient dispersion of activity in these fields of colonial studies."

A final committee of seven began their work immediately, holding one meeting each month. Alexander Carr-Saunders, director of the London School of Economics (LSE), represented social sciences. Audrey Richards, a close and influential friend of Lord Hailey, was brought onto the committee a year later and had a good deal of influence over its subsequent development.

Secretary of State Lord Cranborne addressed the first meeting of the committee. He suggested that the terms of the act referred to "research and enquiry," and that these terms could be given the widest possible interpretation, covering both pure and applied research, such that the committee's function in coordinating research was as important as recommending grants for expenditure. Despite his administrative background, Hailey was equally determined that the committee's goal should be the pursuit of scientific "truth." As the first annual report notes, "the committee should not confine itself to examining proposals put to it by Colonial Government . . . it conceives it as its duty to study the whole field of scientific inquiry; to distinguish the parts of it requiring attention, and to ensure that gaps in it are filled wherever possible to do so."[7] The report goes on to express concern about the "tendency for research problems to be dictated too exclusively by local and temporary interests, without due regard to scientific possibilities." The comprehensiveness and scope of the committee's self-appointed remit inevitably echoed the ambitions and interdisciplinary self-confidence of Hailey's African survey and Worthington's *Science in Africa* (1938).

Small groups of experts were commissioned during 1943 to review the present state of all of the various scientific disciplines. The Colonial Research Committee (CRC) briefed these groups, in particular noting "the inadequacy of the data" from the social sciences and the "difficulties dealing with this subject," partly because "there is no organisation acting for the social sciences." The "special difficulties" in carrying out such research in the colonies were seen equally as due to the lack of U.K. departments "specially responsible for the conduct of detailed investigations" and the nonexistence of departments of social studies within colonial institutes of higher education. The suggested solution was to build up an independent academic research capacity within the colonial territories. The issue of "isolation and restricted opportunities for colonial research workers" would also be "greatly mitigated if centres of research and learning could be developed in the colonies themselves."[8] This would also solve problems of independence and continuity. Up to this point research had often been seen as a luxury by colonial governments, commissioned as necessary to solve particular problems. Audrey Richards was one of the keenest exponents of the development of regional research institutes in the colonies, and she joined the committee at this time. The biological and agricultural sciences already had established field research stations, but for the social sciences the obvious precedent was the Rhodes-Livingstone Institute in Northern Rhodesia, an independent foundation created five years earlier in 1938 (Schumaker 1999). The institute had been set up at the instigation of the colony's governor (with funding from local mining companies) and with a remit to apply anthropology to problems of social change. Makerere (in Kampala, Uganda) and Achimota (in Ghana), which at that point were government-funded technical colleges, were equally cited as places where research facilities could be built up so as to move from being centers of "vocational training" to "real centres of learning in the Colonies" (ibid.).

At the same time the committee received a memo from a Cambridge academic proposing the funding of "fellowships for research in the pure biological, anthropological and geological sciences" with "specifically applied research in the fields of medicine, agriculture, veterinary science and economic geology to be excluded." Such fellows were to be "nominally stationed at Makerere or Achimota."[9] Given Richards's sympathies, one can detect her hand at work in this memo. Following the successful precedent set by Rockefeller and the International Institute for African Languages and Culture, the idea was well received and Hailey proposed that the treasury be asked to fund five such fellowships each year for outstanding scholars. Max Marwick and Aidan Southall were the first social anthropologists to receive these fellowships. However, a lack of "high quality" candidates (partly because no funding was available for research students) led to a later focus on postgraduate training, and a studentship scheme was established.

The Colonial Social Research Group report emphasized the inadequacies and lacunae in extant knowledge.[10] One of the first recommendations of the report was that "the need for social research in the colonies is evident . . . very few social surveys of general standards of living have been done, and of these hardly any have been in charge of trained investigators. In some colonies no general ethnographic surveys have been made, and there are no descriptive accounts of the chief ethnic groups." Again, one senses the enormity of the task foreseen and yet also the need for such detail for rational welfare and development planning. This group of "experts" went on to recommend the founding of a Social Research Council. Recognizing that "the field of social research is so wide that it cannot easily be covered by any one expert," the group saw this new council as playing a coordinating role in the expansion of the social sciences. Again, the limiting factor was seen as the shortage of people with specialized training. The presumption that "knowledge of a particular language or residence in some particular area is sufficient" qualification for research was gently dismissed. Instead, anthropological expertise and skills in conducting large-scale social surveys were particularly prioritized.

Taking their lead from the Colonial Research Committee, the recommendations went on to focus on employment and training issues, emphasising the shortage of trained staff to carry out the necessary research. Isolation, poor conditions, and short-term funding contracts were all seen as pressing problems. Responding to the question of whether special departments or posts in colonial anthropology should be created, the report recommended that the work should fall within the scope of existing departments in U.K. universities, expanding as necessary to cope with increased training demands. Similarly they felt that creating separate "colonial studies" departments was inappropriate as the topic "can only be approached as part of the general study of the field." Establishing departments of social science at Makerere or Achimota was strongly supported and was seen as an "integral part of future programmes in social research."

The report of the Colonial Social Research Group begins ecumenically, admitting that "we have found it impossible to fix any exact boundaries to the field of social research. Because 'primitive' and 'advanced' communities live 'side by side' in the colonial territories research in the social field must be wider in scope than is usual in this country and investigators of more varied types may be required for it." Caution notwithstanding, this statement goes on to attempt to define anthropology as a broadly inclusive project. Later in the report, however, there is a steady slippage from Hailey's call for a multidisciplinary approach to the narrower concerns of academic anthropology. Noting that "in some cases trained anthropologists have been forced to take up other professions," the authors comment that "it is therefore not surprising that there are now few anthropological field workers with the qualifications necessary to undertake the conduct of one of the large scale ethnographic or general social and economic surveys to which we give priority value." The report ends unequivocally with the importance of making provision for the expansion of anthropology and sociology departments "if the increased demands for training envisaged" were to be met. At this point only Oxford, Cambridge, and London had funded anthropology lectureships. This slippage echoes the tensions between Malinowski's espousal of "practical anthropology" and the growing influence of the "scientific" academic anthropology advocated by the followers of Alfred Radcliffe-Brown. The boundaries of the discipline were still far from settled, and the contest between what we now call "pure" and "applied" versions of anthropology was played out within the council. Such conflicts were key in determining the discipline's future.

This one document closely determined the evolution of the new Colonial Social Science Research Council (CSSRC) and its history over the next eighteen years. Much of the goals and issues developed as planned. Formally appointed by legislation the following year, the CSSRC was the first government body to represent, organize, and fund social sciences, and it played a key role in financing and institutionalizing these embryonic disciplines. At the very moment that social anthropology was converting from an informal "band of brothers" into an expanding academic discipline, the CSSRC provided it with financial support and prestige. This was an optimistic time, reflecting the significant influence that LSE anthropologists like Audrey Richards and Raymond Firth had in the making of government policy.

The CSSRC at Work: Institutes and Grants

The CSSRC wasted no time in developing its ambitions. Its first meeting was an informal one, called in June 1944 at the Colonial Office to discuss Audrey Richards's impending fact-finding visit to East Africa. The particular issue in question was a proposal from the principal of Makerere College to develop a humanities degree with a social science component. Richards had no doubt that, on the contrary, developing a research agenda should be the council's first priority. Citing the lack of literature appropriate for teaching, everyone agreed that "emphasis should rest on research *ab initio*, as this would form the basis of the teaching of social subjects later." Monica Wilson, widow of Godfrey Wilson, the first head of the Rhodes-Livingstone Institute (RLI), was mentioned as a possible person to lead such research. Already the importance of the RLI as a model for a training ground for future generations of anthropologists had been recognized.

The first formal meeting of the council was held a month later, with Carr-Saunders of the LSE as chair, and Raymond Firth (now also an LSE professor) as newly appointed secretary. As he had done the previous month, Carr-Saunders again laid out the extensive work facing the council. This time he also pointed to the lack of an umbrella organization to represent the social sciences, which then led him to call for the "closest liaison" between the disciplines. Procedure was discussed, and it was agreed to not rely on formal subgroups of experts, but rather on each member of the council serving as representative for each of the eight disciplines that had originally submitted reports. Firth later produced a discussion document on the council's general policy, suggesting that "linguistic and socio-economic studies" should be "major aims for systematic research in the first instance, covering successive territories." Firth suggested that this would provide "basic data for colonial governments and for research in other disciplines," and also rapidly secure "a body of personnel with some knowledge of colonial conditions and local research techniques." These surveys "would offer opportunity for collaboration among several disciplines (sociology, anthropology, psychology, economics, statistics)." Where would all this start? Given the importance of regional concentration, wrote Firth, "Africa would appear to be an obvious first choice."[11]

At this first meeting there was also extensive discussion both of the perceived training and employment for colonial researchers and of the relative priorities of the different research fields. Indicative of the discipline's dominance, the minutes noted that "the council was of the opinion that the programme of *anthropological* work was most important, as it formed a basis for so many of the other sciences with which it was necessary that it should be closely associated in field work."[12]

There is little doubt that the members of the CSSRC saw themselves as intellectual pioneers, leading the way both in mapping out uncharted territories of African social research problems and in trail blazing the new possibilities for a problem-oriented multidisciplinary social science. The council met almost monthly, and gradually research priorities began to be established. The first annual report exhaustively lists the series of "major" and "urgent" research needs, including "surveys of social and economic conditions in urban and rural areas," "comparative studies of local government," the "effects of migratory labour," "political development in 'plural' communities," not to mention studies of land tenure and colonial administrative law. The council accepted that the "emphasis on the practical applications of research was appropriate."[13]

As the council began to define its work, Firth was asked to circulate an information memo to the colonial governments. He listed the council's primary functions as "the review of the organisation of research in the social sciences in the colonies (including the selection, training, and terms of service of research workers) ii) the scrutiny of particular schemes of research submitted for approval iii) the initiation of proposals for research in fields not otherwise covered and iv) advice as to the publication of results of research."[14] Of these, the heaviest burden on council members was the administration and selection of research grants. The meetings constantly returned to the issue of the shortage of candidates suitable and willing to work in the colonies. For senior scholars, one problem was the difficulty of obtaining leave from their universities. For more junior researchers, the perceived need was for specialist research training—at this time there were no government funds for anthropology research students.

In the very first meeting of the cssrc, Firth proposed to make a preliminary investigation of possible researchers, suggesting that this task would be more successful if done personally "rather than by a formal questionnaire." The council was agreeable, and with no mention of the inevitable disciplinary bias that would be involved, Firth consulted his colleagues and peers. At the following meeting he reported that he had encountered considerable interest and had collected a list of thirty (unnamed) possible candidates, of which six "had expressed willingness to undertake research work under the auspices of the colonial office." No one on the list was considered of high enough calibre to be awarded one of the colonial research fellowships, and Firth suggested that "they would work best in teams, or under the direction of a senior research worker." Firth envisaged an "emergency" training program for this new cadre of young graduates, with metropolitan universities (he named Cambridge, Oxford, and London; and indeed there were only four U.K. anthropology departments—including both University College (UCL) and LSE in London—in existence until after the war) providing the main source of training, and the regional institutes providing social science research workers with "special knowledge of local conditions." Recognizing the contribution that nonacademics and colonial civil servants had made to the discipline, Firth had another proposal for more senior staff such as administrators or schoolmasters. These people needed "the improvement of theoretical equipment in a subject in which some previous training has been received, but not up to modern standards or not being adequate for research." Treading carefully, he proposed that these were to be "specifically termed 'refresher courses' to save susceptibilities."[15] Firth also advocated that the training should encourage "the expansion of knowledge gained in one discipline into a broader social field. . . . The object here should be to weld on to the specialised equipment of the particular research worker a general knowledge of the principles of social and economic structure which will condition so much of the material he will be required to investigate." Amid the rhetoric of interdisciplinarity and team work, the holistic emphasis on the larger context and structure is undeniably anthropological.

Throughout the 1940s, concern over recruitment and training continued to dominate the CSSRC discussions. As the 1947 annual report noted in the gendered language of the time, "the greatest difficulty may be summarised as that of bringing the right man to the right project in the right place at the right time . . . (but) the chief difficulty is still that of finding the right man." The same concerns were voiced by the Colonial Research Council itself, which noted its concern about the "danger of taking second-rate men because of the shortage of first-rate men," adding that "it would be preferable to let the schemes grow as and when first class workers become available."[16]

There was some dispute in the CSSRC about the need for such formal training schemes and whether this idea fit with the council's remit. Carr-Saunders expressed the nonanthropologists' concern about the youth and inexperience of the candidates, such that it "would be quite impossible to allow most of them to go out to the colonies and work independently, even after a period of training."[17] Firth responded by insisting that training would be strictly short term, and without which it would be "impossible to meet the demands which would be made" for sociological researchers. A compromise was agreed: the scheme would be set up, but each application would be submitted to the council for consideration of details of pay, leave, length of training, and so on. Thus in 1947 the CSSRC awarded the first twelve postgraduate studentships. These grants provided six to twelve months of research training, following which students "were required to undertake a specific priority research project of about two year's duration, in one or other of the Colonial territories." The training was deliberately not tied to a specific project in advance, for it was recognized that candidates "may yet have no clear ideas of the exact field of research for which their aptitudes fit them, or of the locality or problem to which they would be most attracted."[18] Among the first students were M. G. Smith, Edwin Ardener, Philip Gardener, John Middleton, and Frank Girling, who subsequently made important contributions to social anthropology. The following year the scheme was extended, somewhat controversially, to allow Fulbright scholars and other American students to receive training at British universities in preparation for "field work in the colonies." In total, twenty-one students received these studentships, and by 1951 the CSSRC annual report showed that the council was much more confident about the recruitment situation, noting that the "field for junior appointments to regional Research Institutes appears to be fairly large." The council awarded few further research fellowships and by 1955 announced that the funds available for individual research were "severely limited," with priority increasingly accorded to the research institutes. Chilver suggested that "it was felt that the discipline had been given a shove," and should now be developing its own resources.[19]

The development of the four regional institutes was the second key function of the CSSRC, and over the fifteen-year period they eventually consumed more than a million pounds of the council's budget, twice as much as that directed at individual research projects. Even the very first meeting of the council in 1944 focused primarily on Max Gluckman's plans to expand the Rhodes-Livingstone Institute in Northern Rhodesia. This organization differed from the others, having been set up as an independent social science research institute in 1938 unattached to a university, but its importance lay in the precedent that it set for the council's own plans for further regional institutes in West and East Africa and the Caribbean. Yet the process of setting up regional centers for social studies was far from straightforward. To whom would they be accountable? Should they be part of the university colleges, or wholly separate? Should Colonial Development and Welfare Act funding go into buildings and infrastructure? Could high quality staff be recruited? In what follows, I focus particularly on Makerere: the plans for the East African Institute for Social Research (EAISR) were the first to develop and were always the most ambitious of the regional research institutes.

Establishing such an institute at Makerere College meant intervening in the fraught politics of regional colonial policy: this was a university college for the whole of East Africa but was located in Uganda, and many were against any attempt at creating an East African federation. There was also institutional politics to attend to. The 1944 Asquith Commission on Higher Education had unequivocally recommended the development of such institutes, but also had strongly advised against the creation of a 'semi-independent' social science unit at Makerere, which might diminish "the authority and prestige of the university."[20] Audrey Richards, the key council advocate for the institutes, was rather differently minded. After her visit to Uganda in 1944 she made a strong case for "a separate institute, that the staff should be free from routine teaching duties, and that the Director should have power to frame research programmes." Such dissension from official policy had to be justified, and the council developed the case that the effective teaching of social studies depended first on the accumulation of "a body of knowledge on sociological and kindred matters in East Africa."[21] Prioritizing research was a way to avoid the danger that staff would have to "devote an undue proportion of their time to routine teaching duties," while still allowing the eventual aim of merging the institute into the university.

A well-resourced research institute was envisaged—equipped with staff, dwellings, and offices. Appropriate candidates for the director were sought out. Raymond Firth recommended William Stanner, an Australian anthropologist who had been a member of Malinowski's seminar. However, strong reservations about Stanner were expressed by the governor of Uganda. These included the concern that he had no economic training, and that in "view of the recent conversion to Christianity of Africans in Uganda it was also advisable that he should not be a militant rationalist." He was nevertheless selected, and he eventually paid a visit to Makerere in 1948 to report on the progress made with the institute. His feedback made much of the enormous political complexities of the situation, questioning even the wisdom of its implementation. This was exactly what the committee did not want to hear, and there was much discussion of other possible locations and of ways of surmounting the difficulties that Stanner seemed to be presenting. Gluckman was secretly pleased, and wrote in 1948 from Oxford in "semi-confidence" to Clyde Mitchell to say that "Stanner has recommended, we hear, that the Makerere Institute be dropped which leaves us unique."[22] Stanner eventually resigned in 1949 and was replaced by Audrey Richards, the initial architect of the EAISR.

Funding by CSSRC was divided up in several ways. Grants were given to individuals for a variety of research topics, ranging within anthropology from studies of African land tenure systems to linguistics, local economies, and "traditional" law. Funding for the regional institutes was less tied to particular research projects. Support was also initially given to the International Institute of African Languages and Cultures to continue its extensive research surveys, including the "Handbook of African Languages" and the "Ethnographic Survey of Africa." While the institute was entirely separate from the London School of Economics, Malinowski's involvement in its founding no doubt contributed to the growing anthropological perception that the CSSRC, given the prominent roles of Firth and Richards, was an LSE affair.

The CSSRC and Anthropology

The history of relations between the CSSRC and anthropology is fascinating. It reveals many of the tensions between the metropolitan academic agenda and the council's more direct concern with colonial "social problems." Given that many key disciplinary figures were on one of the CSSRC committees or were involved with the regional institutes, the disputes also reveal political disagreements between individuals over the appropriate stance for anthropology to take in relation to colonial affairs. A key rift developed between LSE and Oxford, partly fostered by Gluckman's skepticism about a research program too closely directed by the colonial office. As early as 1946, Audrey Richards expressed her concern to her CSSRC colleague Raymond Firth about a seeming lack of commitment from anthropologists to developing regional research infrastructures. Max Gluckman, she writes, "wants to get all the research workers over to England with him—to give them what he calls training in Oxford, preferably for a year." She goes on to suggest that his rationalization for avoiding "the trouble of going back to the field" is his view that "local centres are bad, that short periods of field work are better than long, that there is too much field work being done and not enough theory, and that anyone who works on a government project is betraying their science!" She concludes: "I don't think the Council ought to agree to letting all the research fellows come back for a year to Oxford because Gluckman doesn't want to be in Rhodesia. It seems to me to be a bad precedent, and at present I even think that the Oxford atmosphere of 'down with applied anthropology' and their emphasis on the fact that the climate of Africa is dangerous would not be very good." She ends by pointing out the significance of the move: "I think it is important because it will mean, I fear, the abandonment of our whole local centre policy if we give in on this."[23]

Gluckman had already been frank in his expression of views in another public forum—the Association of Social Anthropologists. In a written response to a memo from Evans-Pritchard proposing the creation of this new association in spring 1946, Gluckman highlighted the "grave danger that the demands of colonial governments for research workers may lead to an excessive concentration on practical problems, to the detriment of basic research, and to the lowering of professional standards and status which would lose the gains of the last 20 years" (Goody 1995). He already knew both of Evans-Pritchard's long antipathy toward Audrey Richards and of his suspicion of applied anthropology, both legacies, Jack Goody suggests, of Evans-Pritchard's animosity with Malinowski.

These differences were openly aired in the next meeting of the council, which was attended by Max Gluckman. In response to the council's view of the importance of the regional institutes, Gluckman argued that it depended on the facilities available, and that at the RLI "there was nothing which could be described as a University atmosphere, and in his opinion the function of a regional institute was to act as an advance base from which to conduct field work rather than as a centre of academic training or excellence." The chair pointed out that the whole purpose of the scheme was to create "regional universities comparable in standing to Universities at home," while Firth accused him of hoping to draw up a plan of local research by "remote control." While arguing for increased funds for the RLI, Gluckman again insisted on the "intellectual stimulus of the home universities" for writing up.[24]

The argument moved on to the relationship of research institutes to "government planning in colonial territories and the problem of applied research to which this gives rise." While everyone agreed that research institutes should concentrate on basic research and "should not obtrude their advice unasked upon territorial governments," Gluckman disagreed with the council's view "that if their assistance was sought in connection with particular investigations . . . they could contribute much and should be ready to do so." The issue was left unresolved. Despite the tensions, and the coded reservations expressed by Firth and Richards about Gluckman "overstretching himself" in the rapid expansion of the RLI, it was agreed to support the RLI plans. No doubt the argument was partly motivated by the interdepartmental rivalry between Oxford and LSE, but it also was the result of fundamentally different attitudes to the role and future possibilities for anthropology in the colonies. In adopting a more avowedly anticolonial stance, Gluckman perhaps missed the opportunity to open up a higher education institute and encourage independent research capacity during the tensions of the federation.

By the late 1940s the relationships between Oxford and LSE as the leading anthropology departments of their day became even more strained. As well as the differing theoretical positions and views on the importance of "applying" social research, the perceived LSE bias of the CSSRC made many in the group unhappy. Richards was alert to this possibility, and in 1946 she wrote to Firth regarding a query he made about CSSRC funding for an LSE research fellow to work in Jamaica. In an aside, she notes that "so far the very strong representation of the School on the CSSRC and CRC has been defensible in part by the fact that we have been responsible for allocation of large sums to other bodies, but not to our own. . . . [This] might be interpreted as letting ourselves in on the ground floor of West Indies social research."[25] Firth later noted, though, that however much the group thought that it was "working in the interests of the profession as a whole, it must have appeared to others that our efforts were too London-based or not strong enough in the face of the other disciplines represented on the council" (1986). In an interview, Firth recalled how he had been warned by Richards's hint that the preponderance of LSE staff on the council would cause jealousy, and he regrets how he had not taken this warning more seriously. Antipathy toward the LSE was both motivated by memories of Malinowski's earlier dominance of the profession (and its funding) and by the view from the Oxford camp that the priority was the discipline's professional status within the academy. The Association of Social Anthropologists of the Commonwealth (ASA)—the scholarly association for academic anthropologists, in pointed distinction to the inclusivity of the RAI—was established the same year by Evans-Pritchard in Oxford.

The split was a vituperative one, with Max Gluckman in Oxford writing a stormy letter to Audrey Richards attacking the LSE "mafia." While he subsequently retracted his outburst, her initial response is fascinating:

> Only Max I do hope this is not going to be a personal quarrel. I disagree with some of the Oxford developments but Firth and I have strenuously stood against the idea that there are two camps. We won't let the students group

themselves like this and we lecture on and discuss both Fortes and EP's [Evans-Pritchard's] material. We certainly kept up our personal relations at the ASA in July. So what is all this talk about 'smashing your influence.' For God's sake don't let us become like two sets of psycho-analysts who turn their scientific hypotheses into religious faiths that you must accept or perish and won't associate with unbelievers. We shall certainly hope that you and some of your ex-team will come up to seminars in London and that any of our East African PhDs will come to Oxford and see you. Perhaps I write with some tone of injury too. I think it is that both EP and Fortes have decided that Council is dominated entirely by the LSE and that they are shut out from it. They admit that they aren't prepared to go on the council or do the extremely heavy work that we have done these last years. (I reckon about ⅓ of my time goes on it in term time). But I don't think they give credit to the fact that if I hadn't fought in the Colonial Office for so long there wouldn't have been any money for anthropology at all. Hence when you make entirely baseless charges I suppose the WORM begins to turn though disclaiming that it has been prodded at all! Well anyhow, for heavens sake don't let us fight![26]

The disagreement spilled out in a heated debate in an ASA business meeting in July 1948. Discussed under "other business," a stoutly worded resolution was passed stating that "the present organisation for the expenditures of funds from the Colonial Development and Welfare fund on anthropological research is not in the best interests of anthropology and its application to colonial problems." The minutes continued, stating that "the interests of anthropology should be represented by persons nominated by the Association," and instructed the secretary to write to the secretary of state to ask him to receive the president of the association, "who would put to him the reasons why the Association had come to these conclusions."[27] When put to the vote the LSE contingent—Firth, Read, Kaberry, and Mair—all abstained, suggesting that the motion was led by Oxford.

Despite the abstentions, a meeting between Secretary of State Creech-Jones and Radcliffe-Brown was sought, and was granted the following month. It is indicative of the influence of the discipline's leading figures at this time that their proposals were treated with such seriousness by the Colonial Office. It is hard to imagine such a meeting occurring even ten years later. A lengthy and uncompromising aide-memoire was sent to the secretary of state regarding the funding of anthropological research. The ASA document made a series of demands, calling first for "a consultative panel consisting of the professors of anthropology of Oxford, Cambridge, the LSE and UCL [University College London] of the London university, which should be consulted with regard to all projects for anthropological research." It went on to ask that any "research worker financed by the committee on social research should be attached to a university department of anthropology during the period of his training and research." These demands served to consolidate not only the discipline but also its oldest departments. The final point was the most controversial, claiming an anthropological monopoly over methodological competence in colonial social research:

> It is said that the majority of the research projects accepted by the committee on social research have in fact been such as can only be effectively carried out by anthropologists. It is desirable that in appointing any person to carry out such projects two things must be taken into consideration: *a) that the person appointed should, before taking up research, have received a thorough training in general social anthropology; b) that before being required to devote attention to some particular problem in which knowledge is required for administration purposes, he should be given sufficient time (in most instances a year) to make a general sociological study of the people or area with which he is concerned.*[28]

In the meeting Radcliffe-Brown, as honorary president, explained that the ASA's main concern was to have more professional control over funding decisions. The Colonial Office response was surprisingly amenable to several of the ideas, including that of a consultative "subject" panel. It recommended in the first instance that its members should be those of the council with a qualification in anthropology, plus those other professors at Oxford, Cambridge, LSE, and UCL not presently on the CSSRC. As a result, a social anthropology and sociology subcommittee panel was subsequently set up, with Evans-Pritchard, Hutton, and Fortes as additional members. This subcommittee panel served as a model for other subject panels, replacing the previous regional committees of the council. Yet anthropology's purism over its particular academic approach to colonial research did not go unchallenged. The Colonial Office memo ended strongly, saying that it "cannot accept the suggestion that the majority of the research projects accepted and recommended by the council have in fact been such as can only be effectively carried out by anthropologists," and that the "final recommendations" would rest with the council and not the consultative panel.

Despite such statements, there is no doubt that these new subject panels signaled the increasing power of British anthropology departments and metropolitan disciplinary agendas over the "colonial social problem" focus of the council. The huge increase in postwar funding for British higher education assured anthropology the institutional security and confidence of an academic identity, even if Colonial Office patronage and the training offered by the regional institutes such as the RLI were still key to the reproduction of the discipline.

The 1950s: Consolidation or Conflict?

By the end of the 1940s, a good deal of individual social research had been commissioned by the CSSRC. Examples in Africa included research on land tenure in Nigeria by Meek and on Basutoland by Sheddick; on native administration in Northern Rhodesia by Epstein and Nyasaland by Mair; and on social organization of the Nandi by Huntingford, the Hausa by M. G. Smith, and the Tiv by Bohannan. Many of these studies had more theoretical influence within the discipline than direct policy relevance. Inevitably, perhaps, given the extant theoretical fashion, many of these studies were holistic accounts of single ethnic groups. Where survey work was conducted, it was usually at the household or local level, for few of the anthropologists were equipped to carry out the territory-wide quantitative surveys that might have been more necessary for national planning purposes. Information coverage was inevitably selective and partial, and hardly served the comprehensive and strategic welfare and developmental blueprint originally envisaged by some in the Colonial Office.

In the 1950s the work of the council gradually changed, particularly as colonial governments were increasingly encouraged to organize their own research into local "problems." Funding by the CSSRC concentrated on the institutes' own research programs and few individual grants were awarded. Yet conflicting interpretations of the council's remit continued. The new anthropology and sociology subcommittee began to meet in 1949, mostly to discuss applications for research fellowships. The initial chair was Godfrey Thomson, but on his resignation in 1950 Evans-Pritchard became chair. Audrey Richards, who was by this time at Makerere running the East African Institute for Social Research, confided her fears about the new chair with Sally Chilver, the CSSRC secretary of the time: "I am depressed because he [Evans-Pritchard] is dead set against local institutes and has made no secret of that. He will vote and finally win his way of getting large grants to English universities, no questions asked and no results expected and those of us who have tried to play the Colonial Office fair will feel HAD."[29] Quite apart from the institutional rivalry and Richard's sense that "the ordinary rules of fair play don't work with him," her main concern was with Evans-Pritchard's dislike of the principle of the devolution of research agendas to the regional institutes like the RLI and the EAISR. Evans-Pritchard's view, echoed by Gluckman, that researchers should return to their "home" universities in the United Kingdom for a six-month break during fieldwork, negated one of the principal rationales for the institutes. The argument revealed not only methodological disagreements but also fundamental political conflicts over disciplinary priorities and what "professionalisation" entailed. Paradoxically, the consolidation of the discipline in U.K. universities depended on this new generation of scholars receiving CSSRC funding for training and fieldwork.

Subsequent letters between Richards and Chilver hint at continuing tensions in the council over the huge funding costs of the regional research institutes, especially as the West African institute became increasingly mired in regional infighting. One might argue that the original insistence on strategic and rational development planning increasingly—and perhaps inevitably—became subsumed within conflicting institutional and academic agendas. In one of Evans-Pritchard's oral reports from the anthropology and sociology subcommittee, he announced that they had strongly recommended that any savings available should be devoted to "independent schemes of research" in areas outside those covered by the institutes' activities or the "special interests" they had developed.[30] Even the chair, the LSE director Carr-Saunders, began to turn against the idea of such institutes, and the view developed that these should be more closely integrated within the new universities. Richards, however, felt that EAISR could train students far more cheaply than otherwise, and that "all the preliminary negotiations and muddles with governments which most other academic research workers have are avoided because we now have good relations with all three Governments." In her letters Richards reflected acutely and wittily on council micropolitics and on the likely sources of opposition, one time writing to Chilver that "I have already told Perham that it is cheaper to finance an Institute than a Scarborough student [referring to a new set of government-funded studentships], and I hope she is smoking that in her pipe." Richards had on her side a well-established set of networks in the Colonial Office, and with Chilver's help she continued to win financial backing for the institutes.

These rivalries developed a new dimension in the 1950s with Gluckman's appointment in Manchester and his growing estrangement from Evans-Pritchard. With the research base and fieldwork access through the RLI a key to Manchester's success at attracting new students, he too began to fear for its future funding. "E-P [Evans-Pritchard] has the will only to exploit the RLI for his students," wrote Gluckman in 1955 to Clyde Mitchell, "and would be pleased if the show broke up and was a failure—since he has publicly stated that research cannot be done well from the Institutes but only from universities. Since in fact the RLI is turning out far better work than Oxford, it would suit him to get a bad Director who would break the show up."[31] The same year Gluckman accused Evans-Pritchard of spreading a rumor that Bill Epstein, one of Gluckman's students, was a card-carrying Communist (and therefore unacceptable as an employee to the RLI trustees).

Whether or not Evans-Pritchard was behind such a slander, Gluckman took the matter deadly seriously, writing at great length to the Northern Rhodesian governor, head of the board of trustees, in order to prevent the rumor from being used as a pretext for wresting control of the institute from the anthropological community. His attempt, however, failed. The CSSRC had at the same time been putting pressure on the institute to develop a closer relationship with the university, and the institute's trustees used the events as a way of appointing a new director who would be more amenable to government influence at a time of growing political unrest in the territory. Henry Fosbrooke, an ex-government sociologist in Tanzania, was appointed in 1955, to the dismay of Gluckman, Mitchell, and others who recognized that the academic freedom of the institute would be increasingly limited. As Mitchell wrote at the time: "In a real test situation like this the CSSRC is powerless for the simple reason that the Trustees decided that they would not consult the CSSRC—for obvious reasons: they knew it would recommend someone on academic grounds not on extraneous grounds—RLI—Rest in Peace." Two years later, as Gluckman finally accepted that his influence had waned and that the "RLI is going to become an adjunct to government," he decided to withdraw all support and contact with the institute.[32] By this time he was leading a highly successful and expanding department in Manchester, and many of his students were working on research projects within the United Kingdom. Gluckman now had less need of the RLI.

The implications of the decrease in council funds available for individual researchers for anthropology should also be seen in the larger context of higher education expansion in the United Kingdom. The Scarborough commission on African and Oriental studies in 1947 had recommended boosting the research capacity and expanding of area studies departments. At the same time the Clapham commission on social science provision (Clapham 1947) had explicitly recommended that the time was not yet right to constitute a U.K.-based social science research council, and that the money instead should be spent on consolidation through earmarked projects and capital grants to institutions. Several new anthropology departments, including Manchester, Durham, and Edinburgh were established as a result, along with new lectureships in existing departments. The discipline was institutionally secure as never before. Yet this expansion was not matched by increased funding for students. Once the sixteen students recruited into the colonial studentship scheme had finished, there was suddenly a dearth of postgraduate funding—a problem that was to occupy ASA throughout the 1950s.

This situation exposed anthropology's reliance on the CSSRC for its students training, and it was not resolved until a new Social Science Research Council was finally established in 1965 at the recommendation of the Heyworth commission (Heyworth 1965). Yet this council, mindful of its remit to produce "useful" knowledge, saw its remit exclusively as British-based social science research. The anthropologists' growing sense of frustration spilt into a submission to the Robbins committee on higher education in 1962 on behalf of sociology and social anthropology. Glass and Gluckman described the constant search for grants for young scholars leading to "senior teachers having to spend a large proportion of their time searching, cap in hand, for small amounts of money from diverse sources" (Glass and Gluckman 1962).

Later still, the Social Science Research Council (the CSSRC's successor) acknowledged in 1968 this change in disciplinary fortune, pointing out that the "present situation with regard to field research by professional social anthropologists is a somewhat static one. Indeed, there are indications that there may be a falling off compared with the very rapid expansion of field research in the fifties" (SSRC 1968). The organization went on to blame this partly on the ending of CSSRC and treasury research grants and studentships. The situation was amelioriated in the same year by the SSRC's own studentship program, but disciplinary nostalgia proved more difficult to cure.

And the Fall . . .

By the mid-1950s the African winds of change were blowing with storm force. If the strength of anticolonial sentiment had been hard to predict, so too was the future of the CSSRC. Riots in Accra in 1948 and in Kampala in 1949, along with the Mau-Mau rebellion in early 1950s Kenya, upset all the cautious timetables for gradual self-government. As Sally Chilver commented, the attitude in the Colonial Office began to shift, with the attitude developing that one had to get out "without getting one's tail caught in the door."[33] These political changes were initially little reflected in the research proposals and programs put before the council. Most of the single-focus ethnographic and sociological surveys continued as before. Audrey Richards provides an interesting example. She kept a careful diary of the political intrigue surrounding the Kabaka's expulsion and subsequent return to Uganda. Yet she published little on the topic. Her Carnegie-funded "Leadership" project at Makerere continued, and her contributions to Faller's *All the King's Men* (Richards 1964) on the Buganda polity made no mention of the complexity of nationalist and anticolonial politics. Only by the late 1950s did the council's attitude begin to change, and it initiated a program of "comparative studies of election procedures," leading to studies of a number of African elections, which involved Lucy Mair and others.

A significant proportion of the remaining council funding supported the production of regional histories. These included the multiauthored three-volume history of East Africa under Donald Low's editorship (1963–1976). The council's energy was also directed toward incorporating the research institutes more closely with the university colleges. During the same period, a new Applied Research Unit was established at the East African Institute for Social Research. This unit was funded by the Ford Foundation, reflecting the increasing dominance of American funding and pragmatic policy interests.

Audrey Richards, now back on the council after completing her five-year appointment at Makerere, received in December 1956 an ominous letter from Arnold Plant, chair of the cssrc. "What I have been trying to decide," he begins, "is whether there is a special case for continuing Treasury finance for Colonial research in this field." His letter reveals how the council was perceived. "I have been thinking about the special problem of ex-dependencies which are attaining independence. I expect the colonial office and the Treasury will be very concerned to avoid involvement in continuing finance, which scientists may wish to see as a corrective to 'misinterpretations of nationalism.' They may feel that any finance . . . [is] likely to be misinterpreted as interference if the UK government puts up the money. I am very likely prickly about this, but I know in another field of an attempt to secure Treasury aid which is being deliberately routed through the British Academy in order that any monies given to scientific research purposes will not be traced back to the Treasury with an implication that they are initiated by UK Government interests."[34] Plant's concern at being viewed as trying to correct "misinterpretations of nationalism" reveals the growing suspicion of colonial-sponsored social research. The possibility of covert indirect funding and the fear of being accused of political interference are indicative of the mood of the times.

Richards was unwilling to accept the full implications of this new political landscape. In her letters to Plant she once again reiterated the importance of ensuring the continuity of research in the social sciences, calling for a "rather energetic re-examination of the whole position of colonial research." Her views on the potentials for research in newly independent states are also deeply revealing. "There are already signs," she wrote in November 1956, "that the new Governments wish to control research in the cultural and historical fields and that they sometimes have objectives beyond those of pure scholarship. Nor are they yet aware of the qualifications needed for directors of research schemes. By continuing to make grants for even a skeleton staff of local administration of research, some measure of control of appointments of this sort would remain in the hands of persons academically qualified, whether in this country or overseas, and a tradition of scholarship might be established."[35]

Aware now of the threat to the future of the CSSRC, Richards immediately began mobilizing her contacts. One of her main arguments in favor of continued colonial funding of the research institutes was that this would preserve their academic freedom. She wrote to her old friend Andrew Cohen, by now governor of Uganda, expressing her concern about the demise of grants to the institutes: "The point is that the social sciences are new in the colonies. They have no government department which understands what they are doing, such as the medical research workers, agriculturalists etc have. They are liable to be concerned with questions of social policy which are controversial and which it would be tempting for the governments of newly self-governing territories, such as the Gold Coast, to try to run." The irony of this statement seems lost on Richards. She goes on to give the example of a Nigerian director "whose motives seem entirely political." In a separate enclosed informal letter to Cohen, she is even more blunt in her recidivist assessment of postcolonial governance: "The universities want local autonomy over social research and to have this research under their own aegis. This means in effect that they will keep their autonomy but do no research."[36]

Ever energetic, Richards fired off numerous letters and began to develop an idea for an organization to replace the CSSRC. She also lobbied for the CSSRC to take a stronger position against its likely demise, which led to a widely circulated 1961 memo that expressed the council's great concern at the likely "break" in the field of social science research, and proposed continued support "for UK scientists to undertake research in the social sciences in colonial territories which become independent." The council firmly recommended its reconstitution as an advisory body to the new Department for Technical Co-operation. The consequences of not doing so included the veiled threat of American and Soviet academic dominance, with "the leading position and international influence of the UK in the study of the social sciences . . . lost to other countries." The memo went on to suggest that the institutes would be under heavy pressure to meet research needs "of immediate practical interest" at the expense of dealing with "the fundamental problems of under-developed countries." This was a paradoxical moment at which to emphasize the institutes' detachment from their applied roots. Despite the strong words, little came of the proposal, and the council wound up its affairs.

Conclusion: Anthropology and the End of Empire

In 1977 the LSE held a series of retrospective seminars exploring the experiences of British anthropologists working in colonial contexts. Richards, Firth, and Chilver all presented papers. They found themselves swimming against a dominant post-Vietnam current that, in a particular reading of texts like Asad (1973), increasingly viewed academic anthropology as simply having been a handmaiden of colonialism. Such a gendered caricature is unfair, reliant as it was on the retrospective presumption of a pure/applied dichotomy that perhaps only made sense from the perspective of a now professionalized academy. It also collapses a number of different historical moments, for as Richards notes, "before the second world war . . . the colonial office . . . gave no financial support to anthropological or any other kind of social science research and might almost be said to be famous for not doing so" (1977: 169). Finally, the caricature does not capture, as described in this essay, the diverse involvement and contradictory political agendas—whether among anthropologists, in the Colonial Office, or in the colonies themselves. Many anthropologists were both ambiguous and tactical in their relationships with colonial authorities; some, like Richards and Firth, negotiated a multiplicity of roles. The focus in this sort of critique, as Peter Pels and Oscar Salemink (1999: n.p.) note, is on "the colonial complicity of *academic* anthropologists" at a time when the "academy" was far from being an established anthropological habitat. If, following Pels and Salemink, we attend to the way "professional methods emerged in direct competition with extra-academic ethnographies," then we can regard academic anthropology as only one aspect of a much broader nexus of ethnographic practices, including those of colonial administrators, missionaries, and independent travelers.

At a general level Stocking is of course right in accepting that "colonialism was a critically important context for the development of anthropology" (1996: 368). Yet this is only the start, not the end, of the explanation. Certainly, as he notes, "important groups within the world of colonial administration had shown themselves willing to accept the scientific status and the utilitarian promissory note of social anthropology" (420). Yet at different moments, the various protagonists played down this possible utility, instead emphasizing the importance of fundamental research. Anthropologists were not alone in this regard, for the CSSRC also played on this rhetorical opposition when it suited them. At one moment Richards describes the CSSRC as "do-gooders trying to organise research which would increase the knowledge we felt to be helpful for 'welfare and development' "; at the next, she emphasises the irrelevance of this work, noting how young anthropologists involved in detailed studies "were learning their jobs . . . and had not the competence to pronounce on the problems of the colony as a whole" (1977: 178). Goody merely revisits this debate when he challenges Kuklick's "globalising" critique of prewar British anthropology and what he calls the presumption that "intellectual traditions are tightly isomorphous with sociopolitical processes" (1995: n.p.). His protestations and counterexamples are significant, but they remain exceptions to a larger set of political rules. Intellectual traditions are always also institutional and political histories.

What were the long-term consequences of colonial patronage for social anthropology? Richards suggests that "the suddenness with which considerable funds became available had . . . dramatic effects which would not have been achieved by a series of small grants" (1977: 186). Anthropology's presence and status within the universities was immeasurably bolstered by the volume of research funding received from the CSSRC. By 1953 there were thirty-eight teaching positions in social anthropology in the United Kingdom (Kuper 1973), an impressive expansion given that up until that moment

in 1937 when Oxford was "taken over" (80), social anthropology was syn-
onymous with the LSE. Much of this expansion came through the creation of
new departments at the School of Oriental and African Studies at the University of London, and at Manchester and Edinburgh, but it also depended
on Colonial Office funding of doctoral and postdoctoral research. As Edwin
Ardener and Shirley Ardener note, "the 'professionalisation' of the discipline
for which the pre-war generation worked was over-whelmingly realised in
the post-war 'bulge'" (1965: 303). Important as university posts were, the
reproduction and expansion of the discipline depended primarily on finding funding for its students.

Here, then, lies the theory/practice paradox at the heart of anthropology's
identity. In order to define itself as first and foremost a metropolitan academic discipline, its practitioners sought to construct a "monopoly of competence" (L'Estoile 1997b) over the study of colonial social change. Anthropology's preeminence within the CSSRC relied on its successful practice of
reformulating "social problems" as scientific ones. The reproduction of its
theoretical credibility and vitality depended on political, financial, and epistemological support from colonial authorities for its research agendas and
fieldworkers. Kuper's (1996: 117) assertion that the "winding up of the CSSRC
did not have much impact" on anthropology does not fully capture the
importance of this symbiosis. The end of empire was also the end of a
complex set of political relations linking scholarly practice with the production of knowledge. It created a lacuna that was only partly filled by the later
emergence of "development" and its new discourse of social change (Ferguson 1997). In the meantime, by working within the ambit of the CSSRC,
anthropologists developed a "monopoly of competence" within a field of
practice that suddenly disappeared. The subsequent identity crisis continues
to define the discipline.

Notes

I would like to thank both Sir Raymond Firth and Sally Chilvers for their help
during the writing of this paper, and Benoît de L'Estoile for his editorial comments.
The financial support of the Leverhulme Foundation and the British Academy is
also gratefully acknowledged.

    1 My account extends beyond 1945 the important social histories of British
anthropology carried out by Kuklick (1992) and Stocking (1996) and complements

the influential synoptic work carried out by Kuper (1996, 1999b). I sketch the larger colonial context surrounding the institutional and intellectual histories of the Rhodes-Livingstone Institute by Brown (1973) and Schumaker (1996, 1999), and reinforce the insistence by Pels and Salemink (1999: 1) that one should not back project the "self-image of twentieth century academic anthropology onto all ethnographic activities that played a role in the formation of the discipline." Through a careful historicization, I add complexity to the vexed debate (Goody 1995, in reference to Kuklick 1992) about anthropology's importance for, and complicity within, the colonial endeavor. The easy characterization of anthropology as handmaiden to colonial rule is no longer possible, and it is the changing historical fortunes of this complex and ambivalent relationship that I seek to uncover.

2 Perham papers, file 685/2, Rhodes House, Oxford.

3 CO 927/1/3, Public Records Office, Surrey (hereafter referred to as PRO).

4 MacDonald to Hailey, 18 March 1940, Brit. Emp. Mss. 342, Rhodes House.

5 MacDonald to Hailey, 18 April 1940, Brit. Emp. Mss. 342.

6 Hailey to MacDonald, 3 May 1940, Brit. Emp. Mss. 342.

7 Colonial Research Committee, first Annual Report, 1943–44, Cmnd. 6535.

8 Colonial Research Council, Progress Report 1942–1943, London School of Economics archives (hereafter referred to as LSE).

9 CO 927/2/1—CRC paper 1943 (57), PRO.

10 Perham papers, file 685/9, Rhodes House.

11 Firth papers, file 2/2, LSE.

12 CSSRC, file 1944, LSE.

13 Colonial Research Committee, First Annual Report, 1943–44, p. 27, Cmnd. 6535.

14 CSSRC, file (44)24, LSE.

15 Memo on training, CSSRC, file 45(3), LSE.

16 Colonial Research Council, 1st meeting of council, 1948 minute 2, 1948, LSE.

17 CSSRC files, minutes of the 8th meeting, 1944, LSE.

18 CSSRC files, Annual report, LSE.

19 Interview by author, 6 March 2000.

20 Asquith Commission, Cmnd. 6647, p. 17.

21 CSSRC files, minutes of the 11th meeting, July 1945.

22 Gluckman to Mitchell, 1 July 1948, Mitchell papers, Mss 1998 5/1 27, Rhodes House.

23 Richards to Firth, 12 August 1946, Firth papers, file 2/3, LSE.

24 CSSRC files, minutes of the 20th meeting (46)27, LSE.

25 Richards to Firth, 12 August 1946, Firth papers, file 2/3, LSE.

26 Richards to Gluckman, 4 November 1948, Richards papers, file 16/19, LSE.

27 ASA papers, file A1/1, LSE.

28 CSSRC, file (48)62, LSE.

29 Richards to Chilver, 14 November 1950, Richards papers, file 16/7, LSE.

30 CSSRC files, meeting minutes, autumn 1952.

31 Gluckman to Mitchell, 16 February 1955, Mitchell MSS box 2 fol. 56, Rhodes House.

32 Gluckman to Mitchell, 8 July 1957, Mitchell MSS box 2 fol. 206, Rhodes House.

33 Interview by author, 6 March 2000.

34 Plant to Richards, 4 December 1956, Richards papers, file 16/11, LSE.

35 Richards to Plant, 12 November 1956, Richards papers, file 16/11, LSE.

36 Richards to Cohen, 3 December 1956, Richards papers, file 16/11, LSE.

Claudio Lomnitz

BORDERING ON ANTHROPOLOGY

Dialectics of a National Tradition in Mexico

The current sense of crisis in U.S. and European anthropology has been widely debated. Beginning with a series of criticisms of the connections between anthropology and imperialism in the 1970s, the critique of anthropology moved to deeper epistemological terrain by interrogating the narrative strategies used by ethnographers to build up their scientific authority and their role in shaping colonial discourses of self and other. The field of anthropology in the United States and Europe is still reverberating from these discussions.[1]

Less well known and less understood, perhaps, is the quieter sense of unease and transformation in anthropological traditions that I refer to here as "national anthropologies." I use this term to indicate anthropological traditions that have been fostered by educational and cultural institutions for the development of studies of their own nation. In this essay I provide a historical interpretation of the gestation of the current malaise in one national tradition, which is Mexican anthropology.[2]

Peripheral nations with early dates of national independence, such as most countries of Latin America, have had national traditions of anthropology that evolved in tandem with European and American anthropology from its inception. The histories of these national anthropologies are still not very well known, in part because of the disjunction between the ways that anthropology is taught in the great metropolitan centers and in national anthropological traditions. Whereas in Britain, France, and the United States anthropological histories are traced back in time within their native traditions, national anthropologies often emphasize ties with great foreign scholars, thereby placing them within a civilizational horizon whose vanguard is abroad. Commenting on this phenomenon, Darcy Ribeiro (1979) once said that his fellow Brazilian anthropologists were *cavalos de santo* (mediums who spoke for their mentors in Europe or the United States). The works of anthropologists of the national traditions thus often appear to be discontinuous with each other. To use an illustration from Mexico, the influence of Franz Boas on Manuel Gamio and of Auguste Comte on the earlier Alfredo Chavero tends to mask the genealogical relations between Gamio and Chavero.

It is therefore not surprising that although the existence of this class of national anthropologies is well known it has not been sufficiently theorized. How does a discipline that owes so much to imperial expansion and globalization—indeed a discipline that has often conceived of itself as the study of racial or cultural others—thrive when its objects of study are the anthropologist's co-nationals? How are theories and methods that are developed in American or European anthropologies deployed in these national traditions? Is there a relationship between the current transformations of national anthropologies and "the crisis of anthropology" writ large?

The study of Mexican anthropology is instructive for the broader class of national anthropologies, because Mexico developed one of the earliest and most successful and internationally influential national anthropologies.[3] The institutional infrastructure of Mexican anthropology is one of the world's largest, and its political centrality within the country has been remarkable. This is linked both to the critical role that Mexico's archaeological patrimony has played in Mexican nationalism and to anthropology's prominent role in shaping national development.

On the other hand, the sense of crisis in contemporary Mexican anthropology moves between two related concerns: the high degree of incorporation of anthropology and anthropologists into the workings and designs of the state, and the isolation and lack of intellectual cohesiveness of the academy. The concern with the co-optation of Mexican anthropology in particular is a recurrent theme. In addition, there appears to be the sort of disjunction between research, criticism, and useful and positive social action ("relevance") that has also been the subject of recent attention in the greater anthropological traditions.

In this essay I show that Mexican anthropology has reached a point in which it must transcend the limitations imposed by its historical vocation as a national anthropology. In order to lend credence to this normative claim, I explore the development of Mexican anthropology from the mid-nineteenth century to the present by focusing on four dynamic processes: the historical relationship between the observations of foreign scientific travelers and the production of a national image (the materials used for this section range from the 1850s to the early 1900s); the relationship between evolutionary paradigms and the development of an anthropology applied to the management of a backward population and its incorporation into "national society" (materials from 1880s to 1920s); the consolidation of a developmental orthodoxy (materials from 1940s to 1960s); and the attempt to move from an anthropology dedicated to the study of "Indians" to one devoted to the study of social class (materials from 1970s to 1990s). Before I move to the historical discussion, however, I begin by contextualizing the current unease in Mexican anthropology.

1968/1995: "Criticism Has Been Exchanged
for an Official Post"[4]

The 1968 student movement produced a generational rupture in Mexican anthropology. Its manifesto carried the disdainful title *De eso que llaman antropología mexicana* (Of That Which Is Called Mexican Anthropology [Warman et al. 1970]), a book that was penned by five members of a group of young professors of the National School of Anthropology who were known in those days as *los siete magníficos*. The magníficos had had the daring to criticize that jewel on the crown of the Mexican Revolution that was *indigenista* anthropology.

By 1968 the identification of Mexican anthropology and official nationalism was at its summit. The new National Museum of Anthropology, which was widely praised as the world's finest, had been inaugurated in 1964, and the National School of Anthropology (ENAH) was housed on its upper floor. The institutional infrastructure of Mexican anthropology was firmly linked to the diverse practices of *indigenismo*, including bilingual education, rural and indigenous development programs throughout the country (concentrated in the Instituto Nacional Indigenista, INI), and a vast research and conservation apparatus that was housed mainly in the Instituto Nacional de Antropología e Historia (INAH). Mexican anthropology had provided Mexico with the theoretical and empirical materials that were used to shape a modernist aesthetics, embodied in the design of buildings such as the National Museum of Anthropology or the new campus of the National University. Further, it was charged with the task of forging Mexican citizenship both by "indigenizing" modernity and by modernizing the Indians, thus uniting all Mexicans in one mestizo community. In Mexico this is what was called indigenismo.[5]

According to the magníficos, then, Mexican anthropology had placed itself squarely in the service of the state, and so had abdicated both its critical vocation and its moral obligation to side with the popular classes. The 1968 generation complained that Mexican indigenismo had as its central goal the incorporation of the Indian to the dominant system, a system that was called "national" and "modern" by the indigenistas but that was better conceived as "capitalist" and "dependent." Mexican anthropology was described as an orchid in the hot house of Mexico's authoritarian state, co-opted and entirely saturated by its needs and by those of foreign capital.

Moreover, the legitimate actions of early indigenistas, their ties to the Mexican revolution, had been exhausted. In the words one of the magníficos, Guillermo Bonfil: "Today we can contrast the reality of Mexican society with the ideals of the Revolution and establish the distance between the two . . . It would be difficult to doubt that in these days we can no longer do justice to the future by maintaining the same programs that were revolutionary 60 years ago. Those programs have either run their course or else they have been shown to be ineffective, useless or, worse yet, they have produced historically negative results" (1970: 42). Thus, the authors of *De eso que llaman antropología mexicana* called for Mexican anthropologists to keep their distance from the state, and to steer clear of a policy (indigenismo) that had the incorporation of the Indian into "national society" as its principal aim. "National society," noted Arturo Warman in the volume, was always an undefined category that simply stood in for what Rodolfo Stavenhagen and Pablo González Casanova had called "internal colonialism" as early as 1963. The aim of Mexican indigenismo had been the incorporation of the Indian into the capitalist system of exploitation, and in so doing it had abandoned the scientific and critical potential of the discipline.[6]

Not surprisingly, tensions grew strong in the National School of Anthropology, and they culminated in the expulsion of Guillermo Bonfil from the school by director Ignacio Bernal. The fact that a number of indigenistas remained loyal to the government during and after the 1968 movement was seen by the *sesentayocheros* (the participants of that movement) as a final moment of abjection, and it marked the end of that school's dominance in Mexican academic settings. Twenty years later, however, Warman—the most well known of the magníficos and author of a number of books critical of Mexico's agrarian policies—accepted first the post of director of the Instituto Nacional Indigenista and later that of secretary of agrarian reform under President Salinas. From this position Warman conducted the government's agrarian policies, which were directed precisely at incorporating Mexican peasants into forms of production geared to the market. Thus the co-optation of the anthropological establishment seemed to repeat itself, complete with its own moment of drama: in March 1995 the Mexico City newspapers reported that Warman was charged with pleading to former President Salinas on behalf of President Zedillo to put an end to a one-day hunger strike.[7]

My contention here is that the vision of anthropology's history repeating itself in a never-ending cycle of state incorporation is a misleading vision. In this essay I seek to elucidate the origins and historical evolution and current exhaustion of the Mexican tradition as a confined, national, anthropology.

The preoccupations that characterized anthropology in Mexico even before its institutional consolidation in the late nineteenth century related to the historical origins of the nation and to the characteristics of its peoples. The study of the origins and of the attributes of the nation's "races" was especially important in Mexico, where independence preceded the formation of a bourgeois public sphere.[8] Until very recently, at least, Mexico has been a country in which public opinion is to a large degree subsidized and dramatized by the state. Anthropological stories of national origins and of racial and cultural difference were therefore useful to governments and they were routinely projected both onto the nation's internal frontiers and abroad. Anthropology has helped to reconfigure the hierarchical relations that develop between sectors of the population, and it has contributed to the formation and presentation of a convincing national teleology. However, in Mexico as elsewhere the strategies and role of the state in shaping the contours of society has been under a major transformation that started in the 1980s. The crisis in anthropology today is not as much about the discipline's absorption by the state as it is about its uncertain role in the marketplace. An enlightened vanguard may no longer realistically aspire to fashion and shape public opinion for internal purposes, and discourses regarding cultural origins and social hierarchies are no longer central to the allure of the country for foreign governments and capitalists. In this context, there is a real need for invention.

Anthropology and the Fashioning of a Modern National Image

The task of shaping an image of national stability, of collective serenity, security, and seriousness of purpose, has never been an easy one in Mexico. Indeed, it was impossible to accomplish in the decades following indepen-

"The Porter and the Baker in Mexico." (In Edward Tylor,
*Anahuac, or, Mexico and the Mexicans, Ancient and
Modern*, 1861)

dence in 1821, when governments had to operate with unstable and insufficient revenue, a foreign debt that was difficult to pay, constant internal revolutions, a highly deficient system of transportation, and frequent foreign invasions. The image of Mexico abroad, an image that had been so important to Mexican politicians and intellectuals even before Alexander von Humboldt published his positive accounts of New Spain, had turned very contrary indeed. Naturalists and ethnographers who followed Humboldt's steps took a decidedly negative view of Mexico's present and a pessimistic view of its future.[9]

A useful point of entry for understanding the labors of the early Mexican anthropologists is a discussion of E. B. Tylor's travel book on Mexico, *Anahuac, or, Mexico and the Mexicans, Ancient and Modern* (1861), which recounts the adventures and impressions that he and the collector Henry Christy had on their trip to Mexico in 1856. To my knowledge, this book has never been published in Spanish, and it is not widely known or read in Mexico. This fact seems odd at first glance, given Mexico's legitimate claim to have been the muse that inspired the discipline that in Oxford was at times referred to as "Tylor's science."[10] The lack of attention to Tylor's Mexican connection seems even stranger given the need that countries like Mexico have had to remind the world that they have not been absent in the process of shaping the course of Western civilization.[11]

However, Mexico's failure to appropriate Tylor's *Anahuac* seems less perplexing after one actually reads the book. Tylor described a Mexico whose presidency had changed hands once every eight months for the past ten years; a country whose fertile coastal regions were badly depopulated, and whose well-inhabited highlands were bandit infested and difficult to travel. The volume also shows a Mexico sharply divided by race, where the whites and half-castes were hated by the Indians who were exploited by them.

Tylor's first vista of Mexico is the port of Sisal in the Yucatan, which for the Mexican reader is an uneasy start in its suggestion of the fragility of Mexico as a polity and its lack of cohesiveness as a nation. As Tylor writes:

> One possible article of export [that] we examined as closely as opportunity would allow [was] . . . the Indian inhabitants. There they are, in every respect the right article for trade: brown-skinned, incapable of defending themselves, strong, healthy, and industrious; and the creeks and mangrove swamps of Cuba only three days' sail off. The plantations and mines that want one hundred thousand men to bring them into full work, and swallow aborigines, Chinese, and negroes indifferently—anything that has a dark skin, and can be made to work—would take these Yucatecos in any quantity, and pay well for them. (16–17)

Tylor's first impression is a disturbing reminder of the fragility of the links between Mexico's people and its territory. His observation revealed what is still today something of a dirty secret, which is that Mayas were indeed being sold as slaves in Cuba at the time. But if Tylor's first impressions were unsettling, Mexican nationalists would find little solace in his conclusions:

That [Mexico's] total absorption [to the United States] must come, sooner or later, we can hardly doubt. The chief difficulty seems to be that the American constitution will not exactly suit the case. The Republic laid down the right of each citizen to his share in the government of the country as a universal law . . . making, it is true, some slight exceptions with regard to red and black men. The Mexicans, or at least the white and half-caste Mexicans, will be a difficulty. Their claims to citizenship are unquestionable, if Mexico were made a state of the Union; and, as everybody knows, they are totally incapable of governing themselves . . . Moreover, it is certain that American citizens would never allow even the whitest of the Mexicans to be placed on a footing of equality with themselves. Supposing these difficulties got over by a Protectorate, an armed occupation, or some similar contrivance, Mexico will undergo a great change. There will be roads and even rail-roads, some security for life and property, liberty of opinion, a flourishing commerce, a rapidly increasing population, and a variety of good things. Every intelligent Mexican must wish for an event so greatly to the advantage of his country . . . As for ourselves individually, we may be excused for cherishing a lurking kindness for the quaint, picturesque manners and customs of Mexico, as yet un-Americanized; and for rejoicing that it was our fortune to travel there before the coming change, when its most curious peculiarities and its very language must yield before foreign influence. (329–30)

Tylor's Mexicans were in most respects an unenlightened people. Mexican schooling was dominated by an obscurantist and corrupt Catholic Church (Tylor mentions the case of a priest who was a highwayman, and discusses the laxity of priestly mores).[12] The legal system gave no protection to ordinary citizens, who were at a structural disadvantage with respect to soldiers and priests. The population avoided paying taxes because the government was ineffective. Indeed, the country as a whole was in the hands of gamblers and adventurers, and Mexican jails offered no prospect of reforming prisoners.

Finally, the ethnologists and historians of the period must have been struck by the Mexican government's incapacity to control the connections between the nation's past and its future, a fact that is demonstrated by Tylor and Christy's activities as collectors of historical trophies, but even more potently by Tylor's remarkable description of Mexico's national museum:

The lower story had been turned into a barrack by the Government, there being a want of quarters for the soldiers. As the ground-floor under the cloisters is used for the heavier pieces of sculpture, the scene was somewhat curious. The soldiers had laid several of the smaller idols down on their faces,

CHAP. IX.

ANTIQUITIES. PRISON. SPORTS.

STATUE OF THE MEXICAN GODDESS OF WAR (OR OF DEATH), TEOYAOMIQUI.
(After Nebel.)
Height of the original, about Nine Feet.

Goddess Teoyaomiqui, Currently Known as Coatlicue.
(In Edward Tylor, *Anahuac, or, Mexico and the Mexicans,
Ancient and Modern*, 1861)

and were sitting on the comfortable seat on the small of their backs, busy playing at cards. An enterprising soldier had built up a hutch with idols and sculptured stones against the statue of the great war-goddess Teoyaomiqui herself, and kept rabbits there. The state which the whole place was in when thus left to the tender mercies of a Mexican regiment may be imagined by any one who knows what a dirty and destructive animal a Mexican soldier is. (222)[13]

Mexican anthropology has had multiple births: the writings of the six-teenth century friars, and especially of Bernardino de Sahagún, are fre-quently cited, but so are those of creole patriots and antiquarians writing in the seventeenth and eighteenth centuries, or the foundation of the International School of American Archaeology and Ethnology in 1911 by Franz Boas, and the creation of the first Department of Anthropology by his student, Manuel Gamio, in 1917.[14] *Anahuac* represents an unacknowledged, but not less-important, point of origin, for Tylor's first book was the sort of travel narrative that anthropologists, including Tylor himself, tried to override with the scientific discipline of anthropology, retaining the sense of discovery and of daring of the genre while reaching for systematization and emotional distance.[15] For Mexican intellectuals, however, *Anahuac* named the unspeakable but omnipresent nightmare of racial dismemberment, national disintegration, and the shameful profanation of the nation's grandeur by the state itself. *Anahuac*, in other words, is a work that both British and Mexican anthropologists would write against. As in a Freudian dream, the primal scene has been carefully hidden, but the development of anthropology in Mexico (and, indeed, in Britain) was to a significant degree shaped by the negative imprint of this book and others like it.

After the publication of *Anahuac*, the situation in Mexico took a different turn than the one that Tylor had envisioned. Instead of being invaded by the United States, Mexico was occupied by France, which took advantage of the U.S. Civil War to regain a foothold on the continent. And although Tylor was not entirely wrong in thinking that a number of Mexicans would welcome the intervention of a great power, civil strife and resistance against the French proved stronger than he had anticipated, and the turn of world events frowned on Mexico's second empire. After its "second independence," however, Mexico had yet to show that it was a politically viable country—one that was capable of embracing progress and attracting foreign investors.

One important move in this direction was the publication of a book written by Vicente Riva Palacio and Manuel Payno, both of whom would later lead the manufacture of a new history of Mexico.[16] *El libro rojo* (The Red Book [1870]) was among the first in a series of lavishly printed and illustrated volumes of the final third of the nineteeth century. It is a brief history of civil violence in Mexico, told by way of an illustrated look at executions and assassinations, much as if it were a book of saints. *El libro rojo* is remarkable for its ecumenical reproach of civil violence: illustrated pages are dedicated equally to Cuauhtemoc and to Xicotencatl (Indian kings who fought on opposite sides during the conquest), to conquistador Pedro de Alvarado and to the Aztec emperor Moctezuma, to Jews burned by the inquisition and to priests massacred by Indians, to marooned African slaves and to a Spanish archbishop. Even more remarkably, the pantheon of martyrs includes heroes on alternate sides of Mexico's civil struggles of the nineteenth century: fathers Hidalgo and Iturbide; the liberals Commonfort and Melchor Ocampo, and the conservatives Mejía and Miramón. Even Maximilian of Hapsburg, who had been executed by the still-reigning president, Benito Juárez, was given equal treatment.

El libro rojo sought to shape a unified Mexico by acknowledging a shared history of suffering. Ideologically this was the course that was later taken under General Diaz (1884–1910).[17] The work of *El libro rojo* was, first, directed to unifying elites, as is shown by its guiding interest in state executions rather than in the anonymous dead produced by civil strife or exploitation. The unification of elites involved taming the nation's war-torn past, and then projecting this freshly rebuilt past into the present in order to shape a modernizing frontier. It is therefore not surprising that the pacification and stabilization of the country that followed slowly after the French intervention required the services of an educated elite (which came to be known as the *científicos*) in order to shape Mexico's image.

The shaping of Mexico's image has been the subject of detailed work by Mauricio Tenorio in his book on Mexico as represented in the Worlds Fairs and elsewhere. I illustrate here the kind of work that was accomplished by this intelligentsia by referring to a book published in English by Justo Sierra and a team of illustrious científicos in 1900, *Mexico, Its Social Evolution*. This work is of special interest not only because Sierra was such a prominent and influential figure in Mexican culture and education, but also because it was printed in English and its lavishly produced illustrations seem to answer point by point the negative comments and images of Mexico offered by Tylor and other travelers.

The first, most fundamental, strategy followed by Sierra's team was to make Mexico's evolution comprehensible and parallel to that of Britain or the United States (that is, to readers of English). Thus, the names of the authors and historical personages were anglicized, from "Jane Agnes de la Cruz" to "William Prieto," and parallels between Mexico's evolution and that of the civilized world were explicitly or implicitly established. Carlos ("Charles") de Sigüenza y Góngora is placed alongside Sir Isaac Newton; Río de la Loza is followed shortly by Auguste Comte; and photographs of museums, hospitals, and courthouses built in Victorian or Parisian styles were displayed on page after page. This mimetic strategy was common among

Mexico's elite literary and scientific circles of the belle epoque, but it is taken up in a punctual manner by Sierra, who endeavors to show that each of the hallmarks of progress exists in Mexico.

Tylor complains of the state of abandon of Mexican education and its subordination to a retrograde church; Sierra provides discussions of the development of Mexican positive science. Tylor smiles ironically at the lack of attention that was given to Mexico's history and patrimony; Sierra shows the National Museum of Anthropology and the ways in which Mexico's once conflict-torn races have been neatly studied and organized in it. Finally, Tylor notes the arbitrariness of Mexico's government, the lack of justice, and of institutions of social reform; Sierra shows the rapid and impressive development of courts of law, of councils, hospitals, schools, museums, and prisons. In short, while Tylor speaks of a country that had been ravaged by revolution, Sierra's book speaks of evolution.

In this dialectic between Tylor's and Sierra's books we can catch a glimpse of the central role that anthropology has had in Mexico's history. In a rather simplified way we could say that the international aspect of anthropology has the capacity to destabilize nationalist images of Mexico. Mexico's national anthropology has worked hard to curb these tendencies by imaging the parallels between Mexico's development and that of the nations that produce anthropologists who travel.

Shaping Narratives of Internal Hierarchy: Organizing Governmental Intervention in the Modernizing Process

In addition to shaping and defending the national image, Mexico's anthropology has had from the beginning a role to play in the criticism and organization of internal hierarchies. Even before the rise of any solid institutional framework for the development of Mexican anthropology, discussions and writings on race and on the historical origins of Mexico's peoples were constantly deployed in order to orient strategies of government. Many examples of this appear in the *Boletín de la Sociedad Mexicana de Geografía y Estadística* (BSMGE), Mexico's oldest scientific periodical (founded in 1839). Statistical and population reports that were drafted in the 1850s and 1860s often carried sections on race, for instance. Thus, Juan Estrada in his report on the Prefectura del Centro of the state of Guerrero says that "of the 25,166 souls in the prefecture, 20,000 are Indians. However, what is painful is that the remaining 5,000 are not educated, nor do they refrain from uniting with the Indians in their designs to exterminate the Hispano-Mexican race" (1852: 74).

In the same period (1845), the Constitutional Assembly of the department of Queretaro gives a more nuanced account of the racial question in its state: "The wise regulatory policy of our government has proscribed for ever the odious distinctions between whites, blacks, bronzed and mixed races. We no longer have anything but free Mexicans, with no differences amongst them except those imposed by aptitude and merit in order to opt for the various destinies of the republic" (Asamblea del Departamento de Guerétoro 1852: 232).[18] However, the authors of the report go on to state: "We would abstain from making this sort of classification [i.e., a racial classification] were it not true that just as politics prefers to treat citizens as essential parts of the nation, so does economics prefer to consider their specific condition, not in order to worsen it but, on the contrary, to seek its improvement. Without a practical knowledge of the peoples [*los pueblos*] we cannot improve their civilization, their morality, their wealth, nor the wants that affect them" (232). The congress then proceeds to discuss the qualities and deficiencies not only of Queretaro's three main races (Indians, mixed-bloods, and creoles), but also important distinctions within the creole race according to level of education. Thus, while the highest class of creoles is circumspect, controlled, and similar to the ancient Spartans, the classes beneath them can be fractious.

Statistics supplied in a report by the state of Yucatán for the year 1852 include detailed discussions of the relationship between race and criminality, showing that Indians are less likely to engage in violent crimes than are mixed-bloods or creoles, because the Indian race is belittled (*apocada*) either naturally or due to degeneration. Correspondingly, the report states, Indians indulge in petty theft, and they do so systematically: "The Indian steals. More than anything he is a thief, and this he is without exception, and in as many ways as he can. However, due to their petty nature, these thefts escape the action of justice, and so are not recorded in the annals of crime" (Sociedad Mexicana 1853: 294). Statistics from the department of Soconusco in Chiapas in the same period divided local races into "Ladinos, Indians, Blacks and Lacandones" (Pineda 1852: 341).

It is clear from these reports that there was not a fixed national system of racial composition but rather that the races, and even to some extent the specifics of their character, varied substantially by region. Even Tylor's classification of Mexican races reflects this, for although he foregrounds the relationship between Indians, half-castes, and Spanish Mexicans, he also mentions the black population in the Veracruz region, and divides Mexican Indians into three types: brown Indians, red Indians, and blue Indians. These so-called blue Indians, known in Mexico at the time as *pintos*, were the troops of General Juan Alvarez that had overrun Mexico City shortly before Tylor's visit; they were described as blue because many of them had a skin disease that erases pigment in large patches.

One of the principal tasks of anthropology as it began to develop in the 1880s was to put into order these regional hierarchies of race and to tie them into a vision of national evolution of the sort that was so successfully displayed in Sierra's *Mexico, Its Social Evolution*. A key strategy for this aim can be found in Alfredo Chavero's work on pre-Columbian history in *Mexico a través de los siglos* (Mexico through the centuries [1888]), a work that develops an evolutionary scheme for pre-Columbian history that implicitly organizes hierarchical relations between the races in the present.

Chavero describes Mexico's pre-Columbian past as if it had been waiting underground for his patriotic generation to bring it back to life. Throughout the ravages of colonial destruction and the revolutions of the nineteenth century, the colossal Mexican past slept under a blanket of soil: "But our ancient history had been saved, and all that could have perished in oblivion shall today rise to our hands. Even if these hands be guided more by daring than by knowledge, they are also moved by love of country, a love that embraces the desire to preserve old memories and ancient deeds just as the great hall of a walled castle keeps the portraits of each of its lords, the sword of the conquistador and the lute of the noble lady" (1888: iv). After claiming the possession of the noble treasures of the past for his country, Chavero proposed an evolutionary story for pre-Columbian Mexico. This story had blacks as the initial inhabitants, but these blacks were weaker and less well suited to most of Mexico's environment than the race that expelled them from all but the torrid tropical zones: the Otomís. For Chavero, then, it is the Otomís who can be truly called Mexico's first inhabitants. However, the Otomís were not much better than the blacks, as they were considered a population of troglodytes who spoke a monosyllabic tongue,[19] a people contemporaneous to humanity's infancy: "Life in those days could be nothing but the struggle for sustenance. Families were formed only by animal instinct. Intelligence was limited inside the compressed crania of those savages . . . And just as nothing linked them to heaven or to an eternal god, so too did they lack any ties to the earth, there was no fatherland [*patria*] for them" (69).

Despite these unpromising beginnings, the inferiority of the Otomís did not deeply scar the nation's pride. Instead, it actually proved useful to understanding contemporary racial hierarchies, for the Otomí initiated an evolutionary movement that culminated with the magnificent Nahoas, a race whose apparition was, according to Chavero, contemporaneous with that of the great civilizations of Egypt, India, and China. Moreover, the Otomí offer a valuable perspective from which to comprehend the condition of the Indians during Chavero's present, for the Otomís were the Indians's Indians— they were the conquered peoples of those who were later, in their turn, conquered. Because of this they allow the Mexican to relativize the Spanish conquest and to diminish its weight in national history: "But did these first peoples acquire any culture? We are not surprised to find them degraded and almost brutish in the historical period. They were torn apart by invasions without receiving new life-blood (*savia*) from the conquerors, and inferior peoples descend and perish when they come into contact with more advanced people. We would be wrong to judge the state of the ancient kingdom of Mexico before the conquest on the basis of our present-day Indians" (67). In one stroke Chavero has established both the grandeur of the Mexican past and the key to comprehending its fall, and so has put aside the painful image that foreigners still projected of Mexico in Chavero's day. Mexico's prehistory and its contemporary moment are thus mapped onto each other and complete one another. The images of the Negro, Otomí, and early Nahoa races illustrate this point: whereas Chavero used archaeological pieces to portray the early Negro and Nahoa races, he relied on a drawing of a contemporary "Indian type" to portray the ancient Otomí. The contemporary "degenerate" Indian type maps onto and indeed substitutes for the missing image of the early and unevolved Otomí, just as the ancient grandeur of the Nahoa completes the image of Mexico's future as it is being shaped by the científico elite.

There is a striking similarity, moreover, between Chavero's description of the degraded Otomís and contemporaneous descriptions by foreigners of the Mexican Indian. For example, the U.S. historian Hubert Bancroft wrote a diary of his travels to Mexico at the time when *Mexico a través de los siglos* was under preparation, and he makes the following comment regarding the pervasive fears among Mexicans of U.S. annexation:

But what the United States wants of Mexico, what benefit would accrue from adding more territory, what the nation has to gain from it I cannot fathom. . . . If there were nothing else in the way, the character of the Mexican people would be objection enough. The people are not the nation here as with us; the politicians are absolute. There is no middle class, but only the high and the low, and the low are very low indeed, poor, ignorant, servile and debased, and with neither the heart or the hope ever to attempt to better their condition. I have traveled in Europe and elsewhere, but never have I before witnessed such squalid misery and so much of it. Sit at the door of your hotel, and you will see pass by as in some hellish panorama the withered, the deformed, the lame and the blind, deep in the humility of debasement, half hidden in their dingy, dirty raiment as if the light of heaven and the eyes of man were equally painful to them, hunchbacks and dwarfs, little filthy mothers with little filthy babes, grizzly gray headed men and women bent double and hobbling on canes and crutches. (1883: 18–19)

In the face of these devastating impressions, Chavero and his generation strived to make Mexico presentable to the patriot, to make it defendable vis-à-vis the foreigner, and especially to attract foreign allies. The success of this great concerted effort of the Porfirian intellectual elite has been discussed by Tenorio, who gives the title "wizards" to the team of Mexican intellectuals and politicians who pulled it off. This is perhaps not much of an exaggeration. Fernando Escalante has reminded us that during most of the nineteenth century, Veracruz, a town that was so plague-ridden that it was known as "the city of death," was nevertheless the favorite city of the creoles, because it was the best way to get out of country.

The special role of Chavero and other early anthropologists was to suggest a certain isomorphism between the past and the present. By creating a single racial narrative for the whole country, these anthropologists could shape the internal frontiers of modernization while upholding a teleology that made progress and evolution an integral aspect of Mexican civilization. Moreover, this strategy involved using history to moralize about the present, which was an immensely popular activity in Mexico that had significant grassroots appeal.[20]

The generation of Porfirian anthropologists would use this evolutionary theory as a frame for shaping Mexico's image, but revolutionary anthropologists would use it to intervene directly in native communities. The key figure in this development is Manuel Gamio, who was so successful that he is generally considered the "father" of Mexican anthropology. Gamio met

Tipo otomí

Cabecita de Teotihuacán

Cabeza gigantesca de Hueyápan

(*above, left*) "Otomí Type."
(*above, right*) "Small Head from
Teotihuacán."
(*right*) "Giant Head from
Hueyápan."
(All in Alfredo Chavero,
México a través de los siglos,
1888)

Franz Boas when Boas founded the International School of American Archaeology and Ethnology in Mexico City in 1910. Boas, as Guillermo de la
Peña (1995: 279) has shown, felt that Gamio was the most promising of the
young Mexican scholars and invited him to do his doctoral work at Columbia.[21] Gamio also received support from Carranza's government even before
its final triumph over Villa, and in 1917 he created the Department of Anthropology of Mexico's agriculture and development ministry. From this
position, Gamio organized a monumental study of the population of the
Valley of Teotihuacán.

In San Juan Teotihuacán, Gamio found a perfect parable for the Mexican
nation. The Valley of Teotihuacán was rich, but its people were poor; the
ancient city was the site of astonishing civilizational grandeur, but the current inhabitants had degenerated due to the Spanish conquest, to exploita-

tion, and to the poor fit between Spanish culture and the racial characteristics of the Indians. Just as important, perhaps, the setting offered up the raw materials for the presentation of a national aesthetics, a strategy that had already been implemented by the authors of *Mexico a través de los siglos* and the architects of Mexico's exhibit at the Paris World's Fair of 1889. This work is continued and deepened by Gamio, who attempts not only to extend the use of an Indian iconography in Mexican publishing and architecture, but also to adopt an indigenizing aesthetic for enlightened classes and to bring a serious engagement with indigenous culture to bear on modern technologies in architecture and cinema.[22]

The elevation of traditional culture for the consumption of elite classes was a matter of some controversy and it was often disdained in the Restored Republic and during the Porfiriato (and it can still be controversial today). For example, when a critic of 1871 described Guillermo Prieto's poetry as *versos chulísimos oliendo a guajolote* (beautiful verses that smell of [the indigenous term for] turkey), this was taken as an insult.[23] Gamio's involvement in the revalorization of indigenous culture was part of a long-term civilizational process for the Mexican elite. On the other hand, unlike his Porfirian predecessors, Gamio felt that the role of the anthropologist was not only to present the past as a vision of a possible future, but also to intervene as the enlightened arm of government, as the arm of science that was best equipped to deal with the management of population, with forging social harmony and promoting civilization. Thus, for Gamio the actions of the anthropologists were the actions of the nation itself. In his prologue to a booklet about the international reactions to *La Población del valle de Teotihuacán*, Manuel Gamio explains that he puts this compendium of flattering comments to print not as an act of self-promotion, but rather because *La Población del valle de Teotihuacán* is "a collective work that has national dimensions." He further states: "The opinions and critical judgments not only praise the scientific methods that preside over the research comprised in this work and the social innovations and practical results that were obtained. There is also in several of the most distinguished foreign judgments the suggestion that a number of other nations follow Mexico's example in favor of the well being and progress of their own people, a judgment that shall undoubtedly satisfy the national conscience" (1924: 2).

On the other hand, the fact that both Teotihuacán and the Department of Anthropology of the Secretaría de Agricultura y Fomento were both national symbols did not make them equal, for whereas Teotihuacan stood for the nation because of the wealth of its territory, the grandeur of its past, and because of its racial and cultural composition (which reflected a four-hundred-year process of degeneration), the Department of Anthropology was the head of the nation from which the promotion of civilization was to come. This is most potently brought home in the instructions that Gamio gave to his researchers before they began fieldwork in Teotihuacan: "We then suggested to our personnel that they shed the prejudices that can arise in the minds of civilized and modern men when they come into contact with the spirit, the habits and customs of the Teotihuacanos, whose civilization has a lag of 400 years. We advised that they should follow strict scientific discipline in the course of their actions, but that they should make every effort to temporarily abandon their modes of thought, expression and sentiments in order to descend in mind and body until they molded to the backward life of the inhabitants" (1924: 51).

The pioneering works of Alexandra Stern have shown the connections that existed between the work of Gamio and other "mestizophilic" nationalists and the eugenics movement.[24] One of the aspects of this relationship that is pertinent to our discussion here is that the view of the current population as degenerate, as having been made to depart from the best developmental possibilities of its race, went along with quite a challenging and revolutionary set of policies. Indeed, as a high government official leading an official project, Gamio had an interventionist role in local society that was entirely different from that of foreign anthropologists. As a result of his recommendation, the government raised the salary of the area's four hundred government employees (who mostly were employed in the archaeological dig and in the various development projects that Gamio promoted) in order to nudge up the salaries that local hacendados paid their peons. Gamio had lands distributed to peasants, and a new road, a railroad station, medical facilities, and schools were built.

The combined power of an integrative scientific method, embodied in anthropology, and its practical use by a revolutionary government was so dizzying that Gamio compared the mission of the Department of Anthropology with the Spanish conquest itself: "We believe that if the attitude of governments continues to be of disdain and pressure against the indigenous element, as it has been in the past, their failure will be absolute and irrevocable. However, if the countries of Central and South America begin, as Mexico has already begun, *a new conquest of the indigenous race*, their failure shall turn into a triumphal success" (1924: 49, emphasis added).

Thus, the discontinuities between Gamio and Porfirian ethnohistorians or ethnolinguists like Chavero or Pimentel are as interesting as their convergence: both believed in the degeneration of Mexican races after the conquest, both believed in the grandeur of Mexican antiquities, and both placed their knowledge in the service of national development. However, the Porfirians did so mainly as part of an effort to present Mexico in the international arena—as a contribution to efforts to bring foreign migrants, foreign investments, and tourism to Mexico—whereas Gamio took these theses and applied them not only to shaping the national image, but also to the art of governing.[25] By doing field research, by creating his own, "integral," censuses, and by intervening in a direct and forceful manner in local reality, Gamio could at once participate in the Porfirian imaging process and help fashion internal frontiers.[26] The similarities and differences between the two anthropological styles parallel the similarities and differences between the Porfirian and the Revolutionary governments: both were modernizing regimes that wished to portray the republic as being led by enlightened and scientific vanguards, but whereas the Porfirian regime placed its bets mostly on providing every possible convenience to foreign capital, the revolutionary governments tried to balance their efforts to attract foreign investors and their commitment to internal social and agrarian reform. This latter formula has been seen in the twentieth century as the one more attractive and desirable in Mexico.

Consolidation of a National Anthropology

When the 1968 generation accused Mexican indigenistas of shaping a strictly national anthropology, Gonzalo Aguirre Beltrán (1992 [1976]: 104) probably rightly accused them back of not having read the indigenistas closely. Aguirre Beltrán went ahead and named a number of cases of studies that had been done by Mexican anthropologists abroad; he could also have listed the active interest that indigenistas from Gamio and Sainz onward showed in exporting Mexican anthropology to other locations. Nevertheless, we can still argue that the 1968 generation was correct on this point, for the anthropology that Mexican indigenistas exported was a national anthropology geared to shaping connections between the ancient past, contemporary ethnic or race relations, and national modernizing projects. As the Mexican governments moved from the early proactive stages of the revolutionary period to institutional consolidation in an era of much industrial growth, the position of anthropology became at once more institutionalized and less capable of challenging the received status quo.

The period that runs roughly from 1940 into the late 1960s is a time when a nationalist orthodoxy prevailed. This is also the time when most of the great state institutions that house Mexico's large professional establishment were built: the Instituto National de Antropología e Historia (1939), the Escuela Nacional de Antropología e Historia (1939), the Instituto Indigenista Inter-americano (1940), the Instituto Nacional Indigenista (1949), the National University's Sección de Antropología (1963), and the new Museo Nacional de Antropología (1964). The growing strength of the Mexican state and the institutional consolidation of anthropology, alongside foreign (principally U.S.) anthropologists' interest in alterity and the delicate position of American researchers in Mexico during the cold war, are all factors that conspired to take the sting off of foreign anthropologists as harsh critics.[27] It is impossible to imagine the kind of candid commentary that we read in Tylor's book regarding, for instance, "what a dirty and destructive animal a Mexican soldier is," being published by a prominent U.S., British, or French anthropologist in this period (which has rather revealingly been labeled "the golden age" of Mexican anthropology).[28]

Instead, foreign anthropologists sought mutually beneficial collaborations or else they were as unobtrusive as possible. They worried about being able to pursue their research interests and about being able to send students to the field. Even so, the orthodoxy of Mexican official anthropology still faced an external challenge, a challenge that is endemic to the very proposition of a nationalized scientific discipline. In this period of industry and progress, the challenge of foreigners was threefold, they could uncover the dark side of modernization, in the tradition of John Kenneth Turner's *Barbarous Mexico*; they could adhere to the Indian and reject the modern; or they could further the political interests of their nations at the expense of the Mexican government. I will briefly exemplify below how these dangers were perceived in this period by examining two incidents.

The first incident occurred in December 1946, when President Miguel Alemán had just taken office. In response to this event, University of Chicago anthropologist Robert Redfield and two high officials of the Mexican government (Mario Ramón Beteta and Alejandro Carrillo) were invited to discuss the president's inaugural speech on Mexican national radio. The discussion generally went off without a hitch, although an attack on Redfield's position by Fernando Jordán appeared later in the newspaper *La Prensa Gráfica.*

After reciting Redfield's impressive scientific credentials, Jordán focused on a question that Redfield raised, which was whether the industrialization of Mexico would not carry with it a radical change in the mores of the Mexican people. Would industrialization not involve the standardization of indigenous cultures? Would it not diminish the beauty of a people that had well-defined ethnic characteristics, a people who gave great personality to Mexico? The radio host who was interviewing Redfield had responded quickly that "the traditional moral structure of the Mexican people is so strong that not even three centuries of Spanish domination were able to change it in the least." However, Fernando Jordán reacted less defensively:

> MEXICAN CURIOS If Mr. Smith, Mr. Adams, or any other tourist who had spent one month in our country had raised the same question, he would have reaffirmed the conception that we have of many of them. We would have thought him superficial and naïve.
>
> However, the question was raised by Dr. Redfield, a professional ethnologist, a renowned sociologist and author of a number of books about Mexico and its aboriginal cultures . . . It is thus impossible to believe that Redfield's question was foolish or idle. But in that case, what does it mean?
>
> In our view it means several things at the same time: Firstly, that Mexico, for the scholar, only has a proper form when it is viewed through the kaleidoscope of native costume, dance, and through the survivals of prehispanic cultures and the "folkloric" misery of indigenous people. But if this is part of Mexico, it is not Mexico itself, and it is not what our nation wishes to preserve. (1946: n.p.)

Jordán is shocked that a famous sociologist could replicate the superficial opinions of a tourist, but he offers an explanation of Redfield's true motives:

> THE ETHNOLOGICAL LABORATORY From another point of view, and given the trajectory of American anthropologists, Redfield's question can be interpreted in a different way. We feel that it expresses the researcher's fear of losing . . . the living laboratory that he has enjoyed since the days of Frederick Starr [another University of Chicago anthropologist]. He fears that he shall no longer be able to vivisect the Otomí, Tztzil, Nahua, or Tarahumara cultures. He trembles at the thought of seeing the Tehuana's dress, or the "curious" rags of the Huichol, being substituted by the overall that is necessary on the shop floor or the wide pants needed in agriculture. He is expressing his ideal of stopping our nation's

evolution in order to preserve the colorful misery of our Indians, a misery that will provide material for a series of books—most of which are soporiferous—in which the concept of culture will be represented by a set of isolated and static "ethnic" attributes that have no relation to the Indian's dynamism. (n.p.)

The foreign anthropologist is interested in exoticizing Indians, in maintaining Mexico as a kind of laboratory or ecological preserve, and not in solving the country's pressing social and economic problems. As such, the anthropologist's opinions and research ideals should be rejected in favor of a more interventionist approach, an approach that is committed to modernization and social improvement. Foreign interest in traditional cultures is welcome insofar as it explores the roots and the potential of the Mexican people, or insofar as it adds its efforts to the practical guidelines set by governmental projects, but when foreigners begin to value the traditional over the modern, what we have is a pernicious form of colonialism.

We should note that Fernando Jordán's own implicit program for the Indians (and this came from a journalist who had studied anthropology in the National School and who favored President Alemán's modernization program) denies anthropology as Redfield understood it. The "internal colonialism" of Mexican anthropology could not uphold diversity over progress, whereas the postcolonial U.S. or European anthropologist could not intervene directly in Mexico, and thus had a vested interest in diversity. National anthropology and metropolitan anthropological traditions relied on one another, but they also denied each other. Thus Gamio could not be a true cultural relativist like his mentor Franz Boas and still retain his brand of applied anthropology (and neither would Boas fully approve of the bewildering variety of applied projects that Gamio liked to juggle). As a result, the degree of mutual ignorance that is tolerated between these traditions in general, and between Mexican and U.S. anthropologies in particular, rests on epistemological conditions that run deeper than mere patriotic rejection or language barriers.

For example, after the publication of the Spanish-language edition of *Five Families* in 1961, Oscar Lewis remarked that

> Some of the [Mexican] reviews [of *Five Families*] seem excellent to me and others very negative. But even in the good ones I feel there is some resentment of the fact it was a North American, a gringo, who has acquainted the world, and even Mexicans, with a little of the misery in which so many families live.
>
> I regret it very much if I have offended some Mexicans with my work. It was

> never my intention to hurt Mexico or Mexicans because I have so much affection for them. . . .
>
> Many times I have suggested that it would be good if some Mexican anthropologists would be willing to leave their Indians for a while and come to my country to study the Neighborhoods of New York, Chicago or of the South. I have even offered assistance in getting grants for them.[29]

Needless to say, the project of Mexicans studying the United States has not yet come to fruition. The very idea of a national anthropology runs against it: What would a book by a Mexican on the United States be used for? Unless, of course, it were a book about Mexicans in the United States, or about American interests in Mexico. There is no public in Mexico, no institutional backing for this product, which would then be destined to be either an erudite curiosity or, worse, a Mexican anthropologist doing the job of the Americans for them.[30] There is no possible symmetry of the sort imagined by Lewis in his well-meaning but also slightly disingenuous comment.

Thus, the threat of a scientific indictment of Mexican modernization by foreign scientists remained, and Mexican reactions to the publication of Oscar Lewis's *Children of Sánchez* (1964) were even more severe than they were to *Five Families*. In a letter to Vera Rubin, Lewis summarized the attack that the Sociedad Mexicana de Geografía y Estadística mounted against his book:

1. The book was obscene beyond all limits of human decency;
2. The Sánchez family did not exist. I had made it up;
3. The book was defamatory of Mexican institutions and of the Mexican way of life;
4. The book was subversive and anti-revolutionary and violated Article 145 of the Mexican Constitution and was, therefore, punishable with a twenty-year jail sentence because it incited to social dissolution;
5. The Fondo de Cultura Económica, the author, and the book were all cited for action by the Geography and Statistics Society to the Mexican Attorney General's Office; and
6. Oscar Lewis was an FBI spy attempting to destroy Mexican institutions.[31]

Much of the Mexican intelligentsia rallied to the cause of Oscar Lewis at this point, including some anthropologists (such as Ricardo Pozas) who had been highly critical of *Five Families* because they saw in the Sociedad Mexicana de Geografía y Estadística's attack the hand of the government trying to keep all eyes off of the destructive effects of Mexican modernization—that is, off of urban poverty. Nevertheless, Arnaldo Orfila, the great Argentine editor and then-director of state-owned Fondo de Cultura Económica, Mexico's most prestigious publisher, was forced to resign from his post, and Lewis published the third edition of *The Children of Sánchez* with a private publisher.

The implications of these two cases are clear. The whole set of views that in Mexico came to be called "officialist," and which more or less served to demarcate the limits of mainstream Mexican anthropology, had a tense relationship both with anthropologists who might romanticize Indians to the degree of rejecting modernization and with those who studied the wrong end of the acculturation process, that is, the unhappily modernized end. If the anthropologists doing the work were American, then these tendencies were all the more menacing. Moreover, the rejection of these foreign works was also a way of reigning in work done by Mexicans, work that could be seen as unpatriotic or as bookish and irrelevant. This was, in fact, pretty much what the official attitude to the 1968 movement boiled down to: student unrest was giving a poor image of Mexico abroad precisely at the time when the nation was on display owing to the Olympic Games.

Conclusion: The Exhaustion of a National Anthropology?

I began this essay by noting the sense of estrangement and of being condemned to eternal repetition that has surfaced in Mexican anthropology in recent years. The sense that anthropology in Mexico is destined to take its place inside a government office, regulating the population, writing the governor's speeches, or presenting a dignified face for the tourist. The sense that Mexican academic anthropology will always be confined to its preexisting public, to a national public that cares only about the solution to the so-called great national problems. The uneasy feeling that nags the student of Mexican anthropology when she or he realizes that Francisco Pimentel was a high official in Maximilian's court, that Alfredo Chavero was the president of the Sociedad de Amigos de Porfirio Diaz, that Gamio was the founder of the Departamento de Asuntos Indígenas, undersecretary of education, and director of the Instituto Indigenista Interamericano, that Caso was founding director of INAH and ENAH, that Aguirre Beltrán was director of INAH, that Arturo Warman is Minister of Agrarian Reform, and so on.

This atavistic sensation is, nonetheless, to some degree a false one. There is a useful corollary to Marx's Eighteenth Brumaire that I think can be usefully applied here, which could be stated on the order of "*moins ça change, moins c'est la meme chose*'" (the less it changes, the less it remains the same). The pattern of absorption of Mexican anthropology by the state is in some respects quite different today from the times when anthropology had a central role to play in national consolidation. The multiplication of state-funded anthropological institutions in the 1970s and 1980s seem to respond more to the growth of the educational apparatus and to state relations with certain middle-class sectors than to the need for anthropologists as technocrats. The existence of certain highly visible anthropologists in government masks the relative decline of the political significance of national anthropology for the Mexican state.

Moreover, in the stages that I outlined above there is a distinct sense of exhaustion of the possibilities of the national anthropology paradigm. It began with the task of fashioning a credible national image that could do the work of harnessing the transnational machinery of progress; from there it complemented this task with an active role in the management of the indigenous population (which in the early twentieth century could mean a concern with the vast majority of the nation's rural population). This development of the anthropological function gained much prestige from the revolutionary government's capacity to distribute land and to mediate in labor and land disputes.

The year 1968 marked a watershed for Mexican national anthropology because the student movement reflected a shift in the relative importance of Mexico's urban population. Correspondingly, the magnificos and others no longer called for absorbing Indians into the nation, but rather argued for a more theoretically inclined anthropology. In fact, each of the major moments of Mexican anthropology, from the científicos to the revolutionaries to the anthropology that blossomed after 1968, has involved a "theoretical inclination." Each has looked to the international field for inspiration or for authority, and intellectual leaders at least have had direct connections with the most prominent leaders of the international field. The apparent paradox, however, is that once theoretical inspiration is channeled to the national anthropology model, dialogue with the international community gets reduced to conversations with area specialists at best. However, as I have shown in detail, there are causes of substance that restrict the relationship between national anthropology and its metropolitan counterparts, for the relationship between these two sorts of anthropologies has more often been one of mutual convenience than of true dialogue, since anthropologies that are devoted to national development must consistently choose modernization over cultural variation, and they must balance studies of local culture with a national narrative that shapes the institutional framework of the field.

In 1968 there was momentary awareness of the conceptual and political confinement that was embedded in "national anthropology," however *De eso que llaman antropología mexicana* was still, unwittingly perhaps, a version of a national anthropology: "Our anthropology has been indigenista in its thematic. Even today it is conceived as a specialization in particular problems. Indigenismo is atomizing and it tends to interpret its materials in an isolated fashion [*en sí mismo*]. *Indigenismo has rejected the comparative method and the global analysis of the societies in which Indians participate*" (37, emphasis added).

The final phase of Mexican national anthropology (the 1970s to the 1980s) was an expansive moment that had a number of things in common with the heady days of Gamio, for the anthropology of this period had to reinvent a nation that no longer had an indigenous baseline but was still centered on taking command of projects of national development. The call to develop a holistic and comparative study of "the societies in which Indians participate" was therefore just as prone to the vices of bureaucratization, theoretical sterility, parochialism, and co-optation by the state as indigenismo had been. Today there may no longer be a viable way of isolating the nation as the anthropologist's principal political and intellectual object, and Mexican anthropology may have to diversify its communitarian horizons and reinvent itself.

Notes

I wish to thank Manuela Carneiro da Cunha, Fernando Escalante, James Fernandez, Friedrich Katz, Ev Meade, and Saul Thomas for their bibliographic suggestions.

1 Ortner 1999 contains reviews of recent books on the crisis in anthropology.

2 The sense that Mexican anthropology is undergoing a difficult transition is reflected in different ways in a number of works, cf. Vázquez León 1987; and Lomnitz 1999, chapter 4. Bartra 1999: 43–48 offers Mexicans a choice between four "intellectual deaths," one of which can be summarized as "death by academy."

3 In 1973 Ralph Beals reviewed the field of Mexican anthropology and concluded that although it had had a relatively minor impact on anthropological theory, Mexican anthropology had played a critical role in the formation of a

national conscience, and that the country had the third-largest number of anthropology professionals, after Japan and the United States (cited in Vázquez León 1987: 139). In fact, however, a number of national anthropologies, especially in Latin America but also elsewhere, have turned to Mexico for inspiration during the twentieth century. It should be noted, however, that Mexico has never been a "pure model" but rather, as in the case of Mexico itself, Mexican-inspired national anthropologies shaped networks of national institutions that were then connected especially to U.S. (or occasionally European) missions: Cornell, Harvard, Chicago, Berkeley, Stanford, UNESCO, and French cultural missions have been some of the institutional partners of these national institutions (for the case of Peru, see Marzal 1981; for Brazil, see Souza Lima, this volume). The influence of Mexican anthropology on the anthropology of the United States receives subtle treatment in Stern 1999a, 1999b; Tenorio Trillo 1999; and Limón 1998, chapter 2.

4   The reference here is to Warman 1970: 34: "Criticism had been substituted by a [official] post [*un nombramiento*]. . . . Anthropology had been rewarded with lifelong benefits in the Instituto de Seguridad Social y Servicios a los Trabajadores del Estado."

5   See Souza Lima, this volume.

6   Scientific research and critical discourse were subsequently (and erroneously, I think) counterposed to the practice of indigenismo: "The state doesn't care about the development of anthropology as a science that is capable of analyzing reality and modifying it deeply. At most it is interested in it as a technique to train restorers of ruins and taxidermists of languages and customs. However, it finds that the schools of anthropology . . . are centers where students gather and study reality in order to transform it, that they fight for democratic liberties and that they maintain a militant attitude on the side of the oppressed" (Andres Medina and Carlos García Mora, cited in Méndez Lavielle 1987: 362).

7   "Culmina el enfrentamiento con Zedillo: Carlos Salinas se va a un 'exilio convenido,'" *Proceso*, 13 March 1995.

8   Guerra and Lamperiere 1998: introduction; Guerra 2000; Escalante 1992; Lomnitz 2000.

9   Foreign negative images of New Spain were the catalyst for some of the most distinguished eighteenth-century historical and anthropological writings by Mexican creoles. For a discussion of this issue, see Gerbi 1973.

10   The British Museum also calls the collector Henry Christy, who accompanied Tylor to Mexico, the godfather of anthropology (British Museum 1965: 1).

11   Unveiling these connections is the painstaking subject of much of the scholarship of recent decades, from Latin American "dependency theory" to Edward Said's *Culture and Imperialism*, but it has also been a constant concern since the late nineteenth century.

12   This is a theme that was well known to English readers after the publication of Thomas Gage's travels in seventeenth-century Mexico.

13   On the subject of the government's care for its antiquities, Tylor tells how

he and Henry Christy literally created markets for antiquities: "At the top of the pyramid [of Cholula] we held a market, and got some curious things, all of small size however" (1861: 275). Henry Christy's ethnographic collection became the most important one of its time, and over half of its registered pieces were Mexican (see British Museum 1965: 11).

14 For standard descriptions of this vision, see Warman 1970; and Lomnitz 1999, chapter 4.

15 Pratt 1992 tracks the connections between travel writing and anthropology.

16 Tenorio Trillo 1996 is the path-breaking book on this subject. For a discussion of *México a través de los siglos,* see pp. 66–71.

17 Widdifield 1996: 61–64; Tenorio Trillo 1996: 30.

18 In a footnote, the Congress of Querétaro contrasts its enlightened view of race with the "horrible anomaly" of slavery in the United States (Asamblea del Departamento de Querétaro 1852 [1845]: 232).

19 "Language is of great value for explaining ethnographic relations. Otomí is a language of an essentially primitive character. The Mexicans call it otomitl, but its true name is hiá-hué. All of the circumstances of this language reflect the poverty of expression of a people that is contemporaneous to humanity's infancy" (Chavero 1888: 65). In his views of indigenous linguistics, Chavero follows the work of Francisco Pimentel (1860a: 370), who argues that monosyllabic languages, such as Chinese and Otomí, have no grammar and are the most primitive. Pimentel (1860b) was also looking for even earlier evolutionary forms within Mexico, such as languages that combined mimicry and speech. In their disdain for Otomí and Chinese, Pimentel and Chavero were following racist trends in European romantic linguistics. See Bernal 1987: chapter 5 (especially 237–38). For a discussion of scientific stereotypes of Mexican Indians, see Buffington 2000: 149–155.

20 Thus, Bancroft writes that "I am really astonished at the great number of pamphlets and books for the young relating to the history of this country, almanacs of history, catechisms of history, treatises on history, etc. These together with the numerous historical holidays and celebrations show as deep and demonstrative a love of country as may be found, I venture to assert, anywhere else on the globe. There is certainly nothing like it in the literature of the United States. Today, the 27th, one hundred years after the event, in this comparatively isolated capital [San Luis Potosí] there are two factions on the plaza almost coming to blows over an Iturbide celebration, the priests insisting that they will do honor to his memory, and the government party swearing that they shall not" (1883: 40–41). In this instance, the date of the commemoration of Mexico's independence becomes the focal point for confrontations between liberals and conservatives. It is possible that Mexican obsessions with history had their roots in the civil wars, although there is certainly much influence from Spanish ideas of lineage and inheritance.

21 Important sources on Gamio include González Gamio 1987; Tenorio Trillo 1999; Stern 1999; Reyes 1991; Buffington 2000; Limón 1998, chapter 2.

22 For example, for a wedding banquet in honor of the Gamio marriage, the

Departamento de Antropología offered their honored guests dishes with titles such as *arroz a la tolteca, mole de guajolote teotihuacano, liebres de las pirámides,* and *frijoles a la indiana.* The invitation to the banquet is reproduced in González Gamio 1987.

23   See the debate in Altamirano 1871, vol. 20: 108–45.

24   Gamio was elected vice president of the Second International Eugenics Congress in Washington, D.C. in 1920 (see Buffington 2000: 154). For a full discussion of Mexican eugenics, see Stern 1999a, chapters 4 and 5, and Stern 1999b.

25   The closest antecedent to Gamio's synthesis may have been the short-lived agrarian experiment carried out by Maximilian. See Meyer 1993.

26   The difference between these two approaches was at the time felt to be so sharp that in the congress for the 1917 constitution the Porfirian científicos were seen as dubious Mexicans, as demonstrated in a speech by Congressman José Natividad Macías on the proposed law of nationality: "Would any of you admit Mr. José Yves Limantour [Diaz's finance minister, born in Mexico of French descent] as a Mexican citizen by birth? Answer frankly and with your hand on your heart. (Voices: No! No!) Would you take as a Mexican by birth Oscar Braniff, Alterto Braniff, or Tomás Braniff? (*Voices: No! No! We wouldn't take any científicos!*) (quoted in Noriega 1967: 255; emphasis added).

27   The impact of the cold war on Mexican anthropology has not yet been studied. The recent revelation that a former director of the National School of Anthropology, Gilberto López y Rivas, spied for the Soviet Union in the United States suggests that this is a significant topic. The effects of Plan Camelot on the intellectual climate in the region are better known (Horowitz 1974). Sullivan 1989 is an important book on the relationship between anthropology and diplomacy in the first half of the twentieth century. On López y Rivas, see Wise 2000; chapter 12; see also two articles that appeared in *Proceso* on 16 April 2000: "Los pasos de López y Rivas como 'espía soviético' en Estados Unidos," by Oswaldo Zavala; and "'Asumo mi responsabilidad y no me arrepiento,' dice el ahora diputado," by Homero Campa.

28   Cf. Téllez Ortega 1987.

29   Oscar Lewis to Arnaldo Orfila, 26 October 1961, quoted in Rigdon 1988: 288–89.

30   Mexican studies of Mexicans in the United States have a tradition dating back to Gamio's *The Mexican Immigrant, His Life-Story* (1931). For a discussion of the ways in which these studies were subordinated to Mexican national interests, often at the expense of the Mexican American perspective, see Limón 1998: chapter 2.

31   Oscar Lewis to Vera Rubin, 12 November 1965, quoted in Rigdon 1988: 289.

Antonio Carlos de Souza Lima

INDIGENISM IN BRAZIL

The International Migration of State Policies

My aim in this essay is to analyze the relations between indigenism and anthropology in contemporary Brazil. Alejandro Marroquín, in his 1977 book *Balances del indigenismo*, offers the following comment on the concept of indigenism: "Indigenism may be defined as a policy implemented by American States in order to solve the problems faced by indigenous populations by means of their integration into the nation. . . . Indigenism is not a science. Nor can it be. It is a policy in the sense that it makes up part of a systematic activity undertaken by public authorities . . . . As with any authentic policy, indigenism must be supported—and indeed is supported—by a certain number of sciences, in particular anthropology, whose constant pressure guides the current course of indigenism" (13). This definition is fully in tune with the official canon of the set of knowledge and practices and forms of exercising power known as indigenism. Having originally emerged in the Mexican national state during the first decades of the twentieth century, these ideas later migrated and spread throughout Latin America in the form of an administrative ideology that helped shape state policies in relation to indigenous populations. Within these shifting national contexts, anthropology appears as a discipline informing the procedures adopted by states in the concrete exercise of their powers. In this essay I wish to examine indigenism as one aspect of a wider setting: namely, the emergence and continued existence of certain forms of power derived from the European conquest. My aim is to expose the ways in which the social inequalities produced by administrative organizations are created and maintained. I start with a critique of the sociological analyses that inform public policies in the Brazilian context and that ingenuously take "social policies" as a set of ways for reducing social inequalities and hierarchies.

With this objective in mind I aim to explore indigenism through the notion of traditions of knowledge—in this case, those traditions associated with the government of ethnically differentiated populations in a colonial context.[1] In order to gain a better understanding of the set of knowledge defined by the terms *Indigenism* and *Anthropology*, I begin here with a historical and anthropological study of the relations of power and domination between public administration and the populations dispersed throughout the Brazilian territory, in particular indigenous peoples.

By "tradition of knowledge," I refer both to the set of knowledge combined and reproduced within shared models of interaction and those objectified within legal devices and codifications designed to subdue, define, classify, hierarchize, regroup, and localize colonized peoples.[2] These operations take place through what I term administrative knowledge and the state agencies empowered to deploy such knowledge. These traditions of knowledge also have an impact on the peoples and organizations that colonize new geographical spaces: in specific terms, they remold their representations of nature and of human societies, setting new coordinates to their mental map. In a colonial context, the authorities concerned with population management define social and geographical space simultaneously through the creation of territories, whose precise definition is determined by complex social hierarchies. Even when colonial administration works toward a better integration of colonizers and colonized, its actions sustain a crucial difference in terms of each group's capacity to act and command. This inequality simply reinforces the colonizer's domination.

In the Brazilian case, we can identify three main traditions among the bodies of knowledge involved in the administration of indigenous peoples. I shall call these the *sertanista* tradition, the missionary tradition, and the mercantile tradition. In the actual day-to-day administration of these dominated populations, it is also possible to identify a fourth tradition, the *scravocrat* tradition, which combines elements from the other three traditions.[3]

By sertanista tradition (the one of greatest interest here) I refer to a set of knowledge with a long history. Despite their alteration over time, these practices go back to the start of Portuguese exploration in Africa, specifically in regions found inland from the coast—the *sertões*.[4] Originally, the term sertanista was used by the Portuguese to refer to the forms of exploration practiced in various parts of the Lusitanian colonial world from the end of the fifteenth century onward (see Monteiro 1994: 7–10, 57–98). This sertanista tradition involved activities such as exploring and delineating the contours of "unknown" geographical spaces and assimilating these to the known world of the explorer. These expeditions created a body of knowledge with strategic value in geopolitical and economic terms, providing a source of information for subsequent commercial exploration. The tradition also worked to produce a description of autochthonous populations, helping the state maintain contacts and trade with these peoples despite its preparations for a war of conquest. In twentieth-century Brazil, as part of an official policy of protecting Indians, the sertanista became a specialist in techniques for attracting and pacifying those indigenous peoples not yet subjected to the state apparatus. These peoples included those without close contacts with the colonial forces and who wished to keep their distance, as well as those groups who were still at war with local segments of colonial Brazilian society and the state.

These traditions, and especially the sertanista tradition, provide the context for examining the migration of the term indigenism to Brazil (along with its associated meanings in the Mexican context)—a process extending from the 1940s until the present day. In the Brazilian case, events such as the official abolition of slavery in 1888, the implementation of a democratic regime in 1889, and the separation of church and state—all vital components in the creation of a federal republic—also provoked a fundamental problem for intellectuals and politicians at the turn of the twentieth century: namely, the issues involved in how to govern a mestizo population made up of numerous indigenous societies (including many still at war with the colonists invading their territories), exslaves, immigrants of European extraction, and creoles. This highly diverse population was, moreover, formed into social networks that existed in relative autonomy to the centers of federal power. Brazilian anthropology was born amid this nationalist thinking, and was deeply affected by the concept of race and by the uncertainties intrinsic to the project of creating a single people out of such a heterogeneous mixture. Mariza Peirano (1981: 1–62, 219–59; 1992: 86–104, 235–50) has shown the underlying pact binding Brazilian anthropology from its outset to the process of nation-building—a pact through which anthropological knowledge, in compliance with various theories in vogue at the time, conjoined with the Brazilian elite's endeavors to create a people and a nation freed from backwardness and dependency.

In this essay, I adopt two analytic postures in examining this topic. First, I take administrative practices and their associated bodies of knowledge as a valid source of material for anthropological study. This source has frequently been subject to denunciations, but never systematic analysis. Second, I assume that the processes leading to the formation of the postcolonial nation-states were heavily influenced by the types of colonialism from which they liberated themselves or against which they constructed their independence (depending on the chosen viewpoint).

These considerations in mind, in the following text I seek to study the uses of the notion of indigenism in Brazilian territory. After examining the origin of the term in Mexico and its migration to Pan-American movements and Brazil, I aim to show how it was adopted and transformed into a distinctive tool by public officials and anthropologists performing bureaucratic and intellectual activities at various levels.

Indigenism in the Mexican Context:
From Literature to State Action

The term indigenism is a product of Hispano-American literature. Originally, it evoked an archetype of the *Indígena*, which can be traced back to the way in which Romanticist ideas were received and interpreted through "social-minded" prose, poetry, and essays in Ibero-American countries as they gained their independence during the nineteeth century. The term also refers to the nation-building projects of the elites who came to power in these new Hispano-American nations, carrying with them a politico-administrative history that retains a certain continuity with the institutions and problems that arose from earlier European colonization.[5] However it was in the Mexican political context following the 1910 revolution that the meaning of indigenism became fixed, designating a particular ideology of governmental action in relation to indigenous populations.[6]

Juan Comas describes the peculiarities that shaped the way this form of administrative ideology and anthropological practice came into being.[7] He links indigenism to a Hispanic colonial tradition that took sociocultural diversity as a topic of interest for a variety of motives (including administrative), but he also associates it with the work of later institutions such as Mexico City's National Museum (which was founded in 1825, then renamed the Museum of Archaeology, History and Ethnology in 1909, and renamed again in 1939 as the National Museum of Anthropology and History), the universities of Columbia, Harvard, and Pennsylvania in the United States, and the various Prussian museums. Comas also cites the founding of the Mexican Indianist Society, which, directly influenced by the 1910 revolution, aimed "to study [the] . . . indigenous races and their evolution" (1964: 14), as well as the International School of American Archaeology and Ethnology, created in 1911, which included Franz Boas as one of its directors. In terms of the influence of national settings on anthropological knowledge, the immediate point of interest here is Mexico's creation of institutions for educational training in anthropology. The model it adopted bore strong resemblance to the colonial schools in other countries: hence, in this sense, the role of state knowledge assumed by anthropology in Mexico was built into the institutions responsible for reproducing the discipline's personnel and producing its discourses. This in itself represents a sizable difference when compared with the Brazilian case where there were no institutions for providing anthropology-based training in the tasks involved in governing indigenous populations.

Comas highlights the crucial role played by Manuel Gamio in the making of Mexican anthropology. The new discipline attempted to put into practice the nationalist precepts of the 1910 revolution; in effect this meant that the administrator became subordinated to the specialist in social sciences, who as keeper of a body of knowledge on the various conflicting human groups was assigned the task of helping steer the moves toward regional integration and development (see Aguirre Beltrán 1957, quoted in Comas 1964: 7). At the time of the revolution, Gamio was professor of archaeology at the Mexico City's National Museum (1911). After obtaining a doctorate in anthropology under Boas at the University of Columbia (1921), he conducted a morphological study of Mexico's indigenous populations (which he termed "regional populations"). He also proposed methods for carrying out public policies and outlined administrative structures that would later be implemented. Gamio later developed an interest in the archaeological study of Mexican indigenous societies, and in his most famous text—*Forjando patria: Pro-nacionalismo* (1916)—he attempted to forge a link between the study of material and intellectual aspects of pre-Columbian civilization and the study of colonial society. This connection, he argued, would enable "a suitably informed approach to any study of the current population, knowledge of which undoubtedly comprises the true gospel of good government. We can therefore perceive the extent to which Archaeology's practical aim is transcendent" (1966: 243).

Gamio defined anthropological fieldwork as a means of testing and defining rational and compensatory policies, intended to correct "the abnormality" impeding the development of the indigenous populations making up the bulk of the national population in Mexico and other Latin American countries. As far as Gamio was concerned, this abnormality was explained by the disinterest, greed, and/or ignorance of the dominant elites, heirs of the European colonizers (1960: 15). To assemble the body of knowledge demanded for pursuing these corrective interventions, Gamio proposed what he termed an "integrated field research method" involving study of the national population from the following viewpoints: quantitative (statistics); qualitative (physical type, language, civilization, or culture); chronological (precolonial, colonial, and contemporary periods); and environmental (regional physiobiology) (1966: 245).

This concern—at once practical and nationalist—appears in a paper presented by Gamio in 1916 as the Mexican delegation's representative at the Second Pan-American Scientific Congress in Washington, D.C. In this text the author proposes setting up anthropology departments with the specific aim of assisting governments in the task of governing indigenous populations. This model was implemented in Mexico in 1917 and lasted until 1924 when the anthropology directorship of the Office of Agriculture and Provisions was created and Gamio was simultaneously named director of the International School of American Archaeology and Ethnology (1916–1920).

It is not my purpose here to delve into the complex relationship between these forms of administrative knowledge and the construction of *mexicanidad* (mexicanity)—a topic vividly explored by Gamio himself and by Luiz Villoro (1996). The crucial point here is that this field research model, based on a highly personal reading of Boas's own proposals, would later be institutionalized in Mexico, acquiring the status of state knowledge and the truth value and power associated with this status.

At the start of the 1930s, the idea surfaced of exporting this Mexican model to the Latin American region. In 1933 Mexico proposed the realization of an Inter-American Indigenist Congress, a suggestion that was ratified in 1938 by the Eighth Pan-American International Congress in Lima (cf. Freire 1990: 54). In order to understand the term's migration to Brazil we need to pause a moment to consider this First Inter-American Indigenist Congress. Also known as the Pátzcuaro congress owing to the location name, the event took place in April 1940. Held during the government of Lázaro Cárdenas (1934–1940), the congress was seen as a triumph for the ideals of the 1910 revolution in which the foundations of indigenist practices can be clearly recognized: agrarian reform, rural education, and a nationalist intellectual movement.[8] These ideas were institutionalized in Mexico in two ways: through the Department of Indigenous Affairs (1936), in terms of indigenism; and through the Department of Anthropology of the National School of Biological Sciences (1938), in terms of anthropological teaching.

Organized in the middle of World War II during a period of intensifying North American geopolitical intervention in Latin America, the Pátzcuaro congress inaugurated the exportation of Mexico's indigenist model and the emergence of an Inter-American indigenism. The founding of the Inter-American Indigenist Institute and of journals such as *América Indígena* and *Boletim Indigenista* created a medium for circulating and debating ideas on methods for administrative intervention in the lives of indigenous populations. A Latin American system of agencies and bodies began to take shape, staffed by specially qualified employees who followed specific training procedures and methods, generally without official links to the universities (except in Mexico), although they maintained relations with institutions close to the United Nations. Later, in 1953, the Inter-American Indigenist Institute became affiliated to the Organization of American States, which enabled the institute to receive funding for applied research from organizations such as UNESCO (cf. Bonfil 1970 [1981]: 88–89). Still heavily influenced by the sertanista tradition, Brazil occupied an idiosyncratic position in this system, keeping itself mostly on the margins of mainstream ideas and practices.

These, then, are some of the elements at work in the formation of indigenism, in the sense connoted by the term when it arrived in Brazil in the 1940s as an applied anthropology; that is, as a set of principles obtained methodologically on the basis of anthropological theories formulated in the United States and Mexico, combined with a set of practical solutions to social problems. Together these elements enabled indigenism to acquire the status of a state knowledge. As such, it addressed a specific issue: namely, solving what the elites in power and the intellectual establishment—though not the populations involved—conceived to be problems, a view born out of a prescriptive vision of the nation-building process and a desire to respond "scientifically" to questions generated in its aftermath. Among these problems, one in particular acquired a crucial geopolitical significance: how to achieve the organized integration of ethnically diverse populations and weakly interconnected social networks only remotely linked to the centers of power.

A Planned Migration: The Historical Background
to the Reception of Indigenism in Brazil

The brief history given above offers an outline of the context in which the set of representations and practices associated with Mexican indigenism was produced. But how did this term migrate to Brazil? How, through whom, and for what purpose did this complex of ideas come to interact with preexisting Brazilian practices for governing indigenous populations, themselves derived from the traditions of knowledge institutionally embedded in the Indian Protection Service (Serviço de Proteção aos Índios [SPI]) first set up back in 1910? (see Souza Lima 1991). How did these traditions of knowledge linked to the government of indigenous peoples and anthropological knowledge interconnect in the Brazilian context? In replying to these questions, we have to go beyond examining the state's dealings with indigenous groups and also look at the role of the National Museum in Rio de Janeiro. Founded in 1818 at the time of the Portuguese court's arrival, the museum was the country's first research institution. Initially it was dedicated to the study of natural history, but later it became the first Brazilian center for research in anthropology.[9]

The 1930s represent a key turning point in the history of the Brazilian government's treatment of indigenous societies. Until then, official action was the responsibility of the SPI, which was charged with the administration of indigenous groups and migrant populations living in remote inland regions well beyond the reach of public administration. These were the sertões—the space of sertanista work. The SPI's principal remits were to pacify and protect indigenous groups, as well as to set up centers of colonization using workforces drawn from these same regions. Article 6 of the 1917 Civil Code placed indigenous peoples in the category of "relatively incapable" persons, alongside minors between sixteen and twenty-one years of age, the insane, married women, and wastrels. Based on this legal coding, the SPI submitted drafts in 1928 for legal powers entitling it to exercise tutelage over all those falling within the juridical category of Indian, but without predefining this category. Here once more we can identify a project for governing sectors of the population whose only means of civil participation is via the state, only this time taking the social form of a tutelary power closely tied to a project for controlling the national territory. At this time direct ownership of "unoccupied" lands fell to Brazil's separate states. This allowed the social networks involved in governing each of these federal regions a wide degree of autonomy. The SPI's top officials were almost all military engineers, a sector heavily influenced by the orthodox positivism of Auguste Comte, which had a profound impact on Brazil from the middle of the nineteenth century onward.

Members of the SPI had always maintained very close ties with the National Museum in Rio de Janeiro—a tradition that began with its founder,

Lieutenant Colonel Cândido Mariano da Silva Rondon.[10] The National Museum was not just a site for housing collections: public bodies regularly asked museum personnel to comment on day-to-day aspects of Brazilian life, with inquiries ranging from concerns about agricultural pests, the exploration of particular minerals, or the feasibility of the government project to transform Indians into a rural labor force (a keenly debated issue at the time the SPI was set up). The opinions provided in the responses of museum personnel carried scientific credibility. During the expeditionary works led by Rondon for expanding the country's network of telegraph lines and exploring ever deeper into the sertões, the National Museum became the main depository for the scientific collections assembled in the process. Moreover, Rondon invited naturalists from the National Museum to accompany the journeys through Brazil's inland regions in order to describe their fauna, flora, and indigenous peoples. Here it is worth noting that the SPI originally made up part of the Ministry of Agriculture, Industry and Commerce—to which the National Museum was also linked—whose objectives included providing support for scientific advances in agriculture and for "civilizing" the rural world.

After the so-called 1930 revolution, the Indian Protection Service entered a phase of severe organizational upheaval. With the 1937 coup d'état and the installation of Getúlio Vargas's nationalist dictatorship, called the Estado Novo (New State), the work of protecting Indians received new resources. As a state prerogative, it became integrated into a wider rhetoric supporting the colonization of Brazil's hinterland—a project renamed the Marcha Para o Oeste (Westward March). In 1939 the National Council for the Protection of Indians (Conselho Nacional de Proteção aos Índios [CNPI]) was set up as part of a vast process involving the creation of state councils focusing on "national tasks" (other councils were created in areas such as geography, the control of scientific and artistic expeditions, national historical and artistic heritage, forestry issues, etc.). High-profile intellectuals were very often appointed to represent the governmental institutions on these councils.[11]

In this new context of territorial and colonial expansion—seen more in theory than in practice—a need emerged for new public officials and with them new ideas (more or less) for governing indigenous populations. The first generation of SPI workers was now retiring or dying out. The initial plan had been for a rapid transformation of the Indian condition, driven by tutelary practices and conceived as a transitory moment associated, in Comtian positivism, with a "fetishistic phase." But this plan was starting to seem

General Cândido Rondon flanked by professors from the National Museum, including Edgard Roquette-Pinto and Heloisa Alberto Torres. The relationship established between the National Museum and the Indian Protection Service was fundamental to the constitution of Brazilian ethnology and indigenism. This picture was taken during the 1920s at the entrance to the museum. (Heloisa Alberto Torres Arquive, National Museum, Federal University of Rio de Janerio)

ever less plausible. Nonetheless, what I term sertanismo, or the sertanista tradition, and the aim of incorporating the Indians into the rural population under official protection, both remained uncontested. It was in this overall setting that the CNPI and SPI established their first contacts with Mexican indigenists.

An invitation to take part in the Pátzcuaro congress arrived via the usual diplomatic channels. In response, the Getúlio Vargas government followed the CNPI's recommendation and sent the anthropologist Edgard Roquette-

Pinto, vice president of the council and exdirector of the National Museum, an academic who still retained long-standing links with the founding group of the SPI. A pioneer in the popularization of science in Brazil, Roquette-Pinto had authored, among many other books, *Rondônia*, which first appeared in 1917 in the series Arquivos do Museu Nacional. *Rondônia* was written as a follow-up to Roquette-Pinto's 1913 journey as the museum's envoy to the Commission of Telegraphic and Strategic Lines from Mato Grosso State to Amazonas State (also dubbed the Rondon commission, which afterward formed the basis for the SPI).[12]

In his report to the CNPI after the Pátzcuaro congress, Roquette-Pinto highlighted those proposals he deemed compatible with the practices of protective tutelage, as well as his own interventions and proposals for the government of Indians based on the Brazilian experience. Hence, there was a clear recognition (and an evident pride) concerning the sertanista heritage and the prestige it had acquired thanks to the propaganda and international contacts established through both diplomacy and the Brazilian press over the first decades of the twentieth century. Although enthusiastic about the news from the congress, the CNPI (which at the time included Rondon and Heloisa Alberto Torres, who represented the National Museum)[13] was unable to establish relations with the Mexican group directed by Manuel Gamio because he was viewed with suspicion by Vargas: a supposed militant from the Mexican Communist Party was on its organizing committee.

Moreover, the CNPI and SPI had always taken the material produced by the North American Bureau of Indian Affairs as their main source of inspiration, in particular wherever land policy was concerned—a topic debated in the CNPI during the drafting of legislation linked to article 154 of the Brazilian Constitution (proclaimed by Vargas in 1937), which dealt with Indian lands. The Mexican position vis-à-vis indigenous peoples seemed only of marginal interest. Nevertheless, in 1943 the Brazilian government did enact the first recommendation of the Pátzcuaro congress, which proposed declaring 19 April as Indian Day throughout the Americas.

However, Brazil's initial lukewarm response was modified during the New State regime. As a result of the bureaucratic rationalization imposed by the regime in its drive to technocratize governmental action, the SPI was forced to look for a new paradigm—one of a recognized scientific nature—for training new personnel, and to revise earlier practices developed under the leadership of officials directly linked to Rondon—a group that considered orthodox positivism to be a scientific guideline in itself. The demands arising from this process led to a new organizational structure for the SPI. This included a Studies Section (set up in 1942, though it only became effective at the end of the decade), the establishment of the internal administrative category of ethnologist, and the implementation of civil service exams for recruiting personnel. At the same time, contacts with Mexican indigenists—who represented an alternative to sertanism—were once more welcomed, leading to a flourishing dialogue within Brazilian institutions that became formalized in texts and spread through publications. The *Boletim Indigenista* (linked to *América Indígena* and published in tandem with it) aimed to supply news and information on indigenism as state policy.

In 1944 Manuel Gamio himself went to Brazil to visit a number of scientific institutions as well as the SPI, and to take part in a session of the CNPI. The latter event was the setting for a resurgence of the dichotomy—typical in the evolution of Mexican thought at the time—between in situ "scientific" studies linked to indigenist issues on one hand, and "university and theoretical" studies on the other. This dichotomy was surmounted by the contribution of Cândido Rondon (and therefore the Brazilian tutelary policy) whose scientific competence was widely recognized. Gamio's visit also sought to obtain Brazil's adhesion to the Inter-American Indigenist Institute. However, Brazil would eventually join only after the war and the end of the dictatorship. An official delegation from the SPI finally participated in the Inter-American Indigenist Congress in 1954.

Ethnology and Indigenism in the 1950s:
The Paths to a Reconversion

Yet despite the delayed response of Brazil's involvement in indigenist issues, we should note a shift here in terms of the receptivity toward indigenist ideas compared to the earlier phase. Although at the start of the 1940s Mexican indigenism was no more than one source of inspiration among others, including the texts being produced in the United States, it did become an important source of dialogue. Some of the Mexican ideas were incorporated into the sertanista theories and practices during the initial phases of the "protectionist" mode of tutelary power in Brazil, which was still being adhered to by members of the CNPI and the SPI's central administration. However, by the end of the 1940s a gradual drift away from the Rondonian model of protection became perceptible (see Freire 1990: 50).[14]

Key posts were taken up by figures such as José Maria da Gama Malcher, one of the first successful public service exam candidates, and Darcy Ribeiro, who was recruited in 1947 to the Studies Section with a diploma from the São Paulo Free College of Sociology and Politics and whose supervisor had been the German anthropologist Herbert Baldus. Armed with a recognized technical and scientific background acquired via formal training, some of these new ethnologists began to question the positions of council members at various opportunities. This provoked a conflict between the CNPI, until then a shrine for the tutelary intelligentsia, and the executive body of the SPI.

This clash between essentially protectionist practices and the formulation of anthropologically inspired rules meant that the distance between the two institutions steadily increased, which continued until Malcher (director of the SPI from 1950 to 1954) partially succeeded in reconciling the two viewpoints. Ribeiro, then head of the SPI Studies Section, was joined in 1952 by Eduardo Galvão, who was appointed to run the Guidance and Support Section, a body that supported plans for local and regional action. In 1954, Roberto Cardoso de Oliveira, who had just acquired a degree in philosophy from the University of São Paulo, also came to work with Ribeiro in the Studies Section. This new generation of ethnologists began to propose tutelary practices based on an alternative set of theoretical paradigms: namely, the theories of cultural contact and acculturation, imported from North American anthropology, combined with the practical guidelines being used by Mexican indigenism that could now be legitimately employed as technical know-how compatible with the new criteria of scientificity in vogue at the time. The conditions were therefore set for questioning the administrative practices that had been in force in Brazil up until this point.[15]

The 1950s were a period of intense transformations in terms of both anthropological research and the indigenist policy pursued by the SPI and the CNPI. The occupation of the northeast portion of Mato Grosso state and the region formed by the Xingu and Araguaia rivers in central Brazil—result of the intense wave of propaganda issued during the New State regime in support of the Westward March—exposed many indigenous groups for the first time to the almost constant presence of "national society." Indeed, both the press and the broadcasting media dwelt on the image of "primitive Brazil," filled in particular by depictions of Xingu societies. Meanwhile, anthropology was taking shape as a discipline. The first Brazilian Anthropology Meeting was held in 1953 at the National Museum; two years later the Brazilian Anthropology Association (Associação Brasileira de Antropologia) was created. Another three meetings took place before the end of the decade.[16] Within the SPI, Galvão and Ribeiro—followed by Cardoso de Oliveira for a brief period from 1950 to 1955—defended a return to protectionist practices built on scientific bases. They joined forces with other SPI officials who, although still influenced by sertanista practices, fell in line with the new directions.[17]

In a section of the 1954 SPI annual report dedicated to the Studies Section, titled "Ethnology and indigenism," Darcy Ribeiro criticized both "traditional ethnological field research" (based on studies of material culture) and acculturation studies, contrasting them unfavorably with an "ethnology with practical aims." In this text, Ribeiro proposes the creation of an annex to the Studies Section, the Museu do Índio (Indian Museum), an institution inspired by indigenism but also designed to train ethnologists and popularize scientific knowledge relating to indigenous issues:

> The Museu do Índio—an institution created and maintained by the SPI Studies Section and therefore fundamentally committed to the aim of safeguarding indigenous populations—obviously cannot remain content with the narrow outlook of traditional ethnology. In consequence, it has recently been directing the research of its technical staff, as well as those groups it sponsors or assists, towards a more active interest in problems relating to the survival of indigenous populations. We expect these new guidelines to produce practical results in three ways: firstly, by creating a knowledge base for improving the SPI's methods for providing assistance; secondly, by allowing greater precision in tackling the problems with which ethnologists have been traditionally concerned by analyzing these problems within the real context in which they operate; and thirdly an enrichment of the topics currently approached in ethnological studies. Hence in addition to kinship terminologies, ergological analyses and so forth, we now expect ethnologists to return from the field with data enabling evaluation of the death, birth and fertility rates of the respective populations, as well as the conditions defining the biotic and ecological interaction between indigenous and rural populations. In addition to mythic corpuses and ritual practices, the ethnologist should assemble all the documents needed to register the change in worldview imposed by the new life-styles Indians are being compelled to adopt, as well as studies of the relations between Indians and neighboring sertanejos, and their reciprocal attitudes and expectations. (1955a: 57)

As in Mexico during this period, UNESCO funded field research in Brazil, which was channeled via the SPI Studies Section. The SPI's official report also contains important information on the role of those members who were looking to provide new grounds for protectionist practices. This material allows us to re-evaluate their careers within indigenism's international social circuits, linked after the war with the fight for the social equality of all peoples within the global processes of decolonialization. A prime example is the International Labor Organization's Permanent Commission meeting of "experts in indigenous issues" (Geneva, March 1954), which drafted subsidiary documents to the International Labor Organization's conventions.[18]

The final part of the report on the Studies Section deals with the Advanced Training Course in Cultural Anthropology—an initiative of the Studies Section/Museu do Índio in collaboration with other institutions—which relied on funding from an institution called Coordination for the Improvement of Higher Education Personnel Foundation (Coordenação de Aperfeiçoamento de Pessoal de Nível Superior).[19] The training program was divided into two modules, the first of which was a systematic apprenticeship in disciplines geared toward field research—a learning period made up of lectures and seminars on a wide range of subjects in order to provide "a conceptual and unified schema for training in direct observation of social phenomena." The second module was comprised of other seminars on the discipline's core topics, based on field research conducted by researchers/lecturers who analyzed its objectives and methods, as well as the results obtained and later published. In addition, the students—all interns from the Museu do Índio—had to devote four hours every day to "classifying documents and ethnographic collections, as well as a number of other museological tasks" (see Ribeiro 1955b: 75). Once financial aid for the research had been secured, the second period of training followed which involved three months of actual field research and resulted in a final dissertation. A new type of training therefore emerged, sanctioned by diploma, which encouraged field experience and was supported by the accumulated know-how of the National Museum (with Luiz de Castro Faria),[20] along with the University of Columbia (Eduardo Galvão) and the Free College of Sociology and Politics (Darcy Ribeiro).

Changes in the political landscape during the second half of the 1950s were crucial in deciding the fate of this venture: the changes' repercussions within the SPI put an end to José Maria da Gama Malcher's leadership, which led in turn to the successive departures in 1955 of Darcy Ribeiro (who would work on increasingly more political projects in the area of public education) and Eduardo Galvão (who joined the Göeldi Museum in Belém). These departures were shortly followed by Roberto Cardoso de Oliveira, who left at the end of 1956. The career trajectory pursued by Cardoso de Oliveira provides a valuable insight into the connections between administration and anthropology over the following years. In 1958 he went to the National Museum, at the invitation of Castro Faria, to help launch a series of teaching courses similar to those found at the Museu do Índio. Shortly thereafter, in 1960, he finished writing up his field research on *O processo de assimilação dos Terena*, originally published in the National Museum's series *Livros*.[21]

Indigenism as a Deontological Stance

From 1955 onward these conceptions of indigenist work in Brazil were no longer able to claim a hegemony over tutelary policy—even only in terms of attacking it, as they had done previously within its power structures. From the end of the 1950s to the eventual abolition of the SPI, ethnologists and ser-tanistas from the CNPI (where the National Museum retained institutional representation) continued planning, studying, and forecasting changes that reflected many of the premises of inter-American (that is, Mexican) indige-nism. In Brazil, the term "applied anthropology" ended up being wholly rejected, at least in this area of research. Brazilian indigenism—conceived as a form of state knowledge applied to the administration of indigenous societies—began to distance itself inexorably from social anthropology.[22]

The end of the 1950s and the start of the 1960s were marked by a series of denunciations against the SPI, including accusations of corruption and even the genocide of indigenous populations. Consequently, even some of the most ardent defenders of state action as an essential mediating force between Indians and non-Indians (and therefore defenders of the necessity for a tutelary institution—the SPI) began to talk about the need for changes. Amid this setting in 1962, Darcy Ribeiro published *A política indigenista brasileira*. This book was reissued in 1970 under the title *Os índios e a civilização*, and it became the key reference work on indigenous problems in Brazil.[23] The ideas in this text correspond to those developed by the SPI Studies Section during the 1950s as well as others found in the UNESCO-funded research projects. The text contains a series of proposals for protectionist action based on "scientific" principles that eventually supplanted the Rondonian protectionist ideology. Ribeiro proposed the implementation of an indigenist policy in the Mexican sense of the term—that is, an applied anthropology and a state knowledge for the government of Indians.

In 1961, the federal government announced its plans for the Xingu Indigenous Park, to be created in a large tract of land situated in central Brazil. Arguments supporting the project came from Ribeiro (focusing on the central problem of how to territorialize indigenous populations); from Cardoso de Oliveira (focusing on the conflicts over land ownership); and above all from Galvão, who used his own ethnographic research in the upper Xingu region to supply scientifically credible arguments based on the notion of cultural area and theories of acculturation. The creation of the Xingu Park involved the definition of a continuous territory of large proportions, designed to maintain indigenous populations in a gradual process of acculturation, structured according to their own aims and interests (see Ribeiro 1955a: 82–97; Cardoso de Oliveira 1955: 173–84; Galvão 1979: 73–115).[24] This upturned the until-then dominant practice of demarcating small territorial areas designed to serve as an interim support for the rapid integration of Indians into the rural workforce. The practical results of importing indigenism's ideas and practices, first sketched in the 1950s, were taking shape. During this changeover a new generation of sertanistas also came to the fore, completing a process initiated at the end of the 1940s.

A similar wave of criticism surfaced in the CNPI, which was made up at the time of prominent anthropologists as well as past directors of the SPI such as Gama Malcher. The idea of a new institutional model was likewise debated, the idea being to strengthen the links between sertanista knowledge and culturalist-style applied anthropology—the latter being the basis, in the eyes of Brazilian anthropologists, of Mexican indigenism.

Two themes stand out from these discussions within the CNPI at the start of the 1960s, a short while before the final crisis and disappearance of the SPI in 1967 and its immediate substitution by the National Indian Foundation (Fundação Nacional do Índio [FUNAI]). The first theme was the need to undertake protectionist action within a new institutional framework. The plan was to create a legally empowered public foundation, directed by a council with deliberative functions whose members would be drawn from both scientific and governmental institutions. The foundation's president would automatically be one of the members of the Directive Council and endowed with executive functions. The second theme was the need for specialized training in a newly created school for indigenism.

In the aftermath of the 1964 coup d'état, however, management of the Brazilian state fell entirely into the hands of the military, and all policy became bound up with the slogan "development and security." This period, particularly after 1968, was marked by the expansion of state powers in

Amazonia, an area perceived to be of paramount geopolitical interest.[25] An Indigenist Council with a consultative status—presented as a space for negotiation and made up entirely of anthropologists—was created, but its impact was limited due to the control exercised by the military.

Yet despite living under a dictatorship, anthropologists did manage to create fertile spaces for the institutionalization of their discipline. The anthropological training courses taught by Cardoso de Oliveira and Castro Faria at the National Museum continued to be offered. Cardoso de Oliveira—who more or less stuck to the guidelines set out by Ribeiro in the 1950s, despite trying to distance himself from them—implemented research projects in which the topic of Indian/non-Indian relations was formulated in terms of interethnic social relations marked by conflict. This funneled the museum's researchers into an increasingly narrow dialogue with authors from Latin America dedicated to the sociology of modernization. In 1968 these courses and projects were combined to form the Post-Graduate Program in Social Anthropology (Programa de Pós-Graduação em Antropologia Social) in the Department of Anthropology at the National Museum, with financial backing from the Ford Foundation and institutional support from the Latin American Research Center at Harvard. Directly or indirectly, this move to create the institutional conditions for anthropological training, especially in field research, had a strong influence on a number of the anthropologists who accompanied Cardoso de Oliveira when he moved to the University of Brasília to start a new postgraduate course in anthropology. Cardoso de Oliveira and his team of researchers trained many students who went on to work for state agencies, FUNAI among them, and the Brasília department maintained fairly strong relations with this sector of government over the ensuing years.[26]

From 1969 onward, FUNAI participated intensively in the state's efforts to extend its reach in the Amazonian region. Directly controlled by the military, one of its primary functions was to establish the first contacts with indigenous populations still outside the social networks connected to public administration. In line with this role, the agency was subordinated to the Ministry of the Interior, which coordinated the different services involved in the colonization of national territory.

Sertanista knowledge thereby gained visibility in the national and international media, since it helped mitigate some of the international criticism of the violence involved in the colonization process. Once again there was an urgent need to increase the number of employees trained to work alongside indigenous populations on a day-to-day basis. As a solution, accelerated intensive training courses were set up from 1970 onward, leading to the creation of the FUNAI category called "indigenist technicians" (or simply "indigenists"). These courses generally had a double role. First, they enabled the official appointment of the many subaltern workers (frequently small agriculturists) who in reality performed the function of heads of indigenous posts—that is, local FUNAI units acting alongside indigenous communities. Due to a lack of basic training, these employees were officially unable to occupy the post of indigenist technician that was created in the new institutional set-up. The training, however, remedied this problem. Second, the courses prepared people recruited via public exams for the same purpose. Fully directed from the outset toward undertaking the daily activities of an indigenous post (e.g., radio use, sanitary and agricultural techniques, forest survival, and FUNAI's bureaucratic routines, etc.) the courses in indigenism (nine in total between 1970 and 1985) gradually added new elements, including courses in anthropology, the history of indigenism (in this case, the origins of the SPI and the sertanista tradition), linguistics, community development, and so on. These disciplines gradually came to be seen as crucial to gaining a better understanding of indigenous problems. In developing this new approach, the generation of FUNAI anthropologists trained by Cardoso de Oliveira in Brasília performed a key role. Some of the teaching staff for these courses became lecturers at the university, which most likely contributed to the dissemination of Mexican indigenism in Brazil.[27] It should be stressed, however, that the administration of these courses was entirely controlled by FUNAI.

These intensive training courses lasted three months. The first phase was theoretical in kind, based on lessons and input from recognized sertanistas, which helped ensure the transmission of knowledge and the formation of relations among the various generations of FUNAI as a bureaucratic entity. A second phase involved the participants being sent to indigenous posts to undertake fieldwork training—which in this case meant all tasks involving the direct intervention of the sertanista and indigenist, under the supervision of an experienced head of post. The theoretical part of the training made frequent use of Darcy Ribeiro's book, *Os índios e a civilização*. The practical part of the training continued to deal with the day-to-day administration of indigenous peoples within an institutional framework dating back to the sertanista tradition, albeit reformed with new elements that reflected the particular reception of the ideas of Mexican indigenism in Brazil.

No long-term training based on a deeper interaction with anthropology was implemented, however, and Brazil never saw the equivalent of the Colonial School. Although references to Mexican indigenism were certainly explicit in the texts and ideas used to reformulate sertanista practices, there was no systematic training based on a project of applied anthropology—in contrast not just to Mexico but also to the British colonial empire, which ran training courses for administrators in university departments. FUNAI's short training courses basically served as a form of institutional socialization, achieved through lectures by experienced sertanistas. The courses also exploited some of the romantic imagery found in the large cities, where the Indian was seen to embody specifically Brazilian values—during a period when foreign capital was entering the country in intensive fashion. This idea was combined with the heroic image of the conquest of new territories, conceived as a form of Christian charity and self-sacrifice. The courses sponsored by FUNAI therefore effectively involved a form of institutional reproduction wavering between bureaucratic rationalization and sectarian co-option, in which the idea of completing a mandate blurred with fulfilling a mission.

This idiosyncratic fusion between the sertanista tradition, whose emblematic figure continues (even today) to be Cândido Rondon, and indigenist knowledge, based on texts such as those of Darcy Ribeiro (which are somewhat inefficient when used as a manual for the day-to-day practice of indigenism in Brazil), inevitably ran up against a contradiction: namely, the developmentalist aims and geopolitical concerns of FUNAI's military directors. For a brief period between 1974 and 1979, the organization's presidency made serious attempts to attract anthropologists emerging from postgraduate courses and integrate them into indigenist activities. Their strategy involved recruiting candidates under the administrative category of anthropologist and running indigenist courses defending the ideals of self-determination and economic autonomy for indigenous populations.[28]

With the creation within FUNAI of a category of technical staff called indigenists, indigenism acquired a concrete body of personnel, sites, and functions that allowed it to expand its political influence and claim particular political spaces as its own. Yet rather than becoming crystallized as a symbol of the state's monopolization of a tutelary role and configuring a set of administrative theories, methods, and practices based on anthropological parameters, the term indigenism migrated yet again—this time within Brazil itself.

The period from 1980 onward saw an abrupt increase in conflicts between the military administration and FUNAI's existing staff. Many of its anthropologists and indigenists were dismissed in 1980 and 1981. In press interviews and scientific meetings, these indigenists responded by presenting themselves as "authentic indigenists," in contrast to those who remained in FUNAI. They found support in alliances established with university anthropologists or in the development of interventionist projects with nongovernmental organizations. Simultaneously, certain alliances formed over the preceding years became much more visible. As part of its opposition to the military regime, the Catholic Church implemented a set of practices and institutions aimed toward political action in defense of certain sectors of society, such as rural workers, laborers, and so on. It thereby became one of the main forces for social uprising. One of these institutions was the Indigenist Missionary Council (Conselho Indigenista Missionário), created in 1972. By this time, missionary indigenism had come to imply a form of missionary action that rather than having conversion as its ultimate aim, was guided by "a preferential option for the poor" developed in the Latin American region after the second Vatican Council.[29]

At the same time, nongovernmental organizations sponsored by European churches and foundations were set up by anthropologists trained on the country's postgraduate programs (some of whom had already worked for FUNAI). Their aim was to coordinate action programs among indigenous peoples, thereby challenging the relative monopoly held by FUNAI in the area of direct intervention—a monopoly endorsed by state laws and the military regime. These new social agents also asserted the indigenist nature of their work. Again we can note the influence of ideas supporting an anthropology of action—or, more generally speaking, forms of action based on anthropology as a discipline, but distinct from those inspired by the Mexican state apparatus.[30]

Indigenism thus became subject to increasingly diverse and volatile interpretations, which from the 1970s onward displayed a kind of deontological stance. The term indigenist also began to accrue a variety of meanings as, for example, someone who worked directly or indirectly in tutelary activities; who undertook engaged research; or, even more generally, who defended the rights of indigenous populations. In light of this, we arrive here at a strange outcome. The terms indigenism and indigenist—completely divested of their original meaning, or at least the meaning they had when introduced into Brazil in the 1950s—became reappropriated by agents, sometimes both actors and authors, located in a wide range of social situations: members of a renewed missionary movement, or anthropologists working in universities or for nongovernmental organizations, or workers employed in technical support programs for the government's large regional development projects. This kind of appropriation and use of the term indigenism—a process still taking place today—began to define activities far removed from applied research programs or indeed any type of work in which anthropological methods and theories could have some impact. Were we to identify a common denominator to these diverse meanings, it would be primarily a recognition of the fact that indigenous societies are forced to rely on government mediators to assist them during a new kind of process— one no longer conceived as forced incorporation under the sway of orthodox positivism as the case at the start of the twentieth century, but rather based on essentially culturalist conceptions, emergent in the 1950s, according to which these societies should be allowed to change at their own pace. We may recall that similar positions had already emerged elsewhere in the world—under British colonialism and the concept of indirect rule, or indeed under Portuguese colonialism—positions vigorously adopted during the processes of decolonialization that followed World War II and debated in forums such as that of the International Labor Organization, which Brazilian indigenists and anthropologists were able to attend.

All contemporary uses of the term indigenism are dominated by ideas of engagement and ethical defense. Compared with the term's original Mexican context, we can note that the Brazilian appropriation modifies the contents of an imported system of representations in response to other knowledge traditions and disciplines. The historical peculiarity of this migratory process lies in the fact that the term lost original aspects of its meaning. Among other changes, it gradually ceased to refer to an applied anthropology, or a state knowledge, or the sense of constructing national communities through the sponsorship of state agencies. In compensation, it acquired new meanings: that of an instrument of critical, militant, or utopic intervention, which displaced it from the world of public administration and its associated practices to the terrain of a kind of university ethics.

These reappropriations obscure the fact that Brazilian anthropology, however distant it may be from applied concerns, has maintained many links with traditions of knowledge that were not institutionalized in the form of academic disciplines. This in turn has led to overlooking a whole universe of popular representations, where we encounter figures such as that of "the Indian," a prototype of minority groups lacking power but romantically transformed into Brazilian national emblems, or that of "the white man," a synthetic image of the colonizer. At another level, declaring an indigenist ethical credo has allowed young anthropologists to adopt fairly naive standpoints in applied projects involving contracts with the state or with nongovernmental organizations. Lacking the requisite preparation for undertaking the role of political mediation implied by these activities, or for deciphering the different meaning systems at work in the production of texts designed to serve as technical evidence in juridical trials, these anthropologists resort to a kind of common sense derived from the sertanista tradition rather than to any theoretical or methodological tools generated by anthropology. It is not just consultancy in indigenous issues where this absence of an adequate system of professional training is exposed. The entire work market for anthropologists depends on a system capable of allying the basic training of doctoral students with the reformulation of issues that are irreducible to the theoretical fetishization of the classics to which the anthropological institution resorts in order to defend its relative (and relatively weak) autonomy from public administration and international development issues.

Adopting an ethical stance is by itself insufficient when considering many dimensions of the public policies relating to the different segments of society, although such a stance may be capable of producing considerable advances at the level of knowledge. The trajectory taken by indigenism in Brazil affords an insight into some of the obstacles to intellectual innovation found in analyzing the relations between state knowledge and university disciplines. Accompanying this trajectory in a deeper fashion allows us to observe key moments in the birth of modern social anthropology in Brazil, as well as its legacies and mutations—a panorama this study can only sketch.

Notes

1 In the wake of the juridical and political independence of the nation-states deriving from European expansion, the political dimensions of the relations between populations identified and/or identifying themselves as indigenous and the conquered spaces cease to be considered as forms of colonialism. For the social sciences produced in these new nations, the term colonialism and its corollaries apply only to the "colonial period"—an ideological construct typical to nationalist chronologies deeply shaped by political inspirations. Inversely, colonialism often

has become a key term in the mostly vague denunciations made in the analytic universe of self-styled postcolonial studies (see the critiques in Thomas 1994: 1–32; and L'Estoile, this volume). Here I use the term to emphasize the virtues of a long-term perspective on the connections (without thereby supposing strict continuities) between, on one hand, the creole elites and forms of colonial power and, on the other, the national elites and forms of power implied in the governance of historically and culturally differentiated populations within the nation-states resulting from European conquest.

2   Here I adopt the notion of tradition of knowledge as defined by Fredrik Barth (1993: 3–25, 339–54).

3   For a development of this viewpoint and an exploration of other traditions, see Souza Lima 2002.

4   See Boxer 1969, chapter 1, for a global view of this process of exploration.

5   This term possesses similarities and differences in relation to so-called Indianism, a concept of singular importance in the Brazilian context. Queiroz 1962: 95–97 provides a literary history of the terms indigenism and Indianism.

6   For a development of the historical context in which indigenism became an ideology of state action, see Nolasco Armas 1981: 67–73; Bonfil 1970 [1981]: 87–96; and Lomnitz, this volume. On the importance of the 1910 revolution and its relations to indigenous and territorial issues, see Williamson 1992: 378–83.

7   Comas was a researcher who basically devoted himself to the study of physical anthropology and archaeology. He was part of the Mexican anthropological establishment—at once a product and a producer of indigenism. The text that I will present was a monograph financed and published by the Inter-American Indigenist Institute, which, as we shall see, emerged out of this movement.

8   On the presidency of Lázaro Cárdenas, see Williamson 1992: 397–400.

9   See Souza Lima 1989 for a study of the relations between natural history museums and indigenism in Brazil.

10   On representations of Rondon's career, see Souza Lima 1991.

11   The CNPI was composed of seven members designated by presidential decree, one of whom had to be from the National Museum.

12   The work was edited in various languages, including German, and from its third edition in 1935 it made up part of the collection *Brasiliana*, which was launched to enshrine Brazilian nationality and its supporters. The work subsequently turned into an instrument for affirming Brazilian ethnology in contrast to the products (above all German) of the hegemonic model of the ethnological study of indigenous populations in America—works written on the basis of long and onerous scientific expeditions, organized by foreigners linked to the Americanist circle and by collectors for European museums. *Rondônia* therefore served as an exemplary work, winning national and international accolades and becoming an emblem of the Brazilian capacity for scientific production. On Roquette-Pinto and his links with the SPI and Franz Boas, see Castro Faria 1998: 149–72.

13   The anthropologist Heloisa Alberto Torres (1895–1977)—who was the daughter of Alberto Torres, one of the main commentators on Brazilian society at

the beginning of the twentieth century—was director of the National Museum from 1938 to 1955, a period in which her wide network of relations in both politics and Brazilian public administration enabled the museum to obtain the resources for training anthropologists to study indigenous peoples. Heloisa Torres also had an important impact on Brazilian indigenist policies owing to her long-standing participation in the CNPI (see Castro Faria 1998: 201–8).

14 On the São Paulo Free College of Sociology and Politics and its role in training researchers in anthropology, see Limongi 1989: 217–33.

15 Darcy Ribeiro, Eduardo Galvão, and Roberto Cardoso de Oliveira later became leaders of a line of research that left its mark on Brazilian anthropology—namely, the studies of interethnic contact. For a historical account of this line of research, see Peirano 1981: 120–71 and, in particular, Oliveira 1987: 495–98. It should be noted that the postgraduate training of Eduardo Galvão (1921–1976), who completed his doctorate at Columbia, was the result of decades of contacts between Heloisa Alberto Torres and Boas. On Galvão's career, see Castro Faria 1998: 187–200, and Gonçalves 1996: 11–23.

16 A set of themes focusing specifically on indigenous societies had already been presented at the time of the first Brazilian Anthropology Meeting: "*Ethnology*, speaker Herbert Baldus; *Acculturation*, speaker Eduardo Galvão; *Indigenist Policy*, speaker Darcy Ribeiro" (Castro Faria 1998: 32).

17 Castro Faria in 1963 produced a very precise assessment of the extent to which the anthropological viewpoint had penetrated into indigenist politics: "During the following three meetings . . . this set of themes remained much the same. At the V Meeting, which occurred in 1961 in Belo Horizonte, the theme of 'Brazilian Indigenist Policy' continued to figure in the program and final report, once more associated with Darcy Ribeiro's name. . . . The discussion of Indigenist Policy involved an attempt to impose the supremacy of scientific criteria over administrative and logistical criteria" (quoted in Castro Faria 1998: 33–34).

18 This report also contained information on the Third Inter-American Indigenist Congress, which was attended by a Brazilian delegation that included José Maria da Gama Malcher and Roberto Cardoso de Oliveira, among others.

19 This governmental agency, designed to train the technical-scientific elites of the administration and higher education system, was part of a global set of "campaigns": the military terminology implied the idea of combating underdevelopment, a rhetoric strongly influenced by the new formulations of social problems that began to take root in Brazil in the 1950s.

20 Luiz de Castro Faria entered the National Museum in 1936 as an unpaid trainee before joining the teaching staff in 1944. One of his first missions was to accompany (and as the National Museum's representative, to control) the 1938 French expedition to Central Brazil led by Claude Lévi-Strauss and Jean Vellard. He later played a crucial role in creating institutional spaces for anthropology and his influence over various generations of anthropologists was fundamental both in Rio de Janeiro and the rest of Brazil. On his career, see Castro Faria 1998: 1–25.

21 The text was republished in 1976 under the title *Do índio ao bugre: O*

processo de assimilação dos Terena. Both editions include a preface by Darcy Ribeiro, demonstrating the work's research links with the works of the SPI Studies Section where it had been initiated.

22   On the denegation of the application of anthropological knowledge in Brazil, see Oliveira and Souza Lima 1983: 277–90; and Souza Lima 1998: 221–68 (see also Oliveira, this volume).

23   After 1939, the Indian Protection Service became part of the Ministry of Agriculture. Darcy Ribeiro headed the Ministry of the Interior in the João Goulart government, which was deposed by military coup in 1964. The 1962 text (Ribeiro 1962) collates reports written during the 1950s when Ribeiro was head of the SPI Studies Section. These reports contain positions similar to those of various documents from the first decade of the twentieth century at the time of the SPI's first attempts to control mediation between Indians and non-Indians. Although not an official government position, it was at least the position of the elite in power at the time who denounced the frictions between the state machinery and the political parties.

24   On the notion of territorialization, see Oliveira 1999: 11–39. On the creation of the Xingu Indigenous Park and the enormous repercussions thereof, see Menezes 2000. On the history of FUNAI, see Souza Lima 2001.

25   Concerning the effects of the politics of the colonization of Amazonia on indigenous societies in the 1970s, see Davis 1977 (see also Albert 1997b: 177–210).

26   On the study project on the relations involved in interethnic friction, see Cardoso de Oliveira 1978 [1972]: 83–130, 151–72, 141–49. On the debates with Ribeiro, see 1978 [1972]:9–17, where Cardoso de Oliveira emphasizes Ribeiro's brief participation in FUNAI's short-lived Executive Council. For the background to the first postgraduate courses in social anthropology, as well as the research projects preceding them, see Corrêa 1995: 25–106, and Rubim 1997. It should be noted that Cardoso de Oliveira's links with the Mexican intellectual context are still alive today.

27   Concerning the courses in indigenism, see Saldanha 1996. My own fieldwork over the last few years has primarily concentrated on studying this phenomenon, through participant observation as well as the collection and analysis of the life histories of sertanistas/indigenists and teachers of these courses. Most of the observations found in the latter part of this text derive from this research.

28   For a description of projects developed by anthropologists linked to universities or nongovernmental organizations among the Ticuna of the Upper Solimões (Amazon) in Amazonas state and the Guarani of Mato Grosso, see Oliveira 1987 and Almeida 1991.

29   On changes in the Catholic Church's activities among indigenous societies, see Pacini 1999, chapter 1.

30   For examples of texts published in Brazil revealing a distinctly indigenist set of references, see Cardoso de Oliveira 1978 [1972]: 197–222; and Bastide 1979: 9–50.

João Pacheco de Oliveira

THE ANTHROPOLOGIST AS EXPERT

Brazilian Ethnology between Indianism and Indigenism

Is it the anthropologist's role to decide whether an individual or a collective can be defined as "indigenous" or, further, to establish the limits of the territory to be officially recognized by the state? As a specialist, does he or she possess the conceptual and methodological tools required for such a definition? In epistemological and ethical terms, should the anthropologist make such a decision, insofar as it implies agreeing to act as a substitute for concrete historical agents (indigenous peoples, class sectors or other social groups, or the state itself) and to assume the role of arbiter between opposed or even antagonistic social interests?

These are all questions inspired by Pierre Bourdieu's reflections (1980) on the attitude that the sociologist should maintain when confronted by intense competition between social actors for social classifications and identities. Perhaps these questions will puzzle anthropologists who do not work with indigenous peoples, or those who over the last two decades have worked in political and institutional contexts outside of Brazil. But while such questions may seem strange and extemporary to the routines of these researchers and teachers, for Brazilian anthropologists these are contemporary dilemmas that permeate their day-to-day relationships with indigenous peoples and with the various state authorities.

Indeed, from the end of the 1980s to the late 1990s different sectors of the state have increasingly turned to the work (qualified as "technical") of anthropologists with specialized training, primarily those incorporated into the academic circuit (universities, museums, and research centers). This demand for collaboration—expressed in the requests for anthropological inquiries and reports[1]—arose out of wider moves to secure juridical and institutional reform in Brazil. These reforms aimed to modify the authoritarian legal practices and administrative structures implanted by the military governments in place from 1964 to 1985. The new political setting was also characterized by the gradual adaptation of national institutions and interests to transnational mechanisms and institutions (1995 to the present). In administrative terms, the demand for collaboration has become focused on the appointment of anthropologists to coordinate work groups formed by the indigenist governmental agency Fundação Nacional do Índio (FUNAI) for the purpose of delimiting indigenous lands.

The novelty of this collaboration has been widely welcomed by anthropologists, judges, and administrators. It is not difficult to comprehend the reasons for such enthusiasm in light of the previous situation: legislation in the area had been based around a centralizing and assimilationist tradition, implemented by an indigenist agency that systematically excluded anthropologists from its activities and ignored the specific nature of anthropological work.[2] However, in contrast to the generally positive appraisal of this recent encounter between anthropologists and state agencies, here I adopt a critical and sociologically relativizing posture: my aim is for this essay to function as a *mauvaise conscience* (bad conscience) capable of bringing to the surface the complexities and risks implied in such collaboration.

In the course of this text, it will become clear that the anthropologist is not bound by the roles and expectations typical to conventional research, but rather comes to define himself or herself (whether by inclusion or opposition) in response to other discourses. In other words, in the split between Indianist and indigenist discourse,[3] between romanticism and political negotiation, anthropologists face the challenge of redefining their own performance—one that meets the demands of the specific context of public inquiries (very different from ethnographic situations), but that equally safeguards the scientific quality of their work, perfecting new conceptual tools and establishing more sophisticated criteria for evaluation.

In the final section of this essay, I draw a parallel between fieldwork in ordinary ethnographic situations and research in administrative and judicial inquiries, while also pointing to the relevance of this localized comparison in a more general discussion. Rather than limiting this debate to anthropology's less-canonical output (such as legal reports), I argue that it should be extended to include ethnography itself and its products.

The Historical Context

Anthropological reports and inquiries in Brazil first appeared in the context of redemocratization, a process that culminated in the declaration of a new constitutional charter in 1988. This was the result of an extensive national debate that lasted for more than a year and involved the consultation and mobilization of civil society as a whole. In the indigenist area, a new visibility was given to all kinds of associations (nongovernmental organizations, professional and scientific associations, the church, trade unions, directly interested groups)—a process that reflected their capacity to put forward useful ideas for securing the rights of minority groups, particularly those of indigenous peoples.

By 1988 the attorney general's office of the republic was immersed in private lawsuits of the federal government for its legal declaration of indigenous areas. Alarmed with the poor quality of the information supplied by the official indigenist body (FUNAI), the office contacted the Brazilian Anthropological Association (Associação Brasileira de Antropologia [ABA]) and requested the expert advice of anthropologists specializing in indigenous populations. Concerned particularly with the financial cost of the compensation payouts being sought, the attorney general's office established an agreement with ABA allowing the former to contract (and remunerate) professionals appointed by the association. These anthropologists would be employed to conduct inquiries and produce legal reports providing proofs and arguments in support of the governmental initiatives.

Also this same year the new constitutional charter was proclaimed. This contained a small but important chapter on indigenous populations, guaranteeing legal recognition of their cultural and linguistic diversity, as well as their distinct forms of organization. In effect, the new legislation reversed a previous tradition of assimilationist policies, whose ultimate goal had been to integrate Indians into the so-called national communion—an objective also made explicit in ordinary laws such as the 1973 Estatuto do Índio (Statute of the Indian; a law still in force today). In addition, governmental protection was declared for the lands traditionally occupied by indigenous populations. In a subsequent decree (1996), the government established norms for the process of identifying the territory of each ethnic group and attributed an important role to the anthropology specialist who would undertake the necessary studies.

During the period of the National Constitutional Assembly, FUNAI remained on the margins of the debates and proposals, while the ABA, the Indigenist Missionary Council (Conselho Indigenista Missionário [CIMI]) and various nongovernmental bodies sent technical information and proposals. Throughout this process, the indigenous leaders made themselves present whenever crucial decisions were required.[4] Yet, shortly before final drafting, FUNAI declared itself contrary to all the proposals, even going so far as to recommend the annulment of the constitutional amendment that established the priority of indigenous rights in the case of land disputes.[5] In complete variance to the desires for democratization expressed in the constitution, FUNAI remained totally opposed to any change in its own administrative practices, and indeed chose a process of "remilitarization" by committing itself to a policy of national security that opposed the creation of indigenous areas in border regions.[6]

The posture adopted by the indigenist agency was only modified at the start of the following decade during the official preparations for the second United Nations Conference on the Environment and Development, which was to be hosted by Brazil (Eco-92).[7] Fearing denouncements by defenders of minority rights and severe criticism from other countries, the Brazilian government quickly undertook a radical revision of its policies in this area. Prominent indigenists and ecologists were appointed to direct the agencies responsible for indigenous peoples and the environment, effectively setting in practice some of the guidelines contained in the constitution years earlier. The aim was to promote a new global and local dynamic to generate new standards in relation to indigenist policy (see Brown 1993; Conklin and Graham 1995; Oliveira 2000).

The Brazilian government's new attitude provoked a positive reaction from international organizations, which led to the release of loans and funding for official indigenist and environmental activities. One of the priorities identified by the World Bank and the European Economic Community was the preservation of the Amazonian rainforest, a project (titled the Pilot Program for Protection of the Tropical Forests) that involved the demarcation of indigenous territories and the creation of new conservation zones. Over the next few years, the governmental sectors responsible for dealing with these issues were formed. These sectors worked to set up technical teams and modify various administrative procedures, establishing guidelines for joint participation and securing the trust of the international agencies that would be providing the necessary resources. In 1995 in the region of Legal Amazonia[8] a program of indigenous land demarcation was initiated (called Programa de Proteção às Terras Indígenas da Amazônia Legal), which was based in FUNAI itself with resources coming from the pilot program.

Once again FUNAI's lack of technical staff surfaced as a limiting factor in this program. A policy was therefore initiated of approaching the universities and the ABA with the express purpose of recruiting anthropologists capable of carrying out the identification of lands claimed by indigenous peoples in lawsuits, many of which had been ignored or downplayed by FUNAI's directors in the 1980s. Hence it was as a corollary of the new setting created by Eco-92 (Oliveira 1993) that professional anthropologists started to be called on to coordinate FUNAI's land identification work groups.[9] Here the anthropologist was drafted to work in conjunction with other specialists (including engineers, cartographers, and a specialist in environmental issues) to produce a technical report that, as explicitly stipulated in Decree 1775/1996, would act as the legal basis for the administrative process of recognizing indigenous land rights.

Inquiries and Their Paradoxes

My aim in this text is not to discuss the impact of these new governmental directives and partnerships (see Ricardo 1994; Oliveira and Almeida 1998), but rather to reflect on the risks and challenges they place on the anthropologist's work. The sheer volume of these official requests justifies such a concern: through the ABA/attorney general's office accord, approximately forty inquiries have taken place since 1988, and according to FUNAI's data (from 1997) there still exist more than 150 indigenous lands to be identified. Taking into account the fact the ABA has around nine hundred associates of which more than two hundred of these study (or have studied) indigenous populations and, furthermore, observing the extent of this collaboration (which involves universities from different parts of Brazil and anthropologists from the main research centers), it is impossible to overestimate the effects of this involvement on anthropological practice. Some academics see this issue as simply a question of personal choice (a process with which the anthropologist may or may not decide to collaborate), while others treat it as an expansion of the work market for anthropologists (and as a sign of positive recognition of their profession). Although all of these professionals make use of their involvement to bolster indigenous demands and interests vis-à-vis the state, I believe this is an issue that affects the expectations and demands placed by society (and particularly the Indians) on the anthropologist. For this reason the issue deserves close attention.

Put simply, my concern is with the complex set of tasks and expectations now being assigned to anthropologists. There has undoubtedly been a substantial advance in ethnographic research on indigenous peoples living within Brazil, as well as in important theoretical developments explaining the dynamics of interethnic contact and the organizational and symbolic forms of these societies. But we need to remain aware that the questions put to anthropologists in the judicial context are highly specific and demand applied knowledge with very detailed conclusions and precise responses.

Can the anthropologist really guarantee that a particular human group is (or is not) indigenous—in other words, that it maintains unbroken links with pre-Colombian populations? And, accepting that such an ethnic group exists, can the anthropologist determine the territory belonging to it with any real precision?

These are very complex issues from the anthropological point of view, yet they are questions for which judges, prosecutors, and lawyers expect precise responses. This is why they use the term "inquiry" (where anthropologists prefer "research") for the investigations conducted for the purpose of producing a report with a high degree of technical-scientific precision.

These preconditions mean that the reports issued during judicial processes can be compared with other official documents making up part of administrative processes and resulting from initiatives taken by the executive power. Here I am referring to the reports produced by "anthropologists" via the "work groups for indigenous land identification" (Oliveira and Almeida 1998: 74–100; Souza Lima 1998: 235–61). In neither case does the production of inquiries and reports look to respond to questions posed by anthropological theory, nor are these inquiry activities financed or sponsored at the initiative of the academic community. Since they are solicited and resourced by other bodies—either by different sectors of the judiciary or by FUNAI itself—the inquiry reports clearly imply the tacit acceptance of certain rules and expectations foreign to the context of anthropological practice per se.

Here my concern is precisely the extent to which the anthropologist can—or should—attempt to reply to such questions without abandoning the conceptual rigor and methodological attentiveness proper to the discipline. This question informs the remainder of my text, where I will focus my discussion on the anthropological criteria that may (or may not) corroborate the knowledge produced in such inquiries, or even call for a reformulation of the theoretical grounding of anthropologists and/or the demands placed on them.

The intervention of anthropologists in judicial and administrative processes should not, strictly speaking, be identified as a modality of applied anthropology; neither does it correspond in any sense to an example of so-

The Anthropologist as Expert 229

called anthropological advocacy (see Maybury-Lewis 1985; Wright 1988), nor may it be seen as a crystallized form of state knowledge.[10] Instead, it should be understood as the exercise of a technico-scientific expertise caught up in a complex play of pressures and negotiations involving different types of social mediators (governmental and nongovernmental organizations, scientific associations and universities, Indians and private interests).

My intention here is to look at some of the dangers and traps that may spring from the collaboration between anthropologists and lawyers, given that this encounter—involving, as it does, the elements of anthropological research, judicial action, and indigenous demands—may not always result in the happiest solutions for everyone, given that each party is motivated by distinct interests and doctrines. Disciplines such as law and anthropology possess their own well-defined methods and sets of doctrines crystallized in written codes and specific bodies of knowledge: hence, it is highly unlikely that the wishes of individual actors (who foresee advantages in this collaboration) can by themselves make a clean slate of the attitudes and traditions previously in operation.

The relatively new nature of this encounter (which derives from the agreement signed in 1988 between the ABA and the attorney general's office) provoked excessively optimistic and slightly nonsensical expectations. The natural euphoria also ended up generating a certain sociological naïveté that led to actors taking as necessary and permanent what was only circumstantial and temporary. The general tone of this text is therefore one of problematizing this encounter between anthropology and law.[11] As such, the exercise proposed here is to rethink—as inspired by the contributions and impasses of modern anthropological research—the questions posed to anthropology in the context of inquiries and reports.

Defining an Ethnic Group

The first question involves the definition of an ethnic group. Common-sense expectations concerning the activities of anthropologists in inquiries and in making reports are fairly similar to the naturalized way in which the various anthropological approaches have conceptualized sociocultural units (Oliveira 1988: 26–28). Just as students of nature are capable of identifying and classifying a specimen from the natural world based on animal and plant morphology, so people tend to presume that, as a specialist, the anthropologist should be capable of identifying and classifying concrete individuals within distinct social units according to the adopted cultural forms. Further compounding this naive supposition, caution has to be taken not to become seduced by simplifications, presuming, for example, that since humans are speaking animals capable of self-classification, the task of identification is made substantially easier (thus opening up a dangerous shortcut into the study of identities).

Indeed such commonplace expectations are far from borne out in reality. Cultural forms fail to reveal the same homogeneity and regularity as genetic transmission, while social units are never so clearly delineated, discontinuous, and permanent as natural genera and species. Above all, social units change with a speed, and in a radical way, unparalleled in natural evolution. Social units abandon old cultural forms and receive (and adapt) additional forms from other societies while simultaneously creating their own new and distinctive forms. Given this scenario of mutability and instability, how can we possibly guarantee that the units in question are still the same?

In some situations the anthropologist's work is made relatively easier, notably when the groups in question retain a strong distinctivity in relation to the cultural dynamics of Brazilian national society. One salient aspect of such distinctiveness is the use of their own language. This also applies to the case—nowadays increasingly rare—of groups who live in a situation of marked isolation; their characterization as an indigenous population can be achieved through the use of absolutely consensual criteria, such as the possession of an exceptionally simple technology or nomadism.

In many other situations, though, the investigation tends to be much more complex and leads to far from consensual results. For example, ethnic groups that have already lost their language and whose culture fails to contrast visibly with that of the region may find their status as indigenous peoples questioned in two ways (in part complementary). First, common sense dictates that historical continuity has already been severed and that, given the acceleration of the process of acculturation, such groups have become fully assimilated and thereby indistinct from the rest of the Brazilian population. Such peoples are conceived as "descendants" or "remnants" who, despite conserving fragments of cultural memory and folklorized traces of customs, can no longer be characterized as Indians. Second, it is similarly argued that the group's original culture has been modified to such an extent, undergoing such a distortion, that nothing typical or authentic remains. Here, an accusation follows of a blatant manipulation of ethnic identity, in which—enticed by clear-cut material advantages—"false Indians" and "inauthentic" indigenous cultures have started to emerge.

Escaping these impasses requires a dialogue with the anthropological conceptualization of ethnic groups. Ever since Barth (1969, 1984, 1988), anthropologists have been working with a fairly precise definition of what constitutes an ethnic group—a definition very different from that commonly accepted. Specific elements of a culture (such as customs, rituals, and shared values) may undergo considerable variations over time or as a result of adaptive adjustments to alterations in their surroundings. What matters, though, is the maintenance of the same organizational form prescribing a unified pattern of interaction between the members and nonmembers of the group in question.

If an ethnic identification corresponds to a classificatory act practiced by a subject within a given situational context, it makes no sense to suppose that a group's self-classifications and those made by others must necessarily coincide. In fact, Moerman (1965) demonstrates precisely the opposite case in a situational analysis of attributions of ethnic identity in the Thailand peninsula. What this and other situational analyses (see Nagata 1974: 348–49) have shown is that classifications performed by different social subjects may vary not only in relation to the value attributed to the terms, but also in relation to the actual boundaries of these elements and in the definition of the nature of the levels of inclusion.

This exposes a large disparity between the anthropological conceptualization of an ethnic group and the nominalist definition given by Oscar Lewis (in a seminar held at the Inter-American Indigenist Institute) and later incorporated into the legislation of various Latin American countries: this definition states that an Indian is anyone who considers himself or herself as such, and is also considered so by the surrounding society. This definition was the source for the characterization of ethnic identity contained in the third article of the Brazilian Statute of the Indian (Law 6.001/73).[12]

The Nature of an Ethnic Group's Continuity

The second question to be considered here is the nature of the historical continuity attributed to an ethnic group. In reading the queries raised by judges, prosecutors, or defense lawyers, the impression created is that ethnic identity is substantial, crystalline, permanent, and independent of internal contexts and divisions. However, the literature on ethnicity contains abundant examples of how reality contradicts this impression.

A non-Brazilian ethnographic account can be cited here as an example of this issue: in a superb description of the case of the Ndendeuli in Africa, Joseph Gallagher (1974) provides a clear demonstration of how the usual commonsense expectations concerning the process of defining an ethnic identity are mistaken. The existence of an identity unifying and singularizing a population is by no means a cultural requirement, a fact that obviously applies to indigenous peoples (including those in Brazil) who have not as yet passed through a process of incorporation within a colonial situation (Wachtel 1992: 46–48; on Brazil, see Oliveira 1999 :8–9).

Far from being a profound expression of a group's unity, ethnonyms often result from a historical accident, frequently a linguistic misunderstanding produced by a play of words or a passing quip. In many cases a dominated group does not exist as an isolated unit, but rather is incorporated into other populations (equally dominated groups or, conversely, sections of the dominant population), becoming divided, subdivided, and added to other groupings of different types. Thus, as fragmented, assembled, and reassembled in various modalities and in different situational contexts, what form of historical and cultural continuity can such a group still present?

Perhaps the only continuity that can be sustained in rebuilding the historical process lived through by such a group is the way in which the group continually refabricates its unity and difference in relation to other groups with which it interacts. The existence of certain native categories of self-identification, as well as distinctive interactive practices, can help delimit a group in relation to others, although the content of these classificatory categories varies substantially and the specific area of sociability fluctuates considerably by expanding and contracting in different situational contexts.

James Clifford arrives at similar conclusions in his description of a judicial dispute between the contemporary inhabitants of the indigenous district of Cape Cod and the Mashpee tribe: "The Indians at Mashpee made and remade themselves through specific alliances, negotiations, and struggles. It is just as problematic to say that their way of life 'survived' as to say that it 'died' and was 'reborn' . . . The history of Mashpee is not one of unbroken tribal institutions or cultural traditions. It is a long, relational struggle to maintain and recreate identities" (1988: 338–39).

The use of biological metaphors to describe social processes can be seriously deceptive, thereby provoking unfounded and unreasonable expectations. The existential modality of ethnic groups and/or cultures bears no resemblance to that of an individual: equating them therefore means eliminating fundamental aspects, homogenizing what is ontologically diverse, and encouraging the emergence of dangerous interpretations and false questions.

The application of biological metaphors to indigenous peoples—especially the more negative kind, such as death, degeneration, or survival—tends to encourage distorted investigations and inappropriate policies from the outset. Attempting to counter the consequences of biological tropes by simply inverting their value attributions from negative to positive—for example, emphasizing the rebirth or historical continuity of indigenous peoples—produces only false solutions compromised from the start by the very problematic impeding the research's advancement. Indeed, it has been as an alternative response to these problems that more technical and apparently distanced terms have been able to flourish—concepts such as integration, assimilation, or detribalization.

As an example from my own work, with this issue in mind I resolved to avoid biological metaphors in my study published in 1999 on the indigenous peoples of northeastern Brazil. This is a regional population that has undergone a process of ethnogenesis over the last fifty years, during which an important part of their current ethnic identity has taken shape. In adopting an alternative approach my aim was to reexamine the theoretical problem of the invention of cultures and the construction or emergence of identities (Hobsbawm 1983: 9–10; Wolf 1982; Wagner 1981), relating these issues explicitly to collective processes and specific social situations, explained by the notion of processes of territorialization.[13]

Defining an "Indigenous Community"

The third question I wish to focus on here is more specific than the characterization of ethnic groups or cultures. Taking into account the practical aims of a judicial inquiry, the question posing itself is the extent to which a contemporary human group making up a distinct unit and recognizing itself as indigenous can be classified as such, despite the profound transformations it may have undergone. Any reply to this question needs to be twofold: with the first addressing the application of a legal definition, and the second turned to convincing a much wider lay public. Here the difficulty arises from the enormous discrepancy in the meanings attributed to the term Indian.

In the first attribution, "Indian" indicates a juridical status within contemporary Brazilian society, endowing its bearer with particular rights as defined in specific legislation. These rights exist only insofar as they refer to a collectivity of which the person is a recognized member; namely, the indigenous community (as stated in the Statute of the Indian) or the indigenous people (a more suitable sociological expression).

In the second attribution, "Indian" indicates a cultural state—a fact clearly indicated by the terms that may in different contexts substitute for it: forest dweller, native, aborigine, savage, and primitive, among others. All clearly mean an inhabitant of the forest who is bound to nature and lacking the benefits of civilization. The prototypical image—portrayed by painters, illustrators, fine artists, children's illustrators, and cartoonists—is of a naked individual who reads only from the great book of nature and who wanders freely through the forest and carries with him or her (or displays on the body) evidence of an exotic and rudimentary culture reminiscent of the beginnings of human history.

In such a vision, the semantic load is already determined: the Indian is effectively an example of a primitive being, archaic in nature and doomed to vanish. Doubtless it is always possible to resort to a Romanticist discourse and invert the preconceptions of evolutionism; moreover, the Indians themselves may deploy such representations to expose the guilty conscience of non-Indians or to incorporate the salvationism of ecological discourse at the turn of the millennium. But even so, this only reinforces the general impression that the place these people really belong is in the past, and that the preservation of primitive peoples in the modern world is an extravagance only made possible in extraordinary and entirely artificial conditions.

To a certain extent, indigenists use such images to correlate contemporary Indians with "good savages" and thus foment a sense of guilt among public opinion over the brutalities practiced during the process of colonization. Yet such arguments only strengthen the belief in the need for a strong protector, a role reserved for the state and performed by its agents (including, of course, a prominent role for the indigenists themselves). In certain cases even some of the interpretations produced by anthropologists, insofar as they focus exclusively on phenomena of alterity, may be appropriated by common sense and public opinion as grounds for legitimizing an atemporal representation of indigenous peoples (for a more developed discussion of this point, see Fabian 1983; Duchet 1985; Oliveira 1999).

The idea of converging these two meanings of "Indian" strikes me as an unpromising and extremely risky undertaking. To give an example: the popular imagery described above—which partly reflects an experience specific to Brazilian society and partly stems from a wider Western imagination concerning the primitive (see, e.g., Diamond 1969; Duchet 1980)—could perhaps be used to justify the official recognition of territory for the Yanomami or a small number of other relatively isolated peoples. But what about all the others? Should they be considered remnants or false Indians? Here we need not consider only extreme cases, such as those of the indigenous peoples of the Brazilian northeast, who are experiencing the kinds of dilemmas extensively reported for the Ndendeuli of Africa and Mashpee of North America. Even peoples who maintain their own language and core institutions, such as the Ticuna, Tucano, Baniwa, and others situated on Brazil's northern frontier, have their status as Indians questioned by loggers, miners, and commercial dealers interested in their lands—indeed, they are deemed acculturated even by some governmental authorities, who use this contention to justify drastically limiting their territorial rights (see Oliveira 1990 for an account of the Calha Norte Project).

It is important to stress the dangers of allowing the juridical definition of an ethnic group as an indigenous community or indigenous people to be dominated by a confused and contestable popular imagery of the Indian, particularly since legal inquiries often occur in situations that are radically different from those supposed by the myth of primitivity. Likewise, the anthropologists' own contributions should avoid vague or evasive digressions: instead, they should carefully explain that they consider and recognize as an indigenous society every collectivity that, first, through its categories and circuits of interaction distinguishes itself from national Brazilian society, and, second, claims itself to be indigenous (that is, descendent—whether in genealogical, historical, or symbolic terms—from a population of pre-Colombian origin).

Manipulations can obviously take place, but I believe this is an essential part of social dynamics and legal virtualities. For the jurist too there is nothing scandalous in admitting that whenever a citizen can be placed in two legal situations, either legislation (or jurisprudence) develops technical norms to determine which status should prevail (and in this case anthropology is unable to provide technico-scientific support), or the faculty for making the decision is left to the interested party. I think this is the direction to be taken in considering the issue of legally recognizing an indigenous people.

The Process of Identifying Indigenous Lands

The main point, however, where all attentions converge in the production of an anthropological inquiry is the definition of the effective limits of
an indigenous territory. As this forms the crux of the judicial dispute, it is
undoubtedly the most sensitive point and here the expert can expect to be
subjected to just about every kind of questioning.

The anthropologist approaching the case must be extremely wary of a
kind of spontaneous ethnology, generated by the norms and categories
present in the legal decrees and administrative acts, reworked and made
explicit by the queries formulated by judges and lawyers, and put into operation by the working conditions (with a stress on the time factor) provided to
the anthropologist. This set of expectations and injunctions, steeped in the
juridical context on which the inquiry is focused, can amount to an almost
autonomous set of guidelines; these in turn may end up directing the investigation without ever being the object of closer attention and reflection on
the part of the anthropologist.

The definition of an indigenous land—in other words, the political process through which the state recognizes the rights of an indigenous community over a stretch of national territory—cannot be described or conceived
according to the coordinates of a natural phenomenon. Far from being
immutable, indigenous areas are always under continual revision, with ad-
ditions, reductions, fusions, and separations. This is not a circumstantial
process arising simply from the state's errors or from pressures imposed by
spurious external interests; rather, it is a constitutive aspect, making up part
of the very nature of the process of territorialization of an indigenous society
within the institutional limits established by the nation-state (Williams 1989;
Oliveira 1999).

Obviously the notion of territory is not in any sense new in the discourse
of the human sciences—indeed it comprises a central element in the classification of political systems and the definition of political units. In contrast
to the nation-state, whose limits are rigidly fixed (since these boundaries
permit the application of law and the exercise of war to be distinguished; see,
e.g., Radcliffe-Brown's classic formula of 1940), indigenous peoples possess
much more fluid territorial borders, which regularly oscillate in response to
demographic variations, warfare expeditions, or migratory movements of
various kinds. For these peoples, the claim over land is not fixed a priori in

the constitution of themselves as a political unit, but may undergo profound changes as a result of the circumstantial convergence of interests and the capacity to assert their claim in the face of pressure from other neighboring societies that share analogous characteristics.

It was a historical fact—the colonial presence—that provoked a new kind of relationship to the territory, setting off transformations in these societies at multiple levels of their sociocultural existence. An ethnic group's moves to claim a specific territory cannot be examined in isolation: any study has to take into account the leaders behind the action and the generation that conceived it, as well as alterations in the productive system, the availability of environmental resources, the combination of indigenous forces in the face of non-Indians at a local level, and the wider historical juncture of the field of indigenist action. As a way of marking the historical and politico-progressive nature of this phenomenon, I prefer to work with the notion of processes of territorialization—a concept I have developed elsewhere (Oliveira 1999)—thereby avoiding the suggestion of immanent qualities implied in the notion of territoriality. The drawbacks of using biological metaphors should never be forgotten, as we saw earlier in relation to the actual definition of ethnic groups.

Continuing with our present line of reasoning, it makes no sense to suppose that an inquiry can establish precisely and definitively the geographical area corresponding to an indigenous people's territory. The proposals of the Indians themselves change because their interests, ideologies, and surroundings also change, just as a people's practices and representations concerning the territory (in other words, what some authors term territoriality) cannot be evaluated outside a specific situational context.

Even if it were possible to establish with any precision the territory occupied by an indigenous people hundreds of years ago, this does not necessarily mean that this is the territory claimed by its contemporary members. Only anthropological research can say how the territory is conceptualized by the ethnic group itself at any given moment. Pressed by the expanding colonial fronts, indigenous peoples have frequently been dislocated hundreds of kilometers away from the areas they once inhabited, then subject to processes of reterritorialization in religious missions, farms, towns, rubber plantations, and so on. How can we define their territory if we persist in thinking of indigenous lands as immemorial and originary, seeking (once more) to lend reality to the myth of primitivity?

Keeping in mind the contextual nature of any proposal for the creation of an indigenous land, the anthropologist needs to describe and evaluate it alongside the social situation that generated it. This approach not only applies to the process of ethnogenesis (Oliveira 1999: 33–34), it is also valid for any analytic endeavor in the human sciences. Hence, the anthropologist is advised to carry out a critical examination of the proposals developed and presented by indigenous leaderships, by the indigenist agency (FUNAI), or by other segments or institutions. It is essential that the expert report (just as any other work of abstraction and generalization) includes a description of the relationship between the anthropologist and the researched group; that it makes the documental sources or gathered testimonies explicit; and that it specifies the informants and stresses the concrete basis of everything that is observed and eventually reported. The impressions and conclusions of the expert himself or herself must be carefully described and justified, thereby helping to ensure an accurate evaluation of the limits and the reliability of the actual research.

Inquiry Situations and Ethnographic Situations

Inquiries and reports stem from a fairly singular research situation, when the conflicts over the definition of an indigenous land have already reached the tribunals or state agencies, and thereby become widely known by Indians and non-Indians alike. The vast majority of informants have a relatively clear view of the aims of the anthropologist's work, knowing very well that what they say could be used in a judicial dispute or in the administrative process to strengthen or reduce their claim's chances of success. Indigenous leaders, indigenous organizations, and nongovernmental organizations also assume the task of clarifying the aims of the work to members of the particular ethnic group, prescribing attitudes and opinions for potential interviewees and even preselecting those whose opinions are more suitable for the demands at hand.

Conducting research in a context that involves decisions on issues vital to the informant is not a simple undertaking: it demands the anthropologist's careful control of investigative methods and techniques, as well as a continual attentiveness in relation to the production of data and multiple intervening factors. A researcher possessing only a general training in anthropology or ethnology will face enormous difficulties in assembling the ethnographic data needed to allow him or her to present the divergent positions (not only between Indians and different sections of Brazilian national society but also between the Indians themselves) and to analyze them critically, without becoming a prisoner to the ideologies promulgated by the different actors (individuals or agencies).

A concrete examination of the inquiry situation—as opposed to the ethnographic situation experienced by anthropologists during fieldwork[14]—shows that here the actions and options are situated at the confluence of three distinct discourses (Indianism, indigenism, and anthropology), each made up of its own suppositions, values, and expectations. The potential overlapping of these three discourses in the inquiry situation implies a certain margin for ambiguity; this can only be overcome by developing a set of criteria capable of establishing the strategic predominance of one of these discourses.

With this in mind, the readings that the social actors and agents may make of the inquiry situation, including the anthropologist's own motives and choices, may take three different directions: the Indianist posture, indigenist activism, and the attentive and critical exercise of anthropology. The first position corresponds to a description of indigenous demands based on unilateral and schematic knowledge of "how these Indians were in the past" (that is, "before the arrival of whites"). This reconstruction is taken to refer back to a golden age, in which social forms were plentiful and cultural forms were authentic. Such an approach results in a static and backward-looking model of society, in which the demands and initiatives of the present must forever be evaluated in relation to the forms and values attributed to an idealized past.

The term "Indianism," by which I designate this posture, itself recalls the literary school of Romantic authors of the nineteenth century. This literature portrayed indigenous peoples as heroic protagonists of a nativist narrative; indigenous customs and institutions were used with no concern for ethnographic rigor or veracity, expressing only the viewpoint (exterior and arbitrary, albeit benevolent) of a white narrator. At root the Indian was little more than an instrument for reaffirming the narrator's own values—a vehicle (a nonrandom one) that allowed him to present his own vision as natural and autochthonous (that is, native and unconnected to imported traditions).

Certain similarities can be detected here between this phenomenon and the orientalism critically analyzed by Edward Said (1979) as a discourse crystallizing and reifying otherness (instead of surpassing it by making its own discursive conditions explicit). Both discourses allow the attribution of meaning to colonial practices and help to justify them. Although Indianism seems to omit the negative aspects of the Other, focusing primarily on a critical reevaluation of the narrator's own society, it implicitly stipulates—by considering indigenous peoples as something bygone and referring only to the past of the Brazilian nation—the conditions that should ideally govern relations between Indians and Brazilians. As a relic of the past, the survival of the Indians depends on the altruistic guardianship of a white patron: this, in turn, is inevitably linked to a nativist view of the state.

The Indianist narrative is expressed in a variety of ways in the concrete situation of inquiry making, as well as in actual fieldwork and in the interpretations deriving from the latter. One point I have already mentioned is the search for an indigenous society in its plenitude: that is, with a precontact organization, an authentic culture, and a territory presumed to be permanent and exclusive. These three aspects act in unison in any such search, each serving to reinforce the other.

Criticizing Indianism by no means implies that the analytic exploration of the indigenous past is unimportant from the viewpoint of its theoretico-interpretive and practical consequences. Like the historian, the anthropologist may conduct documentary research with the aim of determining the land occupied by an indigenous people over a wide period of time, establishing the migratory routes the people took and the cultural exchanges they maintained.

Although the task of ascertaining the accuracy of historical sources—through careful examination and comparison, seeking to contextualize them socially and in relation to the diverging interests of the indigenous peoples and colonization—is somewhat difficult and arduous, the results can be of high value in scientific terms. As unique and specialized knowledge, such material should be made readily available to indigenous peoples themselves and to all those charged with deciding (judicially or administratively) the extent of their territorial rights.

It is highly unlikely that the researcher will be recognized as neutral and impartial by the numerous legal authorities and actors involved. Frequently, representatives of the parties opposing the Indians label him or her—mistakenly—as a romantic (that is, someone nostalgic for the past): this is mostly due to the anthropologist's tendency to focus discussion on past land rights and uses that, in the view of their critics, are totally irrelevant to defining current rights of possession. Conversely, should the anthropologist or historian fail to raise these issues, they will end up legitimating versions of history that ignore or annul indigenous rights.

In the continual ebb and flow of disputes surrounding the holding of an inquiry, it is not rare for the anthropologist—in making the data and analyses from a study available to the population in question—to be accused of manipulation, of undue interference in the process, or even of incitement. On the other hand, the Indians themselves may also refute the presented conclusions, preferring to reaffirm only knowledge obtained by oral tradition and taking historical reconstructions based on written documents as partial, limited, and above all harmful to their own interests.

The second approach to consider is the indigenist one. This operates in the space opened up by the discontinuity between the indigenous society in its original plentitude and the form in which it presents itself today within national society. Hence, the indigenist approach operates within the limits set by alien definitions, shifting between the idealized reconstructions conducted by indigenists and the utilitarian characterizations made in the present day by nonindigenous actors. However, in contrast to the Indianists, their intervention is not aimed at rescuing a lost or neglected reality but rather in arbitrating opposed points of view explicitly located in a competitive situation. The task of arbitration—whether between Indians and non-Indians, or between the Indians themselves—is peculiar to indigenist activity (Oliveira 1988: 222–225). The very term 'indigenist' implies a mediating function, usually performed by staff from the official agency or other bodies (public or otherwise).

The inquiry situation may equally embroil the anthropologist in mediation disputes and transform his or her research into an exercise of arbitration. But by adopting such a path, the anthropologist enters into the dispute for social classifications, exploiting an asymmetric position (that of expert) in order to impose his or her solution on the other actors. The anthropologist thereby becomes wrapped up in a double illusion: on one hand, the temptation to speak from a position of power, abandoning his or her own proper field; on the other hand, the sociological naiveté of imagining that his or her own proposal speaks for a particular group or social force.

In administrative inquiries (in other words, in the reports identifying indigenous lands), the coordinator of the work group can evade the onus of responsibility involved in deciding in favor of a proposal, since the existing norms demand that the expert clearly reports "the community's proposal." As the indigenous people and expert interact in asymmetric conditions, the tendency is for the opinions and arguments of the anthropologist to be directly discussed with the Indians. Rather than producing a sociological analysis of their demands, the work group's coordinator ends up undertaking a process of conciliation and arbitration, in which all efforts are directed toward the generation and ratification of a supposedly unified proposal (albeit equally relative and contextual). In this case, the expert remains less exposed than in the case of judicial reports, since he or she makes themselves present through their endorsement of the community's proposal (which they helped to formulate in their condition of mediator and arbiter; indeed, the community for its part only enters into the decision-making context via the identification report produced by the expert himself or herself).

All of these problems, as well as the strategy of speaking in the name of the community's proposal,[15] derive from the same source: the exclusion of the indigenous people and their representatives from the decision-making process. This creates a space for political mediation that can be filled by the anthropologist, provided the latter accepts acting as an indigenist.

The third posture I wish to examine is that of the expert who limits himself or herself to the exercise of anthropology, seeking to alert judges and administrators to the nature and complexity of the social processes involved in the inquiry situation, as well as the form in which the inquiry and identification reports should be read. This requires the anthropologist to reject the prescriptive formulas of both the Indianist and the indigenist discourses, as well as the reformulation of his or her own contribution as a merely technical activity.

At an institutional level, anthropologists need to fight (individually and collectively) for three key modifications to the administrative system for recognizing indigenous lands. The first and most simple change is to reformulate the expert's working context, looking to distance it from an activity primarily focused on decision making and mediation,[16] and aiming instead to approximate his or her involvement more closely to the encounter that characterizes an ethnographic situation. Fostering this change would be relatively simple. It would be enough for the anthropological work involved to be considered as a preliminary study, produced exclusively by someone with specialized training who simply provides the requisite background information for the later activity of a work group—in reality, a governmental commission of negotiation and arbitration between Indians and non-Indians (see Oliveira and Almeida 1998: 75–79).

A second alteration would involve a different conceptualization of the anthropologist's task, qualifying it as a method of establishing a nexus of meaning, corroborated by ethnographic evidence, between an ethnic organization and a collectively appropriated space. Approached in this fashion, the issue would no longer involve defining the limits of an indigenous land through the proposal of an area to be legally recognized; instead, the anthropologist would be employed to supply ethnographic data and analytic arguments enabling a report's readers to evaluate critically the juridical, anthropological, and political bases of the different proposals formulated by the various social actors, as well as assess the very different sociocultural impacts that would result from the implementation of these distinct proposals.

The anthropologist can and should (since he or she possesses instruments for this) hierarchize these alternatives from the viewpoint of ensuring the well-being and sociocultural continuity of the indigenous collectivity in question, supplying the decision makers with a clear vision of the consequences that may arise from the different options. At an extreme, this includes disqualifying proposals that could place the sociocultural grouping involved in an unacceptable position of risk. Here, the anthropologist is a specialist who performs a rigorous and detailed study but is not the decision-making agent. The technical grounding of his or her arguments will contribute significantly to increasing the transparency of the entire process, thus pressuring the authorities into having to justify, in an equally adequate and consistent manner, their reasons for choosing less-recommendable proposals. But the responsibility and onus of the decision can only fall to those who have effective power at their disposal: namely, the administrative and judicial authorities.

A third change would focus specifically on the administrative context, demanding the abandonment of the paternalistic postures and salvationist pretensions still implicit in the existing procedures in this area. In order for the anthropologist to relinquish the position of spokesperson for indigenous interests (an inheritance from the tutelary regime), it is essential that indigenous peoples possess specific representation in the regular decision-taking mechanisms. Focusing on a very different ethnographic context, Fred Myers (1986) examines the disputes involved in representing the native, pointing out the risks entailed when the anthropologist takes on this role (which is one frequently criticized by the indigenous actors themselves). Except in extremely dramatic and highly exceptional situations, the anthropologist should not foster the illusion that he or she is the spokesperson for indigenous interests, nor heighten any expectations in this direction. The exclusion of indigenous peoples from the process of defining their own lands is something that must be directly censured, and the anthropologist should not allow his or her technical activities to be used as a substitute (or supposed compensation) for the absence of indigenous participation.[17]

It may seem strange that, starting out from the dilemmas of anthropological practice in the inquiry situation, this text ends by suggesting the modification of administrative systems and even juridical conceptions. While these are the indelible marks of the context in which this reflection emerged (specifically, the debate between anthropologists, lawyers, and indigenists in Brazil and the important role played by the ABA at this level), maintaining them in this text has a very particular heuristic function: it expresses a commitment to rooting anthropological knowledge in its conditions of production (as recommended in Asad 1973 and Pels and Salemink 1999). Indeed, with this aim in mind, we could hypothesize that the so-called Brazilian style of doing anthropology (described by Ramos 1988) derives from the fact that it is grounded in the anthropologist's active participation in the legal definition of indigenous lands. This may also explain the special attention that Brazilian anthropologists devote to interethnic relations and conflicts (see, e.g., Ribeiro 1970; Cardoso de Oliveira 1978 [1972]) as well as their continual dialogue with the society to which they pertain, including taking a particular stance in relation to facts and questions that imply value judgments.[18]

More specifically, my interest lies in calling attention to an implicit (and generally little discussed) dimension of "doing anthropology": the practices through which researchers in various ways react to and interfere with their working conditions. For the field researcher, does this simply involve accepting the socially imposed definitions of scientific methodology, taking on the role of a professional responding to a preexisting market? Or is it the inverse: intervening in his or her working conditions, acting to make them more compatible with the potentials and limits of the discipline, while simultaneously remaining attentive to the ethical and political premises always present in some form in any anthropological analysis? Of course, research situations vary greatly and in analytically exploiting this variability, rooting forms of knowledge in their social context, the anthropologist must remain aware of the interventions that he or she performs. Such reflexivity is the only way of ensuring the viability of their activity and the production of the desired type and quality of knowledge.

Developing this kind of detailed scrutiny of anthropology as an exercise implies an on-going critical examination of the procedures involved in research, as well as a greater historical contextualization and comparative analysis from anthropologists as a whole. Where studies of autochthonous populations are concerned, it is imperative to describe not only the relations between anthropologists and the collectivities they study, but above all their forms of participation in the sectorial politics that affect indigenous populations (including land rights, but also other issues). This kind of critical self-evaluation demands that we take into account the institutional devices and concrete historical experiences that configure the initial expectations of those brought together in both inquiry situations and ethnographic research.

In conclusion, inquiries and reports (whether judicial or administrative) constitute a narrative genre very different from theses, monographs, papers, articles, and essays; rather, they possess distinct aims, target a very specific public, have their own funding channels and particular procedural rules, and follow their own distinct methods of evaluation. Above all, they aim to supply information for making decisions on the phenomena they study. This in no sense annuls or disqualifies them as a source of knowledge, nor necessarily reduces them to the performance of roles essentially alien and appended to the role of "an anthropologist." On the contrary, it points to a range of highly complex and urgent theoretical and methodological questions concerning the future development of the discipline as a whole, as well as the definition of legitimate spaces for its professional exercise.

Notes

1 In judicial processes that affect indigenous interests, judges may, for the purposes of clarifying existing doubts or divergences, resort to the specialized services of an anthropologist; the latter must respond to a set of questions formulated by the judge himself or herself, or by lawyers from the parties in litigation. In replying to this request in the form of a technical report (*laudo*), the anthropologist must undertake research (bibliographic or field studies), whose duration and costs will be fixed in mutual agreement with the judge. Following a decision made in 1986 by the Upper Federal Tribunal, anthropologists are the only professionals considered capable of acting as experts (*peritos*) in legal actions relating to indigenous lands (previously engineers, agronomists, and others were also included). Jurists emphasize, though, that inquiries (*perícias*) do not affect the judge's sovereignty: the latter may equally consider the recourse to a technical inquiry superfluous; he or she is likewise free to accept or reject the results presented by the expert (including ignoring their conclusions or requesting a new inquiry).

2 As Oliveira and Almeida 1998: 80 shows for the 1970s and 1980s, FUNAI possesses no "consistent expectations concerning the competence and level of the performance" of the professionals it qualifies as anthropologists.

3 The term "Indianist" is generally used to refer to the Romanticist literature that evolved during the nineteenth century alongside the formation and consolidation of the Brazilian state; these texts aestheticized and glorified indigenous

customs and values, incorporating them as autochthonous and singularizing components of Brazilian nationality. Conversely, the expression "indigenist" is twentieth century in origin and is applied both to government policies relating to indigenous peoples and to the individuals responsible for carrying these out. An analysis of these two terms is more extensively developed in the final section of this essay, where they are taken as indices of two types of discourses present in virtual form in Brazilian society—both of which the anthropologist should avoid in performing his or her activities, as I explain later.

4   For more detailed information on this process, see Santos 1994; Carneiro da Cunha 1986; Ricardo 1994.

5   This especially concerned article 198, paragraph 1, of the Federal Constitution of 24 January 1967, which established in very clear terms the priority of indigenous possession over other modalities of possession or ownership: "Juridical effects of any nature that have as their object the ownership, possession or occupation of lands inhabited by *silvícolas* [Indians] are hereby declared null and void."

6   This was the so-called Calha Norte Project, a governmental program that included various ministries and public bodies and defined priorities and principles for action over a large swathe of Amazonia (see Oliveira 1990).

7   The most representative event in the indigenist and ecological field was the summit held in Rio de Janeiro in 1992. In anticipation of this event, the Brazilian government undertook a radical revision of its indigenist policy, including officially recognizing a number of indigenous territories of sizable proportions.

8   Legal Amazonia was an expression coined in the 1970s as part of an expansionist policy by Brazil's military governments that involved plying the region with tax incentives and development programs. In addition to the states making up the north of the country (according to Brazil's usually geographic division) the area includes the states of Maranhão, Rondonia, Mato Grosso, and Tocantins.

9   Staff specifications in FUNAI include the category of anthropologist, but no technical prerequisite of any kind is demanded for this position beyond a general university education. (This has led to the post being filled by people trained in psychology, architecture, fine arts, economics, or even sometimes social sciences.) In contrast, the ABA only recognizes as full associates—and hence as anthropologists—those who have received specific training at a postgraduate level.

10   For an analysis of the relationship between anthropological knowledge and governmental policies in a colonial context, see L'Estoîle, this volume.

11   Some of the ensuing ideas resulted from a conference delivered in the closing session of the seminar Anthropological Inquiries in Judicial Processes, which was organized by the ABA in December 1991 at the University of São Paulo. This seminar brought together anthropologists, lawyers, and indigenists. The essay was substantially reworked following the colloquium Social Sciences, State and Society, held at the Museu Nacional, Rio de Janeiro, in September 1997.

12   "Indian—or silvícola—designates any individual of Pre-Colombian origin and ancestry, who identifies him or herself, and is identified, as belonging to an

ethnic group whose cultural characteristics distinguish it from national society" (Law 6.001/73, article 3, item 1).

13 By territorialization process I refer to a set of social actions through which a politico-administrative object (in Brazil, the *comunidades indígenas*; in Spanish America, the *reducciones* and the *resguardos*; and in the French colonies, the *ethnie*) is led to transform itself into an organized collectivity, formulating its own identity, instituting decision making and representational mechanisms, and restructuring its cultural forms (including those relating to the environment and the religious universe). It designates an intervention by the political sphere (especially by the state) through which a prescriptive association is established between individuals/groups and geographical limits that have been determined. It is this political act that constitutes ethnic groups by imposing mechanisms of arbitration external to the population in question, themselves resulting from relations of force existing between the different groups represented in this political regime. These constraints are reworked and interiorized by the preexisting cultural reference points; this process also generates new possibilities for action that end up directing indigenous initiatives toward a reconstruction of their political and cultural organization (Oliveira 1999: 21).

14 It should be noted that the ethnographic situation itself is nowadays conditioned by a new political, cultural, and scientific context (see Albert 1995), entirely different from the context in which the research studies of classic ethnologists were undertaken.

15 It is worth observing that the concept of the community's proposal was not an outcome of juridical or administrative acts focused on the technical (or anthropological) nature of the processes involved in recognizing indigenous rights (that is, those initiatives relating in some form to the provisions of the 1988 constitution or decree 1775/96). Instead, it was developed from previous norms in force relating to the work of the indigenist agency (FUNAI), in which the technical content of the function of "anthropologist" is unspecified.

16 Made up by people with different kinds of professional training, the work group is regulated by a schedule of activities that tends to conflict with the rhythm of anthropological research (see Oliveira and Almeida 1998: 84–86).

17 This could be achieved through the incorporation of representatives of the indigenous people into the governmental commission that is examining and evaluating their territorial demands. In terms of the decision-making spheres located at higher and more restricted administrative levels, the indigenous representatives could be appointed by the regional-level and/or national-level indigenous organizations.

18 Irrespective of whether the anthropologist conducts anthropological inquiries or restricts himself or herself to fieldwork in the Malinowskian tradition, the state, society, and the indigenous peoples themselves expect—and in different ways demand—that the anthropologist take a clear and authorized stance in relation to indigenous lands and rights.

Jorge F. Pantaleón

ANTHROPOLOGY, DEVELOPMENT, AND

NONGOVERNMENTAL ORGANIZATIONS

IN LATIN AMERICA

In recent years, Latin American anthropologists have begun to engage in a new kind of relationship with the populations they have traditionally studied (e.g., peasants, indigenous peoples, or the inhabitants of poorer urban districts). This new role has involved their acting as intermediaries between these populations and national and international development agencies, using teaching activities to inform local people about the way the world of development works and the mechanisms they can use to take advantage of development programs.

These activities have become an important career alternative for anthropologists. However, taking part in them demands more than a university diploma: further qualification is required involving specialized postgraduate courses in human development (or sustainable/social/strategic development and so on). The need for retraining in contexts dominated by technocratic discourses (course teachers are usually economists or sociologists) has contributed to a sense of unease among anthropologists, provoking their disagreement with various aspects of the reasoning behind development plans, taken to be reductive of the local realities for which they are intended. Nevertheless, anthropologists are compelled to restrain their critical impulses concerning the content of projects and the discomfort caused by their subordinate position within the domain of public politics, mediating between the demands of those in control of development programs—the representatives of funding agencies and the individuals who run the courses—and the expectations of the target populations.

The terms "development" and "nongovernmental organizations" (NGOS) became part of the same semantic field of actions and perceptions; an expanding universe occupied by multiple social agents working to intervene at various levels of social reality: international, national, state, municipal, communal, and so on. Along with other social scientists, with whom they maintain conflicting and complementary relationships, many anthropologists analyze this world at the same time that they set out guidelines for taking action within it.

In this essay I seek to contribute to an understanding of the meaning and implications of the relationship between anthropologists and development. In the first part of the text I concentrate on the Argentinean and Brazilian cases and sketch a general panorama of the involvement of anthropologists and other social scientists in the profound socioeconomic transformations that have recently taken place in those countries (transformations wherein social development comprises one aspect). In the second part of the essay I propose a critical reading of the recent literature on the ways in which the relationship between anthropology and development has been approached. Rather than provide an exhaustive account of the problems involved, I explore possible lines for future reflection and research.

Development and Its Effects on Practicing Anthropology

Since World War II, economists have occupied a central role in the world of development. Formulation of the theoretical paradigm of development (and so-called developmentalist policies) afforded these professionals new levels of social recognition and participation within the state elite through the formulation and implementation of government policies. Two emblematic cases can be taken from Argentina and Brazil during the governments of Arturo Frondizi (1958–1962) and Jucelino Kubitschek (1956–1961), respectively.[1]

The very notion of Latin America gained new meaning and substance in this context, with the circulation of administrative specialists and models and the creation of international bodies that still play an important role today—the prime example being the Latin American Economic Commission (Comissão Econômica para América Latina), which was formed in 1948 and whose first director was the Argentinean economist Raúl Prebisch. Since then developmentalist projects have undergone various changes, including a broadening of their social range and the inclusion of other disciplines and professionals. In Argentina the role of the social sciences (primarily sociology and, albeit to a much lesser extent, anthropology) was to discover and diagnose the social and cultural aspects supposedly hindering the advance of modernization (a term cultivated by academic sociology at the start of the 1970s). These theoretical and ideological programs were combined with the creation and application of quantitative methods for providing scientific definitions and criteria for the notions of developed and underdeveloped. The indicators for economic and social development were thereby nationalized and regionalized.[2]

In the 1990s development acquired a new impetus as it gathered new meanings and forms. Argentina underwent a rapid process of state reconstruction involving the curtailment of social rights relating to wage labor, citizenship, and other core aspects of the welfare state. Despite the fact that Argentina's system had emerged as a model of success in South America, it was rapidly dismantled during this period. Adjectives accompanying the generic term development (such as "social," "human," and so on) began to appear alongside interventionist projects by international agencies, which filled the space vacated by the state during this period of neoliberalism.[3] The recruitment of social scientists by such agencies and the bodies sponsoring them (such as NGOs) occurred in conjunction with a reduction in the sources of public employment, including positions previously allocated to specialists and professionals in social problems.

This was the setting for the emergence and expansion of NGOs throughout Latin America during a relatively short period of time (less than two decades). Professional politicians also took part in this scramble to monopolize the new bodies and channels of mediation between populations and social programs. From the point of view of NGO activists, this is no more than an anomaly since it runs against the presumed separation between civil society and the state so central to the new forms of representing and implementing these policies. It is therefore not surprising that party activists, government officials, NGO specialists, church activists, and grassroots associations all end up competing for the same resources (aid funds) within the same heavily disputed area.

The very idea of anomaly is compounded by the fact that obtaining funds for social development projects requires the support of governments, since fund providers stipulate the need for partnerships with, or financial contribution from, the states within which the affected populations live. In extreme cases, state agents themselves are forced to become mediators in order to obtain funding support (including organizing and stimulating the setting up of NGOs)—an activity that reveals the extent to which the boundaries of the state (the definition of what is or is not governmental) are contextual and open to dispute.

The involvement of anthropologists in this dispute for a monopoly over the channels of mediation and funding—an area where the development programs are socially constructed—became one of the main routes for their professionalization, while simultaneously helping to confer anthropology with a much higher social and public acceptability in the image of its work in the service of populations, the state, and the new politics.

Starting in 1995, the main funding bodies for social development in Latin America, such as the Inter-American Development Bank (IDB) and the United Nations Development Program (UNDP), significantly increased their loans and technical cooperation activities, not just in Brazil and Argentina but also in other Latin American countries such as Colombia, Guatemala, Venezuela, Chile, and Mexico.[4]

According to official estimates, Brazil has about two hundred thousand entities officially recognized as nongovernmental organizations.[5] The oldest of these concentrate on providing social services and tend to be highly dependent on the state. The newer NGOs mainly aim toward co-management with the Brazilian government. The establishment of consultative council think-tanks involving input from NGOs comprises some of the highest-profile initiatives in the country. These include, for example, the Community Solidarity Program, an initiative for combating poverty and social exclusion.

Brazil appears to have the longest history of NGO activity in Latin America. This activity falls into three periods. The first phase, which continued through the 1960s and 1970s, was dominated by religious organizations pursuing a militant and voluntarist policy that emphasized the potential for grassroots educators to work as mediators. International relations were mainly structured through politics and religion. The second period began in 1979 with the passing of the Amnesty Law and the return of Brazil's political exiles. The third period is characterized by the massive participation of university members and the transformation of NGOs into true spaces of professionalization for young social science graduates. This period also corresponds to a shift in the focus of international relations through the action of multilateral funding agencies, such as the IDB, the UNDP, and the World Bank. The most significant year was 1992, when the Rio 92 Earth Summit took place, which was the first large international conference, sponsored by the United Nations, that looked to establish formal dialogues between governments and NGOs with the overall aim of promoting sustainable development. The Brazilian Association of Non-Governmental Organizations (Associação Brasileira de Organizações Não-Governamentais) was founded the same year. It should be stressed, though, that these changes in the area of social development involved not just the creation of institutions but also a change in attitudes such as those stressing the importance of a commitment to poorer sections of the population.

Brazil also saw the emergence of some of the more subtle analyses of social development programs and NGOs, one of the most outstanding of which was the volume edited by the anthropologist Leilah Landim (1998).[6] This book brings together various contributions from people involved as active participants in the worlds they study: in fact, publication of the book was sponsored by one of the country's main NGOs (the Institute of Religious Studies) to which almost all of the authors are linked. One of the chapters focuses on the National Campaign Against Hunger, which was organized in 1993 by Herbert de Souza (Betinho), a public figure who provides a model example of a grassroots militant sociologist (the book is also dedicated to him).[7] As the book makes clear, the notion of NGO autonomization has a double significance in Brazil: it is at once an analytic tool and an ideal practically implemented by such organizations, primarily in their relations with the government and international funding bodies—entities with which the NGOs themselves are involved in alliances and disputes.

In Argentina during the radical social transformations of the last two decades about eighty thousand NGOs were created, registered, and officially recognized by agencies such as the UNDP, the body responsible for annually publishing the worldwide ranking of human development.[8] The UNDP is also the main international body for officially establishing the key categories of "new social management" that are present in the standardized forms used for drafting projects and whose codes are to be learned by new mediators. The above-mentioned specialization courses in development taken by young university graduates and activists are the main means for the dissemination of this new cosmology, as well as for the scientific and international legitimization of these new social policies structured around notions such as "civil" or "community participation."

In the 1990s a network of postgraduate courses in development, social management, and strategic planning took shape at a continental level, involving the circulation of academic staff and publications. Student intake increasingly included agents from state institutions—the technicians responsible for applying the theories developed by the new key authors. One of the indications of the success of this circuit is the normalization and homogenization of practices of mediation between the officials responsible for implementing policies and the target populations.

The institutions conferring academic legitimacy to the courses (in many cases the same through which funds are channeled) perform a crucial role in internationalizing the key categories of development. The Inter-American Institute for Social Development (INDES/IDB), UNESCO, and the Organization of Ibero-American States for Education, Science and Culture (Organização dos Estados Ibero Americanos para a Educação, a Ciência e a Cultura—OEI) supply both technical consultancy and teaching staff. Additional scientific backing comes from the participation of universities that provide logistical support and issue degree certificates. In the context of a radical restructuring of higher education and an overall reduction in funding for public teaching and research centers, the institutions linked to the network of local universities participating in development are, by contrast, proving adept at securing resources along with an international profile and social recognition. This has helped ensure their survival at a time of crisis.

Books, primers, and statistical summaries have been identified as useful tools in the proposed renewal of means of intervention based on this academic and scientific construction of social problems. One of these works is *Pobreza: Un tema impostergable* (Poverty: An Unavoidable Issue), a collection of essays edited by Bernardo Kliksberg (1993), director of the United Nations Regional Project for State Modernization in Latin America.[9] The book's organization expresses the basic categories structuring this new cosmology. In the first part (subtitled "Problems") the authors—for the most part social economists, specialists in public administration, and sociologists—provide quantitative data exposing the huge socioeconomic inequality produced in the region and the world as a whole during the second half of the twentieth century. The predominant tone is one of denunciation and an attempt to create distance from other policies and institutions working in the area, such as the World Bank and the International Monetary Fund. In the second part of the book ("Solutions"), the aim is to ground the urgent need to formulate proactive policies for redistributing economic resources via "social management": a combination of effective resource management, a commitment to the target populations, and a sensitivity to their demands and "local knowledges" (a category that, as we shall see, refers to the presumed interpretative capacity of anthropological knowledge). The work has all the features of a manual, a common tool of applied/engaged social science.

This process of imposing onto society interventionist models based on scientific knowledge reveals a twofold redefinition of the state: the withdrawal from the management of social policies and the redefinition of the role of specialists. The specialists cease to work as public officials (losing those rights arising from stable employment) in order to take up contracts for specific projects with a limited time span that are dependent on external funding. In turn, this change in the relations between the state and the specialists is linked to the expansion of the university base (an exponential increase in graduates and the creation of new courses linked to development, especially at the postgraduate level) and to the relative contraction of the work market traditionally open to young graduates.

In order for development administrators to work efficiently in close response to the contemporary situation, they require a detailed and precise knowledge of the populations destined to be effected by their actions. Quantifying these populations and measuring their needs comprises one of the main activities of these specialists. The results of this activity (such as the "poverty maps" displaying the geography of underdevelopment) form essential tools in the day-to-day work of anthropologists. Social demand and supply—other key categories—reveal the contextual nature of the positions in the field of development: those who at a given moment or in a particular situation may be localized on the supply side may then be located at other moments or in other contexts on the demand side. Countries, states, municipalities, neighborhoods, and families that succeed in proving they are in a condition of poverty may alternatively demand or supply resources and present or assess projects.

Aid programs are only implemented once the funding bodies have been able to verify the condition of poverty in accordance with scientifically defined technical criteria that have been internationally approved (following standard indicators, such as the Unmet Basic Needs Index).[10] It is precisely while negotiating this recognition that the new technically qualified mediators such as anthropologists make use of their technical know-how and the networks of relations they have built in the development world.

The main elements in the fight for the recognition of poverty are the form and the project, produced in conformity with the vocabulary of internationally recognized classifications. The work of anthropologists and other mediators involves "interpreting demands" and "transmitting requests," respecting the cosmology expressed in the explicit and implicit instructions, based on the belief in development, for filling out application forms for project funding.

Theoretical Debates and Political Positions

There is certainly no consensus among anthropologists concerning the content and consequences of development plans. Some take a stance in favor of practical intervention, while others present themselves as critics of this "power discourse" by questioning the efficacy of intervention and turning the development projects themselves into an ethnographic topic. Both, however, coincide in their perception of the subordinate position occupied by anthropologists in this area.

Two elements make up the commonsense thinking of the anthropologists who specialize in development. The first relates to the discipline's presumed specific nature within the division of labor among the various specialists. Anthropology is thought to be capable of producing a specific kind of knowledge that is "actor-oriented" or designed to capture the viewpoint of the populations in question. Developed in relation to small-scale societies, this approach enables anthropology to make improvements to the projects, modifying (in the field) the distortions arising from the application of generic plans to unique situations. The second element of this commonsense thinking is the shared belief in the fact that the "viewpoint from below" opposes the "viewpoint from above" held by the agents with whom anthropologists compete and in relation to whom they occupy a subordinate position (in the first place, economists, but also engineers and sociologists).

It is significant that one of the best displays of the feelings of anthropologists concerning their experience of the world of development was produced by Lucy Mair (1984), a descendent of a distinguished line of the British school of anthropology, one of the members of Malinowski's group that helped forge the concept of development in the 1930s at the London School of Economics. At that time, when development was linked to the implementation of indirect rule in the African colonies, the main weapon of "functionalist anthropology" against other disciplines and theoretical competitors (such as evolutionism) was precisely the value given to the uniqueness of a kind of knowledge intervention that looked to put the "interest of the natives" in the forefront. This was also the main weapon used by anthropologists "in the field" in the context of their competition with officials from the colonial administration over the capacity to produce knowledge about the local populations.[11] The fact that Mair accompanied the decline of these forms of social intervention during the postwar period confers a particular keenness to her observations about the current situation of anthropologists and their reduction to "local experts" more often asked to provide an evaluation after the failure of particular projects, in a clash of professional reputations in which the dominant viewpoint identifies anthropology with the out-of-date and traditional—and thus, in effect, one of the obstacles to development.

In response to this experience, a reappraisal of anthropology's function acquired momentum in some anthropological circles during the 1990s: its main task came to be seen to act as a critique of development, taken to be a Western tool for dominating non-Western others. In the words of some of the more notable voices of this critical position, development amounts to "a discursive formation," "a power discourse" that separates the powerful from the dominated (see Dahl and Rabo 1992; Hobart 1993).[12]

The main research field of contemporary criticism is the direct observation of the implementation of the plans for development projected by international agencies, in relation to undeveloped and developing populations and, above all, the reappropriations of such projects (and resistance to them) by these target populations, displaying ways of acting and thinking that diverge greatly from those imagined by the "technocrats" of developmentalism.[13]

According to the European Inter-University Development Opportunities Study-Group (EIDOS), anthropologists are particularly well positioned to produce this kind of critique due to their history of questioning the totalizing ambitions of the Western scientific traditions (Hobart 1993). The relation between scientific knowledge and local kinds of knowledge takes the form of an "epistemological dialectic": that is, the increase in any kind of systematic knowledge simultaneously augments the possibility of ignorance; the more knowledge is accumulated through the application of development plans (primarily those at a community level), the more a lack of awareness grows concerning local knowledges. But at the same time as these positions criticize the totalizing view of the West they also reveal an equally homogenized view of anthropology itself, substantializing the relations formed between "defenders of local knowledges" (the anthropologists) and "official defenders of development plans."[14]

Both positions—whether criticizing development or seeking to determine the role that anthropology should ideally perform—share features in common that, despite the supposed theoretical differences, reveal a generalizing idea concerning the anthropologist's work (the defense of local knowledges). This conception fails to problematize the very status of the local, reduced in a dichotomous schema to the dominated, the non-Western, and the like that pushes the analysis back to a position that it had sought to overcome.

It is interesting to note that many of these critiques and the formulation of alternative forms of carrying out projects with local populations come from individuals or groups belonging to departments focused on researching and promoting development.[15] Identifying the position from which criticism is formulated has nothing to do with denouncing a supposed inconsistency but rather with the intention to place into perspective the social conditions of its production and its limits. After all, good intentions notwithstanding, anthropologists are recruited by development programs precisely because they are specialists of the local.

We can also identify another tendency within the critique of development that works in dialogue with these positions—an approach with more ostensibly deconstructivist ambitions, explicitly inspired by Foucault's theses on governmentality. According to this brand of analysis, which spread out from the American universities at the end of the 1980s,[16] developmentalism (like so many other "isms," such as orientalism, colonialism, or indigenism) constituted a truth regime. It was up to the anthropologist to discover the mechanism of domination and at the same time recognize the fact—essential for the discipline's future—that development had provided the seed bed for the emergence of anthropology. In the words of one of the authors who epitomized this viewpoint: "If the colonial encounter determined the power structure in which anthropology took shape, the development encounter has similarly provided the overall context for contemporary anthropology" (Escobar 1997: 498).

This type of claim gave rise to the proposal to distinguish between an anthropology for development and an anthropology of development. The first seeks legitimacy via a "realist epistemology" that recognizes development as a real-world fact. Here participation in development is seen to arise from the failures resulting from verticalist models of applying policies. In this case, the function of anthropology for development is to propose culturally acceptable approaches in which the main voice is that of local populations.[17] On the other hand, the main task of the anthropology of development is to construct a theoretical rather than political identity.[18] The tool for analyzing the practices and representations of power is poststructuralism, a suitable approach "in order to modify the social order that regulates the language production process" (Escobar 1997: 502).

Third World social movements that are resisting capitalism and contemporary models of domination point to the emergence of an era that announces the end of development as the principle driving force behind social life.[19] The true challenge faced by the discipline is to contribute elements that enable these social movements to deepen the political and economic transformations taking place: "Only then will anthropology become truly post-modern, post-savage and—one might add—post-development" (Escobar 1997: 512).

Each of these positions—whether emphasizing political practice (linked to a career as consultant and to anthropology for development) or theoretical production (linked to an academic career and the anthropology of development)—seeks to help build a better world. In general terms, it is necessary to recognize that, along with good intentions, this critical approach has produced a valuable set of ethnographic studies on issues seldom tackled by the discipline until recently. These studies have included research into the institutional frameworks and international circuits making up the world of development, or the participation of local populations in drafting plans for social intervention. At the same time, there has been an expansion in the range of studies to include an analysis of the links between anthropology and other disciplines, such as demographics and economics. The most promising approaches are undoubtedly those that distance themselves from outworn dilemmas reproduced in a new guise (applied anthropology equals "for development" versus theoretical anthropology equals "about development"), or signal the possibility of incorporating the very terms of these dilemmas into a topic of analysis.[20]

However, it is not just past theoretical-political dilemmas that now appear in new forms. We can also see a consistent theme at the level of moral sentiments. The key word here is ambivalence (Ferguson 1997). In the 1930s, anthropology announced the arrival of the world of development. This involved (despite the echoes of evolutionism) placing faith in progressive change—the search for an alternative to the oppression to which the colonial powers subjected the native populations of the African continent. It was also a recognition of the inevitability of social and cultural transformation in the wake of contact. Social and economic progress were only to be welcomed, despite worries concerning the damage inflicted, starting with the poverty that accompanied the process. Thus a configuration very similar to the current one took shape: anthropologists who became involved with development projects (which already provided possibilities for work and research funding) looked to situate themselves on the side of the dominated, thereby assuming a subordinate position at a political and institutional level in relation to other development workers.

Frederick Cooper (1997) and Arturo Escobar (1995) argue that the discursive regime of development took shape in the 1940s, with the Colonial Welfare and Development Act and the *African Survey*, a declaration that sought to respond to the challenges of imperial power; this was followed by the League of Nations and the negotiations for decolonialization by means of a system of mandates, then, finally and above all, with the implantation of developmentalist discourse in the United States after 1949. In contrast to Cooper and Escobar, who both attribute a marginal position to anthropologists during this period, L'Estoile (1997b) shows how British anthropologists from the 1930s onward performed a highly active role in the formulation of colonial projects. Using the terminology involved in development and planning at the time, they transformed government plans for intervention into full-scale study programs like the International Institute of African Languages and Cultures, with their own outlets (such as the journal *Africa*) and the publication of important works for academic circulation.[21]

Conclusion

This short journey through various theoretical-political situations and debates suggests the advantages of a historical and comparative perspective for comprehending the current configuration of the relations between anthropologists and the world of development in Latin America, especially in Brazil and in Argentina. The subordination of anthropologists to other specialists is a historical construction.[22] The defense of anthropological knowledge in the face of the totalizing viewpoints of other disciplines and the adoption of a position in favor of the dominated against the institutional machine of development both reproduce the outcome of academic and institutional relations of force, further strengthening theories and "interdisciplinary teams" that are always hierarchized.

The close relationship observable today between anthropologists and the bodies for social intervention (more or less connected to states) means that anthropologists embody a double agency as critical observers and participating agents. In this play of forces, anthropologists find themselves increasingly close to state functionaries and NGO activists. The future of anthropology in the world of development will depend on the concrete relations established by individuals and groups with political and institutional bodies (such as states, international agencies, and NGOs).

Situated within this play of forces, it will also depend on the forms and degrees of relative power able to be acquired by anthropological knowledge and the academic institutions where it is produced and scientifically validated (such as universities and research institutes).

Notes

1 See Sikkink 1991 for a comparison between developmentalism in Brazil and Argentina. On Brazilian economic thought and developmentalism, see Bielschowsky 2000. For an analysis of the role of economists in the Brazilian state, see Loureiro 1997. On the role of economists in Argentinean developmentalism, see also Neiburg and Plotkin 2003.

2 At the outset the main indicators were related to industrialization: gross domestic product, the import/export balance of good and services, and jobs. It was only later that development came to be measured systematically via social indicators (such as education), until arriving at the present day with the use of "poverty indices" and the "unmet basic needs" coefficient.

3 For discussions of the relation between state transformation and development programs, see, among others, Alayón 1989; Barbeito and Lo Vuolo 1992; Bustelo and Minujín 1991; Golbert and Tenti Fanfani 1994; Grassi, Hintze, and Neufeld 1994; Isuani and Tenti Fanfani 1989; Kliksberg 1992, 1993; Lo Vuolo and Barbeito 1993; Lumi, Golbert, and Tenti Fanfani 1992; Minujín 1993.

4 See UNDP/IDB (1998: 31). The Mexican case is unique, due to the relatively delayed emergence of NGOs (see Piester 1997).

5 This and other statistics are described in UNDP/IDB 1998.

6 The reconstruction of the genesis of NGOs in Brazil presented here owes much to Landim 1993.

7 The title of Landim's chapter, " 'Experiência militante': Histórias das assim chamadas ONGS" (" 'Activist Experience': Histories of the So-Called NGOs"), neatly reflects the social positions from which the authors constitute themselves as analysts of (and intervenors in) their object of study. Other chapters explore themes such as the Catholic youth movement and social action in Rio de Janeiro (by Regina Novaes), practices and representations concerning "Caridade, cidadania e assistência social entre espíritas" (Charity, Citizenship and Social Aid among Spiritualists, by Emerson Giumbelli), and the philanthropy of private companies (by Sergio Goes de Paula and Fabiola Rohden).

8 This information is compiled in the Human Development Index, which was implemented following the publication of the first Human Development Report. The index combines life expectancy and adult literacy rates as well as per capita gross domestic product in more than 130 countries (see Esteva 1999).

9 The work's publication was sponsored by UNDP and the Latin American

Development Center (Centro Latino-Americano para o Desenvolvimento [CLAD]). The preface to the Brazilian edition was written by Herbert de Souza (Betinho). Both UNDP and CLAD help sponsor postgraduate courses in social management in a number of Latin American countries. In Argentina since 1995 these courses have also been implemented in the country's inland provinces, with the support of local government universities.

10 The Unmet Basic Needs Index "qualifies a person or home as poor by directly observing the attainment levels for certain essential needs. Definition of these needs is made through indicators of environmental deficiencies, level of schooling, sanitary conditions and the home's economic capacity" (1997: 107). Assessments undertaken according to this method include the utilization of formulas created by social statistics, such as the "poverty rate" and the production of "poverty maps." The first of these maps was drafted in 1984 in Argentina by the National Statistics and Census Institute (Instituto Nacional de Estadísticas y Censos). Another form of measurement involves the "poverty line" (*linha de pobreza*), however this is considered an indirect method since it looks to deduce poverty levels from income and minimal consumption of food and nonfood goods included in a *cesta básica* (comprising a basket of basic food items—*cesta básica alimentar*—and a basket of nonalimentary goods and services—*cesta de bens e serviços não-alimentares*).

11 Here I draw from the argument put forward in L'Estoile 1997b.

12 Both of these volumes comprise a collection of essays. The first (Dahl and Rabo 1992) is an outcome of the project "Development as Ideology and Folk Model" at the Department of Social Anthropology at Stockholm University. The second (Hobart 1993) arose from the European Inter-University Development Opportunities Study-Group (EIDOS), made up of anthropologists from institutions in Britain, Holland, and Germany.

13 The spirit of the "anthropological defense" of the local and the different can clearly be seen in the book edited by Dahl and Rabo 1992. It contains six articles that thematize the idea of a reproduced and contested reappropriation of power: the "inevitable march of history" in a Cuban village (Rosendahl); the value given to education in Jordan and Syria (Rabo); the meanings of the terms "development" and "modernity" for the women of Lamu Town in Kenya (Fuglesang); the "native viewpoint" in the words of an elder of the Borán tribe in Ethiopia (Dahl and Megerssa); the effect of future-tense language, which makes development a question of moral-religious conversion among the Gapunes of Papua New Guinea (whose core term, Kam-ap ["coming-up"], provides the book's title) (Kulick); and the place of the concept of folk participation (*folkligt deltagande*) in the Swedish aid development institutions (Rosander). It is worth noting the fact that the latter essay is the only one from the book in which the locals are not non-Western but legitimate spokespeople of the practice of development.

14 In the book edited by Hobart (1993) see, for example, the text by Ufford on

the "failures" in the implementation of programs in Indonesia, and, by Arce and Long, on the relations between development bureaucrats and peasants in Jalisco, Mexico.

15 This is the case of the above-mentioned EIDOS group and others, such as the Swedish Agency for Research Cooperation with Developing Countries, the Department of Rural Sociology (Agricultural University, Wageningen), and the Sociology of Development Research Center (University of Bielefeld, Germany). In Europe the training of anthropologists in the area of development increased significantly after 1977 when the Royal Anthropological Institute inaugurated the Development Anthropology Committee. Pursuing identical aims, the American Society for Applied Anthropology in 1981 founded a subsidiary in England, and in 1982 set up, also in England, the Group for Anthropology in Policy and Practice. See Grillo 1985.

16 See Apffel-Marglin and Marglin 1994; Banuri 1990; Ferguson 1990; Rahnema 1986; and, especially, Escobar 1995 and 1997.

17 This explains why this strand of anthropology chooses to become involved in interventionist programs, despite being accused by other development specialists of obstructing the efficiency of projects, as well as being accused of collaborationism by academic anthropologists. See, in particular, Cernea 1995 and Horowitz 1994.

18 Crush 1995; Ferguson 1990; and Escobar himself (1995 and 1997).

19 Also see Escobar's review (1997) of the research undertaken by Nash, Pigg, Ribeiro, and Hvalkov.

20 See Cooper and Packard 1997 and Souza Lima and Barroso-Hoffman 2002. The latter attempts to comprehend the relationship between anthropology, ethnodevelopment, and public policies, especially concerning Brazil's indigenous populations.

21 In other words, cognitive interests and practical interests appeared to be interdependent. Malinowski's appeal to the institute that "this new branch of anthropological science must be clearly *distinguished and treated in its own right*" (1930) should be interpreted in the strongest sense. Malinowski thus explicitly presented the autonomization of social anthropology as a necessary precondition for its practical utility. The new anthropology defined itself as "social" and "functional," in that it claimed to study "native societies" no longer as "primitives," surviving evidence of civilization's past, but rather in the way that these societies function in the present day (L'Estoile 1997b: 351–52).

22 As Grillo (1985) recalls, applied anthropology was a widely resisted minority practice in England between the 1960s and 1970s (the only university chair existing under this name was directed by Mair), and was not acknowledged until the 1980s with the first emergence of the networks of research and action linked to development.

Alban Bensa

THE ETHNOLOGIST AND THE ARCHITECT

A Postcolonial Experiment in the French Pacific

In 1973 I began ethno-linguistic and politico-anthropological research in an area of central-northern New Caledonia, a Pacific archipelago that was taken over by the French in 1853. In less than two centuries the indigenous population, known as the Kanak, had become a minority on their own lands as a result of France's policy of colonization. In 1984 the Kanak embarked on an insurrectionary movement, demanding new institutions capable of laying the grounds for the future independence of this French overseas territory. I endeavored over the next five years to help raise awareness of Kanak civilization and publicize the people's desire for liberation (Bensa 1995). In 1988, the signing of the Matignon Accords restored peace to New Caledonia. In this new climate, Jean-Marie Tjibaou, president of the Kanak Socialist Liberation Front (FLNKS), requested that a Kanak cultural center be constructed in Nouméa, the archipelago's capital. The French state responded by creating the Agency for the Development of Kanak Culture (ADCK) and charged it with launching an international architecture competition to select the project director for the future center. In 1989 Renzo Piano requested my help in preparing the project, and the Italian architect and his team won the competition in 1991. For the next seven years, I continued to work with the Renzo Piano Building Workshop in the creation of the building that would be formally named the Tjibaou Cultural Center. The center was inaugurated on 4 May 1998. In this essay I draw a few lessons from this on-the-job encounter between ethnology and architecture.

An Appeal to Ethnology

For Renzo Piano, the conversion of the Kanak past into a forward-looking architectural project demanded input from anthropology, not because the discipline is seen as a conservatory of bygone exotic practices, but rather because of its capacity to demonstrate the links between the present-day relevance of a cultural demand and its memory (the history of the Kanak people). Usually, when anthropology is called upon outside the research environment it is expected to enrich a situation with a touch of local color or to vouch for the authenticity of certain cultural practices transformed into "custom." In this case, though, the architect did not ask ethnology to affix on the project a label of traditionality, but, on the contrary, to bring the distant past as close as possible in order for its meaning to be vividly felt in the present. With this aim in mind, the builder's intent was for the ethnologist to come up with the components (forms, materials, ideas) that would allow, through the architecture of the structure, the Kanak people to build a modern image of themselves, one retaining links with their past while projecting their community into the future.

The task of integrating the former Kanak world into an image harmonious with their present aspirations implied, for Piano, a delicate synthesis between ethnology and architecture. In fact, the construction of a Kanak cultural center presented him with a perilous choice. Either he could decide to free himself from any reference to the Melanesian world by imagining rigorously functional spaces whose forms would refer to contemporary Western culture alone, or he could immerse himself in a search for plastic correspondences between his creation and the Kanak universe. We should note here that in opting for this second solution, Piano took the opposite approach to the one he took, with Richard Rogers, when designing the Georges Pompidou Center. At the time, the Pompidou project was expressly conceived as a rupture with the old part of Paris and the Halles quarter, and, even more profoundly, as a challenge to the dominant concepts of national heritage. The Georges Pompidou Center forged new relationships with art and culture, made possible by the 1968 uprisings and their aftermath (Piano and Rodgers 1987). By contrast, for Nouméa's Tjibaou Center, Piano worked on the potential continuities between past Oceanic architecture and modern-day European architecture. And by taking this path, he inevitably came face-to-face with ethnology.

The discipline of ethnology, at once empirical and academic, reconstructs the specificities of local populations in all their diversity. Ethnological texts act as a storehouse and attempt to make cultural differences intelligible, thereby providing access to ideas and forms that lie beyond the limits of Western common sense. In the case of New Caledonia, for example, the Kanak worldview can only be grasped through the study of texts based on long-term ethnological research. Nonetheless, it was the architect's task to find a place and meaning for them in his building project. This transition from ethnology to architecture, however, promised to be problematic. How could a human science—closely related to literature and fully absorbed in the virtualities and convolutions of the written text—supply the art of the set square and sliderule with ideas capable of being materialized into walls, roofs, and concourses? Keen to remain as close as possible to the Melanesian world, Piano found a practical solution to this difficult question by inviting an ethnologist to participate directly in the architectural conception.

Involving Ethnology

Today political, economic, or even judicial bodies frequently call on the expertise of all kinds of researchers. Whether it is a question of family rights, public healthcare initiatives, or expert testimony during court inquiries, anthropologists, sociologists, and historians participate in civic life on be-half of their specialty. During their history, the colonies regularly poured out such requests. The authorities in charge of New Caledonia are no exception to this rule, especially when seeking solutions to local conflicts. In relation to linguistic, educational, economic, or land rights issues, there are now count-less reports from experts recounting the history of the archipelago, produc-ing a constant stream of analyses and dispensing advice. Ethnology has not been left behind in exploring this new area of work and has used its field knowledge to provide valuable analytic insights.

The boost that Kanak militants gave to New Caledonia's decolonization process from 1984 onward presented specialists of the archipelago's social and political life with the challenge of interpreting what are still known today as "the events." This situation convinced me to attempt a reevaluation of the scientific knowledge now existing on Kanak society. Along with their dignity, the Kanak acutely desired to regain a wide degree of autonomy across all domains. These aspirations tested ethnology's ability to provide an on-the-spot analysis of the sudden emergence of a previously overlooked people onto the national and international scene. However, while expertise typically involves shedding light on a political debate through expert knowl-edge, my own engagement went some way beyond this. The Kanak national-ist movement's endeavor to make their objectives both understood and recognized led me to cross the border between social science and politics.

What good are the social sciences if they cannot also put their tools and findings to use in aiding much-needed social transformations? My own opinion was that involving ethnology in political debate implied neither its corruption nor its trivialization: rather, by assuming an ethical commitment, ethnology could benefit richly by being forced to reflect on the transient and circumstantial nature of its basic premises. Experts' arguments are difficult to dissociate from political arguments; elucidating a situation is never independent from the desire to transform it; and any report on a problematic situation points the way toward the necessary solutions.

Demonstrating the cultural roots of Kanak demands therefore depended on both ethnology in a classical sense and the individual ethnologist's capacity to convince those people tempted to ignore the Kanak cultural heritage. It is a euphemism to say the majority of New Caledonian Europeans held—and in some more stubborn cases still hold—in poor esteem everything relating to New Caledonian Melanesians. For Jean-Marie Tjibaou it was imperative to combine the Kanak struggle to acquire political power with other initiatives capable of overcoming a long history of scorn and incomprehension, the brunt of which his people have born since the beginning of colonization. Seen from this point of view, past or contemporary research on the Kanak world could clearly help toward a carefully planned revitalization of the Kanak image.[1] Simultaneously, this self-reflexive component to the liberation movement, involving numerous experts from a wide range of disciplines, supplied Tjibaou with a number of crucial arguments.[2] Four difficult years, marked by a series of tragic events, finally resulted in the Matignon Accords in 1988. The accord's signatories recognized the need to work toward "readjusting" all spheres of this French Overseas Territory. This encouraged some researchers to reinforce the positions already acquired by the Kanak and to contribute to their expansion. Personally, I received my first chance to make New Caledonian history and Kanak civilization known to the general public in 1990 with the publication of my book, *Nouvelle-Calédonie: Un paradis dans la tourmente*. This richly illustrated work caught Renzo Piano's attention just when he was hesitating over his decision whether or not to participate in the competition launched for the Nouméa cultural center. Leafing through this book, the architect discovered the Kanak world through a historical ethnology binding analysis with image, an experience that allowed him a deeper introduction to Melanesian plastic art than would a standard museum visit (although following the same logic). By inviting me to help develop the project with his team,

Piano gave me a fresh opportunity to carry the political struggle onto the cultural and symbolic ground where Jean-Marie Tjibaou had so keenly wished it to be pursued (see Tjibaou 1996).

However, the production of knowledge alters significantly when it is directed not toward public authorities but rather toward that singular kind of artist, the architect, and through him the future users of a building. It is no longer a question of updating facts or developing reasoned arguments capable of informing policies but rather of participating in a creative process. In the case of the Tjibaou Cultural Center, the demand was at once more precise—fitting into a team to carry out a tangible project—and more vague since it was not a question of describing particular aspects of the Kanak world (its social organization, political structures, and so forth) but the global knowledge I was presumed to possess as an ethnologist. Since my attention was no longer focused on a personal project or the university supporting my work but instead turned to architecture as an applied art, this knowledge had to be simultaneously well-informed and practical. I was therefore forced to redefine myself in line with the project's aim—the construction of a cultural center—and to embark on a very particular ethnological synthesis, one demanding participation in the architect's decisions.

Working as a Mediator

The main difficulty before me lay in the architectural use of ethnology, bearing in mind that this demanded close discussions not only with the Piano team, but also with the Agency for the Development of Kanak Culture (ADCK).[3] This task of mediation provoked a familiar issue: Does the discourse of the ethnologist risk obscuring or replacing what the people themselves have to say? This question is often raised on the vaguely populist assumption that only the actual members of a group are capable of speaking in its name. I was reproached for "speaking for the Kanak": Why did they need an ethnologist to tell them who they were? This raises two questions, in large part related. First, must we be Muslim to speak of Islam, female to reflect on the feminine condition, serfs to study serfdom, and so on? Second, simply belonging to a community clearly cannot be held to predetermine what a person may have to say about it. More to the point, perhaps, we need to ask what kind of relationship does a native have with his or her community in order for them to be in a position to speak about it to outsiders?

From the Kanak teacher explaining the life of his tribe to the ethnologist, to Éloi Machoro or Jean-Marie Tjibaou presenting their movement's demands to the representatives of the French State, there is a wide range of positions from which people may speak in the name of a given social entity. The ethnologist undoubtedly occupies one of these. Strangely enough, ethnologists are the only people to make a profession of speaking of worlds from which they do not originate but of which they gradually get to know better and better.[4] Their position of outsider slowly alters to the status of associate member, committed to expressing themselves in their own way about the community that has accepted them, while its members continue to make their own voices heard. The role of the ethnologist is not, therefore, to play spokesperson for anyone, but simply to bring the benefit of his or her particular experience to the debate among all of the parties concerned. While such work frequently involves describing practices and suggesting appropriate responses to the demands of the multifarious situations in which he or she becomes embroiled (written texts, research conferences, political meetings, architectural projects, etc.), their particular point of view commands no more legitimacy than those of the representatives of the population concerned. At the most he or she supplies a constructed and individual viewpoint that the cultural agents, Kanak or others, may support or oppose. The creation of a project on behalf of a little-known culture brought together a range of people—Kanak representatives elected by their people,[5] an Italian architect, and French senior civil servants—in pursuit of a common aim. Although not always comfortable, the kind of mediation involved strikes me as indispensable. Just as the Piano team called for an ethnologist, the ADCK requested the collaboration of a "cultural advisor," neither of whom would be Kanak. In passing, it is worth adding that my role would doubtless have been reduced if the great mediators of the Kanak cause and civilization, who died too soon and under tragic circumstances (Éloi Machoro, Jean-Marie Tjibaou, and Yéweiné Yéweiné),[6] had been able to participate in the creation of the cultural center.

From Speeches to Sketches

Once all the theoretical and moral considerations had been taken into account, it remained for us to find concrete and productive methods for reconciling the working (and pondering) methods of the ethnologist and the architect. When it came to space distribution, interior and exterior luminosity of volumes, the height of a ramp, or the shape of a theater, what useful contribution could be made by someone usually devoted to village maps, genealogical inventories, or the documentation of oral traditions? How can one imagine the supposed Kanak ways of conceiving a roof, wandering through a cultural center, enjoying a garden, or organizing traditional festivities in the center's grounds? The task posed for our multidisciplinary team was to construct a building whose particular requirements were neither those of a traditional home nor those of a modern apartment, but rather a public place dedicated to culture and art, which maintained a clear link with that very present yet somewhat mysterious entity called Kanak culture.

During the discussions with architects and engineers, my job was to provide cultural references that could inform and modify the sketches and plans so as to lend them a more Melanesian aspect. Since this strange dialogue had the eventual aim of transforming a thousand-year-old worldview into a contemporary three-dimensional space, how was I to shift from ethnological experience (direct investigations, book writing, class lectures, or conferences) to shaping an image to be crystallized in the form of a building? This task demanded a kind of alchemy in which one knowledge would be reworked by another knowledge in an original synthesis. Once distracted from its usual academic objectives, ethnology can open up to creative imagination—in this case through dialogue with an architect himself anxious not to remain within the confines of architecture. Indeed, for Piano and his team it was essential that the center's lines, walkways, structural forms, and open areas were designed in relation to spaces and preferences that were explicitly or implicitly Kanak. Piano's aim, while remaining attentive to the practical and technical demands of the program, was therefore to come up with a design inspired by the richness of the Melanesian world. As ethnologist, my role was to identify shapes and practices that could guide the builder in his choices. From descriptions and explanations of the roofing of ancient Kanak huts, the layout of the long paths where these huts stood, the habit of avoiding being seen by walking below the esplanades, the use of plant symbolism to express Kanak cosmogony, and the like, the architect captures a line shooting toward the sky, a curve, the shape of a winding path, and the memory of yesterday's texture and color in today's material. As the discussions unfold, the ethnologist's flow of words—a jumble of impressions, emotions, analyses, and anecdotes—slowly filters into the architectural creation, transformed into visual ideas sketched onto paper and then made into building plans, sections, and diagrams. There is nothing more astonishing

Typical elements of the Kanak traditional house—central post, poles, vegetal couverture—surrounded by pines and high poles nearby. (Drawing by Roger Boulay)

Marie-Claude Tjibaou and Octave Togna in conversation with Renzo Piano at Gênes. (Mission des Grands Travaux)

for a specialist in oral and written discourse than to see his words recast by a specialist in the plasticity of concrete forms and become part of the work of an architect keen to achieve his own creation and yet still remain attentive to cultural differences!

In shifting from the fieldwork site to text, and thus from book to construction, we can observe a continual process of metaphorization. As we move further away from the model, the number of features that can be traced back to the initial referent steadily decreases. These remaining signs of the Kanak world are subsequently adapted to the esthetic and technical requirements of the architectural project. The image obtained at the end is not a true reflection but rather, as Renzo Piano suggests, a recollection.

In this exercise of inventing plastic forms, the ethnologist takes a step back to acquire a panoramic view of the world he or she studies, taking advantage of this exterior position in order to highlight its prominent points and sketch its general contours—precisely the opposite approach to the kind adopted when describing a kinship system or mythological traditions to colleagues in a book or a report. But whether working at a distance or in the heart of the society, the ethnologist inevitably produces an image of the community concerned. And this image helps identify the group as a culture. As such, the production of anthropological texts about specific cultures is not antithetical to the design of a building, with a team of architects, similarly intended to signify a particular culture. Both situations basically involve exposing and, where possible, appreciating and celebrating cultural difference. The architect expresses this difference with lines and materials set in space, the ethnologist with his or her research material transformed into texts. Both use their particular styles to give life and body to this mysterious entity called culture. The architect is a painter and sculptor in the same way the ethnologist is always potentially a writer. Their encounter is thus shaped by their creative capacities, just as much as the dialogue between their respective kinds of know-how.

This ethno-architectural experiment emphasized the extent to which everything we perceive as culture is the outcome of the work of mediators, composers, and interpreters—people involved in identifying cultural difference and transforming it into an object. We appreciate a culture as a work of art thanks to the skill of the people showing it to us. By displaying it to us, they create it. This does not mean they invent the culture—something all too easily said nowadays—but that they arrange certain elements of the culture

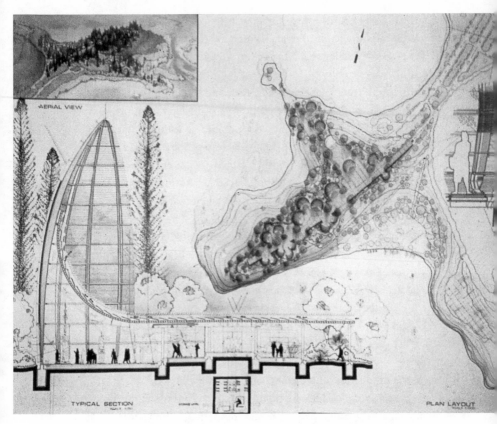

Diagram of the Jean-Marie Tjibaou Cultural Center. (Renzo Piano, 1991)

in order for these to acquire meaning for those unfamiliar with it. In this task, the ethnologist usually endeavors to stay as close as possible to the consistencies and recurrences felt to have been observed in the field. For the architect, on the other hand, an overly formal interpretation of the Kanak culture risks locking the project into a regional style.

Restoration and Creation

As soon as his team won the competition, Piano announced, "we must be careful to avoid copying." The concern to place the Kanak world at the project's center could indeed have turned it into an attempt to produce a

Aerial view of the Jean-Marie Tjibaou Cultural Center. (Photograph by Arnaud Legrain, Mission des Grands Travaux)

carbon copy of this civilization. A nostalgic or, worse still, a museum style of architecture would have made the building little more than a "remake" with folkloric overtones. On the other hand, a building entirely devoid of reference to the Kanak world would have delocalized the project, totally uprooting it from its construction site and from the history of New Caledonia. Both pitfalls had to be avoided: the reconstitution of a traditional Kanak village and the construction of a strictly European building. In order to create a work strongly influenced by the Kanak culture, it thus made ample sense to call on ethnology. However, this discipline, absorbed above all with the distinctiveness and particularity of the local, could not be allowed to limit the architectural team's horizons to New Caledonia's Kanak population. The desire to root the project in the Melanesian context had to be balanced by integrating the project with another set of references, namely those of contemporary architecture.

The cultural center, a building designed to symbolize the Kanak culture in image and space, was only achieved after a lengthy period of esthetic research aimed at displaying the Melanesian world through a technique (modern construction) and materials (concrete, glass, wood, metal) that are in many ways foreign to it. The transition from traditional dwellings made

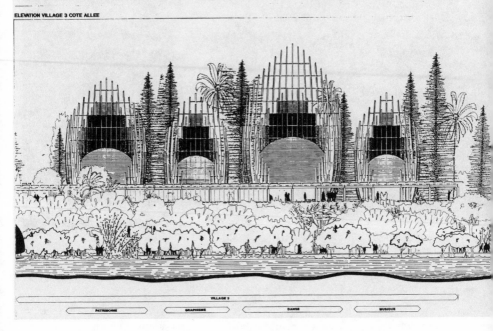

Renzo Piano's architectural rendering of Kanak "huts" in a garden of pine trees for the Jean-Marie Tjibaou Cultural Center. (Renzo Piano Building Workshop)

from trunks, bark, branches, and straw to a cultural center integrating all the most recent advances in the art of construction amounts to a switch from one world into another. Ethnology also proceeds by translation since it transposes into the language of the observer—according to his or her criteria—concepts and practices that are in their original form strictly vernacular. Furthermore, we know that every translation is an interpretation—in other words, a symbolization. The transition from the ancient Kanak dwelling to the most modern construction, just like the transition from field experience to scholarly books sold in the shops of Western capitals, necessitates a complex process of reformulation. Since it involves both a mise en forme and a mise en scène, and since it appeals as much to the senses of sight, hearing, and touch as to the mind, this effort simultaneously combines observation and creativity, analysis and imagination. My strongest impression gained from all my visits to the Tjibaou Center was the sense of being able to grasp, not intellectually but in a definite and immediate way, the concrete effect of this re-creation of the Kanak world through the alliance of ethnology and architecture.

Nevertheless, the Tjibaou Center's "huts" are not huts, no covered walk has ever been seen in New Caledonia, and the center's "Kanak path" corresponds to no real ritual practice. Whereas a colonial exposition would have striven to reproduce "the native dwelling," and an ethnologist would have been inclined to reconstruct an image of the past as truthfully as possible, the building erected at the gateway to Nouméa pushes the Kanak culture beyond its limits. By authenticating this culture, less on behalf of its past than in reference to its future, the ethno-architectural approach breaks with any scrupulous restoration of a former or contemporary reality and thus with the usual definitions of anthropology. Since the discipline's aim is to delimit the contours of discrete and stable cultures, it runs into self-contradiction when it contributes to a "creation," to the invention of shapes or concepts that in some sense did not previously exist. However, practical work can enrich theory, and thus ethnology's encounter with master-builders tends to throw a harsh light on its assumptions: do the discrete and stable social entities that anthropology describes really exist, to the point where ethnologists, like auctioneers, have the right to guarantee their authenticity? Commitment to a project that aims to display and bring to life a people's contemporary experience requires the ethnologist to take into account history in the making and the flow of time. From this point on the self-enclosed ethnic monad and the cultural relativism it nourishes quickly become obsolete. Every social world projects itself into the future, and its ways of inhabiting time make up its identity. If, as Jean-Marie Tjibaou said, this lies "ahead of us," his analysis is as much a prediction of the future as a remark about the present.

Thus, the construction of Nouméa's cultural center reproduced not a past reality but rather a process of identity construction in which ethnologists are both observers and agents. Their discipline is not purely theoretical and descriptive but active, so to speak. In exploiting the performative effect of language, ethnology brings what it reveals into existence and thus parallels the process by which peoples transform and assert themselves. The conjunction of ethnology and architecture demonstrates the creative dimension of anthropological expertise. The barriers between objectivity and subjectivity collapse from the moment that ethnology, like architecture, both analyzes and induces contemporary transformations.

Notes

The publishers of this volume invited the author of this essay to provide, on the theme of expertise, testimony of an unusual experience: the participation of an ethnologist in the work of an architectural team chosen to carry out the construction of a cultural center in New Caledonia, a French Overseas Territory. Another version of this text has been published in *Ethnologie et architecture: Le Centre Culturel Tjibaou. Une réalisation de Renzo Piano* (Paris : Adam Biro, 2000).

1 In 1988 Jean-Marie Tjibaou obtained Michel Rocard's backing to launch a research program on Kanak societies, the origin of numerous theses and publications over the last decade. See Merle 1995; Naepels 1998; Bensa and Leblic 2000.

2 See the 1985 special issue of *Les Temps Modernes*, titled "Nouvelle-Calédonie: Pour l'indépendance."

3 Created by ministerial decree in 1989, this agency has the remit of publicizing Kanak culture (organizing shows, publications, etc.). It also had the task of coordinating the creation of the Tjibaou Cultural Center. As the contracting authority it was responsible for working with the Renzo Piano Building Workshop, which undertook the contract to design the project and supervise its construction.

4 This remark holds true for all ethnology, both of distant and nearby cultures, since the entire point of research is to make the foreign familiar and vice versa.

5 In 1989, Kanak independence activists appointed Marie-Claude Tjibaou, wife of the late leader, and Octave Togna, founder of the nationalist radio (Radio Djiido), as president and director respectively of the ADCK, and thereby also of the cultural center.

6 Eloi Machoro was killed by French police on 20 January 1985; Jean-Marie Tjibaou and Yéweiné Yéweiné were assassinated at Ouvéa on 4 May 1989 by Djubelli Wéa.

"TODAY WE HAVE NAMING OF PARTS"

The Work of Anthropologists in Southern Africa

The extraordinary political transition in South Africa in the early 1990s inspired, among many more momentous initiatives, a number of reflective essays by anthropologists. Curiously, perhaps, these essays did not look forward to what anthropology might contribute to the new South Africa. Rather, they looked back at the historical development of their discipline in the old South Africa.[1] More specifically, they tended to reflect on the classic opposition between two schools of South African anthropology. One was allied with the Apartheid state. Its founder, Werner Eiselen, the first professor of ethnology at an Afrikaans-language university (the University of Stellenbosch), was the intellectual architect of the Apartheid system. His associate, J. A. Engelbrecht, established a department of ethnology at the University of Pretoria. Engelbrecht was succeeded by Eiselen's student and protegé, Pieter Coertze, and Coertze's favored students in turn established departments in the other Afrikaans universities. These Afrikaner ethnologists called themselves *volkekundiges*, or ethnic scientists. They focused theoretically on the concept of culture, and their subject was the traditional culture and social order of the African peoples of South Africa. The other school, founded by Alfred Reginald Radcliffe-Brown, was effectively a local branch of British social anthropology. Associated with the English-language universities, its practitioners were generally opposed to government policy, and were interested in issues of social structure and social change rather than culture and tradition.

The opposition between these two schools became very bitter in the period of high Apartheid between the 1960s and the 1980s, a time when each school was strongly identified with polarized political positions for or against the government.[2] A leading African anthropologist, Mamphela Ramphele, recalls that when Thabo Mbeki, then president of South Africa, was preparing to return from exile, he reproached her for having become an anthropologist. In his eyes, the discipline had been hopelessly compromised by its colonial past. She recalls that she "replied confidently that he needed to distinguish between good and bad Anthropology." She also says "Although a particularly vicious form of anthropology, which provided ethnological justification for segregation, operated in some Afrikaans-speaking universities, there was also another tradition that had earned South African Anthropology a place of honor internationally. Radcliffe-Brown, Monica Wilson, the Mayers and many others had done valuable work that had led to a greater and more sophisticated understanding of South African society" (Ramphele 1995: 164–67).

However, although this simple opposition between a good Anglo anthropology and a bad Afrikaner ethnology fit the polarized climate of South Africa in the 1970s and 1980s, it was beginning to seem somewhat crude as South Africa underwent the great changes of the 1990s, and as intellectuals began to revise their views on the country's history in the light of these changes. To begin with, the conventional classification ignored the extent to which some leading figures of the 1930s did not fit neatly into either camp. For example, the scholarship of Nicholas Van Warmelo, a government ethnologist trained in Germany, had a great deal in common with that of Isaac Schapera, the heir of Radcliffe-Brown, as both Van Warmelo and Schapera freely acknowledged. Even after the war and the advent of the nationalist government with its radical policy of segregation, one of the leading English-speaking South African anthropologists of his generation, W. D. ("David") Hammond-Tooke, a postgraduate student of Schapera and Monica Wilson, spent his apprentice days in the Ethnological Section of the Department of Native Affairs under Van Warmelo, whom he respected (Hammond-Tooke 1997: chapter 5). Further, not everyone was impressed by the liberalism of the Anglo anthropologists. While it is true that the English-language Association for Social Anthropology in Southern Africa welcomed black members, and black scholars were appointed to senior positions at the University of Cape Town and the University of the Witwatersrand in the 1980s, nonwhite anthropologists in the "bush colleges" could be made to feel alienated, and some complained that their concerns and contributions were devalued. (See, e.g., Vawda 1995.)

It is also too simple, and perhaps too convenient, to demonize the Afrikaner volkekundiges. The nationalist ethnological establishment imposed a rigid orthodoxy. Indeed, all of the professors of ethnology at the Afrikaans-language universities were members of a secret society, the Broederbond, which served as the inner establishment of the nationalist movement. Criticism of Apartheid was not tolerated, and fraternization with the Anglo anthropologists was firmly discouraged. On the other hand, some volkekundiges expressed a limited sympathy with mainstream American theories in cultural anthropology, and even with the theoretical ideas of Malinowski (Van Rensburg and Van Der Waal 1999). They were not all racial romantics, let alone closet Nazis (although they were hospitable to some dubious German ethnologists who arrived in South Africa soon after 1945).

This is not to deny that the opposition between the two traditions of anthropology in South Africa was real enough, particularly from the perspective of the practitioners in the South African universities in the 1970s and 1980s. Certainly there were few neutrals. It was difficult for an anthropologist at one of the English-language universities to withdraw from the local battleground and take a lead from the international academic debates. Eileen Krige, Philip Mayer, and, later, David Hammond-Tooke, all attempted at various times to make room for other, politically less charged, concerns in South African anthropology, but as the political confrontation became increasingly critical the options narrowed and political considerations became all-consuming. The crucial fact is that the debate was not only one between two schools of anthropology, but also between the makers of government policy and their opponents. Perhaps terms like "debate," let alone "dialogue," are too weak to describe what was a fraught, bitter, and occasionally dangerous political confrontation, but the point is that the discourse of South African anthropology was ineluctably shaped by the politics of the state. This was necessarily the case for the servants of Apartheid, but it was equally the case for the most bitter opponents of official policy (see Hammond-Tooke 1997, chapter 8; Kiernan 1997).

The Great Debate: Race and Culture

The great debate was about race and culture, tradition and change. More fundamentally, however, it was about the very character of South African society and the nature of its elements. To be sure, this was a debate that transcended the academy, let alone the small community of anthropologists. Indeed, it can be traced back to the nineteenth-century debates between the liberal missionaries and their opponents among the settlers or in the administration.

In addition, the debate was not a peculiarly South African one. Indeed, the most fundamental issue confronting anthropologists in every society has always been the definition of the basic units of human life. Should people be grouped according to race, descent, language, custom, religion, or political allegiance? What are the primordial social groups—tribe, clan, caste, ethnic group, or nation? To complicate matters, there may be multiple affiliations. Moreover, these units may themselves be the building blocks of more complex social systems. Alternatively, they may be merely the internal subdivisions of a larger, encompassing political or economic order that situates and shapes them to its purposes. In that case it becomes of critical importance to determine whether such structures are best understood as colonial or capitalist states, as plural, multiracial, or multicultural societies, or as embryonic nations.

Yet while these are universal issues that have always defined the anthropological debates, there can be few regions of the world in which the characterization of ethnic identities has been more fraught and more tragically formative than in southern Africa. They have also been remarkably unstable. From today's perspective it is easy to imagine that South African history has always been formed by a racial theory that has pitted white against black, but South Africa's divisions have historically been shaped and understood in various ways, and bitterly contested.

Under the rule of the Dutch East India Company (1652–1795), the basic oppositions were those between Christian and pagan, and between free and slave. Racist theories were neither prominent nor clearly articulated during the Dutch period, and social status did not depend on skin color or on origin. Free Christians were accepted at every level of society, and Robert Ross argues that "the system of slavery paradoxically formed a block to development of a racial order" (1993: 5).[3] In the early nineteenth century the Cape became a British colony. The new rulers had little sympathy with the Dutch-speaking farmers (the Boers) and their policies granted some relief to the slaves and the native peoples of the Western Cape. In 1828 free people of color, notably the "Hottentots," were relieved of their legal disabilities, and on 1 December 1834 the slaves in the Cape were emancipated. These initiatives were very largely due to the pressure of the missionary societies, which had been active since the beginning of the nineteenth century. At the same time, missionaries in the field also began to make large-scale conversions of native peoples, thus eroding the old Christian/pagan dichotomy.

The Boers were hostile to these improvements in the legal position of slaves and "Hottentots." So far as the farmers in the interior were concerned, drawing on a Calvinist doctrine of selection and predestination, there was an obvious, God-given opposition between master and servant, made manifest by differences in skin color, language, way of life and religion. These sentiments were alien to the British authorities, but when in 1820 English colonists were settled on the eastern frontier of the colony, the administration began to come under greater pressure to support white settler interests. A secular ideological justification for this policy shift was now available in the form of new scientific theories of race that were becoming current in Europe. By the 1850s, race provided the basis for stratification in the eyes of white settlers and colonial overlords alike (Ross 1993, part 2; Dubow 1995).

Even as the fundamental white/black racial classification established itself in nineteenth-century South Africa, it had to be modified to accommodate subdivisions established on different criteria. The white category itself was divided between two "nations" or "races," Boer and Briton, a division originating in the first third of the nineteenth century as frontier farmers of Dutch extraction contested British overrule and established independent republics in the interior, eventually fighting a war against the British empire at the end of the century. After the establishment in 1910 of the Union of South Africa, the former "Boers" began to consider themselves a local, if not exactly indigenous, nation within the South African state, a self-image symbolized and reinforced when in 1920 Afrikaans replaced Dutch as an official language. The term "Afrikaner" generally replaced the term "Boer." The official Afrikaans dictionary, the *Woordeboek van die Afrikaanse Taal* (1950), defines Afrikaner in two ways, as a racial or a cultural category ("one who is Afrikaans by descent or birth; one who belongs to the Afrikaans-speaking population group"). In general, however, the assumption was that only those who were Afrikaner on both counts were true members of the *Volk*.

South African white electoral politics quickly resolved itself into a competition for power between blocs that were popularly identified as "Afrikaner" and as "English." Afrikaner nationalism became a major political force and an Afrikaner nationalist party held power in a coalition government between 1924 and 1939, and again as a single governing party from 1948 to 1994. These "Afrikaner" and "English" parties inherited native policies that had become established in the second half of the nineteenth century. In very broad terms, the educated Anglo view was that a process of civilization and Christianization would gradually bring the African peoples to a level at which they might share political power with whites. The general Boer—or later, Afrikaner—view was that racial and or cultural differences were too great for assimilation to be desirable or even possible. There were also regional traditions that had evolved in the nineteenth century. The Cape Colony, Natal, and the Boer Republics had different "nonwhite" populations, and had developed divergent administrative traditions. There were debates in Natal and the Eastern Cape as to whether "Christian" or "civilized" natives should be granted a special status, while the Boer Republics, the Transvaal and Orange Free State, insisted on strict segregation.[4] In the Western Cape, the "natives" were a minority. The "Coloureds" constituted the largest single population group. While only a handful of "Coloureds" had been given the vote, there were few legal restrictions on their work or residence, a state of affairs that was regarded as scandalous by the Transvalers. There were similar variations in the treatment of the "Indian" minority. In Natal, the poor Hindu plantation laborers were subject to social and legal handicaps that were not imposed on the smaller and wealthier communities of Muslim traders in the Transvaal, while "Indians" were not even permitted to remain overnight in the territory of the Orange Free State.[5]

It was not only policies that differed. The policies themselves depended on and reinforced racial and cultural classifications, and these also varied between the different regions. The formation of the union necessitated the development of a uniform policy of native administration, and therefore imposed a need for a national system of racial categories.[6] The official solution was to divide the "nonwhites" into three categories, "Coloureds," "Asians," and finally the "Natives," also known as "Bantu" or "Africans." These categories were arranged in a rough hierarchy, with the "natives" at the bottom. Each of these categories was, however, in its own way extremely problematic.

In the early days of Dutch rule, the terms "Hottentot" and "Kaffir" had been used indiscriminately to refer to the native population. The Dutch geographer Olfert Dapper titled his account of the Cape, published in 1668, *Kaffraria, or Land of the Kafirs, Also Named Hottentots.* However, by the middle of the eighteenth century the indigenous peoples of southern Africa were conventionally divided into two groupings, "Hottentots" and "Kaffirs" (or "Caffres"). The term "Hottentots" was applied to the "yellow" native peoples of the Western Cape, the site of the original white colony. This population was made up of small bands of pastoralists, hunters and *strand-lopers* (beachcombers). On the eastern frontier of the colony were "black" peoples who differed from the "Hottentots" in appearance and also in language and in economic and political organization. Pastoralists and farmers with an elaborate iron technology, they were organized into often formidable chiefdoms. They were initally called Kaffirs, a term used by the Portuguese and Dutch for the people they had contacted in East Africa before the South African coast was explored.[7]

Each of these major categories was again, in time, divided into two sections. In the eighteenth century, the peoples of the Western Cape were subdivided into Bushmen and Hottentots. It was generally thought that these peoples had a common origin (see, e.g., Somerville 1979 [1799–1802]: 25, 28), and in accordance with Enlightenment thinking the criterion for differentiating between them was economic. The Bushmen were hunters, the Hottentots pastoralists.

In the nineteenth century, as the colony began to expand and to engage with the Xhosa to the east and the Thlaping to the north, the term Kaffirs came to be restricted to the chiefdoms on the eastern littoral. Similar chiefdoms on the highveld, contacted in the first years of the nineteeenth century, were initially called Bechuanas. The close linguistic relationship between the various Tswana and Sotho languages was acknowledged almost immediately, and the linguistic relationships between the Sotho-Tswana and Nguni languages were often recognized. However, other criteria were generally also adduced to distinguish them. For example, W. H. C. Lichtenstein, a German scientist who in 1806 participated in one of the first expeditions to the "Bechuana," wrote: "That the Beetjuanas are of the same origin as the other Kaffers has been agreed upon, but they differ considerably in many ways from the others particularly in a higher degree of culture. Their physique is very much like the lean strong stature of the Kaffers," he added, "but as a rule they are more delicate" (1973 [1806]: 65).

The term "Bechuana" was used as a group name by the Rolong and Hurutshe people, who were the first to be encountered by scientific travelers from the Cape (see, e.g., Lichtenstein 1973 [1806]:65). However, the term was not used as a self-description by all the people now termed "Tswana." The notable exceptions were the Kgatla and Eastern Kwena, who tended to prefer the term "Sotho," which was also widely used by many other groups north of the Orange River. Nevertheless, the description "Bechuana" was used to cover most of the peoples now termed Tswana and Sotho in the nineteenth century. For example, the first study of Southern Sotho—which was done by Eugène Casalis, a missionary attached to Mosheshwe—was titled *Etudes sur la langue Séchuana* (1833).

Another German scholar, Wilhelm Bleek, who had been trained in the tradition of Indo-European philology, introduced systematic linguistic criteria in the mid-nineteenth century for the classification of the peoples of southern Africa, the main Bantu languages being grouped into two categories, "Setshuana" and "Kafir." He also introduced the term "Bantu" in 1862 as an umbrella term for these languages (Doke and Cole 1961: 62–64). In the early twentieth century Bryant introduced the neologism "Nguni," which gradually took the place of "Kaffir." "Kaffir" had become a derogatory term, and, moreover, was now increasingly being used to refer specifically to the Xhosa-speaking peoples of the Eastern Cape as distinguished from the "Zulu," thus creating the need for another umbrella term (Marks and Atmore 1970).

Bleek's coinage, Bantu, gradually became the preferred local scientific term for the erstwhile "natives." It was used by the official historian George McCall Theal in his influential study, published in 1910, titled *Ethnography and Condition of South Africa before* A.D. *1505*. In 1922, at the time that the first linguistic and ethnographic department was established in South Africa at the University of Cape Town, the Witwatersrand University Press was set up to publish a new scholarly journal, titled *Bantu Studies*, to cover the studies of South Africa's native peoples. Strangely enough, the official announcement proclaimed that despite its name, the journal would promote "the scientific study of Bantu, Hottentot and Bushman,"[8] suggesting that even in some scientific quarters "Bantu" was regarded as a synonym (or even a euphemism) for "native." Complicating matters—or perhaps, from another point of view, simplifying the classificatory problem—an umbrella term to cover all the "Bushmen" and "Hottentots" was introduced in 1928 by Leonard Schultze, a German physical anthropologist. Schultze proposed the term "Khoisan" to describe what he took to be the common racial stock of the Bushmen and Hottentots, and in 1930 Schapera adopted this coinage for his ethnographic survey, which he titled *The Khoisan Peoples of South Africa: Bushmen and Hottentots*. Later, "Khoi" and "San" became the preferred alternatives to "Hottentot" and "Bushmen." However, these peoples were no longer regarded as significant elements of the South African population. The "Hottentots" had become assimilated into the "Cape Coloured" population, and the "Bushmen" were now regarded as remote and numerically insignificant (indeed probably "disappearing") peoples—picturesque, perhaps, but of mainly scientific interest.

By the early twentieth century, the "Bantu" were generally thought to belong to a single race and also to share a linguistic and cultural heritage. Linguists now referred to the large African language family to which the

South African groups belonged as "Bantu," a term that grouped the South African peoples together with the bulk of the African population south of a line drawn from southern Cameroon in the west to southern Kenya in the east. The common assumption was that linguistic, racial, and cultural criteria would tend to coincide, although one or another criterion might be deemphasized. Theal, for example, pronounced that "the Bantu tribes of Africa south of the Zambesi vary so greatly in appearance, in speech, in customs, and in intellect, that it is evident they do not form one homogenous race, still the manner of construction of the various dialects in use by them being the same, and the one ruling tenet in the religion of them all being identical, they can be classed as a family group by themselves" (1910: 143).

The "Bantu" accounted for approximately three-quarters of the total population of South Africa. But if the category of peoples described by scientists and—as time went on—by the authorities as "Bantu" in South Africa were thought of at one level as a single group, they were nevertheless also believed to be divided into various "tribes," except for a problematic category of "detribalized natives." These tribes were supposed to constitute the fundamental social and national divisions of the Bantu. Nevertheless the definition and significance of these tribal units turned out to be extremely contentious.

There were two competing ways of classifying the native or Bantu population. One was based on linguistic criteria, usually eked out with observations on culture and race. The other approach was founded on the belief that the natural condition of Africans was to live under the authority of chiefs, and that as a consequence their tribal affiliation was primary. However, the tribes or chiefdoms, as the political units were called, did not neatly coincide with the cultural or linguistic divisions. Communities that were evidently of different origin, and were linguistically and culturally distinct, often fell under the rule of a single chief. Was the natural native community made up of the subjects of a chief, however diverse their origins, or was it a descent group of some kind, even though it might not constitute a political community? And were there perhaps nations or cultural groups that incorporated a number of chiefdoms?

The missionary anthropologist Henri Junod defined "the Thonga tribe," living on both sides of the Mozambique/Transvaal border, with a population he estimated at three-quarters of a million. These people were by no means homogeneous. According to Junod, they should be divided into six main clusters on cultural and linguistic grounds, and they were ordered into a great number of chiefdoms. Junod also admitted that the various parts of "the Thonga tribe" had no tradition of common identity, that there was no indigenous name for the whole grouping, and that the various "clans," or political divisions, had different traditions of origin. He conceded that the collective term "Thonga" was not used by the people themselves but rather was applied to them by their neighbors. (In fact, in the way of these things, "Thonga" is a pejorative Shona term for peoples without cattle.) On the other hand, Junod argued that all Thonga spoke dialects of a common language and shared some cultural features that set them off from the Zulu speakers to the south, to whom they were otherwise obviously related (1912, vol. 1: 13–19).

The integrity of Junod's "Thonga" category is not immediately evident. However, it has been plausibly argued that it made sense in the context of more practical considerations. Junod's classification was based on the field of operations of his missionary society, the Swiss Romande mission. The missionaries standarized the language and fostered assumptions of linguistic and cultural unity. Wittingly or not, they were in the business of nation building (Harries 1989: 85–90). Incidentally, in South Africa itself another term, "Shangaan," was established to refer to people from Mozambique. This term was taken from a breakaway group of Gaza Nguni that had split off from Shaka's Zulu chieftaincy and established itself in southern Mozambique under their chief, Soshangane. In the Witwatersrand gold mines, "Shangaan" came to be used generally for Mozambicans, and then was diffused to areas of "Thonga" settlement in the Transvaal (Harries 1989: 86).

The most sophisticated attempt to classify "the Bantu tribes of South Africa" was undertaken by the government ethnologist N. J. Van Warmelo in a study published in 1935, and it demonstrated the delicacy and difficulty of this enterprise. Van Warmelo received his doctorate from the Colonial Institute in Hamburg. Although he was trained as a linguist, he deployed historical and ethnological criteria, paid attention to the current landholding and political circumstances, and drew attention to what he called "tribal decay" (1935: 5). Discussing his criteria for classification, Van Warmelo suggested that a purely historical approach was impractical because the sources were inadequate, and in any case tribes had divided and migrated, had absorbed foreign elements and been conquered and forcibly dispersed, and had even changed their cultures. A classification according to cultural traits was not possible in practice since there were too many gaps in what was then known and too much had changed in many areas. There remained language, which was the most reliable basis for classification: "For in the days when many tribes were being broken up, and their culture and all its outward visible signs, such as homesteads and the products of arts and crafts, destroyed, the language survived with the speakers" (1935: 7).

The Single Society

It is apparent that although a simple logic of racial discrimination provided the basic framework for the classification of South Africa's population in the twentieth century, the principles underlying the classification were diverse and even contradictory. This was a matter of concern to academic specialists such as the anthropologists, but despite the fact that these categorical distinctions arose within official and popular discourses of the white group, they were widely accepted in every section of the society. The main political movements on the nonwhite side were organized in terms of the same classificatory system. The "natives" had been brought together in a single state for the first time with the establishment of the Union of South Africa in 1910. While the union was being negotiated between white political groups, a "South African Native Convention" was held in Bloemfontein to protest against the exclusion of nonwhites from the franchise. In 1912 the South African Native National Congress was formed, its name being changed in 1925 to the African National Congress. In 1954 an alliance of congress parties was set up, bringing together the African National Congress with the older Indian National Congress (Gandhi's organization), and introducing two newly established and numerically insignificant groups, the Coloured Peoples' Congress, and the white Congress of Democrats, a front organization for the Communist Party.

A radical challenge to this established racial division was presented by an academic movement that emerged in the 1920s, which argued that South Africa was a single society. To be sure, it was driven by extreme and dangerous internal divisions, but these arose from the structure of the single society itself. Moreover, the various sections of the society were becoming increasingly integrated politically and economically. The outstanding advocate of this one-society thesis was the historian William Miller Macmillan.[9] In his view, some of the most insidious proponents of a segregationist policy were the ethnologists, whose strategy was to focus on apparently conservative tribal peoples living on the native reserves. Dismissing conventional ethnography as antiquarian, and complaining that it drew attention away from the actualities of South African life, Macmillan pointed out that as early as 1915 "barely half the natives of the Union appeared to have homes except on land owned ... by Europeans" (1929: 312). The reserves were in any case grossly inadequate even for their residual populations, and the traditional institutions of rural Africans had been shattered.

Macmillan declared war on all the anthropologists without discrimination, but in fact the social anthropologists at the universities of Cape Town and the Witwatersrand generally accepted his analysis. Radcliffe-Brown, South Africa's first professor of social anthropology, agreed that traditional social organization had been radically undermined, and he insisted that the organization even of a Transkeian tribe could be understood only in the context of the national state and economy. Agreeing with the proponents of the single society thesis that this society was undergoing radical transformations, the "social" anthropologists focused their attention on the erosion of local cultural identities, the growth of labor migration, and the imposition of an overriding binary division between white and black. The leading ethnographer of the English school, Isaac Schapera, investigated social, economic, and religious changes among the Kgatla of the Bechuanaland Protectorate, setting their institutions in the context of colonial society and the wider economy of southern Africa. The same perspective shaped the classic ethnography of a Transkeian people published in 1936 by Monica Hunter (better known under her married name, Wilson), which was tellingly titled *Reaction to Conquest: Effects of Contact with Europeans on the Pondo of South Africa.*

In 1934, Schapera edited a book titled *Western Civilization and the Natives of South Africa: Studies in Culture Contact*, which opens with the chapter "The Old Bantu Culture." After this chapter, however, the volume moves to a description of culture change, land shortages, labor migration, Christianity, and urbanization, with little reference to local cultural variations or traditional forces. In 1937, Schapera summed up the situation in southern Africa in this way:

> Of the Bantu as a whole it can be said that they have now been drawn permanently into the orbit of Western civilization. They do not, and probably will not, carry on that civilization in its purely European manifestations. It is more likely that in certain directions at least they will develop their own local

variations. But these variations will be within the framework of a common South African civilization, shared in by both Black and White, and presenting certain peculiarities based directly upon the fact of their juxtaposition. Already such a civilization is developing, a civilization in which the Europeans at present occupy the position of a race-proud and privileged aristocracy, while the Natives, although economically indispensable, are confined to a menial status from which few of them are able to emerge with success . . . But despite all this, the Bantu are being drawn more and more into the common cultural life of South Africa. (386–87)

The single society thesis directed ethnographers to consider rural communities in relation to the state, and fostered social, economic, and political studies. However there was, of course, an established alternative, dominant in most metropolitan centers, which was to study cultural traditions and culture areas. *The Bantu-Speaking Tribes of South Africa*, also edited by Schapera and published in 1937, dealt only with Bantu-speaking populations within the borders of South Africa and the three British protectorates in southern Africa and excluded the substantial Nguni and Sotho offshoots in Zimbabwe and Zambia, along with the Thonga of Mozambique, but it seems to have been conceived as a culture area survey. It is true that a consistent attempt was made to depict uniformities in the "Southern Bantu" region rather than to record every last local "tribal" difference, a notable departure from more orthodox culture area studies.[10] Nevertheless, this volume must be seen as a contribution to a more conventional culture area tradition of study, and so as representing, at least in part, an alternative to the projects inspired by the single society thesis. It is significant that the original plan was to have as coeditors of the volume Schapera and the archsegregationist, Eiselen, although in the end Eiselen withdrew and moved out of academia to take a position in native administration.

In the metropolitan centers of the discipline the cultural area tradition remained predominant, or at least was thought of as respectable. Within British social anthropology, Malinowski's Trobriand monographs, or the work of Charles Seligman and Edward Evans-Pritchard in the Sudan, were largely ahistorical studies of supposedly traditional ways of life. Even after World War II, Evans-Pritchard, for example, tended to dismiss studies of change either as a branch of "applied anthropology" (which like any applied field was obviously less academically serious and interesting than the pure form of the discipline) or as "sociology," with the implication that such studies were the business of another, less prestigious, discipline (see L'Estoile

1997b). When Hilda Kuper wrote her account of the Swazi, she had to divide it for publication into two volumes, the first of which consisted of a long discussion of the traditional system, while the second dealt with changes in the colonial period in response to a system of racial domination. The International African Institute decided to publish only the first volume (*An African Aristocracy*), leaving the second volume (*The Uniform of Colour*) to be published by the Witwatersrand University Press.

There was, however, a counterattack by the more radical South African anthropologists (see Kuper 1996, chapter 6). This was associated particularly with Max Gluckman, who was a student of Winifred Hoernlé and Radcliffe-Brown and a political radical. Gluckman published some of the most innovative analyses of rural society from the one-society perspective, demonstrating that even in the heart of Zululand, a region famous for cultural conservatism, cultural change, and complex social interactions between white and black shaped everyday life (see, e.g., Gluckman 1958). Gluckman was banned in 1939 by the South African government from doing further field research in Zululand, and he took a position at the Rhodes-Livingstone Institute in Northern Rhodesia during World War II. After the war, he and his colleagues pioneered the study of urban politics and labor migration in Central Africa. In 1949 he was appointed to the foundation chair in social anthropology at Manchester University, where he introduced the South African critique of cultural studies into the very heart of British social anthropology.

Developing the Single Society Theory

The fundamental premise of the single society thesis was that ethnic or tribal identities would wither away as overarching social, political, and economic institutions evolved and a common "civilization" emerged. The opposite view was that of the segregationists, who were associated largely with the Afrikaner nationalist camp. For them, integration and ethnic assimilation were anathema, threatening both the national identity of the Afrikaner people and the integrity of the white race. The project of Apartheid aimed to shore up the divisions, seen as natural divisions, within the South African population: that is, between Afrikaner and English; between white and black; between Asian, colored, and Bantu within the "non-European" population; and, finally, within the Bantu category, between tribes or nations.

The expertise of (Afrikaans-speaking, nationalist) anthropologists was called on to define the appropriate subgroupings within the Bantu category. There was also an attempt to develop a special theory, which came to be called the "ethnos" theory. As a variant of traditional Romantic Volk theory, its central assumption was that every authentic ethnic group had a distinctive culture, without which its members were lost and miserable. A subsidiary premise was that members of such a group would prefer to marry endogamously, so that the ethnos tended to become also a biological group.[11]

But although they had a very general theory about the importance of primordial identities, these official ethnologists faced intractable difficulties when it came to identifying communities that shared these identities. The African chiefdoms of the nineteenth century had been smashed by British and Boer armies, and in some areas in any case there had never been sufficiently large-scale units to form the basis for modern administrative divisions. These were problems familiar from experiments with indirect rule elsewhere in Africa, but they were present here in much starker form, since the changes imposed by a century of white overrule in an industrializing society had been far greater than elsewhere on the continent. However, the Bantu were officially represented as a language family and were divided into ten "national units" based on broadly linguistic and geographical criteria. Within each section a conveniently conservative line of chiefs was identified and established as the ruling family.[12]

For their part, liberal and radical critics of Apartheid insisted that the divisions invented or reinforced by the Apartheid system were artificial, dangerous fictions imposed on what was increasingly an integrated (though profoundly conflict-ridden) economic and political system, within which there were many shared values. The single society orientation became the orthodoxy in the next generation in the English-language universities in South Africa, and as the Apartheid system became increasingly repressive, a new wave of academic studies recast the single society model in marxist terms. The undertaking was led by historians, who introduced a modified version of the marxist three-stage model of social evolution (see Saunders 1988: 165–85). Traditionally the African people had lived in small chiefdoms recruited by descent and organized into lineages. Then in the late seventeenth century or early eighteenth there was a general transition to a (quasi-feudal) state system. Finally, all of these independent political units were conquered by whites and absorbed into the capitalist state, and their peoples were reduced to a uniform status of landless peasantries and labor migrants.

The ethnographic studies carried out by anthropologists in these universities were designed to demonstrate the effects of Apartheid. The distinctive ethnographic objects became the churches in the black townships, the migrants' hostels and associations, the rituals and songs associated with labor migration, the impact of migration on the rural domestic group, and the displaced peoples deposited by resettlement schemes or deprived of their squatter rights on white farms. All this, of course, was against the background of an ideology that insisted on the importance of primordial differences, not only between white and black but within the black population, and a policy that was constructing pseudo-traditional tribal governments, while the state labored—brutally but ultimately unsuccessfully—to reverse the flow of people into the urban areas.

The single society thesis reinforced the tendency of English-speaking South African anthropologists to limit their ethnographic curiosity to the boundaries of the state. This concentration was buttressed by the international cultural boycott of the 1970s and 1980s. South African scholars now turned in upon themselves. Comparisons were rarely made with countries to the north, including even Botswana and Zimbabwe. However, the model also discouraged comparisons within South Africa itself. The marxist perspective that became current in the English-speaking universities had no place for tradition, ethnicity, and culture; or rather, these appeared only as mystifications in the service of a politics of divide and rule. Any concern with cultural differences was suspect, as potentially serving the interests of Apartheid. All of the oppressed were in the same boat. Ethnic identities were the creation of white initiatives (see Vail 1989). It was assumed that the single society was divided vertically into classes or racial castes, but not horizontally into ethnic groups.

Coloured, Hottentot, and Bushmen

The classic South African ethnographies, published between the 1920s and the 1940s, had dealt with Bantu-speaking rural populations; indeed, in this period only one comparable study, Winifred Hoernlé's study of the Nama, was devoted to a Hottentot or Khoi group.[13] In the 1960s, anthropologists from the University of Cape Town began to make ethnographic studies of "Hottentot" or "Coloured" communities in the Cape and in Namibia (see Carstens 1966). However, in the ideological climate created by Apartheid the designation of the subjects of these studies became a matter of the most acute sensitivity.

Legally the nonwhite, Afrikaans-speaking peoples in the Western Cape were members of a specific caste, termed "coloured," within the Apartheid system. (The designation "coloured"—or more specifically "Cape coloured," or "so-called coloured" in the terminology of dissent—came into use in the middle of the nineteenth century.) The roots of most of the population lay in formerly "Hottentot," slave,[14] or "Baster"[15] communities, but the Hottentot connections were played down by all concerned, as were slave antecedents. The term "Hottentot" thus became a term of abuse.

By the twentieth century people referred to as "Cape coloured" were dominantly Afrikaans speakers and were usually members of (segregated) Dutch Reformed Church congregations. They also bore Afrikaans names. It was further widely believed that their ancestry could be traced to white forbears, and they were sometimes represented as being of "mixed race," a characterization emphasized by some "coloured" intellectuals who developed a myth of origin of their community as having been created at the moment of the arrival of the Dutch by the rape of local women by European sailors. This supposed racial mixture was also sometimes emphasized to distinguish the Cape coloureds from the Xhosa peoples who began to settle in Cape Town and to compete with them for jobs.

The promiscuous mixture of cultural, religious, linguistic, and racial criteria was characteristic of South African discourse, and the problematic nature of the underlying assumptions became especially evident when these criteria were flagrantly incompatible with each other. The "coloured" people, for example, were supposed to be racially distinct but they were native Afrikaans speakers and by and large members of the Dutch Reformed Churches. From the 1960s some liberal Afrikaners advocated the inclusion of the coloureds in the Afrikaner nation, on the grounds that cultural identity trumped race. This was an option that was seductive for many colored people, but at the same time the government was forcibly moving tens of thousands of so-called coloureds from their old-established homes in the centers of the Cape's cities and towns. As the political situation became increasingly polarized, the preferred strategy among both political activists and social scientists was instead to represent them as "black South Africans," on the argument that their consciousness and the conditions of their lives were shaped by Apartheid in the same way as the lives of the rest of the disenfranchised proletariat.

The emergence of an inclusive "coloured" category, and the debates that it fostered, had the consequence that in social anthropology "Hottentot" studies disappeared into a very different sort of project—that is, the study of the landless, voteless, "coloured" peoples of the Western and Northern Cape. The trajectory followed by Bushmen studies was very different. This was because the field fell outside the scope of South African anthropology as it had come to be defined. Research was concentrated in Botswana, with outliers in Namibia, and it was therefore not constrained by the academic boycott. Following Lorna Marshall's pioneering study of the !Kung in the 1950s,[16] a new wave of foreign ethnographers began to work in Botswana. South African–based social anthropologists showed no interest in the revival of Bushmen studies, which seemed irrelevant to their new concerns. Rather, research on Bushmen was shaped by the very different agendas of (mainly) American anthropology.

The great theoretical debate that came to shape Bushmen studies focused on the !Kung and had to do with the definition of their historical and evolutionary status. Richard Lee's famous study was carried out in the tradition of American evolutionism. He produced an ecologically driven account of the adaptation of hunter-gatherers to a semidesert environment, and he presented his findings as a contribution to the reconstruction of the transition to the upper Paleolithic in Africa. The !Kung came to serve as the ethnographic exemplars of a universal stage of human evolution (Lee 1979; Lee and DeVore 1968). This representation was challenged by a revisionist school, which argued that all of the Bushmen had been subjugated and incorporated for centuries by pastoralist peoples, black and white, and that it was absurd to treat them as the last African representatives of an ancient hunter-gatherer way of life. Rather, they were the underclass of a single, hierarchical social system (Wilmsen 1989).

There was also debate about the ethnic identity of these peoples and their proper designation. In a familiar move, tainted colonial labels were replaced with a scientific nomenclature that was based on vernacular terminology. Schapera had given his imprimatur in 1930 to the term Khoisan, used to designate the "Hottentot-Bushmen" category as a whole. Monica Wilson led the next generation of South African anthropologists in replacing the terms "Bushmen" and "Hottentot" by "San" and "Khoi," respectively, although "San" was in fact a derogatory Khoi ("Hottentot") word for hunters.

In the 1980s the distinction between "Bushmen" and "Hottentot" itself came into question. Linguistic classifications cross-cut the division between hunters and herders, and historical evidence showed that some populations moved from hunting to herding and back again (Barnard 1992, chapter 2). In Botswana, ethnic or linguistic labels were disputed by development workers, who redesignated the Bushmen or San as "Sarwa." This derogatory Tswana ethnic label was now redefined by political activists to mean "remote peoples." The term was designed to apply to poor and weak communities in the north and west of the country, and it was intended to be an economic or geographical indicator rather than an ethnic label. In practice, however, impoverished "Kgalagadi" were not identified as Sarwa, however poor they may have been and however remote their homes from the rail line. Also not identified as Sarwa were the small groups of "Hottentots," who were sharply distinguished from "Sarwa" by the peoples of the Kalahari. What happened in effect what that development personnel took over the traditional (and derogatory) Tswana term for "Bushmen."

Although local political influences were by no means irrelevant, from the 1960s onward Bushmen studies developed largely within the framework of a cosmopolitan anthropological discourse. There was a certain, perhaps neglected, convergence between the revisionists in Bushmen studies and the single society theorists in South Africa, for both insisted on the processes of incorporation and domination. There was also an interesting difference of emphasis, however. For South African scholars, it seemed obvious that the structuring forces were exerted by the state or by the highly corporate and centralized mining capitalist system, which was in turn closely associated with the state. For the largely American-based revisionists working in Botswana and Namibia, the state was ignored. The power to influence local communities was attributed instead to the vague global forces of imperialism and capitalism that play such a central role in the modern demonology of the American Left. Perhaps this is not a very significant difference: it can be argued that at the fundamental level at which the very nature of the ethnographic object is in question, the main currents of South African anthropology and Bushmen ethnography converged on a common theoretical perspective.

Both the one society school in South Africa and the revisionists in Botswana took the view that ethnic groups were effectively invented by some higher power (the state, the imperialist order, the capitalist system) to serve its own nefarious purposes. The researcher's task was first to deconstruct this fiction, and then to constitute new subjects of research. These were once more defined in relation to the state, but were now identified as the real products of political and economic exploitation. In South Africa, the victims of Apartheid became the objects of anthropology. In Botswana, attention was shifted from the "Bushmen" or "San" to the underclass, the Fourth World at the mercy of the Third.

From Single Society to Rainbow Nation

The transition to a democratic political system may be regarded, from one point of view, as a huge social experiment, testing the established theories about South African society. The old Apartheid theory predicted that Africans would always express a primordial loyalty to tribal identities. However, it soon became clear that the African National Congress had a huge following among black South Africans almost everywhere in the country. It is true that a few of the old Bantustan parties retained some measure of support, most significantly in the Zulu-speaking region, but even there the electorate divided neatly into two, a rural section in the KwaZulu heartland, which was loyal to the Zulu nationalist movement, Inkhatha, and on the other hand the Natal-based, generally Christian and urban section that voted for the African National Congress. (This division between a conservative rural population and an outward-looking population in the towns and cities had been a major theme of English-language ethnography.)

In the first two open South African elections, in 1994 and 1999, a majority of "coloreds" voted for the Afrikaner Nationalist Party. Indians were divided between the "white" parties and small Indian parties. However, the overwhelming majority of African voters supported the African National Congress, and most whites voted for the historically white parties—their votes apparently expressing "racial" identifications that had been entrenched from the middle of the nineteenth century. It could be argued, however, that class was decisive, not race, for a century of racial discrimination had produced a close correspondence between race, education, housing, employment patterns, and income (see Lodge 1999, especially chapter 3).

None of this surprised the English-language anthropologists. However, they began to acknowledge difficulties in conceptualizing the social and cultural processes that were emerging in the new South Africa. Writing an editorial introduction to a 1997 collection of essays by English-language South African anthropologists, Patrick McAllister remarked that their discipline was "emerging from the corner it painted itself into in the dark days of apartheid," during which it had been characterized by "the preoccupation with political economy analyses." ("Political economy" is the euphemism, borrowed from the Americans, for marxism.) McAllister and his colleagues had now come to recognize "that culture needs to be reintroduced into the answers we give to explain social practice" (1997: 2–3). Addressing his former marxist self with something like wonder, another South African anthropologist, Andrew Spiegel, remarked that ethnographers active in the countryside had to admit that "something has (or appears to have) survived, persisted or continued, and that one cannot assume that incorporation into an industrial environment results in a complete overturning and replacement of what existed and occurred before" (1997: 10).

These efforts are straws in the wind, signaling tentative movements in the direction of ethnographic work that is more responsive to local conceptions of the world. There are alternative possibilities, however. A number of anthropologists, English and Afrikaner, have found comfort in a postmodernist relativism (a theory that states that no useful distinction is to be made between a theory and an ideology). Others, again, have abandoned abstract problems of theory in favor of applied research, which is much in demand these days. Historically, research projects in Anglophone social anthropology in South Africa were often motivated by opposition to Apartheid, capitalism, or colonialism. The challenge now is to serve the state, rather than to oppose it. But socially responsible research may not be enough. Soon it will be necessary to face up to the intellectual challenge being formulated by the African National Congress. The new state is developing its own view of South Africa. Positive discrimination is legally entrenched. President Mbeki fosters talk of an "African Renaissance," and he offers a tentative welcome to Afrocentric ideas. Perhaps the anthropologists will have to enter into fresh debates on familiar themes, arguing once again about the most basic issues, the character of the single society, and the nature of the units into which the South African population divides, or is divided.

Notes

I am very grateful to Benoît de L'Estoile for his stimulating editorial suggestions on an earlier draft of this paper, which was published in French in the journal *Synthèses*. Isaac Schapera and Robert Ross also kindly read and commented on an earlier draft. The title of this paper is taken from a well-known World War II poem by Henry Reed. It describes an instructor pointing to the parts of a gun and teaching the recruits how to use them.

1 See, for example, Gordon 1990; Gordon and Spiegel 1993; Hammond-Tooke 1997; Kiernan 1997; Kuper 1999b, chapter 9; Ramphele 1995; Van Rensburg and Van der Waal 1999; Vawda 1995.

2 A clear statement of this opposition between Afrikaans and English anthropology in South Africa may be found in Martin West's inaugural lecture as professor of social anthropology at the University of Cape Town (West 1988).

3 I rely heavily here on the analysis in Ross 1993, especially chapter 3.

4 For a sophisticated discussion of the different traditions of native administration before the union, see Hamilton 1998: chapters 3–4.

5 The "Asian" or "Indian" population was concentrated in Natal, though there was also a substantial settlement in the Transvaal. The heterogeneous peoples yoked together as "Indians" included Hindu descendants of South Indian indentured laborers in the plantations of Natal; educated "free Christians"; and Muslim Punjabi-speaking traders, descended from independent immigrants, who worked mainly in their own small businesses and were settled largely in the Transvaal. Mahatma Gandhi, who arrived in South Africa in 1893 to work as a lawyer, formed the Natal Indian Congress in 1894 and remained in the country for two decades as the leader of a South African Indian political movement. In spite of his efforts, however, a South African "Asian" or "Indian" political identity was never strongly developed.

6 It would be fascinating to make a study of the changes of racial classification in the South African census and the Cape Colony census. In the last census of the Cape Colony, in 1904, there were seven major categories divided into forty subdivisions.

7 *Kafir*, or unbeliever, was the term used by Arabs for people in the interior of Africa, and it was adopted by the Portuguese and Dutch.

8 In 1941, the name of the journal was changed to *African Studies*.

9 On Macmillan, see Saunders 1988: 47–75 and Macmillan 1975.

10 A similar format was retained by Hammond-Tooke a generation later when he edited a revised version of the volume (see Hammond-Tooke 1974). I published a criticism of the approach in a review article titled "Culture Area or Political System?" (Kuper 1976).

11 The theoretical approach of the ethnos school is summarized and discussed in Hammond-Tooke 1997, chapter 6.

12 Hammond-Tooke 1997, chapters 5–6.

13 Hoernlé's papers on the Nama, published between 1913 and 1925, were edited by Peter Carstens and published in 1985 under the title *The Social Organization of the Nama*.

14 The slaves were themselves not ethnically homogeneous. Though most of the slaves had been brought from the Dutch East Indies, a significant number came from Madagascar and Mauritius. A distinct category emerged in the Cape, defined

by religion. These were the Muslim "Cape Malays." They lived in the very heart of Cape Town and were descended from slave artisans imported from the Dutch East Indies.

15 The term Baster, or Bastard, in use in the early nineteenth century, was applied to independent groups of Khoi origin but Boer culture living beyond the boundaries of the colony. It was also used to refer to people of mixed origin (slave and "Hottentot," or the descendants of white intermixtures with slaves or "Hottentots").

16 See Marshall 1976 for her collection of essays on the !Kung.

REFERENCES

Aguirre Beltrán, Gonzalo. 1957. *El proceso de aculturación: Problemas científicos y filosóficos*. Mexico: Universidade Autónoma de México.

——. 1992 [1976]. *Obra polémica*. Mexico: Fondo de Cultura Económica.

Alayón, Norberto. 1989. *Asistencia y asistencialismo ¿Pobres controlados o erradicación de la pobreza?* Buenos Aires: Humanitas.

Albert, Bruce. 1995. "Anthropologie appliqué ou 'anthropologie impliquée.'" In *Les applications de l'anthropologie: Un essai de réflexion collective depuis la France*, ed. Jean-François Baré. pp. 87–118. Paris: Karthala.

——. 1997a. "'Ethnographic Situation' and Ethnic Movements: Notes on Post-Malinowskian Fieldwork." *Critique of Anthropology* 17 (1): 53–65.

——.1997b. "Territorialité, ethnopolitique et développement: À propos du mouvement indien en Amazonie Brésilienne." *Cahiers de l'Amérique Latine* 23: 177–210.

Albert, Bruce, and David Kopenawa. 2003. *Yanomami, l'esprit de la forêt*. Paris: Fondation Cartier pour l'Art Contemporain, Actes Sud.

Alexandre, Valentim. 2000a. "Questão nacional e questão imperial em Oliveira Martins." In *Velho Brasil, novas Áfricas: Portugal e o império (1808–1975)*. Porto: Afrontamento.

——. 2000b. "O império colonial no século XX." In *Velho Brasil, novas Áfricas: Portugal e o império (1808–1975)*. Porto: Afrontamento.

Almeida, Rubem Ferreira Thomaz de. 1991. "O projeto Kaiowá-Ñandeva: Uma experiência de etnodesenvolvimento junto aos Guarani-Kaiowá e Guarani-Ñandeva contemporâneos do Mato Grosso do Sul." Master's thesis, National Museum, Federal University of Rio de Janeiro.

Altamirano, Ignacio Manuel. 1871. *Diários (Obras completas)*. Vol. 20. Mexico: Conaculta.

Amselle, Jean-Loup, and Elikia M'bokolo, eds. 1998 [1985]. *Au cœur de l'ethnie*. Paris: La Découverte.

Anderson, Benedict. 1991. *Imagined Communities: Reflections on the Origin and Spread of Nationalism*. London: Verso.

Apffel-Marglin, Frédérique, and Stephen A. Marglin, eds. 1994. *Decolonizing Knowledge: From Development to Dialogue*. Oxford: Clarendon Press.

Ardener, Edwin, and Shirley Ardener. 1965. "A Directory Study of Social Anthropologists." *British Journal of Sociology* 16: 295–315.

Arendt, Hannah. 1966. *The Origins of Totalitarianism.* New York: Harcourt Brace and World.

Aron, Raymond. 1959. "Introduction." In *Le savant et le politique*, by Max Weber. Paris: Plon.

Asad, Talal. 1991. "Afterword: From the History of Colonial Anthropology to the Anthropology of Western Hegemony." In *Colonial Situations: Essays on the Contextualization of Ethnographic Knowledge*, ed. George W. Stocking Jr. pp. 313–24. Madison: University of Wisconsin Press.

——, ed. 1973. *Anthropology and the Colonial Encounter.* New York: Humanities Press.

Asamblea del Departamento de Querétaro. 1852 [1845]. "Notas estadísticas del Departamento de Querétaro, formadas por la asamblea constitucional del mismo, y remitidas al supremo gobierno. . . ." *BSMGE* 3: 169–236.

Balandier, Georges. 1950a. "Aspects de l'évolution sociale chez les Fang du Gabon." *Cahiers Internationaux de Sociologie* 9: 76–106.

——. 1950b. "Problèmes économiques et problème politiques au niveau du village Fang." *Bulletin de l'Institut d'Etudes Centrafricaines* 1: 49–64.

——. 1951. "La situation coloniale: Approche théorique." *Cahiers Internationaux de Sociologie* 11: 44–79.

——. 1952. " Contribution à une sociologie de la dépendance." *Cahiers Internationaux de Sociologie* 12: 47–69.

——. 1955. *Sociologie dynamique de l'Afrique Noire.* Paris: PUF.

Balandier, Georges, and Jean-Claude Pauvert. 1952. *Les villages gabonais: Aspects démographiques, économiques, sociologiques. Projets de modernisation.* Brazzaville: Mémoires de l'Institut d'Études Centrafricaines.

Bancroft, Hubert. 1883. «Observations on Mexico» (manuscript).

Banuri, Tariq. 1990. "Development and the Politics of Knowledge: A Critical Interpretation of the Social Role of Modernization." In *Dominating Knowledge: Development, Culture and Resistance*, ed. Frédérique Apffel-Marglin and Stephen A. Marglin. Oxford: Clarendon Press.

Barbeito, Alberto C., and Rubén Lo Vuolo. 1992. *La modernización excluyente: Transformación económica y estado de bienestar en la Argentina.* Buenos Aires: Losada/Unicef.

Barnard, Alan. 1992. *Hunters and Herders of Southern Africa: A Comparative Ethnography of the Khoisan Peoples.* Cambridge: Cambridge University Press.

Barth, Fredrik. 1969. "Introduction." In *Ethnic Groups and Boundaries: The Social Organization of Culture Difference*, ed. Fredrik Barth. pp. 9–38. Bergen: Universitets Forlaget; London: George Allen and Unwin.

——. 1984. "Problems in Conceptualizing Cultural Pluralism, with Illustrations from Somar, Oman." In *The Prospects for Plural Societies*, ed. David Maybury-Lewis. pp. 77–87. Washington, D.C.: American Ethnological Society.

——. 1988. "The Analysis of Culture in Complex Societies." *Ethnos* 3–4: 120–42.

——. 1993. *Balinese Worlds.* Chicago: University of Chicago Press.

Bartra, Roger. 1999. *La sangre y la tinta: Ensayos sobre la condición postmexicana.* Mexico: Océano.

Bashkov, Ira. 1991. "The Dynamics of Rapport in a Colonial Situation: David Schneider's Fieldwork on the Islands of Yap." In *Colonial Situations: Essays on the Contextualization of Ethnographic Knowledge*, ed. George W. Stocking Jr. pp. 170–242. Madison: University of Wisconsin Press.

Bastide, Roger. 1974. *Sociologia e psicanálise.* São Paulo: Melhoramentos/EDUSP.

——. 1979. *Antropologia Aplicada.* São Paulo: Editorial Perspectiva.

Bateson, Gregory. 1942. "Morale and National Character." In *Civilian Morale*, ed. Goodwin Watson. pp. 71–91. New York: Houghton Mifflin.

Bateson, Gregory, and Margaret Mead. 1942. *Balinese Character: A Photographic Analysis.* New York: New York Academy of Sciences II.

Bausinger, Hermann. 1993 [1971]. *Volkskunde ou l'ethnologie allemande: De la recherche sur l'antiquité à l'analyse culturelle*, translated by Dominique Lassaigne and Pascale Godenir. Paris: Éditions de la MSH.

Bazin, Jean. 1998. "A chacun son Bambara." In *Au cœur de l'ethnie*, ed. Jean-Loup Amselle and Elikia M'bokolo. pp. 87–127. Paris: La Découverte.

Bender, Gerald. 1980. *Angola sob domínio português.* Lisbon: Sá da Costa.

Benedict, Ruth. 1934. *Patterns of Culture.* Boston: Houghton Mifflin.

——. 1989 [1946]. *The Chrysanthemum and the Sword: Patterns of Japanese Culture.* Boston: Houghton Mifflin.

Bennett, John W., and Michio Nagai. 1953. "The Japanese Critique of the Methodology of Benedict's 'Crysanthemum and the Sword.'" *American Anthropologist* 55: 404–11.

Bensa, Alban. 1995. *Chroniques Kanak: L'ethnologie en marche.* Paris: Survival International France.

——. 1990. *Nouvelle-Calédonie: Un paradis dans la tourmente.* Paris: Gallimard (Découvertes). [Revised and expanded edition is *Nouvelle-Caledonie: Vers l'emancipation.* Paris: Gallimard. 1998].

Bensa, Alban, and Isabelle Leblic, eds. 2000. *En pays Kanak.* Paris: Maison des Sciences de l'Homme.

Bernal, Martin. 1987. *Black Athena: The Afrocentric Roots of Classical Civilization.* Vol. 1. New Brunswick: Rutgers University Press.

Bielschowsky, Ricardo. 2000. *Pensamento econômico brasileiro: O ciclo ideológico do desenvolvimentismo.* Rio de Janeiro: Contraponto.

Biondi, Jean-Pierre, and Gilles Morin. 1992. *Les anticolonialistes (1881–1961).* Paris: Robert Lafont.

Bloch, Marc. 1995. *Histoire et historiens.* Paris: Colin.

Boas, Franz. 1966 [1932]. "The Aims of Anthropological Research." In *Race, Language and Culture.* pp. 243–259. New York: Free Press.

Bonfil, Guillermo. 1970. "Del indigenismo de la revolución a la antropología crítica." In *De eso que llaman antropología mexicana*, ed. Arturo Warman, Guillermo Bonfil, Margarita Nolasco, Mercedes Olivera, and Enrique Valencia. Mexico: Editorial Nuestro Tiempo. [Published in Portuguese in *Antropologia e indigenismo na América Latina*, ed. Carmen Junqueira and Edgar de Assis Carvalho. pp. 87–100. São Paulo: Cortez. 1981].

Bonneuil, Christophe. 1999. "Le Muséum National d'Histoire Naturelle et l'expansion coloniale de la IIIème république (1870–1914)." *Revue d'histoire de la France d'Outre-Mer*, 86 (322–23): 143–69.

Bourdieu, Pierre. 1980. "L'identité et la représentation: Eléments pour une réflexion critique sur l'idée de région." *Actes de la recherche en sciences socials* 35: 63–72.

———. 1981. "Décrire et prescrire: Les conditions de possibilité et les limites de l'efficacité politique." *Actes de la Recherche en Sciences Sociales* 38: 69–74.

———. 1994. "Rethinking the State: Genesis and Structure of the Bureaucratic Field." *Sociological Theory* 12 (1): 1–18.

Boxer, Charles R. 1969. *The Portuguese Seaborne Empire, 1415–1825*. New York: Alfred A. Knopf.

Brévié, Jules. 1936. "Science et colonisation." In *Trois études de Monsieur le Gouverneur Général Brévié*. Dakar: Imprimerie du Gouvernement Général de l'AOF.

Brian, Eric. 1994. *La mesure de l'etat: Administrateurs et géomètres au XVIIIème siècle*. Paris: Albin Michel.

British Museum. 1965. *Henry Christy: A Pioneer of Anthropology*. London: British Museum.

Brown, Richard. 1973. "Anthropology and Colonial Rule: Godfrey Wilson and the Rhodes-Livingstone Institute, Northern Rhodesia." In *Anthropology and the Colonial Encounter*, ed. Talal Asad. London: Ithaca Press.

Brown, Michael F. 1993. "Facing the State, Facing the World: Amazonia's Native Leaders and the New Politics of Identity." *L' Homme* 33 (2–4): 307–26.

Buffington, Robert. 2000. *Criminal and Citizen in Modern Mexico*. Lincoln: University of Nebraska Press.

Bustelo, Eduardo S., and Alberto Minujín. 1991. *La política social en los tiempos del cólera*. Buenos Aires: Unicef Argentina.

Cabral, Amílcar. 1978. *Obras escolhidas*. Porto: Seara Nova.

Caetano, Marcelo. 1974. *Depoimento*. Rio de Janeiro: Record.

Calvet, Louis-Jean. 1981. *Lingüística y colonialismo*. Madrid: Júcar.

Cardoso de Oliveira, Roberto. 1955. "Relatório de uma investigação sobre terras em Mato Grosso." In *Serviço de Proteção aos Índios—1954*. pp. 173–84. Rio de Janeiro: SPI/Ministério da Agricultura.

———. 1960. *O processo de assimilação dos Terena*. Rio de Janeiro: Museu Nacional.

———. 1978a [1972]. "Possibilidades de uma antropologia da ação." In *A sociologia do Brasil indígena*. Rio de Janeiro: Tempo Brasileiro.

———. 1978b [1972]. *A sociologia do Brasil indígena*. Rio de Janeiro. Tempo Brasileiro.

———. 1976. *Do índio ao bugre: O processo de assimilação dos Terena*. Rio de Janeiro: Francisco Alves.

Carneiro da Cunha, Manuela. 1986. *Antropologia do Brasil: Mito, história, etnicidade.* São Paulo: Brasiliense.

———, ed. 1987. *Os direitos do índio: Ensaios documentos.* São Paulo: Brasiliense.

———. 1992. *Legislação indigenista no século XIX.* São Paulo: Comissão Pró-Índio/Edusp.

Carstens, Peter. 1966. *The Social Structure of a Cape Coloured Reserve.* Cape Town: Oxford University Press.

Castelo, Cláudia. 1999. *O modo português de estar no mundo.* Porto: Afrontamento.

Castro Faria, Luiz de. 1998. *Antropologia: Escritos exumados 1. Espaços circunscritos; Tempos Soltos.* Niterói, Brazil: EDUFF.

Cernea, Michael M. 1995. "Social Organization and Development Anthropology." 1995 Malinowski Award lecture, Society for Applied Anthropology, World Bank, Washington, D.C.

Chamboredon, Jean-Claude. 1982. "Émile Durkheim: Le social, objet de science." *Critique* 445–46: 460–531.

Chanet, Jean-François. 1996. *L'ecole républicaine et les petites patries.* Paris: Aubier.

Châtelet, François. 1976. "La question de l'histoire de la philosophie aujourd'hui." In *Politiques de la philosophie*, ed. Dominique Grisoni. pp. 29–53. Paris: Bernard Grasset.

Chauleur. 1934. *La région nord.* Typescript, ANFOM/Cameroun C 888. Monographies. 145 pp.

———. 1943. "Esquisse ethnologique pour servir à l'étude des principales tribus des territoires du Cameroun sous mandat français." *Bulletin de la Société d'Études Camerounaises.*

Chavero, Alfredo. 1888. *México a través de los siglos—Historia antigua de la conquista.* Vol. 1. Barcelona: Espasa and Cia.

Chilver, Elizabeth M. 1957. "A New View of Africa: Lord Hailey's Second Survey." *The Round Table: A Quarterly Review of British Commonwealth Affairs* 48: 120–29.

Chombart de Lauwe, Paul-Henri, and J. Deboudaud. 1939. "Carte schématique du Cameroun." *Journal de la Société des Africanistes* 9 (2): 197–204.

Clapham, S. J. 1947. "Report of the Committee on the Provision for Social and Economic Research" (CMD6868- Clapham ctte). London: House of Commons. Official Reports.

Clifford, James. 1988. "Identity in Mashpee." In *The Predicament of Culture: Twentieth-Century Ethnography, Literature, and Art.* Cambridge, Mass.: Harvard University Press.

Cohen, William B. 1971. *Rulers of Empire: The French Colonial Service in Africa.* Stanford: Stanford University Press.

Cohn, Bernard. 1990. "The Census, Social Structure and Objectification in South Asia." In *An Anthropologist among the Historians, and Other Essays.* pp. 224–54. Delhi: Oxford University Press.

Comas, Juan. 1964. *La antropología social aplicada en Mexico: Trayectoria y antologia.* Mexico: Instituto Indigenista Interamericano.

Conklin, Alice L. 1997. *A Mission to Civilize: The Republican Idea of Empire in France and West-Africa, 1895–1930*. Stanford: Stanford University Press.

Conklin, Beth A., and Laura R. Graham. 1995. "The Shifting Middle Ground: Amazonian Indians and Eco-Politics." *American Anthropologist* 97 (4): 695–710.

Coombes, Annie E. 1994. *Reinventing Africa: Museums, Material Culture, and Popular Imagination in Late Victorian and Edwardian England*. New Haven: Yale University Press.

Cooper, Frederick. 1997. "Modernizing Bureaucrats, Backward Africans and the Development Concept." In *International Development and the Social Sciences: Essays on the History and Politics of Knowledge*, ed. Frederick Cooper and Randall Packard. pp. 4–92. Berkeley: University of California Press.

Cooper, Frederick, and Randall Packard, eds. 1997. *International Development and the Social Sciences: Essays on the History and Politics of Knowledge*. Berkeley: University of California Press.

Copans, Jean. 1975. *Anthropologie et impérialisme*. Paris: Maspero.

Corrêa, Mariza. 1982. *As ilusões da liberdade: A escola de Nina Rodrigues e a antropología no Brasil*. Ph.D. diss. São Paulo University.

———. 1995. "A antropologia no Brasil (1960–1980)." In *História das ciências sociais no Brasil*, Vol. 2, ed. Sergio Miceli. São Paulo: Editora Sumaré.

Crawford, Elisabeth, Terry Shinn, and Sverker Sörlin, eds. 1993. *Denationalizing Science: The Context of International Scientific Practice*. Dordrecht: Kluwer.

Crush, Jonathan. 1995. "Introduction: Imagining Development." In *Power of Development*, ed. Jonathan Crush. New York: Routledge.

Dahl, Gudrun, and Annika Rabo, eds. 1992. *Kam-ap or Take-off: Local Notions of Development*. Stockholm: Stockholm Studies in Social Anthropology.

Darnell, Regna. 1986. "Personality and Culture: The Fate of the Sapirian Alternative." In *Malinowski, Rivers, Benedict, and Others: Essays on Culture and Personality*, ed. George Stocking Jr. pp. 156–83. Madison: University of Wisconsin Press.

Davis, Shelton H. 1977. *Victims of the Miracle: Development and the Indians of Brazil*. New York: Cambridge University Press.

Delafosse, Maurice. 1921. "Sur l'orientation nouvelle de la politique indigène dans l'Afrique Noire." *Renseignements Coloniaux et Documents Publiés par le Comité de L'Afrique Française* 6: 145–52.

———. 1925. *Les civilisations négro-africaines*. Paris: Larose.

Delavignette, Robert. 1946. *Service africain*. Paris: Gallimard.

Deschamps, Hubert. 1931. "La vocation coloniale et le métier d'administrateur." *Renseignements Coloniaux* 10: 497–500.

Diamond, Stanley. 1969. *Primitive Views of the World*. New York: Columbia University Press.

Dias, Jorge. 1953. *Estudos do caráter nacional português*. Lisbon: Junta de Investigações do Ultramar.

———. 1961a. "Os elementos fundamentais da cultura portuguesa." In *Ensaios etnológicos*. Lisbon: Junta de Investigações do Ultramar.

——. 1961b. "A expansão ultramarina portuguesa à luz da moderna antropologia." In *Ensaios etnológicos*. Lisbon: Junta de Investigações do Ultramar.

Dias Duarte, Luiz Fernando. 2000. "Anthropologie, psychanalyse et 'civilisation' du Brésil dans l'entre-deux-guerres." *Revue de Synthèse* 121 (3–4): 325–44.

Dimier, Véronique. 1999. «Construction et enjeu d'un discours colonial scientifique sur l'administration coloniale comparée, vers 1930–vers 1950.» Ph.D. dissertation, University of Grenoble.

Doke, Clement M., and Desmond T. Cole. 1961. *Contributions to the History of Bantu Linguistics*. Johannesburg: Witwatersrand University Press.

Drouot, Henri. 1950. "Au rond-point folklore." *Annales de Bourgogne*, 221–22.

Dubow, Saul. 1995. *Illicit Union: Scientific Racism in Modern South Africa*. Johannesburg: Witwatersrand University Press.

Duchet, Michèle. 1980. *Anthropologie et histoire au siècle des lumières*. Paris: Maspero.

——. 1985. *Le partage des savoirs: Discours historique et discours ethnologique*. Paris: La Découverte.

Dugast, Idelette. 1948. "Essai sur le peuplement du Cameroun." *Bulletin de la Société d'Études Camerounaises* 21–22: 19–34.

——. 1949. «Inventaire ethnique du Sud-Cameroun.» Cahors: Mémoires de l'Institut Français d'Afrique Noire, Centre du Cameroun.

——. 1954. "Banen, Bafia and Balom." In *Peoples of the Central Cameroons; Ethnographic Survey of Africa*. London: International African Institute.

——. 1955, 1959. *Monographie de la tribu des Ndiki (Banen du Cameroun)*. 2 vols. Paris: Institut d'Ethnologie.

Dumont, Louis. 1951. *La tarasque*. Paris: Gallimard.

——. 1980 [1966]. *Homo Hierarchicus: The Caste System and Its Implications*. Translation by Mark Sainsbury, Louis Dumont, and Basia Gulati. Chicago: University of Chicago Press.

Durkheim, Émile. 1975. "L'etat." In *Textes—Fonctions sociales et institutions*. Vol. 3. pp. 172–78. Paris: Minuit.

Éboué, Félix. 1931. "Les peuples de l'Oubangui-Chari: Essai d'ethnographie, de linguistique et d'économie sociale." *Bulletin de l'Afrique Française, Renseignements Coloniaux et Documents*. Archives Congolaises 17.

Elias, Norbert. 1972. "Process of State Formation and Nation Building." In *Transactions of the Seventh Congress of Sociology*. Vol. 3. Geneva: International Sociological Association.

——. 1982. "Scientific Establishments." In *Scientific Establishments and Hierarchies*, ed. Norbert Elias, Herminio Martins, and Richard Whitley. pp. 3–69. Dordrecht: Reidel.

——. 2000 [1939]. *The Civilizing Process: Sociogenetic and Psychogenetic Investigations*. Translated by Edmund Jephcott, edited by Eric Dunning, Johan Goudsblom, and Stephen Mennell. Oxford: Blackwell.

——. 1989 [1968]. "Introducción." In *El proceso de la civilización. investigaciones sociogenéticas y psicogenéticas*. pp. 9–46. Mexico: Fondo de Cultura Económica.

[Prologue to the 1968 German edition. Transalated in *The Civilizing Process: Sociogenetic and Psychogenetic Investigations.* Oxford: Blackwell, 2000].

———. 1996. *The Germans: Power Struggles and the Development of Habitus in the Nineteenth and Twentieth Centuries.* New York: Columbia University Press.

Escalante, Fernando. 1992. *Ciudadanos imaginarios.* México: El Colegio de México.

Escobar, Arturo. 1995. *Encountering Development: The Making and Unmaking of the Third World.* Princeton: Princeton University Press.

———. 1997. "Anthropology and Development." *International Social Science Journal* 154: 497–516.

Esteva, Gustavo. 1999. "Development." In *The Development Dictionary: A Guide to Power as Knowledge,* ed. Wolfgang Sachs. London: Witwatersrand University Press; Zed Books.

Estrada, Juan. 1852. "Estado libre y soberano de guerrero; Datos estadísticos de la prefectura del centro." *BSMGE* 3: 71–75.

Fabian, Johannes. 1983. *Time and the Other: How Anthropology Makes Its Objects.* Cambridge: Cambridge University Press.

———. 2000. *Out of Our Minds: Reason and Madness in the Exploration of Central Africa.* Berkeley: University of California Press.

Fabiani, Jean-Louis. 1988. *Les philosophes de la république.* Paris: Éditions de Minuit.

Fabre, Daniel. 1998. "L'ethnologie française à la croisée des engagements (1940–1945)." In *Résistants et résistance,* ed. Jean-Yves Boursier. pp. 319–400. Paris: L'Harmattan.

Faure, Christian. 1989. *Le projet culturel de Vichy: Folklore et Révolution nationale 1940–1944.* Paris: Éditions du CNRS/Presses Universitaires de Lyon.

Febvre, Lucien. 1954. "Avant-Propos." *Encyclopédie française—Le bien-être et la culture.* Vol. 14 (Societé de Gestion de l'Encyclopédie Française). Paris: Larousse.

Ferguson, James. 1990. *The Anti-Politics Machine: "Development," Depolitization, and Bureaucratic Power in Lesotho.* Cambridge: Cambridge University Press.

———. 1997. "Anthropology and Its Evil Twin: 'Development' in the Constitution of a Discipline." In *International Development and the Social Sciences: Essays on the History and Politics of Knowledge,* ed. Frederick Cooper and Randall Packard. pp. 150–75. California: University of California Press.

Firth, Raymond. 1936. *We the Tikopia: A Sociological Study of Kinship in Primitive Polynesia.* London: George Allen and Unwin.

———. 1986. "The Founding and Early History of the ASA." *Annals of the ASA* 7: 4–9.

Foucault. Michel. 1979. "Governmentality." *Ideology and Consciousness* 6: 5–21.

———. 1994 [1973]. *The Order of Things: An Archaeology of the Human Sciences.* New York: Vintage Books.

França, José-Augusto. 1985. *A arte moderna em Portugal.* Lisbon: Bertrand.

Freire, Carlos Augusto da Rocha. 1990. *Indigenismo e antropologia: O conselho nacional de proteção aos índios na gestão rondon (1939–1955).* Master's thesis, National Museum, Federal University of Rio de Janeiro.

Freyre, Gilberto. 1940. *O mundo que o português criou.* Lisbon: Livros do Brasil.

Gage, Thomas. 1699. *A New Survey of the West-Indies*. London: M. Clark.

Gallagher, Joseph T. 1974. "The Emergence of an African Ethnic Group: The Case of the Ndendeuli." *International Journal of African Historical Studies* 7 (1): 1–26.

Gallo, Donato. 1988. *O saber Português: Antropologia e colonialismo*. Lisbon: Heptágono.

Galvão, Eduardo. 1979. *Encontro de sociedades: Índios e brancos no Brasil*. Rio de Janeiro: Paz e Terra.

Gamio, Manuel. 1922. *La población del valle de Teotihuacán*. 2 vols. Mexico: Secretaría de Agricultura y Fomento.

——. 1924. *Opiniones y juicios sobre la obra La población del valle de Teotihuacán*. Mexico: Secretaría de Agricultura y Fomento.

——. 1931. *The Mexican Immigrant, His Life-Story*. Chicago: University of Chicago Press.

——. 1960. *Forjando patria*. Mexico: Editorial Porrua.

——. 1966. *Consideraciones sobre el problema indígena*. México: Instituto Indigenista Interamericano.

García Mora, Carlos, ed. 1987–1988. *La antropología en México: Panorama histórico*. 15 vols. Mexico: INAH.

Geertz, Clifford. 1995. *After the Fact: Two Countries, Four Decades, One Anthropologist*. Cambridge, Mass.: Harvard University Press.

——. 2001. *Available Light: Anthropological Reflections on Philosophical Topics*. Princeton: Princeton University Press.

Gerbi, Antonello. 1973. *The Dispute of the New World: The History of a Polemic, 1750–1900*. Pittsburgh: University of Pittsburgh Press.

Gerholm, Tomas, and Ulf Hannerz. 1983. "Introduction: The Shaping of National Anthropologies." *Ethnos* 47 (1): 5–35.

Girardet, Raoul. 1972. *L'idée coloniale en France*. Paris: La Table Ronde.

Glass, D.V., and Max Gluckman. 1962. "The Social Sciences in British Universities: Memorandum to the Robbins Committee on Higher Education Submitted by the Council of the British Association for the Advancement of Science on Behalf of the Committee of Section N (Sociology)." *Advancement of Science* (July): 1–7.

Gluckman, Max. 1958. *An Analysis of a Social Situation in Modern Zululand*. Manchester: Manchester University Press.

Golbert, Laura, and Emilio Tenti Fanfani. 1994. "Nuevas y viejas formas de pobreza en la Argentina." *Sociedad* 4: 85–103.

Gonçalves, Marco Antonio. 1996. "Introdução." In *Diários de campo: Entre os tenetehara, kaioá e índios do Xingu*, ed. Eduardo Galvão. Rio de Janeiro: Editora UFRJ/Museu do Índio-FUNAI.

González Gamio, Angeles. 1987. *Manuel Gamio, una lucha sin fin*. Mexico: Unam.

Goody, Jack. 1995. *The Expansive Moment: Anthropology in Britain and Africa, 1918–1970*. Cambridge: Cambridge University Press.

Gordon, R. 1990. "Early Social Anthropology in South Africa." *African Studies* 49 (1): 15–48.

Gordon, R., and A. Spiegel. 1993. "Southern Africa Revisited." *Annual Review of Anthropology* 22: 83–105.

Gorer, Geoffrey. 1943. "Themes in Japanese Culture." *Transactions of the New York Academy of Sciences* 2 (5): 106–24.

——. 1948. *The American People*. New York: Norton.

——. 1953. "National Character: Theory and Practice." In *The Study of Culture at a Distance*, ed. Margaret Mead and Rhoda Métraux. pp. 57–83. Chicago: University of Chicago Press.

——. 1955. *Exploring English Character*. London: Cresset Press.

Grassi, Estela, Susana Hintze, and Maria Rosa Neufeld, eds. 1994. *Políticas sociales, crisis y ajuste estructural*. Buenos Aires: Espacio Editorial.

Greenhalgh, Paul 1987. *Ephemeral Vistas: The "Expositions Universelles," Great Exhibition and World Fairs, 1851–1939*. Manchester: Manchester University Press.

Grillo, Ralph D. 1985. "Applied Anthropology in the 1980s: Retrospect and Prospect." In *Social Anthropology and Development Policy*, ed. Ralph D. Grillo and Alan Rew. London: Tavistock Publications.

Guerra, Francois Xavier. 2000. "The Implosion of the Spanish American Empire: Emerging Statehood and Collective Identities." In *The Collective and the Public in Latin America: Cultural Identities and Political Order*, ed. Luis Roniger and Tamar Herzog. Brighton, U.K.: Sussex Academic Press.

Guerra, Francois Xavier, and Annick Lamperiere. 1998. *Los espacios públicos en Iberoamérica: Ambigüedades y problemas, siglos XVIII–XIX*. Mexico: Fondo de Cultura Económica.

Gulick, John. 1973. "Urban Anthropology." In *Handbook of Social and Cultural Anthropology*, ed. John J. Honigmann. pp. 979–1029. Chicago: Rand McNally College Publishing Co.

Hailey, Lord. 1938. *An African Survey: A Study of Problems Arising in Africa South of the Sahara*. Oxford: Oxford University Press.

Hamilton, Carolyn. 1998. *Terrific Majesty*. Cambridge Mass.: Harvard University Press.

Hammond-Tooke, W. David, ed. 1974. *The Bantu-Speaking Peoples of Southern Africa*. London: Routledge and Kegan Paul.

——. 1997. *Imperfect Interpreters: South Africa's Anthropologists 1920–1990*. Johannesburg: Witwatersrand University Press.

Handler, Richard. 1986. "Vigorous Male and Aspiring Female: Poetry, Personality, and Culture in Edward Sapir and Ruth Benedict." In *Malinowski, Rivers, Benedict, and Others: Essays on Culture and Personality*, ed. George W. Stocking Jr. pp. 127–55. Madison: University of Wisconsin Press.

——. 1988. *Nationalism and the Politics of Culture in Quebec*. Madison: University of Wisconsin Press.

——. 1989. "Anti-Romantic Romanticism: Edward Sapir and the Critique of American Individualism." *Anthropological Quarterly* 62 (1): 1–14.

Hardy, Georges. 1932. "Rapport général." In *Congrès International et Intercolonial de la Société Indigène.* Exposition Coloniale Internationale de Paris, 5–10 October 1931.

Harries, Patrick. 1989. "Exclusion, Classification and Internal Colonialism: The Emergence of Ethnicity among the Tsonga-Speakers of South Africa." In *The Creation of Tribalism in Southern Africa*, ed. Leroy Vail. London: James Currey.

Harris, Marvin. 1968. *The Rise of Anthropological Theory.* New York: Crowell.

Herskovits, Melville J. 1941. *The Myth of the Negro Past.* New York: Harper and Row.

——. 1948. *Man and His Works.* New York: Knopf.

Herzfeld, Michael. 1993. *The Social Production of Indifference: Exploring the Symbolic Roots of Western Bureaucracy.* Chicago: University of Chicago Press.

Heyworth, Lord. 1965. *Report of the Committee on Social Studies* (Heyworth report). HMSO Command 2660, London.

Hobart, Mark, ed. 1993. *An Anthropological Critique of Development: The Growth of Ignorance.* London: Routledge.

Hobsbawm, Eric. 1983. "Introduction." In *The Invention of Tradition*, ed. Eric Hobsbawm and Terence Ranger. Cambridge: Cambridge University Press.

——. 1987. *The Age of Empire, 1875–1914.* London: Weidenfeld and Nicolson.

Hoernlé, Winifred. 1985. *The Social Organization of the Nama, and Other Essays.* Edited by Peter Carstens. Johannesburg: Witwatersrand University Press.

Horowitz, Irving L., ed. 1974. *The Rise and Fall of Project Camelot: Studies in the Relationship between Social Science and Practical Politics.* Cambridge: MIT Press.

Horowitz, Michael M. 1994. "Development Anthropology in the Mid-1990s." *Development Anthropology Network*, 12 (1–2): 1–14.

Hsu, Francis L. K. 1972. "Introduction: Psychological Anthropology in the Behavioral Sciences." In *Psychological Anthropology*, ed. Francis L. K. Hsu. pp. 1–15. Cambridge: Schenkman.

Hunter, Monica. 1936. *Reaction to Conquest: Effects of Contact with Europeans on the Pondo of South Africa.* London: Oxford University Press.

Hyam, Ronald. 1999. "Bureaucracy and Trusteeship in Colonial Empire." In *The Oxford History of the British Empire*, ed. Judith Brown and William Roger Louis. Oxford: Oxford University Press.

Inkeles, Alex. 1972 [1961]. "National Character and Modern Political Systems." In *Psychological Anthropology*, ed. Francis L. K. Hsu. pp. 201–40. Cambridge: Schenkman.

"Inventaire ethnique et linguistique du Cameroun sous mandat français. Documents mis à jour au 31/12/1933 et communiqués par M. le Commissaire de la Republique." 1934. *Journal de la Société des Africanistes* 4 (2): 203–8.

Isuani, Ernesto A., and Emilio Tenti Fanfani. 1989. *Estado democrático y política social.* Buenos Aires: Eudeba.

Jackson, Walter. 1986. "Melville Herskovits and the Search for Afro-American Culture." In *Malinowski, Rivers, Benedict, and Others: Essays on Culture and Personality*, ed. George W. Stocking Jr. pp. 95–126. Madison: University of Wisconsin Press.

Jeffries, Charles, ed. 1964. *A Review of Colonial Research 1940–1960.* London: Department of Technical Co-operation, HMSO.

Joffo, Joseph. 2001. *Un sac de billes.* Paris: Hachette Livre.

Jordán, Fernando. 1946. "En torno a la pregunta de un antropólogo." *La Prensa Gráfica,* 16 December.

Junod, Henri A. 1912. *The Life of a South African Tribe.* 2 vols. Neuchatel: Imprimerie Attinger.

Kaplan, David, and Robert A. Manners. 1972. *Culture Theory.* Englewood Cliffs, N.J.: Prentice-Hall.

Kardiner, Abram. 1939. *The Individual and His Society.* New York: Columbia University Press.

Kardiner, Abram, and Edward Preble. 1961. *They Studied Man.* Cleveland: World Publishing Co.

Kiernan, Jim. 1997. "David in the Path of Goliath: South African Anthropology in the Shadow of Apartheid." In *Culture and the Commonplace,* ed. Patrick McAllister. Johannesburg: University of Witwatersrand Press.

Kliksberg, Bernardo, ed. 1992. *¿Cómo enfrentar la pobreza? Aportes para la acción.* Buenos Aires: Grupo Editor Latinoamericano.

———, ed. 1993. *Pobreza: Un tema impostergable. Nuevas respuestas a nivel Mundial.* Mexico City: Fondo de Cultura Económica.

Klukhohn, Clyde. 1949. *Mirror for Man.* New York: McGraw-Hill.

Kuklick, Henrika. 1992. *The Savage Within: The Social History of British Anthropology 1885–1945.* Cambridge: Cambridge University Press.

Kuper, Adam. 1973. *Anthropology and Anthropologists: The Modern British School.* London: Allen Lane.

———. 1976. "Culture Area or Political System?" *Africa* 46 (3): 291–94.

———. 1988. *The Invention of Primitive Society: Transformations of an Illusion.* London: Routledge.

———. 1996 [1973]. *Anthropology and Anthropologists: The Modern British School.* London: Routledge.

———. 1999a. *Culture: The Anthropologist's Account.* Cambridge, Mass.: Harvard University Press.

———. 1999b. *Among the Anthropologists: History and Context in Anthropology.* London: Athlone.

———. 2004. "Existe-t-il une 'école européenne' en anthropologie?" *Critique* 680–81: 150–59.

Kuper, Hilda. 1947a. *An African Aristocracy: Rank among the Swazi.* London: Oxford University Press; International African Institute.

———. 1947b. *The Uniform of Colour: A Study of White-Black Relationships in Swaziland.* Johannesburg: Witwatersrand University Press.

Labouret, Henri. 1931. *À la recherche d'une nouvelle politique indigène dans l'ouest Africain.* Paris: Éditions Du Comité De l'Afrique Française.

Laferté, Gilles. 2001. "Le comte Lafon, un nouvel arrivant devenu entrepreneur de la tradition bourguignonne." *Territoires contemporains, Cahiers de l'*IHC 6: 41–60.

———. 2002. *Folklore savant et folklore commercial: Reconstruire la qualité des vins de Bourgogne.* Ph.D. dissertation, École des Hautes Études en Sciences Sociales, Paris.

Landim, Leilah. 1993. *A invenção das* ONG's*: Do serviço invisível à profissão inexistente sem nome.* Ph.D. dissertation, National Museum, Federal University of Rio de Janeiro.

———, ed. 1998. *Ações em sociedade: Militância, caridade, assistência etc.* Rio de Janeiro: ISER-NAU.

Leal, João. 1999a. "Jorge Dias: Os maconde de Moçambique." *Etnográfica—Revista do Centro de Estudos de Antropologia Social* 1.

———. 1999b. *Psicologia étnica e identidade nacional em Portugal: História e permanências de um tema.* Arrábida. Mimeograph.

———. 2000. "A antropologia portuguesa entre 1870 e 1970: Um retrato de grupo." In *Etnografias portuguesas (1870–1970): Cultura popular e identidade nacional.* Lisbon: Dom Quixote.

Lebovics, Herman. 1992. *True France: The Wars over Cultural Identity, 1900–1945.* Ithaca: Cornell University Press.

Leclerc, Gérard. 1972. *Anthropologie et colonialism.* Paris: Fayard.

Lee, Richard B. 1979. *The* !Kung San*: Men, Women, and Work in a Foraging Society.* Cambridge: Cambridge University Press.

Lee, Richad B., and Irven Devore, eds. 1968. *Man the Hunter.* Chicago: Aldine.

Leenhardt, Maurice. 1938. "L'Océanie." In *Congrès de la recherche scientifique dans les territoires d'outre-mer.* Exposition Internationale de Paris, 1937. Paris: Association Colonie-Sciences.

Leiris, Michel. 1950. "L'ethnographe devant le colonialisme." *Les Temps Modernes* 6 (58): 357–74.

Leite, Dante Moreira. 1969 [1954]. *O caráter nacional brasileiro: História de uma ideologia.* São Paulo: Pioneira.

Leite, Jurandir Ferrari Carvalho. 1993. "Quantas são as terras indígenas?" *Resenha & Debates*, Textos 1.

Leroi-Gourhan, André, and Jean Poirier. 1953. *L'ethnologie de l'union française.* Paris: Presses Universitaires de France.

L'Estoile, Benoît de. 1994. "l'anthropologue face au monde moderne: Malinowski et la rationalisation de l'anthropologie et de l'administration." *Genès*, 17: 140–63.

———. 1997a. "Au nom des 'vrais africains': Les élites scolarisées de l'Afrique coloniale face à l'anthropologie (1930–1950)." *Terrain* 28: 87–102.

———. 1997b. "The 'Natural Preserve of Anthropologists': Anthropology, Scientific Planning and Development." *Social Science Information* 36 (2): 343–76.

———. 1997c. "Africanisme et africanism: Esquisse de comparaison franco-britannique." In *L'africanisme en questions*, ed. Anne Piriou and Emmanuelle Sibeud. pp. 19–42. Paris: EHESENs, Centre d'Études Africaines.

———. 1999. "Une petite armée de travailleurs auxiliaires: La division du travail et ses enjeux dans l'ethnologie française des années 1930." Paper submitted to the colloquium Recherches Collectives dans les Sciences Sociales, Centre de Recherches Historiques, Paris.

——. 2003. "From the Colonial Exhibition to the Museum of Man: An Alternative Genealogy of French Anthropology." *Social Anthropology/Anthropologie Sociale* 11 (3): 341–61.

——. (forthcoming). "Internationalisation and Scientific Nationalism: The International Institute of African Languages and Cultures in the Interwar Period." In *Anthropology and Imperialism in Africa*, ed. Robert J. Gordon and Helen Tilley. Manchester: Manchester University Press.

L'Estoile, Benoît de, and Michel Naepels. 2004. "Frontières de l'anthropologie." *Critique* 680–81.

Levi, Primo. 1989 [1986]. *Les naufragés et les rescapé: Quarante ans après Auschwitz.* Translated by André Maugé. Paris: Gallimard.

Lévi-Strauss, Claude. 1973 [1959]. "Le champ de l'anthropologie." In *Anthropologie structurale deux.* Paris: Plon.

Lévy-Bruhl, Lucien. 1925. "L'Institut d'Ethnologie de l'Université de Paris." *Revue D'ethnographie et de Traditions Populaire* 23–25: 1–4.

——. 1929. "Rapport d'activité de l'Institut d'Ethnologie pour 1929." *Annales de l'Université de Paris* 417–22.

Lewis, Oscar. 1961. *Antropología de la pobreza: cinco familias.* Mexico: Fondo de Cultura Económica. [Spanish translation of *Five families: Mexican case studies in the study of poverty.* New York: Basic Books, 1959.]

——. 1964. *Los Hijos de Sánchez: autobiografía de una familia mexicana.* Mexico: Fondo de Cultura Económica. [Spanish translation of *The children of Sánchez: Autobiography of a Mexican family.* New York: Random House, 1961.]

Lichtenstein, W. Hinrich C. 1973 [1806]. *Foundations of the Cape: About the Bechuanas.* Cape Town: Balkema.

Limón, José. 1998. *American Encounters: Greater Mexico, the United States, and the Erotics of Culture.* Boston: Beacon Press.

Limongi, Fernando. 1989. "A escola livre de sociologia e política em São Paulo." In *História das ciências sociais no Brasil*, vol. 1, ed. Sérgio Miceli. São Paulo: Editora Sumaré.

Lindesmith, Alfred R., and Anselm L. Strauss. 1950. "A Critique of Culture and Personality Writings." *American Journal Review* 15: 587–600.

Linton, Ralph. 1936. *The Study of Man.* New York: Appleton-Century.

Lodge, Tom. 1999. *South Africa Politics since 1994.* Cape Town: David Philip.

Loizos, Peter, ed. 1977. "Anthropological Research in British Colonies. Some Personal Accounts." *Anthropological Forum* 4 (2).

——. 1930. "The Rationalization of Anthropology and Administration." *Africa* 3: 405–30.

Lomnitz, Claudio. 1999. *Modernidad indiana: Nueve ensayos sobre nación y mediación en México.* México: Planeta.

——. 2000. "Nationalism as a Practical System: A Critique of Benedict Anderson's

Theory of Nationalism from the Vantage Point of Latin America." In *The Other Mirror*, ed. Miguel Angel Centeno. Princeton: Princeton University Press.

Loureiro, Maria Rita. 1997. *Os economistas no governo*. Rio de Janeiro: Fundação Getulio Vargas.

Lo Vuolo, Rubén, and Alberto Barbeito. 1993. *La nueva oscuridad de la política social: Del estado populista al neoconservador*. Buenos Aires: Miño y Dávila Editores.

Lowie, Robert H. 1980 [1945]. *The German People: A Social Portrait to 1914*. New York: Octagon Books.

Lumi, Susana, Laura Golbert, and Emilio Tenti Fanfani. 1992. *La mano izquierda del Estado: La asistencia social según los beneficiarios*. Buenos Aires: Miño y Dávila Editores.

Macmillan, William M. 1929. *Bantu, Boer, and Briton: The Making of the South African Native Problem*. London: Faber and Gwyer.

——. 1975. *My South African Years*. Cape Town: David Philip.

Maget, Marcel. 1953. *Guide d'étude directe des comportements culturels*. Paris: Civilisations du Sud.

——. 1968. "Problèmes d'ethnographie européenne." In *Ethnologie générale*, ed. Jean Poirier. pp. 1247–1338. Paris: Encyclopédie de la Pléiade.

——. 1993. "A propos du Musée des ATP de sa création à la libération (1935–1944)." *Genèses: Sciences Sociales et Histoire* 10: 90–107.

Mair, Lucy. 1984. *Anthropology and Developement*. London: Macmillan Press.

Malinowski, Bronislaw. 1930. "The Rationalization of Anthropology and Administration." *Africa* 3: 405–430.

——. 1937. "Preface." In *The Savage Hits Back*, by Julius E. Lips. London: Lovat Dickson.

Manson, William C. 1986. "Abram Kardiner and the Neo-Freudian Alternative to Culture and Personality." In *Malinowski, Rivers, Benedict, and Others: Essays on Culture and Personality*, George W. Stocking Jr. pp. 72–126. Madison: University of Wisconsin Press.

Marcus, George E. and Michael J. Fischer. 1986. *Anthropology as Cultural Critique: An Experimental Moment in the Human Sciences*. Chicago: University of Chicago Press.

Margarido, Alfredo. 1975. "Le colonialisme portugais et l'anthropologie." In *Anthropologie et impérialisme*, ed. J. Copans. Paris: Maspero.

Mariot, Nicolas. 2002. " 'Nos fleurs et nos cœurs': La visite présidentielle en province comme événement institué." *Terrain* 38: 79–96.

Marks, Shula, and Anthony Atmore. 1970. "The Problem of the Nguni: An Examination of the Ethnic and Linguistic Situation in South Africa before the *Mfecane*." In *Language and History in Africa*, ed. David Dalby. pp. 120–32. London: Frank Cass.

Marques, A. H. de Oliveira. 1986. *História de Portugal*. Vol. 3. Lisbon: Palas Editores.

Marroquín, Alejandro. 1977. *Balances del indigenismo: Informe sobre la política indigenista en América*. México: INI.

Marshall, Lorna. 1976. *The !Kung of Nyae Nyae*. Cambridge Mass.: Harvard University Press.

Martonne, Édouard de. 1930. *Le savant colonial*. Paris: Larose (Vies Coloniales).

Marzal, Manuel. 1981. *Historia de la antropología indigenista: México y Perú*. Lima: Pontificia Universidad Católica del Perú.

Mauss, Marcel. 1969 [1921]. "La Nation." In *Oeuvres*, vol. 3. Paris: Minuit.

Maybury-Lewis, David. 1985. "A Special Sort of Pleading: Anthropological Advocacy at the Service of Ethnic Groups." In *Anthropology and Advocacy: First Encounters*, ed. Robert Paine. St. Johns, Canada: Institute of Social and Economic Research, Memorial University of Newfoundland.

McAllister, Patrick. 1997. "Introduction." In *Culture and the Commonplace*, ed. Patrick McAllister. Johannesburg: University of Witwatersrand Press.

Mead, Margaret. 1969 [1928]. *Coming of Age in Samoa*. Harmondsworth, U.K.: Penguin.

——. 1953. "The Study of Culture at a Distance." In *The Study of Culture at a Distance*, ed. Margaret Mead and Rhoda Métraux. pp. 3–53. Chicago: University of Chicago Press.

——. 1962 [1953]. "National Character." In *Anthropology Today: Selections*, ed. Sol Tax. pp. 396–421. Chicago: University of Chicago Press.

——. 1965 [1942]. *And Keep Your Powder Dry: An Anthropologist Looks at America*. New York: Morrow Quill.

——. 1978. "End Linkage: A Tool for Cross-Cultural Analysis." In *About Bateson*, ed. John Brockman. pp. 169–231. London: Wildwood Home.

Mead, Margaret, and Rhoda Métraux, eds. 1953. *The Study of Culture at a Distance*. Chicago: University of Chicago Press.

Mendes Corrêa, Antônio Augusto Esteves. 1945. *Raças do império*. Porto: Portucalense.

Mendez Lavielle, Guadalupe. 1987. "La quiebra política (1965–1976)." In *La antropología en México: Panorama histórico*, vol. 2, ed. Carlos García Mora. pp. 339–438. Mexico: INAH.

Menezes, Maria Lucia Pires. 2000. *Parque indígena do Xingu: A Construção de um território estatal*. Campinas: EdUnicamp.

Mercier, Paul. 1951. *Les tâches de la sociologie*. Dakar: IFAN.

Merle, Isabelle. 1995. *Expériences coloniales. Nouvelle-Calédonie (1853–1920)*. Paris: Belin.

Meyer, Jean. 1993. "La junta protectora de las clases menesterosas: Indigenismo y agrarismo en el segundo imperio." In *Indio, nación y comunidad en el siglo diecinueve*, ed. Antonio Escobar. pp. 329–64. Mexico: CIESAS.

Minujin, Alberto, ed. 1993. *Desigualdad y exclusión: Desafíos para la política social en la Argentina de fin de siglo*. Buenos Aires: Unicef/Losada.

Moerman, Michael. 1965. "Ethnic Identification in a Complex Civilization: Who Are the Lue?" *American Anthropologist* 67 (5/1): 1215–230.

Monteiro, John. 1994. *Negros da terra*. São Paulo: Companhia das Letras.

Moreira, Adriano and José Carlos Venâncio, eds. 1999. *Luso-tropicalismo: Uma teoria social em questão*. Lisbon: Veja.

Moutinho, Mário. 1982. "A etnologia colonial portuguesa e o estado novo." In *O fascismo em Portugal* (Atas do Colóquio). Lisbon: A Regra do Jogo.

———. 2000. *O indígena no pensamento colonial português*. Lisbon: Edições Universitárias Lusófonas.

Myers, Fred. 1986. "The Politics of Representation: Anthropological Discourse and Australian Aborigines." *American Ethnologist* 13: 138–53.

Naepels, Michel. 1998. *Histoires de Terres Kanakes*. Paris: Belin.

Nagata, Judith A. 1974. "What Is a Malay? Situational Selection of Ethnic Identity in a Plural Society." *American Ethnologist* 1 (2): 331–50.

Neiburg, Federico, and Mariano Plotkin. 2003. "Elites estatales, elites intelectuales y ciencias sociales en la Argentina de los años 60. El Instituto Torcuato di tella y la nueva economía." *E.I.A.L. Estudios Interdisciplinarios de América Latina y el Caribe*, 14 (1): 119–49.

Noiriel, Gérard. 1988. *Le creuset Français. Histoire de l'immigration XIXᵉ–XXᵉ siècles*. Paris: Éditions du Seuil.

———. 1999. *Les origines républicaines de Vichy*. Paris: Hachette.

Nolasco Armas, Margarita. 1981. "A antropologia aplicada no México e seu destino final: O indigenismo." In *Antropologia e indigenismo na América Latina*, ed. Carmen Junqueira and Edgar de Assis Carvalho. pp. 67–86. São Paulo: Cortez.

Nordman, Daniel, and Jean-Pierre Raison. 1980. *Sciences de l'homme et conquête coloniale: Constitution et usage des sciences humaines en Afrique (XIXe-XXe siècles)*. Paris: Presses de l'École Normale Supérieure.

Noriega, Raúl, ed. 1967. *50 discursos doctrinales en el congreso constituyente de la revolución mexicana, 1916–1917*. Mexico: Instituto de Estudios Históricos de la Revolución Mexicana.

Oliveira, João Pacheco de. 1987. "Fricção interétnica." In *Dicionário de ciências sociais*, ed. Benedicto Silva. Rio de Janeiro: Fundação Getúlio Vargas.

———. 1988. *O nosso governo: Os ticuna e o regime tutelar*. São Paulo: Marco Zero—CNPq.

———. 1990. "Frontier Security and the New Indigenism: Nature and Origins of the Calha Norte Project." In *The Future of Amazonia: Destruction or Sustainable Development?* ed. David Goodman and Anthony Hall. pp. 155–76. London: Macmillan Press.

———. 1993. "Três modelos de intervenção, remilitarização e relexos da UNCED." *Reseña & Debate* 2. PETI / Museu Nacional.

———. 1999. "Una etnologia dos 'índios misturados': Situação colonial, territorialização e fluxos culturais." In *A viagem da volta: Etnicidade, política e reelaboração cultural no nordeste indígena*. Rio de Janeiro: Contracapa.

———. 2000. "Indian Politics in Contemporary Amazonia." Paper presented at the Third Annual Oxford Conference on Amazonia 7–9 December 2000. University of Oxford.

Oliveira, João Pacheco de, and Alfredo Wagner Berno Almeida. 1998. "Demarcação e reafirmação étnica: Um ensaio sobre a FUNAI." In *Indigenismo e territorialização: Poderes, rotinas e saberes coloniais no Brasil contemporâneo*, ed. João P. de Oliveira. Rio de Janeiro: Contracapa.

Oliveira, João Pacheco de, and Antonio Carlos de Souza Lima. 1983. "Os muitos fôlegos do indigenismo." *Anuário Antropológico* 81: 277–90.

Ortner, Sherry. 1999. "Some Futures of Anthropology." *American Ethnologist* 26 (4): 984–91.

Oulmont, Philippe. 1999. "De 'ma petite patrie' à Buchenwald. Un inspecteur primaire sous l'Occupation: Enseignement de l'histoire et patriotisme vécu." *Cahiers Jean Jaurès* 152: 131–52.

Pacini, Aloir. 1999. *Pacificar: Relações interétnicas e territorialização dos Rikbaktsa*. Master's thesis, National Museum, Federal University of Rio de Janeiro.

Partridge, William L., and Elizabeth M. Eddy. 1978. "The Development of Applied Anthropology in America." In *Applied Anthropology in America*, ed. William L. Partridge and Elizabeth M. Eddy. pp. 3–45. New York: Columbia University Press.

Paxton, Robert. 1972. *Vichy France: Old Guard and New Order 1940–1944*. New York: Columbia University Press.

Peer, Shanny. 1998. *France on Display: Peasants, Provincials, and Folklore in the 1937 Paris World's Fair*. Albany: State University of New York Press.

Peirano, Mariza. 1981. "The Anthropology of Anthropology: The Brazilian Case." Ph.D. dissertation, Harvard University.

——. 1992. *Uma antropologia no plural: Três experiências contemporâneas*. Brasília: EdUnB.

Pélissier, René. 1979. "Institutions africanistes portugaises." In *Le naufrage des caravelles: Études sur la fin de l'empire portugais (1961–1975)*. Paris: Éditions Péllissier.

Pels, Peter. 1996. "The Pidginization of Luguru Politics: Administrative Ethnography and the Paradoxes of Indirect Rule." *American Ethnologist* 23(4): 738–61.

——. 1997. "The Anthropology of Colonialism: Culture, History, and the Emergence of Western Governmentality." *Annual Review of Anthropology* 26: 163–83.

Pels, Peter, and Oscar Salemink. 1999. "Introduction: Locating the Colonial Subjects of Anthropology." In *Colonial Subjects: Essays on the Practical History of Anthropology*, ed. Peter Pels and Oscar Salemink. pp. 1–52. Ann Arbor: University of Michigan Press.

Peña, Guillermo de la. 1995. "Nationals and Foreigners in the History of Mexican Anthropology." In *The Conditions of Reciprocal Understanding*, ed. James W. Fernandez and Milton B. Singer. pp. 276–303. Chicago: University of Chicago Center for International Studies.

Pereira, Rui. 1988. "Antropologia Aplicada na Política Colonial Portuguesa." Master's thesis, New University of Lisbon.

Piano, Renzo, and Richard Rodgers. 1987. *Du plateau Beaubourg au Centre Georges-Pompidou.* Paris: Éd. du Centre Pompidou.

Piester, Kerianne. 1997. "Targeting the Poor: Politics of Social Policy Reforms in Mexico." In *The New Politics of Inequality in Latin America: Rethinking Participation and Representation*, ed. Douglas A. Chalmers, Carlos M. Vilas, Katherine Hite, Scott B. Martin, Kerianner Piester, and Monique Segarra. 469–88. Oxford: Oxford University Press.

Pimentel, Francisco. 1860a. "Discurso sobre la importancia de la lengüística, leido por el sr. D. Francisco Pimental al tomar asiento por primera vez en la Sociedad de Geografía y Estadística el 22 de agosto de 1861." *BMSGE* 7: 367–71.

——. 1860b. "Lengua pantomímica de Oaxaca, en sesion del 19 de diciembre de 1861, leyó el sr. socio D. Francisco Pimentel la siguiente proposicion." *BSMGE* 8: 473.

Pina Cabral, João de. 1991. *Os contextos da antropologia.* Lisbon: Difel.

Pineda, Emilio. 1852. "Descripcion geográfica del departamento de Chiapas y soconusco." *BMSGE* 3: 341.

Pison, Guy. 1943. "L'enquête d'architecture rurale du chantier 1425." *Techniques et Architecture*, 11–12.

Pollak, Michael. 1979. "Paul F. Lazarfeld, foundateur d'une multinationale scientifique." *Actes de la Recherche en Sciences Sociales* 25: 45–59.

Porto, Nuno. 2002. "O museu e o arquivo do império (o terceiro império português visto do Museu do Dundo, Companhia de Diamantes de Angola)." In *Trânsitos coloniais: Diálogos críticos luso-brasileiros*, ed. Cristiana Bastos, Miguel Vale de Almeida, and Bela Feldman-Bianco. pp. 117–32. Lisbon: ICS.

Pratt, Mary Louise. 1992. *Imperial Eyes: Travel Writing and Transculturation.* New York: Routledge.

Queiroz, Maria José de. 1962. *Do indianismo ao indigenismo nas letras hispanoamericanas.* Belo Horizonte: Imprensa da UFMG.

Radcliffe-Brown, Alfred R. 1940. "Introduction." In *African Political Systems*, ed. Edward Evans-Pritchard and Meyer Fortes. Oxford: Oxford University Press.

Rahnema, Majid. 1986. "Power and Regenerative Processes in Micro Spaces." *International Social Science Journal* 117: 361–75.

Ramos, Alcida R. 1988. "Ethnology Brazilian Style." *Cultural Anthropology* 5 (4): 452–57.

——. 1998. *Indigenism: Ethnic Politics in Brazil.* Madison: University of Wisconsin Press.

Ramphele, Mamphela. 1995. *A Life.* Cape Town: David Philip.

Redfield, Robert. 1930. *Tepoztlán, a Mexican Village: A Study of Folk Life.* Chicago: University of Chicago Press.

Reyes, Aurelio de los. 1991. *Manuel Gamio y el cine.* Mexico: UNAM.

Ribeiro, Darcy. 1955a. "Seção de estudos." *Serviço de Proteção aos Índios—1954.* Rio de Janeiro: SPI.

——. 1955b. "Curso de aperfeiçoamento." *Serviço de Proteção aos Índios—1954.* Rio de Janeiro: SPI.

———. 1962. *A política indigenista brasileira.* Rio de Janeiro: Serviço de Informação Agrícola do Ministério da Agricultura.

———. 1970. *Os índios e a civilização: A integração das populações indígenas no Brasil moderno.* Rio de Janeiro: Editora Civilização Brasileira.

———. 1979. "Antropologia ou a Teoria do Bombardeio de Berlim" (Interview by Edilson Martins). *Encontros com a Civilização Brasileira* 12: 81–100.

Ricardo, Carlos Alberto. 1994. "Os índios e a sóciodiversidade nativa contemporânea no Brasil." In *A Temática Indígena na Escola,* ed. Aracy Lopez da Silva and Luís D. Benzi Grupioni. pp. 29–60. Brasília: MEC, MARI, UNESCO.

Rich, Paul B. 1986. *Race and Empire in British Politics.* Cambridge: CUP.

Richards, Al. 1964. "Authority Patterns in Traditional Buganda and Traditional Values and Current Political Behaviour." In *The King's Men,* ed. Lloyd A. Fallers. Oxford: Oxford University Press.

———. 1977. "The Colonial Office and the Organisation of Social Research." *Anthropological Forum* 4: 168–89.

Rigdon, Susan. 1988. *The Culture Facade: Art, Science, and Politics in the Work of Oscar Lewis.* Urbana: University of Illinois Press.

Riva Palacio, Vicente, and Manuel Payno. 1870. *El libro rojo.* Mexico: Diaz de León y White.

Rivet, Paul. 1931. "Organisation des etudes ethnologiques." *Congrès des Recherches Scientifiques Coloniales.*

———. 1936. "Ce qu'est l'ethnologie." *Encyclopédie Française,* vol. 7. Paris: Larousse.

Rivière, Georges-Henri. 1939. "Le folklore: L'artisanat et les métiers régionaux." *La Renaissance* 22 (2) (Special Issue: L'Art Français à l'Exposition de New York).

———. 1942. "Le folklore paysan: Notes de doctrine et d'action." *Études Agricoles d'Economie Corporative* 2 (4): 291–316.

———. 1973. "Le chantier 1425: Un tour d'horizon, une gerbe de souvenirs." *Ethnologie Française* 3 (1–2): 9–14.

Rogers, Susan Carol. 2001. "Anthropology in France." *Annual Review of Anthropology* 30: 481–504.

Roquette-Pinto, Edgard. 1917. *Rondônia.* Rio de Janeiro: Museu Nacional Archives.

Rosas, Fernando. 1994. *História de Portugal—O Estado Novo,* vol. 7. Lisbon: Estampa.

Ross, Robert. 1993. *Beyond the Pale: Essays on the History of Colonial South Africa.* Hanover, N.H.: Wesleyan University Press.

Roume, Ernest. 1929. "Avant-propos." *Outre-Mer* (March): 3–5.

Rubim, Christina de Rezende. 1997. "Os programas de pós-graduação em antropologia social do Museu Nacional, Universidade de Brasília, Universidade de São Paulo e Universidade Estadual de Campinas." *Horizontes Antropológicos* 13(7): 97–128.

Rueschemeyer, Dietrich, and Theda Skocpol, eds. 1996. *States, Social Knowledge, and the Origins of Modern Social Policies.* Princeton: Princeton University Press; New York: Russell Sage Foundation.

Said, Edward W. 1979. *Orientalism.* New York: Vintage Books.

———. 1993. *Culture and Imperialism*. New York: Knopf.

Saldanha, Luiza. 1996. "Escola de heróis: Os cursos de formação de técnicos em indigenismo da FUNAI, 1970–1985." Master's thesis, Federal University of Rio de Janeiro.

Santos, Silvio Coelho dos. 1994. "Os direitos dos indígenas no Brasil." In *A temática indígena na escola*, ed. Aracy Lopez da Silva and Luís D. Benzi Grupioni. pp. 87–105. Brasília: MEC, MARI, UNESCO.

Sapir, Edward. 1985a [1924]. "Culture, Genuine and Spurious." In *Selected Writings of Edward Sapir in Language, Culture, and Personality*, ed. David G. Mandelbaum. pp. 308–31. Berkeley: University of California Press.

———. 1985b [1934]. "The Emergence of the Concept of Personality in a Study of Cultures." In *Selected Writings of Edward Sapir in Language, Culture, and Personality*, ed. David G. Mandelbaum. pp. 590–97. Berkeley: University of California Press.

Saunders, Christopher. 1988. *The Making of the South African Past: Major Historians on Race and Class*. Cape Town: David Philip Publishers.

Schapera, Isaac. 1930. *The Khoisan Peoples of South Africa: Bushmen and Hottentots*. London: Routledge.

———, ed. 1934. *Western Civilization and the Natives of South Africa: Studies in Culture Contact*. London: George Routledge and Sons.

———. 1937. "Cultural Changes in Tribal Life." In *The Bantu-Speaking Tribes of South Africa: An Ethnographical Survey*, ed. Isaac Schapera. London: George Routledge and Sons.

———. 1939. "Anthropology and the Native Problem." Presidential Address to Section E., *South African Journal of Science* 36: 89–103.

Scheper-Hughes, Nancy. 1995. "The Primacy of Ethical Propositions for a Militant Anthropology." *Current Anthropology* 36 (3): 409–20.

Schneider, David M., and Richard Handler. 1995. *Schneider on Schneider: The Conversion of the Jews and Other Anthropological Stories*. Durham: Duke University Press.

Schöttler, Peter. 1995. "Marc Bloch et Lucien Febvre face à l'Allemagne nazie." *Genèses: Sciences Sociales et Histoire* 21: 75–95.

Schumaker, Lynette. 1996. "A Tent with a View: Colonial Officers, Anthropologists, and the Making of the Field in Northern Rhodesia, 1937–1960." *Osiris* 11: 237–59.

———. 1999. "Constructing Racial Landscapes: Africans, Administrators, and Anthropologists in Northern Rhodesia." In *Colonial Subjects: Essays on the Practical History of Anthropology*, ed. Peter Pels and Oscar Salemink. Ann Arbor: University of Michigan Press.

Schweber, Libby. 2002. "Wartime Research and the Quantification of American Sociology: The View from 'The American Soldier.'" *Revue d'Histoire des Sciences Humaines* 6: 65–93.

Sen, Amartya. 1989. *On Ethics and Economics*. London: Blackwell Publishers.

Seyferth, Giralda. 1989. "As ciências sociais no Brasil e a questão racial." In *Cativeiro e Liberdade*, orgs. Jaime Silva, Patrícia Birman, and Regina Wanderley. pp. 11–31. Rio de janeiro: UERJ.

Shapin, Steven. 1992. "Discipline and Bounding: The History and Sociology of Science as Seen through the Externalism-Internalism Debate." *History of Science* 30: 333–69.

Shweder, Richard A. 1979. "Rethinking Culture and Personality Theory. Part I: A Critical Examination of Two Classical Postulates." *Ethos* 7 (3): 255–78.

SIEMPRO (Sistema de Información, Monitoreo y Evaluación de Programas Sociales). 1996. *Política Social y Pobreza* (Módulo 1). Buenos Aires: Presidencia de la Nación.

Sierra, Justus, ed. 1900. *Mexico: Its Social Evolution.* 2 vols. Mexico City: J. Ballescá and Co.

Sikkink, Kathryn. 1991. *Ideas and Institutions: Developmentalism in Brazil and Argentina.* Ithaca: Cornell University Press.

Sociedad Mexicana de Geografía y Estadística. 1853. "Estadística de Yucatán, publicase por acuerdo de la R. Sociedad de Geografía y Estadística, de 27 de enero de 1852." BMSGE, 238–339.

Société de Gestion de l'Encyclopédie Française. 1935–1966. *Encyclopédie française.* 21 vols. Paris: Larousse.

Somerville, William. 1979 [1799–1802]. *Narrative of His Journeys to the Eastern Cape Frontier and to Lattakoe 1799–1802.* Cape Town: Van Riebeeck Society.

Souza Lima, Antonio Carlos de. 1989. "Os museus de história natural e a construção do indigenismo no Brasil." *Comunicações do* PPGAS 13.

——. 1991. "O Santo Soldado: Pacificador, bandeirante, amanasador dos sertões, apóstolo da humanidade. Uma leitura de *Rondon conta sua vida,* de Esther de Viveiros." *Comunicações do* PPGAS 21.

——. 1995. *Um grande cerco de paz: Poder tutelar, indianidade e formação do estado no Brasil.* Petrópolis: Vozes.

——. 1998. "Os relatórios antropológicos de identificação de terras indígenas da Fundação Nacional do índio: Notas sobre o estudo da relação entre Antropologia e Indigenismo no Brasil, 1968–1985." In *Indigenismo e territorialização: Poderes, rotinas e saberes coloniais no Brasil contemporâneo,* ed. João P. de Oliveira. pp. 221–68. Rio de Janeiro: Contra Capa Livraria.

——. 2001. "Fundação nacional do Índio." In *Dicionário histórico-biográfico brasileiro,* vol. 2, ed. Alzira A. de Abreu, Israel Belloch, Fernando Lattman-Weltman, and Sergio T. N. Lamarão. pp. 2426–432. Rio de Janeiro: Ed. Fundação Getúlio Vargas.

——. 2002. "Tradições de conhecimento na gestão colonial da desigualdade: Reflexões a partir da administração indigenista no Brasil." In *Trânsitos coloniais: Diálogos críticos luso-brasileiros,* ed. Cristiana Bastos, Miguel Vale do Almeida, and Bela Feldman-Bianco. pp. 151–72. Lisbon: Imprensa de Ciências Sociais.

Souza Lima, Antonio Carlos, de and Maria Barroso-Hoffman, eds. 2002. *Etno-*

desenvolvimento e políticas públicas: Bases para uma nova política indigenista. Rio de Janeiro: Contracapa/LACED.

Spiegel, Andrew D. 1997. "Continuities, Culture and the Commonplace: Searching for a New Ethnographic Approach in South Africa." In *Culture and the Commonplace*, ed. Patrick McAllister. Johannesburg: University of Witwatersrand Press.

Spindler, George D., and Louise Spindler. 1983. "Anthropologists View American Culture." *Annual Review of Anthropology* 12: 49–78.

SSRC (Social Science Research Council). 1968. *Research in Social Anthropology: A Social Science Research Council Review*. London: SSRC.

Starn, Orin. 1986. "Engineering Internment: Anthropologists and the War Relocation Authority." *American Ethnologist* 13 (4): 700–20.

Stauder, Jack. 1980. "Functionalism Abroad: A Theory in Question." In *Anthropology: Ancestors and Heirs*, ed. Stanley Diamond. The Hague: Mouton.

Stern, Alexandra. 1999a. "Eugenics beyond Borders: Science and Medicalization in Mexico and the U.S. West, 1900–1950." Ph.D. dissertation, University of Chicago.

———. 1999b. "Buildings, Boundaries, and Blood: Medicalization and Nation-Buildings on the U.S.-Mexico Border, 1910–1930." *HAHR* 79 (1): 41–81.

Stocking, George W. Jr. 1968. *Race, Culture and Evolution. Essays in the History of Anthropology*. New York: Free Press.

———. 1976. "Ideas and Institutions in American Anthropology: Thoughts Toward a History of the Interwar Period." In *Selected Papers from the American Anthropologist*, vol. 2, pp. 1–44. Washington, D.C.: American Anthropological Association.

———. 1983. "Afterword: A View from the Center." *Ethnos* 47 (1): 172–86.

———. 1986. "Essays on Culture and Personality." In *Malinowski, Rivers, Benedict, and Others: Essays on Culture and Personality*, ed. George W. Stocking Jr. pp. 3–12. Madison: University of Wisconsin Press.

———. 1996. *After Tylor: British Social Anthropology 1881–1951*. Madison: University of Wisconsin Press.

Stoetzel, Jean. 1955 [1954]. *Without the Crysanthemum and the Sword. A Study of Youth in Post-War Japan*. New York: Columbia University Press.

Sullivan, Paul. 1989. *Unfinished Conversations: Mayas and Foreigners between Two Wars*. New York: Knopf.

Suzuki, Peter T. 1980. "A Retrospective Analysis of Wartime 'National Character' Study." *Dialectical Anthropology* 5 (1): 33–46.

———. 1981. "Anthropologists in the Wartime Camps for Japanese Americans: A Documentary Study." *Dialectical Anthropology* 6 (1): 23–60.

Téllez Ortega, Javier. 1987. "La época de oro (1940–1968)." In *La antropología en México: Panorama histórico*, vol. 2, ed. Carlos García Mora. pp. 289–341. Mexico: INAH.

Tenorio Trillo, Mauricio. 1996. *Mexico at the World's Fairs: Crafting a Modern Nation*. Berkeley: University of California Press.

——. 1999. "Stereophonic Scientific Modernisms: Social Science between Mexico and the United States, 1880s–1930s." *Journal of American History*, 1156–187.

Theal, George McCall. 1910. *Ethnography and Condition of South Africa before* A.D. *1505*. London: George Allen and Unwin.

Thiesse, Anne-Marie. 1991. *Écrire la France: Le mouvement littéraire régionaliste de langue française entre la Belle Époque et la Libération*. Paris: Presses Universitaires de France.

——. 1997a. *Ils apprenaient la France: L'exaltation des régions dans le discours patriotique*. Paris: Éditions de la MSH.

——. 1997b. "Régionalisme et ambiguïtés vichystes. La revue *Terre Natale*." *La Revue des Revues* 24: 121–29.

Thomas, Nicholas. 1994. *Colonialism's Culture: Anthropology, Travel, and Government*. Cambridge: Polity Press.

Thomaz, Omar Ribeiro. 2002. *Ecos do Atlântico Sul: Representações sobre o Terceiro Império Português*. Rio de Janeiro: Editora da UFRJ-FAPESP.

Tilly, Charles. 1975. "Reflections on the History of European State-Making." In *The Formation of National States in Western Europe*, ed. Charles Tilly. pp. 3–83. Princeton: Princeton University Press.

Tjibaou, Jean-Marie. 1996. *La présence kanak: Écrits et dits de Jean-Marie Tjibaou*, ed. Alban Bensa and Éric Wittersheim. Paris: Odile Jacob.

Turner, John Kenneth. 1911. *Barbarous Mexico*. Chicago: C. H. Kerr and Co.

Tylor, Edward B. 1861. *Anahuac, or, Mexico and the Mexicans, Ancient and Modern*. London: Longman Green Longman and Roberts.

UNDP/IDB (Programa de las Naciones Unidas para el Desarrollo y Banco Interamericano de Desarrollo). 1998. *El capital social: Hacia la construcción del índice de desarrollo sociedad civil de Argentina*. Buenos Aires: Edilab.

Vail, Leroy, ed. 1989. *The Creation of Tribalism in Southern Africa*. London: Currey.

Van Gennep, Arnold. 1937–1958. *Manuel de folklore français contemporain*. Paris: Picard.

Van Rensburg, Fanie, and Kees Van Der Waal. 1999. "Continuity and Change in South African Cultural Anthropology (*Volkekunde*): Issues of Essentialism and Complexity." *South African Journal of Ethnology* 22 (2): 45–58.

Van Warmelo, Nikolaas J. 1935. *A Preliminary Survey of the Bantu Tribes of South Africa*. Pretoria: Government Printer.

Varagnac, André. 1938. *Définition du folklore, suivi de notes sur folklore et psychotechnique et sur L'agriculture temporaire, la préhistoire et le folklore*. Paris: Société d'Éditions Géographiques, Maritimes et Coloniales.

Vawda, Shahid. 1995. "The Other Anthropology: A Response to Gordon and Spiegel's Review of Southern African Anthropology." *African Studies* 54 (1): 128–31.

Vázquez León, Luis. 1987. "La historiografía antropológica contemporánea en México." In *La Antropología en México: panorama histórico*, vol. 1, ed. Carlos García Mora. pp. 176–94. Mexico: INAH.

Velay Vallantin, Catherine. 1999. "Le congrès international de folklore de 1937." *Annales Histoire et Sciences Sociales* (March–April): 481–506.

Villoro, Luís. 1996. *Los grandes momentos del indigenismo en México*. México City: El Colegio de México/El Colegio Nacional/Fondo de Cultura Económica.

Wachtel, Nathan. 1992. "Note sur le problème des identités collectives dans les Andes méridionales." *L'Homme* 32 (122–24): 39–51.

Wagner, Peter, Björn Wittrock, and Richard Withley, eds. 1990. *Discourses on Society: The Shaping of the Social Science Disciplines*. Dordrecht: Kluwer.

Wagner, Peter, Björn Wittrock, and Hellmut Wollmann. 1991. "Social Science and the Modern State: Policy Knowledge and Political Institutions in Western Europe and the United States." In *Social Science and Modern States: National Experiences and Theoretical Crossroads*, ed. Peter Wagner, Carol H. Weiss, Björn Wittrock, and Hellmut Wollmann. pp. 28–85. Cambridge: Cambridge University Press.

Wagner, Roy. 1981. *The Invention of Culture*. Chicago: University of Chicago Press.

Wallerstein, Immanuel et al. 1996. *Open the Social Sciences: Report of the Gulbenkian Commission on the Restructuring of the Social Sciences*. Stanford: Stanford University Press.

Warman, Arturo. 1970. "Todos santos, todos difuntos." In *De eso que llaman antropología mexicana*, ed. Arturo Warman, Guillermo Bonfil, Margarita Nolasco, Mercedes Olivera, and Enrique Valencia. Mexico: Editorial Nuestro Tiempo.

Weaver, Thomas, ed. 1973. *To See Ourselves: Anthropology and the Modern Social Issues*. Glenview, Ill.: Scott, Foresman and Co.

Weber, Florence. 1989. "Les études rurales dans la France des années 30: Un apogée oublié." *Recherches Sociologiques* 20 (3): 367–81.

———. 1996. "Les visiteurs des jardins ouvriers. De la cérémonie à l'entre-soi (Ivry, 1909–1939)." *Genèses: Sciences Sociales et Histoire* 22: 40–63.

———. 2000. "Le folklore, l'histoire et l'etat en France." *Revue de Synthèse* 121 (3–4): 453–67.

———. 2003a. "L'ethnologie et l'etat en France, des années trente aux années cinquante." In *Histoire des politiques du patrimoine*, ed. Loïc Vadelorge and Philippe Poirier. Paris: La Documentation Française.

———. 2003b. "Politiques du folklore en France, 1930–1960." In *Pour une histoire des politiques du patrimoine*. pp. 269–300. Paris: Comité d'Histoire du Ministère de la Culture/Fondation Maison des Sciences de l'Homme.

———. 2003c. "Marcel Maget et le service de foklore paysan de la corporation paysanne, 1937–1944." Paper presented at the conference Du Folklore à l'Ethnologie: Institutions, Musées, Idées en France et en Europe de 1936 à 1945, 19–21 March, Paris.

Weber, Florence, and Tiphaine Barthelemy. 1989. *Les campagnes à livre ouvert: Regards sur la France rurale des années 30*. Paris: PENS/Éditions ÉHÉSS.

Weber, Florence, and Bertrand Müller. 1999 "Des recherches collectives au croisement de l'histoire et de l'ethnographie (1935–1939)." Paper presented at the international colloquium Histoire de la Recherche Collective en Sciences Sociales au XXe Siècle, Centre de Recherches Historiques, 4–6 November, Paris.

——. 2003 "Réseaux de corresponants et missions folkloriques: Le travail d'enquête en France, vers 1930." *Gradhiva* 33: 43–55.

Weber, Max. 1949. "'Objectivity' in Social Science and Social Policy." In *The Methodology of the Social Sciences*, translated and edited by Edward A. Shills and Henry A. Finch. pp. 49–112. New York: Free Press.

——. 1968 [1922]. *Economy and Society: An Outline of Interpretive Sociology*, ed. G. Roth and C. Wittich. Berkeley: University of California Press.

——. 1958a. "Politics as a Vocation." In *From Max Weber: Essays in Sociology*, ed. Hans Gerth and C. Wright Mills. pp. 77–128. New York: Oxford University Press.

——. 1958b. "Science as a Vocation." In *From Max Weber: Essays in Sociology*, ed. Hans Gerth and C. Wright Mills. pp. 129–56. New York: Oxford University Press.

West, Martin. 1988. "Social Anthropology in a Divided Society." Inaugural Lecture Series. University of Cape Town.

Whitley, Richard. 1984. *The Intellectual and Social Organization of the Sciences.* Oxford: Clarendon Press.

Widdifield, Stacie G. 1996. *The Embodiment of the National in Late Nineteenth Century Mexican Painting.* Tucson: University of Arizona Press.

Williams, Brackette F. 1989. "A Class Act: Anthropology and the Race to Nation across Ethnic Terrain." *Annual Review of Anthropology* 18: 401–44.

Williamson, Edwin. 1992. *The Penguin History of Latin America.* London: Penguin.

Wilmsen, Edwin N. 1989. *Land Filled with Flies: A Political Economy of the Kalahari.* Chicago: University of Chicago Press.

Wise, David. 2000. *Cassidy's Run: The Secret Spy War over Nerve Gas.* New York: Random House.

Wolf, Eric. 1982. *Europe and the People without History.* Berkeley: University of California Press.

Worthington, Edgar B. 1938. *Science in Africa: A Review of Scientific Research Relating to Tropical and Southern Africa.* London: Oxford University Press.

Wright, Robin. 1988. "Anthropological Presuppositions of Indigenous Advocacy." *Annual Review of Anthropology* 17: 365–90.

Yans-Mclaughlin, Virginia. 1986. "Science, Democracy, and Ethos: Mobilizing Culture and Personality for World War II." In *Malinowski, Rivers, Benedict, and Others: Essays on Culture and Personality*, ed. George W. Stocking Jr. pp. 184–217. Madison: University of Wisconsin Press.

CONTRIBUTORS

ALBAN BENSA teaches anthropology at the École des Hautes Études en Sciences Sociales in Paris. He is also head of the Laboratoire Genèse et Transformations des Mondes Sociaux at the Centre National de la Recherche Scientifique. Among his publications are *Les chemins de l'alliance: L'organisation sociale et ses représentations en Nouvelle-Calédonie* (with J. C. Riviere, 1982); *Chroniques Kanak: L'ethnologie en marche* (1995); and *L'ethnologue et l'architecte: Ethnologie et architecture, le Centre Culturel Jean-Marie Tjibaou* (2000), an account of his collaboration with the architect Renzo Piano.

MARCIO GOLDMAN teaches social anthropology in the Graduate Program in Social Anthropology at the Museu Nacional, Federal University of Rio de Janeiro. He is a researcher for the Conselho Nacional de Desenvolvimento Científico e Tecnológico and is the author of *Razão e diferença: Afetividade, racionalidade e relativismo no pensamento de Lévy-Bruhl* (1994); *Alguma antropologia* (1999); and coeditor with Moacir Palmeira of *Antropologia: Voto e representação política* (1996).

ADAM KUPER teaches anthropology at Brunel University in London. His main publications include *Anthropology and Anthropologists* (1978); *Wives for Cattle: Bridewealth and Marriage in Southern Africa* (1982); *The Invention of Primitive Society: Transformations of an Illusion* (1988); *The Chosen Primate: Human Nature and Cultural Diversity* (1994); *Among the Anthropologists: History and Context in Anthropology* (1999); and *Culture: The Anthropologists' Account* (2002).

BENOÎT DE L'ESTOILE teaches social anthropology at the École Normale Supérieure and at the École des Hautes Études en Sciences Sociales (Paris) and is a researcher at the Laboratoire Genèse et Transformations des Mondes Sociaux at the Centre National de la Recherche Scientifique. He has published widely on the production of anthropological knowledge and the building of the colonial state in France and Great Britain. He is coeditor of *Ocupações de terra e transformações sociais* (with Lygia Sigaud, forthcoming), and of *Frontières de l'anthropologie* (with Michel Naepels, 2004).

CLAUDIO LOMNITZ is Distinguished University Professor of Anthropology and Historical Studies at the New School University. He is author of *Evolución de una sociedad rural* (1982); *Exits from the Labyrinth: Culture and Ideology in Mexican Nacional Space* (1993); *Modernidad indiana: Nueve ensayos sobre mediación y política* (1999); *Deep Mexico, Silent Mexico: An Anthropology of Nationalism* (2001); and *Death and the Idea of Mexico* (forthcoming).

DAVID MILLS is Anthropology Coordinator at the U.K Centre for Learning and Teaching—Sociology, Anthropology and Politics at the University of Birmingham. As well as conducting research on the contemporary teaching and practice of anthropology within universities, he is writing a political history of the discipline.

FEDERICO NEIBURG teaches social anthropology in the Graduate Program in Social Anthropology at the Museu Nacional, Federal University of Rio de Janeiro. He is a researcher for the Conselho Nacional de Desenvolvimento Científico e Tecnológico and for the Fundação de Amparo a Pesquisa do Estado do Rio de Janeiro. He is the author of *Identidad y conflicto en la Sierra Mazateca* (1988) and *Os intelectuais e a invenção do peronismo na Argentina* (1997).

JOÃO PACHECO DE OLIVEIRA teaches ethnology in the Graduate Program in Social Anthropology at the Museu Nacional, Federal University of Rio de Janeiro. He is a researcher for the Conselho Nacional de Desenvolvimento Científico e Tecnológico and coordinator of the Laboratório de Pesquisas em Etnicidade, Cultura e Desenvolvimento at the Museu Nacional. Among his publications are *O nosso governo: Os ticuna e o regime tutelar* (1988); *Indigenismo e territorialização: Poderes, rotinas e saberes coloniais no Brasil contemporâneo* (1998); *Ensaios de antropologia histórica* (1999); and *A viagem da volta: Etnicidade, política e reelaboração cultural no nordeste indígena* (1999).

JORGE F. PANTALEÓN teaches anthropology at Montreal University in Canada. He obtained his Ph.D. in social anthropology from the Graduate Program in Social Anthropology, Museu Nacional, Federal University of Rio de Janeiro, and the focus of his research is on the anthropology of economics and development in Argentina.

OMAR RIBEIRO THOMAZ teaches in the Anthropology Department at the University of Campinas. He is also a researcher for the Centro Brasileiro de Análise e Planejamento. Among other publications, he is the author of *Ecos do atlântico sul: Representações sobre o terceiro império português* (2002).

LYGIA SIGAUD teaches social anthropology in the Graduate Program in Social Anthropology at the Museu Nacional, Federal University of Rio de Janeiro, and also is a researcher for the Conselho Nacional de Desenvolvimento Científico e Tecnológico. She is author of *Os clandestinos e os direitos* (1979) and *Greve nos engenhos* (1980), and is coeditor, with Benoît de L'Estoile, of *Ocupações de terra e transformações sociais* (forthcoming).

ANTONIO CARLOS DE SOUZA LIMA teaches social anthropology in the Graduate Program in Social Anthropology at the Museu Nacional, Federal Univer-

sity of Rio de Janeiro. He is also a researcher for the Conselho Nacional de Desenvolvimento Científico e Tecnológico, and coordinator of the Laboratório de Pesquisas em Etnicidade, Cultura e Desenvolvimento at the Museu Nacional. He is
author of *Um grande cerco de paz: Poder tutelar, indianidade e formação do estado no
Brasil* (1995) and is coeditor, with Maria Barroso-Hoffman, of the trilogy *Bases para
uma nova política indigenista (Etnodesenvolvimento e políticas públicas; Além da
tutela;* and *Estado e povos indígenas)* (2002).

FLORENCE WEBER teaches sociology and ethnology at the École Normale
Supérieure, where she is head of the Social Sciences Department. Among her
publications are *Le travail à-côté: Étude d'ethnographie ouvrière* (1989 [2001]);
L'honneur des jardiniers: Les potagers dans la France du XXᵉ siècle (1998); *Le guide de
l'enquête de terrain* (with Stéphane Beaud, 1997); and an annotated anthology of
texts by Max Weber (2001).

INDEX

Library of Congress Cataloging-in-Publication Data

Empires, nations, and natives :
anthropology and state-making /
Benoit de L'Estoile, Federico Neiburg,
and Lygia Sigaud, editors.
p. cm.
Includes bibliographical references and
index.
ISBN 0-8223-3628-6 (cloth : alk. paper)
ISBN 0-8223-3617-0 (pbk. : alk. paper)
1. Political anthropology. 2. Political
customs and rites. 3. Politics and
culture. I. L'Estoile. Benoit de.
II. Neiburg, Federico G.
III. Sigaud, Lygia.
GN492.E46 2005
306.2—dc22   2005010072

3585 272

DATE DUE